Colección Támesis
SERIE A: MONOGRAFÍAS, 331

A COMPANION TO
MARIO VARGAS LLOSA

Tamesis

Founding Editors
†J. E. Varey

†Alan Deyermond

General Editor
Stephen M. Hart

Series Editor of
Fuentes para la historia del teatro en España
Charles Davis

Advisory Board
Rolena Adorno
John Beverley
Efraín Kristal
Jo Labanyi
Alison Sinclair
Isabel Torres
Julian Weiss

SABINE KÖLLMANN

A COMPANION TO MARIO VARGAS LLOSA

TAMESIS

© Sabine Köllmann 2014

All Rights Reserved. Except as permitted under current legislation
no part of this work may be photocopied, stored in a retrieval system,
published, performed in public, adapted, broadcast,
transmitted, recorded or reproduced in any form or by any means,
without the prior permission of the copyright owner

The right of Sabine Köllmann to be identified as
the author of this work has been asserted in accordance with
sections 77 and 78 of the Copyright, Designs and Patents Act 1988

First published 2014
Paperback edition 2020

ISBN 978 1 85566 269 8 hardback
ISBN 978 1 85566 340 4 paperback

Tamesis is an imprint of Boydell & Brewer Ltd
PO Box 9, Woodbridge, Suffolk IP12 3DF, UK
and of Boydell & Brewer Inc.
668 Mt Hope Avenue, Rochester, NY 14620-2731, USA
website: www.boydellandbrewer.com

A CIP catalogue record for this book is available
from the British Library

The publisher has no responsibility for the continued existence or accuracy of
URLs for external or third-party internet websites referred to in this book,
and does not guarantee that any content on such websites is,
or will remain, accurate or appropriate

Typeset by BBR, Sheffield

CONTENTS

Preface	vii
Introduction	1

PART 1: A LIFETIME OF READING AND WRITING

1	Two Sides of a Vocation: Writer and Intellectual	11
2	Truth and Lies: Literary Theory and Criticism	22
3	Journalism and Essays: from Art to Politics	44

PART 2: THE NARRATIVE WORK

4	Prelude: *Los jefes* (1959)	81
5	Experimenting with Form and Language: Narratives of the 1960s and 1970s	86
6	Towards the Total Novel: *La guerra del fin del mundo* (1981)	150
7	Experimenting with Genres: Novels of the 1980s and After	169
8	Interlude: the Demons of Literature and Politics (*El pez en el agua*, 1993)	213
9	The Return of the Grand Design: *La Fiesta del Chivo* (2000), *El Paraíso en la otra esquina* (2003) and *El sueño del celta* (2010)	223

PART 3: WORKS FOR THE THEATRE

10	Life's Dreams: the Storyteller on Stage	279

Suggestions for Further Reading	302
Bibliography	306
Index	318

PREFACE

The Nobel Prize in Literature 2010 for Mario Vargas Llosa was the culmination of a long and illustrious career, in the course of which he has become famous for his novels, but also notorious for his (often polemical) participation in intellectual and political debates. Both areas of his writing, fiction as well as essays and journalism, are ongoing endeavours which he pursues with the same vigour today as he did fifty years ago. The aim of this book is to provide readers with an overview and a general evaluation of Vargas Llosa's large body of work, and to discuss the contradictory reactions which he provokes.

This *Companion* differs from the approach of other introductions to Vargas Llosa which divide his work into different phases, corresponding to the changes in his political opinion. It challenges the received opinion about his notorious development: supposedly from a youthful Marxist writer, supporter of the Cuban revolution, who wanted literature to play a part in radical social change, to a liberal, right-wing propagandist of free-market politics who, nonetheless, continues to produce great literature that manages to transcend his political opinions. By contrast, this book highlights the many continuities in his long writing career: within his fiction, it follows recurring themes, formal features and patterns of language – three main factors, according to Vargas Llosa's theory, in transforming reality into fiction. In terms of literature's role in society it shows the continuity between his famous early statement that 'literature is fire' and the importance he ascribes to fiction in his Nobel Lecture, as a rebellious force encouraging a critical, nonconformist spirit.

The first part of this book discusses Vargas Llosa's literary theory and criticism as it has developed over the years. This is complemented by a survey of his political essays and journalism, highlighting his conception of the dual role of writer and intellectual.

The main part focuses on the fictional work. Combining a roughly chronological treatment with a thematic approach, it gives prominence to Vargas Llosa's narrative work. His short stories of 1959 already contain many of the characteristics that would later become a trademark of his fiction. Formal experimenting emerges as one of the common features of his earlier novels in which he developed narrative techniques influenced by, amongst others, Flaubert and Faulkner. At the same time, he experimented with language, trying to find a way of reproducing the slang of youth gangs, the jargon of the military, popular language, and the melodrama of radio serials.

An important point in Vargas Llosa's approach to literature is his ambition to encompass the complexity of reality in a work of fiction. A highlight in his quest for the 'total novel' is the 1981 *La guerra del fin del mundo* [*The War of the End of the World*] which successfully combines technical and structural complexity with a way of telling a story that can be read on many different levels: as an adventure story, a historical novel, but also as a political novel integrating his strong anti-ideological convictions into an immensely rich narrative.

After this central masterpiece, the focus of Vargas Llosa's fiction shifted to experimenting with different genres: erotic fiction, thrillers, writing about art (ekphrasis), a reworking of Greek myths, metafiction, and not least the memoirs that his political interlude engendered. The study highlights common themes that run through this very diverse body of work, giving it unity and coherence: authoritarianism, machismo, the father, the outsider, the relationship between reality and fiction, and the role of storytelling, to name just a few.

The last chapter devoted to Vargas Llosa's narrative work demonstrates how *La Fiesta del Chivo* [*The Feast of the Goat*] of 2000 picked up a number of these diverse strands and reunited them with the totalizing ambition of his earlier novels. The analysis of this great dictatorship novel and of the novels that have followed it more recently, *El Paraíso en la otra esquina* [*The Way to Paradise*] (2003) and *El sueño del celta* [*The Dream of the Celt*] (2010), reveals the extent of continuity and coherence in Vargas Llosa's more than fifty years of writing.

In the third and final part of the book, a look at his theatrical work shows how Vargas Llosa transposes the topics that mark his narrative work to a different medium. This includes the ambiguities of reality and fiction which he explores on the stage, in recent years even as an actor himself.

Suggestions for further reading complement this comprehensive overview of Mario Vargas Llosa's work, which is aimed at enabling undergraduate and graduate students to evaluate the differing reactions to this by now canonic, but nonetheless controversial Hispanic author. For the general reader interested in the Nobel Prize winner this book provides an introduction to his complex and fascinating fictional universe, giving an idea of its unity, while adding essential information about his intellectual and political background.

Wherever possible I have used published English translations of quotations; the others are mine. The dates given for Vargas Llosa's works in the text of this study refer to the year of their first publication and correspond to the bibliography at the end of this book, listing his works in chronological order of publication. But the page numbers of quotations in my text refer to the editions I have actually used, which are referenced in the footnotes.

INTRODUCTION

The Peruvian author Mario Vargas Llosa is one of the major Latin American literary figures of the last five decades. A prolific writer, he has so far published sixteen novels,[1] some shorter narrative works, eight plays, a children's book, five major critical studies of other writers, and a large number of essay collections concerning literature, politics and wider social and intellectual issues, many of which derive from the journalistic work that he has always pursued in parallel with his fictional writing. From the beginning of his career, literature and politics were two sides of his vocation as a writer that have coexisted and influenced each other.

Born in the Peruvian town of Arequipa on 28 March 1936, Mario Vargas Llosa spent a happy early childhood with his mother and her family in Cochabamba, Bolivia, where he learnt to read and write. Encouraged by his maternal family, he developed a passion for literature which would determine his whole life. He found that the 'magic' of fictions opened up worlds, allowing him to 'break the barriers of time and space' and to turn 'dreams into life and life into dreams'.[2] Although writing stories proved to be a difficult undertaking which required discipline, patience and lots of reading and imitating the great masters, he found it a delightful occupation. It was not until unhappiness disrupted his existence that reading and writing became a necessity, providing refuge and relief from the shock of his father, whom he had believed to be dead, re-entering his peaceful life. Mario was eleven years old and living in Piura when his mother revealed to him that his father was, in fact, alive and that they would move to Lima to live with him. In his Nobel Lecture Vargas Llosa describes how, from that moment onwards, literature became his 'reason for living' ('mi razón de vivir'):

---

[1] During the final proof-correcting stage of this book, Vargas Llosa's seventeenth novel was published: *El héroe discreto* [The Discreet Hero] (Madrid: Alfaguara, 2013). Set in contemporary Peru it alternates between two stories, with some familiar protagonists such as Lituma, Don Rigoberto with his wife Lucrecia and son Fonchito.

[2] Mario Vargas Llosa, 'In Praise of Reading and Fiction', Nobel Lecture, 7 December 2010, <http://nobelprize.org/nobel_prizes/literature/laureates/2010/vargas_llosa-lecture_en.html> [accessed 27 October 2012]. There is also a printed version of this text: *In Praise of Reading and Fiction. The Nobel Lecture*, trans. Edith Grossman (New York: Farrar, Straus and Giroux, 2011). I continue to quote from the online version.

Perdí la inocencia y descubrí la soledad, la autoridad, la vida adulta y el miedo. Mi salvación fue leer, leer los buenos libros, refugiarme en esos mundos donde vivir era exaltante [sic], intenso, una aventura tras otra, donde podía sentirme libre y volvía a ser feliz. Y fue escribir, a escondidas, como quien se entrega a un vicio inconfesable, a una pasión prohibida. La literatura dejó de ser un juego. Se volvió una manera de resistir la adversidad, de protestar, de rebelarme, de escapar a lo intolerable.[3]

[I lost my innocence and discovered loneliness, authority, adult life, and fear. My salvation was reading, reading good books, taking refuge in those worlds where life was glorious, intense, one adventure after another, where I could feel free and be happy again. And it was writing, in secret, like someone giving himself up to an unspeakable vice, a forbidden passion. Literature stopped being a game. It became a way of resisting adversity, protesting, rebelling, escaping the intolerable.][4]

The father intended to disrupt, even cure his son Mario's unmanly passion for literature by sending him to the Leoncio Prado Military Academy. All he achieved was widening his son's knowledge of Peruvian society, raising his social awareness and providing him with the material for his first novel which, years later, would catapult him onto the international literary scene.

In 1952 Mario Vargas Llosa returned to Piura where, during his final year at school, he was able to direct his first – unpublished – play, *La huida del inca* [The Inca's Escape], in a performance at the local theatre. Back in Lima, the rebellion against his father continued with his refusal to study at the conservative Catholic university, preferring to enrol at the much more politicized National University of San Marcos, where he joined a clandestine Marxist group called Cahuide. That, too, provided material for a novel – *Conversación en la catedral* [*Conversation in the Cathedral*][5] – as did his experiences as a journalist for newspapers and the radio. At the age of 18 he took the rebellious decision to marry his aunt Julia, a divorcee ten years older than him, and in 1959 he left for Europe on a scholarship to complete a doctorate at the Complutense University in Madrid. The following year the couple moved to Paris – a dream come true for the aspiring writer and lover of French literature and culture. Despite the financial necessity of juggling several odd jobs Vargas Llosa managed to have a collection of short stories

---

[3] Mario Vargas Llosa, 'Elogio de la lectura y la ficción', Nobel Lecture, 7 December 2010, <http://nobelprize.org/nobel_prizes/literature/laureates/2010/vargas_llosa-lecture_sp.html> [accessed 27 October 2012].

[4] Vargas Llosa, 'In Praise of Reading and Fiction'.

[5] Mario Vargas Llosa, *Conversación en la catedral* (Barcelona: Seix Barral, 1985); Mario Vargas Llosa, *Conversation in the Cathedral*, trans. Gregory Rabassa (New York: HarperCollins, 2005).

published – *Los jefes* [The Leaders] (1959)[6] – while working on his first novel. Against all odds, he had turned himself into a professional writer. He later divorced Julia Urquidi and married his cousin Patricia Llosa who has accompanied – and managed – his life of writing ever since.

When, in 1962, the 26-year-old's *La ciudad y los perros* [*The Time of the Hero*][7] became the first Latin American novel to win the Biblioteca Breve prize awarded by the Spanish publishing house Seix Barral, it helped to spark the so-called Boom of Spanish American fiction. A much-debated phenomenon, the Boom owes its name to the fact that, during the 1960s, a number of innovative novels by Latin American writers appeared in quick succession, bursting into the consciousness of a Western reading public due to their publication or distribution, promotion and quick translation in Europe. The most influential writers of the Boom were the so-called Big Four: the Argentinian Julio Cortázar, the Mexican Carlos Fuentes, the Colombian Gabriel García Márquez, and Vargas Llosa, the youngest of the four. Living and working outside their native countries, and meeting frequently in the stimulating intellectual atmosphere of Paris, Barcelona or other European cities, they developed a common Latin American identity across national borders which replaced the regional outlook of previous generations of writers from Spanish America. A wider perspective went hand in hand with a wider aesthetic: instead of traditional realism the Boom authors adopted experimental techniques able to reflect the complex and ambiguous relationship between fiction and reality.

An important extraliterary factor in uniting this group of writers during the 1960s was their enthusiastic support for the Cuban Revolution which had made culture an important part of its political strategy. Between 1965 and 1971 Vargas Llosa was involved with the Cuban cultural institute *Casa de las Américas*, served on the board of its journal and was a juror for the literary prize of the same name. This political dimension of the Boom appealed to Western readers who followed the Cuban socialist experiment with sympathy and fascination. The link between literature and politics contributed further to the success of Spanish American authors in those years and had a lasting effect on the reception of Latin American fiction. But the unifying power of the ideological consensus of the 1960s ended abruptly with the Padilla Affair in 1971. The Cuban poet Heberto Padilla was arrested for criticizing the Castro regime and forced to undergo a humiliating ritual of self-denunciation. A wave of protest against such Stalinist practices went through previously

---

[6] Mario Vargas Llosa, *Los jefes* (Barcelona: Bruguera, 1983). The English translations of these short stories are included in Mario Vargas Llosa, *The Cubs and other Stories*, trans. Gregory Kolovakos and Ronald Christ (London: London: Faber and Faber, 1991).

[7] Mario Vargas Llosa, *La ciudad y los perros* (Barcelona: Seix Barral, 1983); Mario Vargas Llosa, *The Time of the Hero* (London: Picador, 1986).

pro-Cuban intellectual circles around the world. Vargas Llosa drafted a letter of protest to Fidel Castro which was signed by such influential left-wing artists as Sartre, Simone de Beauvoir, Jorge Semprún, Pier Paolo Pasolini and many others.[8] At the same time, Vargas Llosa publicly resigned from *Casa de las Américas* and cancelled other commitments in Cuba. The protest movement had the support of Carlos Fuentes, but other major Boom writers were less forthright in their criticism of Castro. A deep rift had emerged which divided the group and marked the end of the Boom. It also ended personal friendships such as that between Vargas Llosa and García Márquez who, to this day, remains a close associate of the Cuban regime and friend of Fidel Castro – famously denounced by Vargas Llosa as Castro's 'cortesano' [literally: courtier, but with the association of courtesan].[9]

After this rupture Vargas Llosa reconsidered his own attitude to socialism and, over the years, distanced himself more and more from the Left. His insistence on freedom of speech as the foundation of a free society turned him into a highly controversial, even vilified figure in circles where his persistent criticism of Cuba was regarded as a betrayal of his former leftist ideals. This influenced the reception of his literary output of the 1970s[10] which was seen as a sign of Vargas Llosa's 'sell-out' to the market, with 'lighter' novels replacing the highly complex works of the previous decade. But he continued his experimenting with form and language in novels that used shifting narrative levels and different points of view in a new way, exploring the language of radio broadcasts, newspaper reports and letters (private as well as formal), and added a new element: the exploration, within the novel, of how fiction works. In 1981 he conducted his own television programme on Panamericana Televisión, *La Torre de Babel* [The Tower of Babel], which touched on all things cultural.[11]

Vargas Llosa developed a distinctly liberal, anti-ideological position, influenced by his readings of Isaiah Berlin and Karl Popper. This was reflected in his 1981 novel *La guerra del fin del mundo* [*The War of the End of the World*].[12] The dual concern for literature and politics continued to shape his

---

[8] Mario Vargas Llosa, 'Carta a Fidel Castro', in *Contra viento y marea, I (1962–1972)* (Barcelona: Seix Barral, 1986), pp. 250–2.

[9] Vargas Llosa used this expression at the 1986 assembly of PEN International in New York. See Mario Vargas Llosa, 'Respuesta a Günter Grass', in *Contra viento y marea, III (1964–1988)* (Barcelona: Seix Barral, 1990), pp. 394–400 (p. 399).

[10] For an account of how the critics who initially praised Vargas Llosa's novels retrospectively condemned them as reactionary, see Juan E. De Castro, *Mario Vargas Llosa. Public Intellectual in Neoliberal Latin America* (Tucson: The University of Arizona Press, 2011), pp. 13–16.

[11] At the time of writing (November 2012), some of these programmes can be watched on YouTube, <http://www.youtube.com>.

[12] Mario Vargas Llosa, *La guerra del fin del mundo* (Barcelona: Plaza y Janés, 1982); Mario Vargas Llosa, *The War of the End of the World* (London: Faber and Faber, 1986).

essayistic and journalistic work as well as his fiction, where he dealt with social and political issues in parallel with metafictional questions about the relationship between reality and fiction. His notorious move to a liberal (some would say neo-liberal or conservative)[13] position, vigorously promoting free-market policies in texts, lectures and interviews at every opportunity, continued to provoke outrage and influenced the evaluation of his literary work. Some critics demonized him both for his writing and his political position, while others tended to disconnect Vargas Llosa as a writer from his opinions as an intellectual in public debate. All this time, his commitment to questions of individual liberties in a social context remained unchanged.

In the late 1980s Vargas Llosa's deep concern about the Peruvian government's nationalization programme made him enter politics. Not a natural politician, and without the necessary hunger for power, he ran as a candidate in Peru's 1990 presidential elections. During the campaign his strong convictions, principled attitude and honest approach, speaking the truth about necessary austerity measures, did not always work in his favour. Existing power structures forced him to enter into an alliance with the established forces of the Right, a move that discredited him in the eyes of the electorate.[14] He lost the elections to Alberto Fujimori, who took over a number of Vargas Llosa's policies, but without the liberal democratic foundation. When Fujimori's regime became more and more dictatorial Vargas Llosa unrelentingly drew the world's attention to the abuses of power in Peru and appealed to the international community for sanctions against his home country. Fujimori's regime unleashed a vicious campaign denouncing him as a traitor and threatened to strip him of his citizenship. At that point Spain's socialist Prime Minister Felipe González offered Vargas Llosa Spanish citizenship, which he accepted (he continues to hold dual nationality).

In the past two decades, Vargas Llosa has received an impressive range of awards from institutions and organizations reaching right across the political spectrum for both his literature and his political commitment to freedom and democracy,[15] which proves that he is widely respected in his dual role as writer

---

[13] Ignacio Ramonet, 'Vargas Llosa, neocon with a Nobel', *Le Monde diplomatique*, 23 December 2010, <http://mondediplo.com/2010/12/23vargasllosa> [accessed 27 October 2012].

[14] His consultant at the time, Mark Malloch Brown, wrote afterwards: 'He was seen as a man guiltily straining to keep a closet door shut with the bad secret of his allies behind it. He began as a champion of change and ended up being perceived as a protector of privilege.' Mark Malloch Brown, 'The Consultant', *Vargas Llosa for President* (*Granta*, 36 (1991)), 87–95 (p. 93).

[15] See the full list of honours and distinctions, and the dedications quoting his literature as well as his political commitment, on his official website, <http://www.mvargasllosa.com/distin.htm>. See also my essay 'Vargas Llosa as "the man who writes and thinks"', in *Vargas Llosa and Latin American Politics*, ed. Juan E. De Castro and Nicholas Birns (New York: Palgrave Macmillan, 2010), pp. 173–88.

and intellectual. Nevertheless, he frequently alienates people of the Left as well as the Right with his non-partisan, independent positions and his often polemical contributions to public discourse. Like his fiction, which covers a broad range of genres and topics, his political positions are not easy to categorize. His promotion of liberal free-market economics, often applauded by neo-conservative organizations, coexists with a defence of gay rights and strong attacks on nationalism and anti-immigration movements. His insistent criticism of populist tendencies in Latin America and his continued attacks on Cuba and on Venezuela's Hugo Chávez stand next to a passionate denunciation of Israeli settlements in Palestinian territory. Categories of Left and Right, Third World and Western prove too simplistic to describe his beliefs. The common denominator is freedom: Vargas Llosa supports the individual's human and civil rights, and postulates respect for democratic processes and institutions which make it possible to live in freedom.

In 2010, Mario Vargas Llosa received the prize that many thought he would never get: the Swedish Academy awarded him the Nobel Prize in Literature for 'his cartography of structures of power and his trenchant images of the individual's resistance, revolt and defeat'. Twenty-eight years later than his erstwhile friend and rival Gabriel García Márquez, and after many years of media speculation during which his name was regularly brought up as a candidate for the Nobel, Vargas Llosa himself claimed that the announcement took him completely by surprise. He and his wife even thought it might be a hoax when, very early in the morning of 7 October 2010, they received the phone call informing them about the award. For a long time a rumour had been commonly accepted that his militant liberalism and his unreserved criticism of collectivist political models would make him unelectable in the eyes of the Swedish Academy. 'I have taken all the precautions necessary for them never to give it to me', Vargas Llosa had joked the previous year when asked about the Nobel Prize.[16] When his name was announced as the 2010 Laureate, there was genuine surprise. The general reaction in the press during the next few days and weeks was one of delight, especially in the Spanish-speaking world: A 'triumph for Spanish language fiction' and 'shared by the whole of Latin America' were typical reactions, but also the statement that 'the Swedish Academy has honoured itself' by taking the long-overdue step to honour Vargas Llosa. 'Finally!' was one of the most read comments, as in the editorial of *El País* on October 8: 'Mario, al fin'. After the Nobel came nobility: in February 2011 it was announced that the King of Spain would

---

[16] Rory Carroll, 'Mario Vargas Llosa surprised and delighted by Nobel prize win', *The Guardian*, 7 October 2010, <http://www.guardian.co.uk/books/2010/oct/07/mario-vargas-llosa-nobel-prize-literature> [accessed 27 October 2012].

bestow the title of 'Marqués' on Vargas Llosa for his 'universally recognized, extraordinary contribution to Spanish language fiction'.[17]

By all accounts, Vargas Llosa lived through one of the most turbulent and intense times of his life between the Nobel announcement in October 2010 and the beginning of 2011, when things gradually returned to normal and his voice rejoined the public debate with a characteristically polemical, but well-argued article on the controversy surrounding the Wikileaks website and its notorious founder Julian Assange.[18] As we will see, the events of this period illustrate better than anything two crucial concepts of Vargas Llosa's literary theory: his understanding of writing as a passion and a vocation that needs to be pursued with rigour and discipline; and the ambiguous relationship between reality and literature, where real-life events can take on the quality of fiction. Or, as Vargas Llosa himself put it during the Nobel Banquet Speech: 'Let us toast ... Sweden, that strange kingdom that seems to have performed, for a privileged few, the miracle of turning life into literature and literature into life.'[19]

---

[17] Mábel Galaz, 'Es un honor ser marqués a la vez que Del Bosque', *El País*, 5 February 2011, <http://www.elpais.com/articulo/agenda/honor/ser/marques/vez/Bosque/elpepigen/20110205elpepiage_2/Tes> [accessed 27 October 2012].

[18] Mario Vargas Llosa, 'Lo privado y lo público', *El País*, 16 January 2011, <http://www.elpais.com/articulo/opinion/privado/publico/elpepiopi/20110116elpepiopi_10/Tes> [accessed 27 October 2012]. Vargas Llosa, the ardent defender of freedom of speech, came out as not in favour of Wikileaks's 'universal voyeurism', a 'destruction of confidentiality' which he judged to be a manifestation of barbarism and frivolity. The article is now included in his book *La civilización del espectáculo* (Madrid: Alfaguara, 2012), pp. 152–6.

[19] Mario Vargas Llosa, 'Nobel Banquet Speech', 10 December 2010, <http://nobelprize.org/nobel_prizes/literature/laureates/2010/vargas_llosa-speech.html> [accessed 27 October 2012].

PART 1:
A LIFETIME OF READING AND WRITING

1

Two Sides of a Vocation: Writer and Intellectual

When news of the Nobel Prize reached Mario Vargas Llosa in New York, it found him doing what he has done all his life: reading and writing. That autumn, he was teaching two courses on fiction at Princeton University and had started his day early to prepare a class on the importance of point of view in fiction, which he was going to illustrate with examples from Alejo Carpentier. He later described how, during those early hours, the rereading of *El reino de este mundo* [*The Kingdom of this World*] (1949) had worked its magic on him.[1] But that fateful morning, the pleasure of reading which has been so important to him throughout his life was thoroughly disturbed. Vargas Llosa has always believed in literature as a vocation requiring the writer's full dedication, an activity which structures the entire life and needs to be pursued with discipline and total commitment. He has modelled himself on the French writer Gustave Flaubert who regarded creating fiction as an exclusive, all-encompassing endeavour, not to be shared with other distracting activities. 'Writing is the commitment of your entire personality, and I think it's the only way you can succeed as a writer – with discipline and also [with a certain] stubbornness', Vargas Llosa told his students at Princeton.[2] But from the moment the news of the award became public, reading and writing, those quiet, solitary activities which, nevertheless, can be enormously pleasurable and enriching, became impossible. The writer's strict daily routine was turned upside down, his well-organized life descended into turmoil, and his voice as a regular columnist for the Spanish newspaper *El País* and other papers around the world suddenly fell silent. Nevertheless, when asked about the curse of the Nobel that had hit so many previous recipients who became unable to produce new work, he declared defiantly: 'I will always be writing. Death will find me with my pen in hand.'[3] His highest ambition, he said, had

---

[1] Mario Vargas Llosa, 'Catorce minutos de reflexión', *El País*, 10 October 2010, <http://www.elpais.com/articulo/opinion/Catorce/minutos/reflexion/elpepiopi/20101010elpepiopi_11/Tes> [accessed 27 October 2012].

[2] Jennifer Greenstein Altmann, 'Novelist Vargas Llosa imparts writing insights to students', *News at Princeton*, 4 October 2010, <http://www.princeton.edu/main/news/archive/S28/59/50G40/index.xml?section=featured> [accessed 27 October 2012].

[3] 'Mario Vargas Llosa Says Nobel Prize Changed His Life: "Death Will Find Me

never been to receive the ultimate literary prize, but 'to know that my books would be read in the way that I read the books which changed my life'.[4]

Vargas Llosa drafted his Nobel Lecture in the middle of other commitments. When the day of the awards ceremony in Stockholm came, the events surrounding the lecture took on the quality of one of his own fictions. That morning Vargas Llosa found himself completely out of voice. Under the gaze of the world press, looking extremely pale and worried, he was rushed off to hospital where he received an injection which managed to restore his vocal cords, just in time for the delivery of the speech. But his voice, so used to public speaking, began to crack again during the lecture, this time due to emotion, when he reached the part in his speech where he thanked his wife of forty-five years. 'She does everything and does everything well', he read out sobbing, and many listeners found themselves moved to tears, reaching for a handkerchief. The first Nobel Prize winner to cry during his acceptance speech, Vargas Llosa saved the situation by a characteristically ironic turn of phrase. He said about his wife Patricia, that she 'is so generous that even when she thinks she is rebuking me, she pays me the highest compliment: "Mario, the only thing you're good for is writing"'.

'Elogio de la lectura y la ficción' [In Praise of Reading and Fiction] condenses Vargas Llosa's ideas about fiction and its role in society into a compelling intellectual autobiography. It is an account of his readings and writings, of people and places that have shaped his life and made him into the writer and intellectual that he is today. But above all, the Nobel Lecture is a passionate apologia for the transforming power of fiction, and for the important social function that literature fulfils for humankind:

> Por eso, hay que repetirlo sin tregua hasta convencer de ello a las nuevas generaciones: la ficción es más que un entretenimiento, más que un ejercicio intelectual que aguza la sensibilidad y despierta el espíritu crítico. Es una necesidad imprescindible para que la civilización siga existiendo, renovándose y conservando en nosotros lo mejor de lo humano. Para que no retrocedamos a la barbarie de la incomunicación y la vida no se reduzca al pragmatismo de los especialistas que ven las cosas en profundidad pero ignoran lo que las rodea, precede y continúa.[5]

With My Pen In Hand"', *Huffington Post*, 3 November 2010, <http://www.huffingtonpost.com/2010/11/03/vargas-llosa-says-nobel-p_n_778573.html> [accessed 27 October 2012].

[4] Javier Rodríguez Marcos, 'El "terror feliz" de un premio Nobel', *El País*, 4 November 2010, <http://www.elpais.com/articulo/cultura/terror/feliz/premio/Nobel/elpepicul/20101104elpepicul_1/Tes> [accessed 27 October 2012].

[5] Mario Vargas Llosa, 'Elogio de la lectura y la ficción', Nobel Lecture, 7 December 2010, <http://nobelprize.org/nobel_prizes/literature/laureates/2010/vargas_llosa-lecture_sp.html> [accessed 27 October 2012].

[That is why this must be repeated incessantly until new generations are convinced of it: fiction is more than an entertainment, more than an intellectual exercise that sharpens one's sensibility and awakens a critical spirit. It is an absolute necessity so that civilization continues to exist, renewing and preserving in us the best of what is human. So that we do not retreat into the savagery of isolation and life is not reduced to the pragmatism of specialists who see things profoundly but ignore what surrounds, precedes, and continues those things.][6]

This urgent appeal to the 'new generations' to take literature seriously reflects the concern about the trivialization of culture that Vargas Llosa has voiced in a number of essays during the last few years, and which he has now assembled in *La civilización del espectáculo* [The Civilization of Entertainment] (2012).[7] He denounces the view of literature as pure entertainment in our postmodern societies which have turned everything into a spectacle. In fact, reading means stepping outside ourselves, engaging with the fictional lives of others, a move which helps us 'to break out of confinement and change and improve'. 'Good literature', he says in the Nobel Lecture, 'erects bridges between different peoples, and by having us enjoy, suffer, or feel surprise, unites us beneath the languages, beliefs, habits, customs, and prejudices that separate us.' This idea that 'literature creates a fraternity within human diversity' and 'introduces into our spirits nonconformity and rebellion, which are behind all the heroic deeds that have contributed to the reduction of violence in human relationships' can be traced right back to the beginning of his career. It belies the received opinion that Vargas Llosa's ideas have changed drastically, not only in the field of politics but also in his concept of literature. If we follow Vargas Llosa's understanding of the function of reading and writing step by step back in time we find the same basic concepts. About ten years ago, an essay called 'Literature and Life' (2001) highlighted the uniting, humanizing effect of reading fiction:

Those of us who read Cervantes, Shakespeare, Dante or Tolstoy understand each other and feel part of the same species because, in the works that these writers created, we learn what we share as human beings, what is common to all of us beneath the wide range of differences that separate us. And there is no better defence against the stupidity of prejudice, racism, xenophobia, religious or political sectarianism or autarchic nationalism than this invariable truth that appears in all great literature: that men and

---

[6] Mario Vargas Llosa, 'In Praise of Reading and Fiction', Nobel Lecture, 7 December 2010, <http://nobelprize.org/nobel_prizes/literature/laureates/2010/vargas_llosa-lecture_en.html> [accessed 27 October 2012].

[7] Mario Vargas Llosa, *La civilización del espectáculo* (Madrid: Alfaguara, 2012).

women across the world are equal, and that it is unjust that they are subject to discrimination, repression and exploitation.⁸

These ideas about the humane qualities of literature correspond to his journalism where, as we will see, he defends human rights and attacks nationalism, religious fanaticism, racist discrimination and authoritarianism. Literary and political goals coincide.

Further back, during the 1990s, Vargas Llosa's statements about the social function of literature were less forceful, with a certain dose of scepticism, but he nevertheless insisted:

> Pero, sí creo con firmeza que, sin renunciar a entretener, la literatura debe hundirse hasta el cuello en la vida de la calle, en la experiencia común, en la historia haciéndose, como lo hizo en sus mejores momentos … porque nada aguza mejor nuestro olfato ni nos hace tan sensibles para detectar las raíces de la crueldad, la maldad y la violencia que puede desencadenar el ser humano, como la buena literatura.⁹

> [I do, however, firmly believe that literature, without refusing to entertain, has to immerse itself deep in life on the streets, in common experiences, in history in the making, as it did in its best moments … because nothing sharpens our senses as much, and nothing makes us more able to detect the roots of cruelty and evil, of the violence that human beings are capable of unleashing, as good literature does.]

Another decade earlier, Vargas Llosa's texts of the 1980s already contain the concept of stepping out of oneself and adopting a different perspective through reading, which makes the reader less likely to accept reality as it is – a potentially dangerous process in illiberal societies, as he points out:

> Vivir vidas que uno no vive es fuente de ansiedad, un desajuste con la existencia que puede tornarse rebeldía, actitud indócil frente a lo establecido. … Salir de sí mismo, ser otro, aunque sea ilusoriamente, es una manera de ser menos esclavo y de experimentar los riesgos de la libertad.¹⁰

> [Living through lives that one does not have is a source of tension, a maladjustment to one's existence that can turn into rebelliousness, into a

---

⁸ Mario Vargas Llosa, 'Literature and Life', in *Touchstones. Essays on Literature, Art and Politics*, select., trans. and ed. John King (London: Faber and Faber, 2007), pp. 135–49 (p. 137).

⁹ Mario Vargas Llosa, 'Dinosaurios en tiempos difíciles', in *Friedenspreis des deutschen Buchhandels 1996. Mario Vargas Llosa. Ansprachen aus Anlass der Verleihung*, ed. Börsenverein des Deutschen Buchhandels (Frankfurt am Main:Verlag der Buchhändler-Vereinigung, 1996), pp. 35–48 (pp. 39–40). This article is now also included in his latest essay collection, *La civilización del espectáculo* (pp. 212–26).

¹⁰ Mario Vargas Llosa, 'El arte de mentir', *Contra viento y marea, II (1972–1983)* (Barcelona: Seix Barral, 1986), pp. 418–24 (p. 424).

defiant attitude toward things as they are. ... Stepping outside of oneself, being someone else, even in an illusionary manner, is a way of being less of a slave and experiencing the risks of freedom.]

In the highly charged political atmosphere of the 1970s Vargas Llosa's self-reflexive essays on literature were primarily concerned with defending his freedom as a writer to create authentic literature which does not necessarily have to correspond to his personal opinions outside literature. This was a fall-out from the Padilla Affair and the subsequent attacks on Vargas Llosa for his uncompromising criticism of Cuba. But even in this decade of texts defending literature's freedom to be irresponsible he pointed to the basic human concerns that fiction raises: 'Una obra es "literaria" cuando las experiencias que consigue apresar con palabras y según un orden dado, a más de tener un valor colectivo, expresan dentro de determinadas circunstancias sociales e históricas lo "humano", algo much más permanente que lo social e histórica a secas' [A work is 'literary' when the experiences that it successfully renders by putting them into words and into a certain order capture, within the framework of social and historical circumstances, that which is 'human'; and that is something much more enduring than plain social and historical reality].[11]

As far back as 1967, in his famous acceptance speech for the Rómulo Gallegos Prize, we find an ardent defence of literature which has strong echoes in the Nobel Lecture of forty-three years later. Under the programmatic title 'La literatura es fuego' [Literature is Fire], Vargas Llosa says about fiction:

> Ella contribuye al perfeccionamiento humano impidiendo el marasmo espiritual, la autosatisfacción, el inmovilismo, la parálisis humana, el reblandecimiento intelectual o moral. Su misión es agitar, inquietar, alarmar, mantener a los hombres en una constante insatisfacción de sí mismos, su función es estimular sin tregua la voluntad de cambio y de mejora.[12]

> [It contributes to human improvement, preventing spiritual atrophy, self-satisfaction, stagnation, human paralysis and intellectual or moral decline. Its mission is to arouse, to disturb, to alarm, to keep men in a constant state of dissatisfaction with themselves: its function is to stimulate, without respite, the desire for change and improvement.][13]

---

[11] Ricardo Cano Gaviria, *El buitre y el ave Fénix. Conversaciones con Mario Vargas Llosa* (Barcelona: Anagrama, 1972), p. 38.

[12] Mario Vargas Llosa, 'La literatura es fuego', in *Contra viento y marea, I (1962–1972)* (Barcelona: Seix Barral, 1986), pp. 176–81 (p. 179).

[13] Mario Vargas Llosa, 'Literature is Fire', in *Making Waves*, ed. and trans. John King (London: Faber and Faber, 1996), pp. 70–4 (p. 72).

The humanizing effect of literature, inciting the desire to change and improve reality, which he described in this and other texts from the 1960s, corresponds to the 2010 Nobel Laureate's ardent appeal to recognize the role of fiction as a motor of progress: 'Nothing has sown so much disquiet, so disturbed our imagination and our desires as the life of lies we add, thanks to literature, to the one we have'. As Vargas Llosa reiterated in his Nobel Lecture, readers become 'infected with longings' leading them to 'permanently question a mediocre reality' – a clear link to the memorable formula he used as the title of an essay, back in 1966, to define literature's role in society: 'Una insurrección permanente' [A Permanent Insurrection].[14]

Vargas Llosa's understanding of literature has remained consistent throughout his career. But in the context of the 1960s, with its general enthusiasm for the Cuban revolution, the rhetoric of radicality[15] that pervades 'La literatura es fuego' could easily be misunderstood in a political sense. The vocabulary of militant political action that Vargas Llosa used there to great emotional effect was bound to raise the false expectation that his fiction would contain a recognizably socialist message – hence the accusations by some critics that his literature of the 1970s represented a betrayal of his ideals. He described literature as 'angry and rebellious', as 'militancy', 'protest', 'aggression', 'insurrection'; he characterized the writer as an 'unruly social element' whose mission it is to stir up, agitate and alarm people, in order to fight 'exploitation' and 'blinding inequalities' with 'fire' and 'the sharpest weapons' available, even with – verbal – 'violence' (all translations are John King's). Although Vargas Llosa made it clear that, in whatever circumstances, literature would always be rebellious since it springs from the writer's dissatisfaction with the world – 'el escritor ha sido, es y seguirá siendo un descontento' [the writer has been, is, and will continue to be, dissatisfied] – the forceful rhetoric of 'La literatura es fuego', with its metaphors of fire and uproar, firmly established the association of literature with a battle against political oppression. That impression was reinforced by an explicitly political passage about Latin America's socialist future:

> Pero dentro de diez, veinte o cincuenta años habrá llegado a todos nuestros países, como ahora a Cuba, la hora de la justicia social y América Latina entera se habrá emancipado del imperio que la saquea, de las castas que la explotan, de las fuerzas que hoy la ofenden y reprimen. Yo quiero que esa hora llegue cuanto antes y que América Latina ingrese de una vez por todas en la dignidad y en la vida moderna, que el socialismo nos libere de nuestro anacronismo y nuestro horror. ('La literatura es fuego', p. 179)

---

[14] Mario Vargas Llosa, 'Una insurrección permanente', in *Contra viento I*, pp. 107–10.
[15] See my study *Vargas Llosa's Fiction & the Demons of Politics* (Oxford: Peter Lang, 2002), pp. 39–45.

[But within ten, twenty or fifty years, the hour of social justice will arrive in our countries, as it has in Cuba, and the whole of Latin America will have freed itself from the order that despoils it, from the castes that exploit it, from the forces that now insult and repress it. And I want this hour to arrive as soon as possible and for Latin America to enter, once and for all, a world of dignity and modernity, and for socialism to free us from our anachronism and our horror.] ('Literature is Fire', p. 73)

Vargas Llosa made public the background to this statement in an interview with Ricardo Setti:[16] the Cuban regime suggested to him to make a gesture in favour of the revolution by publicly donating the Rómulo Gallegos Prize money to a fund supporting Che Guevara while privately receiving the sum back through diplomatic Cuban channels for his own use. Vargas Llosa indignantly refused this unworthy farce and decided instead to introduce into his acceptance speech in Venezuela, at that time hostile to Castro, the above statement in support of Cuba. This was acknowledged by the Cuban regime, and Vargas Llosa received praise for this welcome public statement, 'el grito de Caracas' [the cry from Caracas].[17] He did, however, take care to complement his bold declaration of support for the revolution with a claim to absolute freedom for the writer: 'Pero cuando las injusticias sociales desaparezcan, de ningún modo habrá llegado para el escritor la hora del consentimiento, la subordinación o la complicidad oficial. Su misión seguirá, deberá seguir siendo la misma; cualquier transigencia en este dominio constituye, de parte del escritor, una traición' ('La literatura es fuego', p. 180) [But when social injustices disappear, this will not mean that the hour of consent, subordination and official complicity will have arrived for the writer. His mission will continue, must continue, to be the same: any compromise in this area will be a betrayal] ('Literature is Fire', p. 73).

Vargas Llosa's concept of the creative impulse as a spontaneous, irrational process based on the writer's 'demons' (see the discussion in chapter 2 below) is obviously incompatible with the notion of literature in the service of an extraliterary goal. In the 1960s he felt this dilemma very deeply, but he was convinced: the duty of a writer to create good literature cannot be compromised by his political goals. In a text written in La Havana in 1966 about 'the role of the intellectual in national liberation movements' ('El papel del intelectual en los movimientos de liberación nacional') he therefore introduced the distinction between 'creador' [creator] and 'intelectual' [intellectual]: 'en el artista, el elemento determinante no es nunca racional, sino espontáneo, incontrolable, esencialmente intuitivo. Y el escritor no puede

[16] Ricardo A. Setti, ... *sobre la vida y la política: Diálogo con Vargas Llosa* (México: Kosmos Editorial, 1989), pp. 147–50.
[17] Setti, p. 150.

poner ese elemento al servicio de nada, de una manera premeditada' [for an artist, the determining creative factor is never rational, but spontaneous, incontrollable, essentially intuitive. And the writer cannot use this creative factor, in a premeditated manner, in the service of anything].[18]

Instead of giving in to the pressures of writing literature in support of a cause, Vargas Llosa argued in favour of accepting, even welcoming this tension between the role of writer and intellectual, and turning it into a creative force. Throughout his long career he has pursued this dual role, always claiming that discrepancies between the two sides of his vocation are unavoidable:

> That element which rushes out spontaneously from the most secret corner of one's personality imposes a special colouring upon the story one is trying to write, establishes hierarchies among the characters which sometimes subtly overturn our conscious intention, adorns or impregnates that which we are narrating with a meaning or symbolism which, in some cases, not only does not coincide with our ideas but can even go so far as to substantially contradict them.[19]

But while this and other similar statements over the years were meant to defend the writer's freedom in creating an autonomous fictional world, in recent times they seem to have backfired: Vargas Llosa has become increasingly irritated that his literature wins acclaim whereas his political opinions are vilified. This happened, for example, in the way that his dictatorship novel *La Fiesta del Chivo* [*The Feast of the Goat*][20] was received in 2000: Vargas Llosa, 'the prophet of neoliberalism and North American capitalism who cannot differentiate between victims and persecutors', as the Spanish author Manuel Vázquez Montalbán said, nevertheless 'reclaimed progressive territory' in his fiction: 'in this novel, he seems to be the liberal novelist who is opposed to a dictator'.[21] Ten years later, the Nobel Prize provoked similar reactions. The French paper *Le Monde Diplomatique* published an article with the title 'Romancier flamboyant, doctrinaire convulsive. Les Deux Mario Vargas Llosa' [Ardent Novelist, Raging Doctrinaire. The Two Mario Vargas Llosas].[22] The Spanish actor Guillermo Toledo made a similar

---

[18] Mario Vargas Llosa, 'El papel del intelectual en los movimientos de liberación nacional', in *Contra viento I*, pp. 105–6.

[19] Mario Vargas Llosa, *Literature and Freedom* (St Leonards, Australia: Centre for Independent Studies, 1994), p. 4.

[20] Mario Vargas Llosa, *La Fiesta del Chivo* (Madrid: Alfaguara, 2000); Mario Vargas Llosa, *The Feast of the Goat*, trans. Edith Grossman (New York: Farrar, Straus and Giroux, 2001).

[21] Thomas Bodenmüller, 'Yo no me voy a poner a juzgar la novela de Vargas Llosa', entrevista con Manuel Vázquez Montalbán, *Iberoamericana*, 1.3 (2001), 173–80 (p. 177).

[22] Ignacio Ramonet, 'Romancier flamboyant, doctrinaire convulsive. Les Deux Mario

distinction saying that, while Vargas Llosa earned the Nobel Prize on literary grounds, one must not forget his 'ultracapitalist and neoliberal' position which makes him a 'very dangerous right-winger'.[23] The singer and friend of Vargas Llosa, Joaquín Sabina, came to his defence with the statement: 'sus novelas son mucho más de izquierda, a pesar suyo, que las de muchos escritores de izquierda' [his novels are – unintentionally – much more left-wing than those of left-wing writers].[24] And the official Cuban newspaper *Granma* led with the title: 'Nobel de la literatura, Antinobel de la ética' [Nobel in Literature, Anti-Nobel in Ethics].[25]

In 2005 Vargas Llosa received the Irving Kristol Award from the American Enterprise Institute, a neo-conservative US think-tank associated with the 'Fundación Internacional para la Libertad' [International Freedom Foundation] whose founding member and President Vargas Llosa is. In his acceptance speech 'Confessions of a Liberal'[26] he complained about the 'schizophrenic process' by which critics try to disconnect his fiction from his opinions in public debates. Instead, he asked to be seen 'as a unified being, the man who writes and thinks', since 'both activities form part of a single, inseparable reality'. This is in accordance with the dual role Vargas Llosa has always defined for himself, as a creator of fictions and, at the same time, as a commentator on society and politics.

The idea of the writer as an intellectual engaged in public debate goes back to his admiration for Sartre, whose conviction that words are acts shaped his own concept of literature in the 1950s and 1960s. He firmly believed in the social obligation of a writer to participate in public debate and contribute to the solution of social problems. In the 1970s, Vargas Llosa focused on the particular Latin American context of underdevelopment and political problems, such as disinformation and censorship, a situation in which the privilege of having an education and control over language carried with it the need to 'assume a social responsibility: at the same time that you develop a personal literary work, you should serve, through your writing but also

---

Vargas Llosa', *Le Monde Diplomatique*, November 2010, <http://www.monde-diplomatique.fr/2010/11/RAMONET/19856> [accessed 27 October 2012].

23 Laura Jurado, 'Willy Toledo: "Vargas Llosa es un derechista muy peligroso"', *El Mundo*, 8 October 2010, <http://www.elmundo.es/elmundo/2010/10/08/baleares/1286554322.html> [accessed 27 October 2012].

24 'Joaquín Sabina se pronunció en contra del veto a Mario Vargas Llosa', *El Comercio*, 16 March 2011, <http://elcomercio.pe/espectaculos/728391/noticia-joaquin-sabina-se-pronuncio-contra-veto-mario-vargas-llosa> [accessed 27 October 2012].

25 'Nobel de la literatura, Antinobel de la ética', *Granma*, 8 October 2010, <http://www.granma.cu/espanol/noticias/8octu-novel.html> [accessed 27 October 2012].

26 Mario Vargas Llosa, 'Confessions of a Liberal', 2005 Irving Kristol Lecture AEI Annual Dinner, <http://www.aei.org/speech/22053> [accessed 27 October 2012].

through your actions, as an active participant in the solution of the economic, political and cultural problems of your society'.[27]

In a 1987 survey for the French *Magazine Littéraire* about the role of the intellectual Vargas Llosa made it clear that, despite his changes in political opinion, he never put into question the moral responsibility which the writer has 'in parallel' with his artistic responsibility.[28] It was this moral responsibility that led him to enter politics in the late 1980s. But the obligations of a politician turned out to be quite different from the moral stance that an independent intellectual is able to take. Since then he has resumed his dual role of creating fictions and contributing to public debate with articles, lectures, interviews, open letters and pronouncements in favour or against a political issue or party. In an essay of 2006 he defended the novelist Günter Grass in the controversy aroused by the German writer's shocking revelations in his autobiography,[29] which seemed to put into question his credibility as a committed intellectual. Despite their bruising polemical exchanges in the 1980s about European left-wing attitudes to Latin America[30] Vargas Llosa praised Grass on this occasion for being one of the last authors to believe that the role of writer is 'the most formidable one', since it means not only entertaining but also educating, guiding and orienting the reader by giving lessons, launching 'diatribes, polemics' and generally stirring up public opinion. A proper intellectual in the old-fashioned sense of the word,

> Günter Grass es el último de esa estirpe, a la que pertenecieron un Victor Hugo, un Thomas Mann, un Albert Camus, un Jean-Paul Sartre. Creían que ser escritor era, al mismo tiempo que fantasear ficciones, dramas o poemas, agitar las conciencias de sus contemporáneos, animándolos a actuar, defendiendo ciertas opciones y rechazando otras, convencidos de que el escritor podía servir también como guía, consejero, animador o dinamitero ideológico.[31]
>
> [Günter Grass is the last in a line of writers to which a Victor Hugo, a Thomas Mann, an Albert Camus, a Jean-Paul Sartre, belonged. They

---

[27] Mario Vargas Llosa, 'Social Commitment and the Latin American Writer', *World Literature Today*, 52 (1978), 6–14 (p. 6).

[28] Mario Vargas Llosa, 'Les Français vus de l'étranger par Jürg Altwegg, Mario Vargas Llosa et Stanley Hoffman', *Le rôle des intellectuels de l'affaire Dreyfus à nos jours* (*Magazine Littéraire*, 248 (1987)), 56–8 (p. 57).

[29] In his autobiography *Beim Häuten der Zwiebel* [Peeling the Onion] (Göttingen: Steidl, 2006) Grass revealed that, as a seventeen-year-old soldier towards the end of the Second World War, he became for a couple of months a member of the infamous SS. This caused a scandal and played into the hands of those who had always disputed the left-wing intellectual's role as a moral conscience in postwar West German society.

[30] See Mario Vargas Llosa, 'Freedom for the Free?', in *Making Waves*, pp. 200–4.

[31] Mario Vargas Llosa, 'Günter Grass, en la picota', *El País*, 27 August 2006, <http://elpais.com/diario/2006/08/27/opinion/1156629605_850215.html> [accessed 26 August 2013].

believed that, in addition to imagining fictions, dramas or poems, being a writer consisted of stirring up their contemporaries' conscience, inciting them to act, defending certain options while rejecting others, with the conviction that the writer could also serve as a guide, advisor, animator or ideological incendiary.]

Considering the controversial reactions that Vargas Llosa's own interventions provoke, he himself assumes this role as 'dinamitero', exploding myths, prejudices, received opinions and inciting an open debate. The article on Grass is also a defence of his own position as a writer engaged with the great social, political, cultural and moral topics. He fully identifies with the role of intellectuals such as Grass and his German colleague Hans-Magnus Enzensberger whom he praises as 'un gran agitador de conciencias y algo así como un barómetro de todos los grandes problemas de nuestro tiempo' [a great agitator of our conscience and something like a barometer of all the big problems of our times].[32]

The Nobel Lecture of 2010 is the best example of how Vargas Llosa intertwines literature and politics. Its account of what shaped him as a writer is closely linked to his political concerns: he underlines his abhorrence of authoritarianism, of dictatorships, political violence and religious fanaticism; he warns about the dangers of nationalism, that 'incurable plague of the modern world'. The speech brings out what is at the basis of both his literary and his political ideas: the coexistence of differing ideas; understanding and tolerance of 'the other'; and, above all, freedom. As we will see, the twin concerns of politics and literature also tie in with his fiction where not only dictators, violent fanatics and nationalistic idealists take centre stage, but also writer figures and storytellers. Despite some shifts of emphasis over the years, the different levels of Vargas Llosa's work – fiction, literary theory and criticism, and socio-political commentary – show a remarkable coherence.

---

[32] Enzensberger received the 2002 Prince of Asturias Prize for Communication and the Humanities. Mario Vargas Llosa, 'Agitador de conciencias', *ABC*, 16 May 2002, <http://www.abc.es/hemeroteca/historico-16-05-2002/abc/Cultura/agitador-de-conciencias_99723.html> [accessed 27 October 2012].

2

Truth and Lies: Literary Theory and Criticism

A large number of essays, lectures and interviews in which Vargas Llosa explores his understanding of literature bear witness to his continuous interest in the theoretical aspects of literary creation. To name just a few landmark texts: in 1966 he delivered the programmatic lecture *La novela* [The Novel],[1] an exposition of his ideas about novel writing; a year later he declared that 'literature is fire', elaborating on the rebellious nature of fiction in his famous Rómulo Gallegos Prize speech;[2] the critical study of *García Márquez. Historia de un deicidio* [History of a Deicide], published in 1971,[3] begins with a definition of Vargas Llosa's own understanding of fiction; *Historia secreta de una novela* [Secret History of a Novel], also from 1971,[4] tells the story of how he wrote *La casa verde* [*The Green House*];[5] and 1972 saw the publication of a book-length interview conducted by Ricardo Cano Gaviria called *El buitre y el Ave Fénix* [The Vulture and the Phoenix],[6] which touched on all important aspects of Vargas Llosa's literary theory. Later essays such as 'El arte de mentir' [The Art of Lying][7] and the prefaces to his plays of the 1980s examined the ambiguities between truth and lies, such as the appropriately named 'Las mentiras verdaderas' [Lies That Tell the Truth], introduction to *La señorita de Tacna* [*The Young Lady from Tacna*] (1981).[8] He returned

---

[1] Mario Vargas Llosa, *La novela. Conferencia pronunciada en el Paraninfo de la Universidad de la República, el 11 de agosto de 1966* (Montevideo: Fundación de Cultura Universitaria, 1969).

[2] Mario Vargas Llosa, 'La literatura es fuego', in *Contra viento y marea, I (1962–1972)* (Barcelona: Seix Barral, 1986), pp. 176–81; Mario Vargas Llosa, 'Literature is Fire', in *Making Waves*, ed. and trans. John King (London: Faber and Faber, 1996), pp. 70–4.

[3] Mario Vargas Llosa, *García Márquez. Historia de un deicidio* (Barcelona: Barral Editores, 1971).

[4] Mario Vargas Llosa, *Historia secreta de una novela* (Barcelona: Tusquets, 1971).

[5] Mario Vargas Llosa, *La casa verde* (Barcelona: Argos Vergara, 1980); Mario Vargas Llosa, *The Green House* (London: Picador, 1986).

[6] Ricardo Cano Gaviria, *El buitre y el Ave Fénix. Conversaciones con Mario Vargas Llosa* (Barcelona: Anagrama, 1972).

[7] Mario Vargas Llosa, 'El arte de mentir', in *Contra viento y marea, II (1972–1983)* (Barcelona: Seix Barral, 1986), pp. 418–24.

[8] Mario Vargas Llosa, 'Las mentiras verdaderas', in *La señorita de Tacna* (Barcelona: Seix Barral, 1981), pp. 9–12; Mario Vargas Llosa, 'Lies That Tell the Truth', in *Three plays*.

to this notion in 1990, in a preface to the collection of his literary criticism called *La verdad de las mentiras* [The Truth of Lies].[9] The borders between Vargas Llosa's essays on other writers and his own theory of writing fiction are often blurred, such as in *A Writer's Reality* (1990),[10] the text of a series of lectures given at Syracuse University in 1988. In 1997 he published *Cartas a un joven novelista*[11] where, in a series of *Letters to a Young Novelist*,[12] he explains his ideas about writing novels. In a systematic and instructive manner, this textbook for the aspiring writer revisits the crucial points of Vargas Llosa's literary theory, including the technicalities of transforming reality into fiction.[13] More recently Vargas Llosa has published a number of important essays in journals such as *Letras Libres*, containing his thoughts on the novel's future ('La muerte de la novela' [The Death of the Novel], 1999),[14] on the role of fiction in society (for example, 'Un mundo sin novelas' [A World Without Novels], 2000)[15] and in history ('El viaje a la ficción' [The Journey to Fiction], 2008).[16] He integrated some of these ideas into his 2010 Nobel Lecture.[17]

The literary theory that Vargas Llosa has developed is highly self-referential. It reflects his own way of writing realist narrative fiction and deals with the questions: What drives a writer to invent fictional worlds? How does he or she go about transforming reality into fiction? What relation does this fiction have to life? And what effect does a work of fiction have on the reader? His key concepts in dealing with these questions are the 'demonios' [demons] that nourish a writer's vocation; the 'elementos añadidos' [added

---

The Young Lady from Tacna. Kathie y el Hippopotamus. La Chunga, trans. David Graham-Young (London: Faber and Faber, 1990), pp. 5–7.

[9] Mario Vargas Llosa, *La verdad de las mentiras. Ensayos sobre literatura* (Barcelona: Seix Barral, 1990).

[10] Mario Vargas Llosa, *A Writer's Reality* (London and Boston: Faber and Faber, 1990).

[11] Mario Vargas Llosa, *Cartas a un joven novelista* (Barcelona: Planeta, 1997).

[12] Mario Vargas Llosa, *Letters to a Young Novelist*, trans. Natasha Wimmer (New York: Farrar, Strauss & Giroux, 2002).

[13] The title is reminiscent of Rainer Maria Rilke's *Letters to a Young Poet* (London: Penguin, 2011). Of Rilke's letters only the first two actually contain advice on writing poems, but the first letter especially touches on areas essential to Vargas Llosa's own *Letters*: the exclusiveness of a literary vocation, the transformation of the writer's own experience into art and the resulting authenticity of the work.

[14] Mario Vargas Llosa, 'La muerte de la novela', *Letras Libres*, 1 (1999), 14–16.

[15] Mario Vargas Llosa, 'Un mundo sin novelas', *Letras Libres*, 2 (2000), 38–44.

[16] Mario Vargas Llosa, 'El viaje a la ficción', in *El viaje a la ficción. El mundo de Juan Carlos Onetti* (Lima: Alfaguara, 2008), pp. 11–32.

[17] Mario Vargas Llosa, 'Elogio de la lectura y la ficción', Nobel Lecture, 7 December 2010, <http://nobelprize.org/nobel_prizes/literature/laureates/2010/vargas_llosa-lecture_sp.html> [accessed 27 October 2012]; Mario Vargas Llosa, 'In Praise of Reading and Fiction', Nobel Lecture, 7 December 2010, <http://nobelprize.org/nobel_prizes/literature/laureates/2010/vargas_llosa-lecture_en.html> [accessed 27 October 2012].

elements] of form, structure and language; the truth and lies of a 'total' novel; and the rebellious nature of fiction.

In Vargas Llosa's view, a writer responds to a strong sense of vocation that arises out of a disagreement with the world as it is. There can be manifold individual reasons for this rejection of reality, and for the writer's passionate desire to create an alternative, invented world. His theoretical texts of the 1960s and 1970s highlight the 'demons' which he tries to 'exorcize' by writing:

> hechos, personas, sueños, mitos, cuya presencia o cuya ausencia, cuya vida o cuya muerte lo enemistaron con la realidad, se grabaron con fuego en su memoria y atormentaron su espíritu, se convirtieron en los materiales de su empresa de reedificación de la realidad, y a los que tratará simultáneamente de recuperar y exorcizar, con las palabras y la fantasía, en el ejercicio de esa vocación que nació y se nutre de ellos, en esas ficciones en las que ellos, disfrazados o idénticos, omnipresentes o secretos, aparecen y reaparecen una y otra vez, convertidos en temas. (*Deicidio*, p. 87)

> [events, people, dreams, myths, whose presence or absence, life or death made him averse to reality; that became deeply engraved in his memory and tormented his mind, turned into the material for his endeavour to rebuild reality, and that he tries to simultaneously retrieve and exorcize, by means of words and imagination, carrying out this vocation which they engender and nourish, in fictions where they appear again and again, disguised or identical, omnipresent or secret, transformed into subject matter.][18]

Vargas Llosa distinguishes between three categories of 'demons' (see *Deicidio*, pp. 102–3): apart from personal obsessions ('demonios individuales') the collective experience of certain historical or social events can leave a lasting mark on the writer's imagination (what he calls the 'demonios sociales o históricos' [social or historical demons] clearly visible, for example, in his recurring themes of dictatorship and political violence); his third category is cultural experiences which influence the fictional reconstruction of reality ('demonios culturales' [cultural demons], such as events experienced through books or films).[19] The conversion of a writer's obsessions into the themes of his fiction happens in an involuntary manner. According to Vargas Llosa, the writer is not free to choose his subject matter, it imposes itself. He goes so far as to say that only by letting the 'demons' determine what to write about, literature becomes truly authentic: 'me parece difícil que

---

[18] Because Vargas Llosa's theory predominantly refers to his own way of writing, it seems justified, even in his pronouncements about the writer in general, to use the male pronoun only.

[19] This distinction makes the interpretation of Vargas Llosa's 'demons' in mere psychoanalytical terms questionable, for example as Armando Perreira does in his study *La concepción literaria de Mario Vargas Llosa* (México: Universidad Nacional Autónoma de México, 1981).

se llegue a ser un creador – un transformador de la realidad – si no se escribe alentado y alimentado desde el propio ser por aquellos fantasmas (demonios) que han hecho de nosotros, los novelistas, objetores esenciales y reconstructores de la vida en las ficciones que inventamos' (*Cartas*, pp. 29–30) [it seems unlikely to me that anyone will become a creator – a transformer of reality – if he doesn't write encouraged and nourished from the depths of his being by those ghosts (or demons) who've made us novelists determined protesters and reconstructors of life in the stories we tell] (*Letters*, p. 22).

Vargas Llosa's terminology of the writer's 'demons' and their 'exorcism' caused some controversy.[20] His predilection for drastic comparisons and shocking metaphors made him describe the writer as a 'vulture', feeding on 'the putrid flesh of history',[21] whose job it is to 'cannibalize' or 'ransack' his own experiences for his writing (*Deicidio*, p. 101). He has since modified that terminology, without abandoning his basic ideas: the writer feels the need to come to terms with things that occupy his mind in an obsessive manner; these things thrust themselves on him as the subject matter of his fiction and enable him to create authentic literature.

Vargas Llosa sees the writer as a 'slave' to the urgent, passionate desire to deal with his obsessions in fiction and to express his discontent with life: 'Porque el escritor, que es el hombre más libre frente a los demás y el mundo, ante su vocación es un esclavo'[22] [Because the writer, who is the freest person imaginable with respect to other people and the world, is a slave to his vocation].[23] He has repeatedly compared this vocation to a tapeworm eating away at a person's substance, needing to be fed continuously. Just as the tapeworm becomes an integral part of that person's life, and cannot be abandoned (see *Cartas*, pp. 7–20; *Letters*, pp. 3–14), the vocation to create fiction becomes the dominant feature of a writer's existence, demanding his complete dedication: 'Ella es una pasión y la pasión no admite ser compartida', he wrote in 1966 ('Bondy y la vocación', p. 117) [Literature is a passion and passion does not allow itself to be shared] ('Bondy and the Vocation', p. 63). In the 1997 *Cartas a un joven novelista* he reiterated this thought, concluding with a memorable *antimetabole* (the rhetorical figure which repeats the same words in reverse order)[24] summing up his notion of the writer: 'la vocación

---

[20] See, for example, Angel Rama and Mario Vargas Llosa, *García Márquez y la problemática de la novela* (Buenos Aires: Corregidor-Marcha, 1973).

[21] Mario Vargas Llosa, 'The Latin American Novel Today', *Books Abroad*, 44.1 (1970), 8–16 (p. 12).

[22] Mario Vargas Llosa, 'Sebastián Salazar Bondy y la vocación del escritor en el Perú', in *Contra viento I*, pp. 111–35 (p. 117).

[23] Mario Vargas Llosa, 'Sebastián Salazar Bondy and the Vocation of the Writer in Peru', in *Making Waves*, pp. 59–69 (p. 63)

[24] Vargas Llosa is fond of this figure and often uses it to create an intellectual paradox, for example when he said that winning the Nobel Prize turned 'life into literature and literature into

literaria se alimenta de la vida del escritor ni más ni menos que la longínea solitaria de los cuerpos que invade. Flaubert decía: "Escribir es una manera de vivir". En otras palabras, quien ha hecho suya esta hermosa y absorbente vocación *no escribe para vivir, vive para escribir'* (*Cartas*, p. 17; my italics) [the literary vocation feeds off the life of the writer just as the tapeworm feeds off the bodies it invades. As Flaubert said: 'Writing is [a] way of living'. In other words, those who make this enchanting and engrossing vocation their own *don't write to live but live to write*] (*Letters*, pp. 11–12; my italics). The compulsive and exclusive manner of creating fiction goes hand in hand with Vargas Llosa's view of writing as hard work which requires great discipline and a 'constant sacrifice'.[25] For him inspiration does not exist: 'Sobre mí no caía jamás esa fuerza divina: a mí cada sílaba escrita me costaba un esfuerzo brutal' [I was never visited by that divine force: each syllable I wrote cost me a horrendous effort] (*Historia secreta*, pp. 48–9).

In his attempt to describe the creative process – 'alquimia que me fascina porque la entiendo menos cuanto más la practico'[26] [alchemy [that] fascinates me because the more I practise it, the less I understand it][27] – Vargas Llosa frequently uses the dichotomy 'realidad real/realidad ficticia' [real reality/ fictional reality]. Fictional reality reflects, but also negates real reality and compensates for its shortcomings. His 1971 study *García Márquez. Historia de un deicidio* says of the writer's creation: 'es dos cosas a la vez: una reedificación de la realidad y un testimonio de su desacuerdo con el mundo' [it is two things at once: a rebuilding of reality and a testimony of the writer's disagreement with the world] (*Deicidio*, p. 88). He further elaborates this point in a passage that remains fundamental to his understanding of novel writing:

> Escribir novelas es un acto de rebelión contra la realidad, contra Dios, contra la creación de Dios que es la realidad. Es una tentativa de corrección, cambio o abolición de la realidad real, de su sustitución por la realidad ficticia que el novelista crea. Este es un disidente: crea vida ilusoria, crea mundos verbales porque no acepta la vida y el mundo tal como son (o como cree que son). La raíz de su vocación es un sentimiento de insatisfacción contra la vida; cada novela es un deicidio secreto, un asesinato simbólico de la realidad. (p. 85)

---

life' (see 'Introduction', above), or express the mutual dependency of two factors as in the title of his publication *La libertad de la cultura. La cultura de la libertad* [The Freedom of Culture. The Culture of Freedom] (Santiago de Chile: Fundación Eduardo Frei, 1985).

[25] Cano Gaviria, p. 63.

[26] Mario Vargas Llosa, 'El teatro como ficción', in *Kathie y el hipopótamo* (Barcelona: Seix Barral, 1983), pp. 9–13 (p. 12).

[27] Mario Vargas Llosa, 'Theatre as Fiction', in *Three plays*, pp. 81–4 (p. 83).

[Writing novels is an act of rebellion against reality and against God, against God's creation that is reality. It is an attempt to correct, change or abolish real reality, to substitute it with the fictional reality that a novelist creates. The latter is a dissident: he creates verbal worlds, an illusion of life, because he does not accept life and the world as they are (or as he thinks they are). At the root of his vocation is a feeling of discontent with life; every novel is a secret deicide, a symbolic murder of reality.]

Although the notion of 'deicide' is not so prominent in his later theoretical writings,[28] the view of creating fictional reality as an attempt to overthrow 'real reality' and erect an alternative cosmos remains at the centre of Vargas Llosa's theory. In one of his *Letters to a Young Novelist* he underlines this point:

Estoy convencido de que quien se abandona a la elucubración de vidas distintas a aquella que vive en la realidad manifiesta de esta indirecta manera su rechazo y crítica de la vida tal como es, del mundo real, y su deseo de sustituirlos por aquellos que fabrica con su imaginación y sus deseos. (*Cartas*, pp. 11–12)

[I'm convinced that those who immerse themselves in the lucubration of lives different from their own demonstrate indirectly their rejection and criticism of life as it is, of the real world, and manifest their desire to substitute for it the creations of their imagination and dreams.] (*Letters*, p. 7)

Despite being dependent on the writer's own experiences, the imaginary world of a novel has to have a life of its own in order to be convincing. It has to go beyond pure referential truth and become an autonomous world: 'El mundo así forjado, de palabra y fantasía, es literatura cuando en él lo añadido a la vida prevalece sobre lo tomado de ella' [The world thus forged, of words and imagination, constitutes [proper] literature when, in it, what is added to life prevails over what is taken from it].[29] According to Vargas Llosa's theory, the so-called 'elementos añadidos', the 'added elements' that a novelist chooses, determine whether a fictional world gains autonomy from the real-life events it is based on. These added elements can consist of 'his resentment, his nostalgia, his criticism' (*Deicidio*, p. 86) of the things that his imagination contributes, and also of the order that the novelist imposes on the fictional world by using certain narrative strategies. Unlike the irrational

---

[28] On the eclectic mix of ideas that have influenced Vargas Llosa's concept of the creator God, and on the parallels between his theory of the writer's rebellion against God's creation and Albert Camus's *L'homme révolté*, see my study *Vargas Llosa's Fiction & the Demons of Politics* (Oxford: Peter Lang, 2002), pp. 47–53.

[29] Mario Vargas Llosa, *La utopía arcaica. José María Arguedas y las ficciones del indigenismo* (México: Fondo de Cultura Económica, 1996), p. 85.

manner in which a writer finds his subject matter, the actual process of turning life into fiction constitutes a rational choice of literary devices on his part. As a verbal recreation of the world, he gives the novel structure by choosing a time frame and a space in which it develops; he decides on style, point of view, type of narrator and what Vargas Llosa calls 'nivel de realidad' [level of reality] (for example, realistic or fantastic). It is these narrative techniques, together with elements of the imagination, that determine whether a fictional creation has the necessary power of persuasion to transport the reader into a world of its own ('El poder de persuasión' is the heading of one of Vargas Llosa's *Cartas*): 'Esta es la curiosa ambigüedad de la ficción: aspirar a la autonomía sabiendo que su esclavitud de lo real es inevitable y sugerir, mediante esforzadas técnicas, una independencia y autosuficiencia' (p. 38) [This is the curious ambiguity of fiction: it must aspire to independence knowing that its slavery to reality is inevitable, and it must suggest through sophisticated techniques an autonomy and self-sufficiency] (*Letters*, p. 29). Vargas Llosa names four such techniques, or added elements, which he regards as essential in creating an autonomous fictional world:

1. 'La muda o el salto cualitativo' [shifts or qualitative leaps]: these terms refer to narrative devices that bring about a significant change in the character of a narration. This can be a sudden shift in the spatial or temporal frame, a surprising change of narrator or a shift on the level of reality, such as when a hitherto realistic account takes on a magical quality.
2. 'Los vasos comunicantes' [communicating vessels] are montage techniques such as intercalated dialogues on different levels of time or space, or between different people, where, for example, a conversation between protagonists A and B suddenly jumps to a dialogue between A and C. The resulting spatial or temporal juxtapositions have the effect of revealing hidden connections between events on different strata of a narrative.
3. 'Las cajas chinas' [Chinese boxes] consist of telling a story within a story (within a story within a story and so forth) in the manner of *The Thousand and One Nights*. Vargas Llosa explains this technique as a 'symbiosis or association of elements with a mutually unsettling effect on each other' (*Letters*, p. 101).
4. 'El dato escondido' [the hidden fact] refers to 'significant silences' (*Letters*, p. 109) in the narration of events. The novelist leaves out essential information in order to create suspense, ambiguity, or special narrative interest, either by distorting the chronological order ('dato escondido en hipérbaton' [hidden fact created by hyperbaton]) or by eliminating key information altogether ('dato escondido elíptico' [hidden fact created by ellipsis]).

These narrative strategies help to establish the fictional creation as an autonomous world, independent of its real model, but also independent of its creator, since the author is supposed to disappear effortlessly behind the narration. This is an ideal modelled on Flaubert whom Vargas Llosa quotes with the words: 'L'artiste doit être dans son oeuvre comme Dieu dans la création, invisible et tout-puissant; qu'on le sente partout, mais qu'on ne le voie pas'[30] [The artist must be in his work like God in his creation, invisible and all-powerful; he must be everywhere felt, but never seen][31] – hence Vargas Llosa's preoccupation with the narrator as the most important fictional creation within a novel whose way of telling the story, 'showing or hiding himself, lingering or surging ahead, being explicit or elusive, talkative or taciturn, playful or serious' (*Letters*, pp. 42–3) decides on its power of persuasion.

The technical side of creating a fictional world is where, according to Vargas Llosa, the novelist is totally responsible for his success or failure: 'La literatura es puro artificio, pero la gran literatura consigue disimularlo y la mediocre lo delata', he says (*Cartas*, p. 47) [Literature is pure artifice, but great literature is able to hide the fact while mediocre literature gives itself away] (*Letters*, p. 38). Successful novels, made up of the 'lies' of fiction pretending to be true, convey a special kind of truth, a 'truth that can only be expressed in a furtive and veiled fashion, disguised as something it is not'[32] ('mintiendo, expresan una curiosa verdad, que sólo puede expresarse disimulada y encubierta, disfrazada de lo que no es').[33] The dichotomy 'verdad/mentira' [truth/lie] becomes more and more important in Vargas Llosa's theory, where he often uses oxymoron[34] to express the ambiguous nature of literature: 'la verdad de las mentiras' [the truth of lies], 'la mentira verdadera' [the truthful lie], 'la verdad mentirosa' [the lying truth], etc. As he explains: 'Esta verdad no reside en la semejanza o esclavitud de lo escrito o dicho —de lo inventado— a una realidad distinta, "objetiva", superior, sino en sí misma, en su condición de cosa creada a partir de las verdades y mentiras que constituyen la ambigua totalidad humana' ('Las mentiras verdaderas', p. 11) [This truth doesn't lie in any similarity or slavish adherence of the spoken or written word (what is created) [*sic*] to a higher 'objective' reality, but in

---

[30] Mario Vargas Llosa, *La orgía perpetua. Flaubert y 'Madame Bovary'* (Barcelona: Seix Barral, 1975), p. 145.

[31] Mario Vargas Llosa, *The Perpetual Orgy. Flaubert and 'Madame Bovary'*, trans. Helen Lane (London: Faber and Faber, 1987), pp. 124–5.

[32] Mario Vargas Llosa, 'The Truth of Lies', in *Making Waves*, pp. 320–30 (p. 320).

[33] Mario Vargas Llosa, 'La verdad de las mentiras', in *La verdad de las mentiras*, pp. 5–20 (p. 6).

[34] The rhetorical figure which combines opposites. On the importance of oxymoron in Vargas Llosa's writing see my forthcoming article 'Mistrust and mastery: Goethe, Victor Hugo, Mario Vargas Llosa and the art of rhetoric', *Rhetorica*, 2014.

itself, as something created from the raw material of truth and falsehood which make up the ambiguous totality of human experience] ('Lies That Tell the Truth', p. 6). Novels are able to reflect the contradictory nature of human beings and respond to the reader's wish to have varied and multidimensional experiences in fiction which he or she cannot have in reality:

> Sus órdenes artificiales proporcionan refugio, seguridad, y en ellos se despliegan, libremente, aquellos apetitos y temores que la vida real incita y no alcanza a saciar o conjurar. ... Gracias a [la ficción] somos más y somos otros sin dejar de ser los mismos. En ella nos disolvemos y multiplicamos, viviendo muchas más vidas de la que tenemos. ('La verdad de las mentiras', pp. 12, 19)

> [Its artificial orders give refuge and security and also allow the free display of those appetites and fears that real life provokes but cannot satisfy or exorcize. ... Thanks to fiction we are more and we are others without ceasing to be the same. In it we can lose ourselves and multiply, living many more lives than the ones we have.] ('The Truth of Lies', pp. 325, 329)

The type of novel that is best suited to achieve this effect on the reader is what Vargas Llosa calls the 'novela total' [total novel], able to encompass a whole world in all its aspects. He finds this 'totalizing ambition' achieved in novels as far apart as the late fifteenth-century chivalric novel *Tirant lo Blanc* by Joanot Martorell and García Márquez's most famous novel, *Cien años de soledad* [*One Hundred Years of Solitude*] (1967), both works that he has written about extensively. *Tirant lo Blanc*, he says, combines historical, military, social, cultural, romantic, sexual and psychological aspects with a mythical level to deliver a 'total' picture of the reality of its time. This turns it into a subversive work which breaks all borders and shows reality as it is, without didactic attempt: 'era una cosa tremendamente subversiva, porque desbarataba toda clase de tabúes, desvanecía toda clase de supercherías' [it was tremendously subversive because it broke all kinds of taboos and lifted all kinds of smokescreens] (*La novela*, p. 19). He values it as a novel which can be read and enjoyed on many different levels. The same goes for *Cien años de soledad*, 'novela que es, simultáneamente, cosas que se creían antinómicas: tradicional y moderna, localista y universal, imaginaria y realista' [a novel that is, simultaneously, many things believed to be mutually exclusive: traditional and modern, local and universal, fantastic and realistic] (*Deicidio*, pp. 79–80). It is also an example of a fictional microcosm which reflects the wider world in all its facets: the fictional Macondo, setting of a number of García Márquez's works, plays host to a whole range of human experiences. In the same way Faulkner, another of Vargas Llosa's literary models, created Yoknapatawpha County as the setting of most of his novels, and Juan Carlos Onetti, subject of Vargas Llosa's latest book-length critical study, invented his fictional microcosm of Santa María, a place that gains autonomy by having 'una historia, geografía, tradición, mitología y problemática social que le son propias' [a proper history, geography, tradition, mythology, and its own set of social problems] (*El viaje*, p. 85). These totalizing narratives are the ones that have drawn Vargas Llosa himself as a reader into their invented universe. As a novelist, he aims to provide his own readers with equally seductive verbal counter-worlds, able to complement real life with a wide spectrum of experiences in fiction.

Vargas Llosa's totalizing ambition is modelled on what he himself found in the work of authors such as Martorell, Faulkner, García Márquez, Tolstoy and Balzac. The latter's declared ambition to capture 'the private history of nations' in his vast collection of interconnected novels, *La Comédie Humaine* [*The Human Comedy*], is an ideal that Vargas Llosa strives after. He uses a quotation from Balzac as the epigraph of his 1969 *Conversación en la catedral* [*Conversation in the Cathedral*]:[35] 'Il faut avoir fouillé toute la vie sociale pour être un vrai romancier, vu que le roman est l'histoire privée des nations' [One has to have explored every sphere of social life to be a true novelist, since novels are the private history of nations]. While Vargas Llosa has not created anything comparable to García Márquez's Macondo, Faulkner's Yoknapatawpha County or Onetti's Santa María, he has, however, invented a protagonist who appears in several of his works: Lituma, in various phases of his life and often accompanied by his raucous friends, 'los Inconquistables' [the Unconquerables], is a character who creates a secret, underlying continuity between a number of novels and plays, as we will see. Vargas Llosa calls him his response to the 'tentación balzaciana',[36] the temptation to create a fictional universe stretching over several individual works in the manner of the French author. Like Balzac, he hopes to provide the reader with an 'integrating vision' ('esa visión integradora', 'Un mundo sin novelas', p. 39) of human existence in all its shades, on all different levels of life, where the ambiguities and contradictions of reality are able to coexist.

This special quality of literature responds to a deep-rooted desire in human nature to want more, and different, things than are possible in real life. In the epigraph to his study of Flaubert, one of his most important 'cultural demons', Vargas Llosa quotes the French writer's statement that 'the only way to tolerate existence is by loosing oneself in literature as in a perpetual orgy' (a quotation that provides the title of the book).[37] According to Vargas

---

[35] Mario Vargas Llosa, *Conversación en la catedral* (Barcelona: Seix Barral, 1985); Mario Vargas Llosa, *Conversation in the Cathedral*, trans. Gregory Rabassa (New York: HarperCollins, 2005).

[36] José Miguel Oviedo, *Espejo de escritores* (Hanover, NH: Ediciones del Norte, 1985), p. 163.

[37] *La orgía*, p. 9, quoted in the original French: 'Le seul moyen de supporter l'existence, c'est de s'étourdir dans la littérature comme dans une orgie perpétuelle'.

Llosa, fiction is able to fulfil the desire to overcome reality's limitations and let the reader live different lives – but only temporarily. The reader, just like the author of a work of fiction, returns to reality even more aware of its limitations, which reinforces the initial rebellious impulse to wish for a different reality. This is the 'permanent insurrection' that Vargas Llosa talked about in his literary theory of the 1960s and 1970s, something he later preferred to call 'permanent conspiracy' ('The Truth of Lies', p. 330):

> Soñar, escribir ficciones (como leerlas, ir a verlas o creerlas) es una oblicua protesta contra la mediocridad de nuestra vida y una manera, transitoria pero efectiva, de burlarla. La ficción, cuando nos hallamos prisioneros de su sortilegio, embelesados por su engaño, nos completa, mudándonos momentáneamente en el gran malvado, el dulce santo, el transparente idiota que nuestros deseos, cobardías, curiosidades o simple espíritu de contradicción nos incitan a ser, y nos devuelve luego a nuestra condición, pero distintos, mejor informados sobre nuestros confines, más ávidos de quimera, más indóciles a la conformidad. ('El teatro como ficción', p. 12)

> [Dreaming, creating works of fiction (the same as reading, going to plays, suspending disbelief) is an oblique way of protesting against the mediocrity of life and it is also an effective, if cursory way of ridiculing it. Fiction, when we find ourselves under its spell, bewitched by its artifice, makes us feel complete, by transforming us momentarily into those great villains, those angelic saints, or those transparent idiots, which we are constantly being invited to become by our desires and aspirations, our cowardice, our inquisitiveness or simply our spirit of contradiction, and when it returns us to our normal state, we find we have changed, that we are more aware of our limitations, more eager for fantasy and less ready to accept the status quo.] ('Theatre as Fiction', p. 83)

Over the years, Vargas Llosa's highly idiosyncratic literary theory has provoked criticism and debate, and even scholars close to the author, such as José Miguel Oviedo, conceded that the theory is only valid when applied to himself: 'El único defecto de la "teoría" es que cuando empieza a alejarse de Vargas Llosa y de su objeto de estudio, su aplicabilidad resulta menos segura' [the only deficiency of the 'theory' is that, when it begins to move away from Vargas Llosa and his object of study, its usefulness becomes less certain].[38] Nevertheless, Vargas Llosa looks at other writers' work using the concepts he has developed to explain his own way of writing. Starting with the life of an author, he searches for the 'demons' which might have influenced a particular author's fictional creations, going on from there to analyse and evaluate his or her processes of turning these life experiences into art. In an eclectic manner

---

[38] José Miguel Oviedo, *Mario Vargas Llosa: la invención de una realidad* (Barcelona: Seix Barral, 1982), pp. 346–7.

he combines a rather old-fashioned kind of biographical approach with a close reading of the texts, taking into account narrative strategies, stylistic and rhetorical patterns, and investigating the intricacies of the narrator, but never without contextualizing his analysis of the text. The beginnings of this method are already visible in the thesis that Vargas Llosa submitted in 1958, at the end of his studies at the National University of San Marcos in Lima: *Bases para una interpretación de Rubén Darío* [Foundations for an Interpretation of Rubén Darío], published in 2001 when Vargas Llosa received an Honorary Doctorate from San Marcos.[39]

Literary criticism has always featured prominently in Vargas Llosa's journalistic writing which he has pursued in parallel with his creative endeavours. The bibliography on his official website[40] shows that, as a teenager, he was already regularly writing articles on Peruvian novelists for *El Comercio* and other papers.[41] Book reviews and other occasional texts on writers remain an important part of his newspaper contributions to date, and a number of these have been included in his various essay collections. There are some authors he returns to again and again, with shorter articles or longer essays, since they have contributed in significant ways to his formation as a writer: Jorge Luis Borges, whose prose left him 'in utter amazement' when he first read it (*A Writer's Reality*, p. 3), remains in his judgement 'the most important thing to happen to imaginative writing in the Spanish language in modern times'.[42] Vargas Llosa admires his style as much as his combination of cosmopolitanism, the mastery of 'a far-ranging cultural sphere', with the local topics of his Argentinean homeland. Georges Bataille and his notion of 'Evil' ('le mal') as the other, irrational side of human nature,[43] was enormously influential on Vargas Llosa's own fictional exploration of the world of dark and antisocial instincts. There is also the already mentioned Joanot Martorell on whose 'total novel' he has published a small book under the title *Carta de batalla por Tirant lo Blanc* [Tirant lo Blanc's Battle Letter] (1991), bringing together three essays from 1969, 1970 and 1991.[44] As critic, Vargas Llosa concentrates on those authors he counts among his most fruitful

---

[39] Mario Vargas Llosa, *Bases para una interpretación de Rubén Darío, tesis universitaria 1958* (Lima: Universitaria Nacional de San Marcos, 2001).

[40] <http://mvargasllosa.com/biblio.htm>

[41] See also Miguel Angel Rodríguez Rea, *Tras las huellas de un crítico: Mario Vargas Llosa, 1954–1959* (Lima: Fondo Editorial de la Pontificia Universidad Católica del Perú, 1996).

[42] Mario Vargas Llosa, 'The Fictions of Borges', in *Wellsprings*, trans. Kristin Keenan de Cueto, John King and Jonathan Titler (Cambridge, MA and London: Harvard University Press, 2008), pp. 26–46 (p. 29).

[43] See Mario Vargas Llosa, 'Bataille or the Redemption of Evil', in *Making Waves*, pp. 117–26.

[44] Mario Vargas Llosa, *Carta de batalla por Tirant lo Blanc* (Barcelona: Seix Barral, 1991).

'cultural demons'. Talking about these writers he also talks about himself, not least in the many lectures he gives in academic institutions. His critical interests clearly lie in the aspects of fiction that concern him in his own writing. He readily admits that other forms of literature, such as the French Nouveau Roman, seem 'boring' to him (see *Orgía*, pp. 49–50). His collection of critical essays *La verdad de las mentiras* (1990, extended 2002) contains a highly personal – and as such debatable – canon of what he regards as the great works of twentieth-century fiction.

Apart from these shorter essays of criticism he has published a number of in-depth studies of writers particularly close to his heart, starting with *García Márquez. Historia de un deicidio* (1971). This 670-page book is an extremely detailed study of the Columbian author's literature along the lines of Vargas Llosa's own creative theory. The first part, called 'La realidad real' [Real Reality], on the writer's biography and his personal, social and cultural 'demons', is followed by a thorough investigation of 'La realidad ficticia' [Fictional Reality] of García Márquez's work and his invented world of Macondo. Vargas Llosa looks at *Cien años de soledad* under the aspect of the 'total novel', analysing its various points of view: narrator, time, space and level of reality. In a compelling chapter on the novel's narrative strategy he documents how García Márquez's style, especially the patterns of enumeration, repetition and hyperbole, create the magical realism for which this work has become famous. Vargas Llosa's analysis of how these rhetorical devices create a distinct narrative rhythm is illuminating. He comes to the conclusion: 'Por el ritmo hechizante, la forma se convierte en contenido' [through its entrancing rhythm, form turns into contents] (*Deicidio*, p. 588), and highlights the mutual dependency of subject matter and form as a mark of successful fiction (see p. 594). His examination of the 'hidden facts' in *Cien años de soledad* helps to understand the effect he is trying to create in his own fiction by using the same narrative device. He could be talking about one of his own fictional creations when he writes of the 'dato escondido en hipérbaton' in this novel: 'Ese vacío premeditado sugiere, ese silencio habla, esa mutilación turba, intriga, contamina al resto del relato cierto enigma, cierta zozobra, y obliga al lector a intervenir en la narración para llenar ese hueco significativo, añadiendo, adivinando, inventando, en complicidad activa con el narrador' [This deliberate empty space suggests something, this silence talks, this mutilation confuses and intrigues the reader, contaminating the rest of the story with a certain mystery, a certain disquiet, requiring the reader's intervention in the narration to fill this significant void by adding, guessing, inventing something, in active complicity with the narrator] (p. 271). Vargas Llosa's lucid analysis of García Márquez's style and narrative strategies goes far beyond the biographical criticism that one might expect from the importance he ascribes to the writer's 'demons'.

The 'Life and Work' approach seems prominent again in Vargas Llosa's

1975 study *La orgía perpetua: Flaubert y 'Madame Bovary'* [*The Perpetual Orgy. Flaubert and 'Madame Bovary'*], but here, too, he goes on to examine the narrative techniques that make *Madame Bovary* 'the first modern novel' (see *Orgía*, pp. 245–77). The study is divided into three parts. In the first, as Vargas Llosa states provocatively, he speaks more about himself than Flaubert, since the protagonist Emma Bovary is one of his most fruitful 'demons', instilling him with a sense of what literature can do on a personal level. The ambiguous relationship between life and fiction, exemplified in this character, also plays a role in his reaction as a reader. He recounts the 'cathartic effect' on him of Emma's suicide:

> Recuerdo haber leído en esos días, con angustiosa avidez, el episodio de su suicidio, haber acudido a esa lectura como otros, en circunstancias parecidas, recurren al cura, la borrachera o la morfina, y haber extraído cada vez, de esas páginas desgarradoras, consuelo y equilibrio, repugnancia del caos, gusto por la vida. El sufrimiento ficticio neutralizaba el que yo vivía. ... Emma se mataba para que yo viviera. (*Orgía*, pp. 25–6)

> [I remember having read, during those days, the episode of her suicide with anxious, avid anticipation, having hastened to my reading and rereading of this scene as others in similar circumstances take to religion and the parish priest, to drinking, or to morphine, and having each time found consolation and a sense of proportion, a revulsion against chaos, a taste for life in those heartrending pages. The fictional suffering neutralized the suffering I was experiencing in real life. ... Emma was killing herself in order that I might live.] (*Orgy*, pp. 16–17)

In this first part of the book he also develops his theory of the most important ingredients that a novel needs to bewitch its readers: rebelliousness, violence, melodrama and sex. These components can be found in all of Vargas Llosa's own works:

> En otras palabras, la máxima satisfacción que puede producirme una novela es provocar, a lo largo de la lectura, mi admiración por alguna inconformidad, mi cólera por alguna estupidez o injusticia, mi fascinación por esas situaciones de distorsionado dramatismo, de excesiva emocionabilidad ... y mi deseo. *Madame Bovary* es pródiga en estos ingredientes, ellos son los cuatro grandes ríos que bañan su vasta geografía. (p. 20)

> [In other words, the maximum satisfaction that a novel can bring me is to arouse, as I read, my admiration for this or that revolt against the established order, my anger at some stupidity or injustice, my fascination for melodramatic situations, for excessive displays of emotion ... and my secret desire. *Madame Bovary* is chock-full of these ingredients, they are the four great rivers that irrigate its vast geography.] (p. 12).

The second part of the investigation contains an anecdotal account of the novel's gestation, its possible sources, and the personal circumstances of Flaubert as a man of letters, before going on to discuss the narrative strategies of *Madame Bovary*. In this part of the study, the dual focus on the author and his work, and the link between the two, is always present. Thematically, Vargas Llosa looks at marginality as a characteristic of the writer as well as his protagonist; he uncovers a binary structure running through the novel, reflecting the writer's dual nature as a person living a life and at the same time observing and creating; and he analyses how Flaubert created *Madame Bovary* as an autonomous world, erasing the traces of his own authorial intervention. He highlights Flaubert's influential invention of the free indirect style, able to represent 'el funcionamiento de la conciencia sin recurrir ... a sus manifestaciones externas' (p. 260) [the functioning of consciousness without having recourse to its external manifestations] (p. 226). In response to the criticism that Vargas Llosa's theoretical notions received from Angel Rama and others after his publication of *Historia de un deicidio*, he justifies the application of his concepts, stating the purpose of his detailed analysis: 'La cronología y la palabra, el tiempo y el narrador son, naturalmente, una indestructible unidad; su separación es artificial, pero no hay otra manera de mostrar cómo funciona *la pesada y complicada máquina* que permite a una ficción dar la ilusión de la verdad, fingir la vida' (p. 194) [Chronological order and words, time and the narrator are, naturally, an indestructible unity; separating them is an artificial procedure, but there is no other way of showing the workings of *the ponderous and complicated machinery* that enables a fiction to create the illusion that it is true, to pretend to be alive] (p. 168). It is through the artificial separation and analysis of the elements constituting this work of fiction that, in the last part of his study, he is able to support his evaluation of *Madame Bovary* as the first modern novel.

Another novelist on whom Vargas Llosa has written extensively since as long ago as 1955 is his compatriot José María Arguedas, and in 1996 he published the book-length study *La utopía arcaica. José María Arguedas y las ficciones del indigenismo* [The Archaic Utopia. José María Arguedas and the Fictions of Indigenism]. His particular fascination with Arguedas's work lies in the context of socio-political commitment in which it was written. For Vargas Llosa, Arguedas represents better than anyone the dilemma of the Latin American writer and his social responsibility in a country plagued by underdevelopment and marred by a crass ethnic, social, linguistic and cultural divide. The privilege of having an education and the means of expression in such a society – doubly important in Arguedas's case since he grew up experiencing both the Hispanic and indigenous culture of Peru – raises the expectation that a writer should produce literature in the service of progress: 'Ningún escritor latinoamericano de la generación de Arguedas pudo ignorar la presión que se ejercía sobre él a favor del compromiso' [No

Latin American writer of Arguedas's generation could ignore the pressure on him in favour of commitment] (*Utopía*, p. 25). The case of Arguedas allows Vargas Llosa to exemplify his long-held conviction that literature in the service of a cause is incompatible with the rebellious nature of fiction as an authentic expression of the writer's demons. Good intentions do not necessarily produce good novels, since the premeditated elements of committed literature can stand in the way of authenticity. Vargas Llosa shows how, in his view, *Todas las sangres* [Blood of All Races] (1964) is an example of such well-meaning writing – 'impregnada de preocupaciones ideológicas y políticas de principio a fin' [steeped in ideological and political preoccupations from beginning to end] (p. 243) – but ultimately a failure for its lack of internal fictional persuasiveness. On the other hand, *Los ríos profundos* [*Deep Rivers*] (1958) delivers a portrait of social reality by way of an accomplished piece of fictional writing, 'un libro [que] seduce por la elegancia de su estilo, su delicada sensibilidad y la gama de emociones con que recrea el mundo de los Andes' [a book [that] seduces through the elegance of its style, its delicate sensibility, and the scale of emotions with which it recreates the Andean world] (p. 176). Vargas Llosa exposes the pitfalls of trying to combine moral responsibility and artistic judgement:

> esta situación abre las puertas de la literatura a toda clase de oportunismos y chantajes. ... ¿Cómo llamar fracasada una novela que protesta contra los opresores de las masas sin parecer sirviente del opresor? ... José María Arguedas experimentó este terrible dilema y hay huellas de ese desgarramiento en su obra y en su conducta ciudadana. (pp. 27–8)

> [this situation opens the door to all sorts of opportunism and blackmail affecting literature. ... How can you call a novel a failure which protests against the oppressors of the masses without appearing to serve the oppressor? ... José María Arguedas experienced this terrible dilemma, and traces of that split are present in his work and in his conduct as a citizen.]

Vargas Llosa understands Arguedas's tragic life along these lines. He examines the strong link between the author's life and his work, culminating in Arguedas's last unfinished novel *El zorro de arriba y el zorro de abajo* [*The Fox from Up Above and the Fox from Down Below*] (1971) in which he anticipated his own suicide.

La utopía arcaica is unique among Vargas Llosa's critical works since it is part literary criticism, part political manifesto. It takes Arguedas's work as a starting point to discuss the literary and ideological movement of *Indigenismo* in defence of the rights of Peru's indigenous population. Much less impressionistic than some of Vargas Llosa's other book-length studies, this volume undertakes a thorough review of the movement's philosophical background and comes to the conclusion that *Indigenismo* is a backwards-looking, conservative, collectivist, anti-liberal and anti-modern project, rooted more in fiction than in reality. The ambiguous expression 'ficciones del indigenismo' in the study's title is an example of how Vargas Llosa has transferred his dual concept of reality and fiction to politics and ideology. The 'fictions of indigenism' are not only the novels he examines here, but also the illusions of the ideological movement in real life. In *A Writer's Reality* he had explained that 'ideology in Latin America was fulfilling this task for many people; that ideology was the way they incorporated fiction into their lives' (*A Writer's Reality*, p. 149). This is one of the main points of *La utopía arcaica*, contrasting the useful fictions of literature with the harmful fictions of ideology. In line with its hybrid character, the critical study of his fellow countryman's literature ends with a summary of Peruvian politics from General Velasco Alvarado's agrarian reform to the mass exodus of the indigenous population to the cities, their development away from indigenist ideals to an innovative informal economy, and the terror of the Maoist 'Sendero Luminoso' [Shining Path] insurgents. It culminates in an attack on Alberto Fujimori, the Peruvian president at the time who had defeated Vargas Llosa in the 1990 elections, and his authoritarian politics.

Following on from his work on Flaubert, in 2004 Vargas Llosa published a study of another nineteenth-century French novelist whose work helped him to endure the depressing reality of his years at the Leoncio Prado military school, as he relates in the opening chapter to *La tentación de lo imposible. Victor Hugo y 'Los Miserables'* [*The Temptation of the Impossible. Victor Hugo and 'Les Misérables'*].[45] The embodiment of the 'total novel', *Les Misérables* contains every ingredient that engages Vargas Llosa the reader with a fictional work: 'La revolución, la santidad, el sacrificio, la cárcel, el crimen, hombres superhombres, vírgenes o putas, santas o perversas, una humanidad atenta al gesto, a la eufonía, a la metáfora' (*La tentación*, p. 15) [Revolution, sanctity, sacrifice, prison, crime, men who were supermen, women who were virgins or whores, saintly or wicked, a whole cast of characters shaped by theatricality, euphony, and metaphor] (*The Temptation*, p. 1). In an amusing chapter Vargas Llosa shows how Victor Hugo's own life was as rich and extraordinary as his fictional inventions, and how his real-life personality was as grandiose and formidable as the narrator of his novel. In Vargas Llosa's view, this omniscient, omnipotent narrator, whom the author of *Les Misérables* tries to pass off as 'Victor Hugo' himself (see *La tentación*, pp. 43–52), is the most important – fictional – protagonist of the novel: 'Omnisciente y exuberante, el narrador es también un narciso, un exhibicionista nato. No puede dejar de nombrarse, de citarse, de recordarnos

---

[45] Mario Vargas Llosa, *La tentación de lo imposible. Victor Hugo y 'Los Miserables'* (Madrid: Alfaguara, 2004); Mario Vargas Llosa, *The Temptation of the Impossible. Victor Hugo and 'Les Misérables'*, trans. John King (Princeton: Princeton University Press, 2007).

que está ahí y que él decide lo que se cuenta y cómo se cuenta. Su silueta se antepone continuamente a la de los personajes hasta borrarlos' (p. 30) [Omniscient and exuberant, the narrator is also a narcissist, a born exhibitionist. He cannot stop mentioning himself, quoting himself, reminding us that he is there and that it is he who decides what is told and how it is told. He continually appears in front of the characters, to the point of blotting them out altogether] (p. 14).

Vargas Llosa analyses the various narrative strategies used to guide the reader closely through the vast fictional universe of *Les Misérables*, and the effects that the narrator's tricks, such as pretended modesty and the withholding of information, produce. This narrator, he says, reveals a 'deicidal' ideology, 'contaminada de pies a cabeza de este prurito totalizador' (p. 201) [consumed as he is with this obsession with totality] (p. 158). That is why Vargas Llosa regards *Les Misérables* as 'the last great classical novel', whereas *Madame Bovary*, published six years earlier, is the 'first great modern novel' due to its invisible narrator:

> Con *Los Miserables* el narrador llega a la cumbre de la inconsciencia, como si adivinara que el magnífico espectáculo que nos brinda es su canto de cisne ... Ahí está, legislando, tronando, autoritario, impúdico, seguro de que ejerce sobre el lector el mismo dominio absoluto que tiene sobre sus personajes, convencido de que quien lo oye —lo lee— le cree religiosamente lo que cuenta por lo inspirado que es, lo bellas que son sus palabras y lo fogoso de sus argumentos. (pp. 49–50)

> [With *Les Misérables*, the narrator reaches the pinnacle of unconsciousness, as if he had somehow guessed that the magnificent spectacle that he is giving us is his swan song ... There he is, legislating, thundering on, authoritarian, shameless, certain that he has the same absolute control over the reader as he has over his characters, convinced that whoever listens to him, or reads him, believes religiously in what he is saying because of his inspiring nature, the beauty of his words, and the passion of his arguments.] (pp. 31–2)

In studying Victor Hugo's most famous work Vargas Llosa uses a different approach from his other critical essays, adapting to the nineteenth-century character of the novel in question. He looks at the events and themes that structure the fictional universe of *Les Misérables*, and he studies characterization, highlighting the typecasting that Hugo uses to imbue his fictional creation with a poignant socio-political message. There is 'the saint', 'the angel with a dirty face', 'the just' and, amongst a number of others, 'the fanatic', a type particularly close to Vargas Llosa's own concerns. The protagonist Javert, a policeman on a fanatical hunt to bring escaped convict Jean Valjean to justice, in the end lets him go after the convict shows mercy towards him in a face-to-face confrontation. The narrator explains Javert's change of mind by his discovery of the existence of goodness, that is to say of God, but Vargas Llosa begs to differ: 'En realidad, ha descubierto la existencia de verdades contradictorias, de valores incompatibles entre sí, la inexorable confusión del bien y del mal en ciertas experiencias humanas' (p. 105) [In fact, he has discovered the existence of contradictory truths, of incompatible values, the inexorable confusion between good and evil that occurs in certain human experiences] (p. 79). The 'contradictory truths' being one of the most important concepts of Vargas Llosa's thinking since his discovery of Isaiah Berlin's philosophy in the 1980s (see below, pp. 56–7), this interpretation shows how closely his literary criticism is linked to his political reasoning, which will be discussed in chapter 3.

In the final part of his book on Victor Hugo, Vargas Llosa looks at how the writer and political activist managed to integrate his political concerns and social criticism into his narrative work without it affecting the internal persuasiveness of his fiction. Vargas Llosa reviews the criticism that Hugo's novel provoked at the time for rendering a distorted image of society, misrepresenting historical events such as Waterloo, and exaggerating social injustices. He agrees that *Les Misérables* overemphasizes certain issues that were very important to Victor Hugo, such as the injustices of the penal system. But this is precisely what makes the work a true representation of Hugo's demons, in other words a work of fiction and not of documentation or historiography. For Vargas Llosa the novel is a formidable fictional creation which irresistibly draws the reader into its universe and fills him or her with the nostalgia, indignation, pity or revulsion that a successful novel is able to arouse. It is thus able to fulfil its subversive function: 'no hay la menor duda … de que *Los Miserables* es una de esas obras que en la historia de la literatura han hecho desear a más hombres y mujeres de todas las lenguas y culturas un mundo más justo, más racional y más bello que aquel en el que vivían' (p. 223) [But there is no doubt … that, in the history of literature, *Les Misérables* is one of the works that has been most influential in making so many men and women of all languages and cultures desire a more just, rational, and beautiful world than the one they live in] (pp. 176–7). The subversive effect of great novels, Vargas Llosa says, summarizing his approach to literary criticism, lies in the 'espléndidas realidades que construyen las ficciones logradas, en las que la belleza de la palabra, la elegancia de la construcción y lo efectivo de las técnicas hacen que incluso lo más feo, bajo y vil resplandezca como logro artístico' (p. 221) [splendid realities that successful fictions construct, in which the beauty of the words, the elegance of the construction, and the effectiveness of the techniques are such that even the most ugly, low, and abject things shine forth as artistic triumphs] (p. 175).

Vargas Llosa again takes up this point about the paradoxical effect of literature in his most recent work of literary criticism, the 2008 study *El viaje a la ficción. El mundo de Juan Carlos Onetti* [The Journey to Fiction.

The World of Juan Carlos Onetti]. In the conclusion to this study about the Uruguayan writer whose fictional world is dominated by anti-heroes suffering from failure and despair, he states:

> Lo que hay en el mundo de Onetti de amargo y pesimista, de frustración y sufrimiento, cambia de valencia cuando, seducidos por la sutileza y astucia de su prosa, entramos en su mundo, lo vivimos, gozando con lo que en él sucede aunque al mismo tiempo suframos y nos desgarremos con el espectáculo de las miserias humanas que él exhibe. Ése es el misterio de la obra literaria y artística lograda: deleitar sufriendo, seducir y encantar mientras nos sumerge en el mal y el horror. (*El viaje*, p. 233)

> [The bitterness and pessimism, frustration and suffering that can be found in Onetti's world changes significance when, seduced by the subtlety and astuteness of his prose, we enter into his world, live through it, enjoying what goes on, even though we simultaneously suffer and get upset about the spectacle of human misery that it exhibits. That is the mystery of an accomplished literary and artistic work: it delights by making us suffer, it seduces and bewitches by submerging us into evil and horror.]

The study's eponymous preface is an essay exploring the role of fiction in the development of humankind. It traces the necessity of human beings to tell, and listen to, stories in order to live through experiences other than their own, a factor which, according to Vargas Llosa, was essential in overcoming the fear of the unknown and the desire, driven by the imagination, to develop new kinds of life. But the imaginary worlds of fiction also complemented real life where it was necessary to suppress certain instincts, desires and fears in order for human beings to live together in a civilized society. The retrieval of this other side, 'esa otra vida negada y reprimida' [this other life, denied and repressed] (p. 29) is one of the purposes of fiction, a point Vargas Llosa had made in previous essays about Georges Bataille. Fiction re-establishes freedom by opening up the possibility to explore pathways which in reality should be closed. This issue of the ambiguous relationship between fiction and reality in Onetti's fictional universe, 'la dialéctica entre la realidad y la ficción' (p. 65), has long fascinated Vargas Llosa: he even mentioned the Uruguayan writer in his acceptance speech for the Rómulo Gallegos Prize in 1967 as 'the great Onetti ... who has not received the recognition that he deserves' ('Literature is Fire', p. 74). As Vargas Llosa interprets it, Onetti's work is

> casi íntegramente concebida para mostrar la sutil y frondosa manera como, junto a la vida verdadera, los seres humanos hemos venido construyendo una vida paralela, de palabras e imágenes tan mentirosas como persuasivas, donde ir a refugiarnos para escapar de los desastres y limitaciones que a nuestra libertad y a nuestros sueños opone la vida tal como es. (*El viaje*, p. 32)

[almost entirely conceived to show the rich and subtle way in which human beings have come to construct, next to real life, a parallel one, made of words and images as untrue as they are persuasive, in which we take refuge to escape from the disasters and limitations that life as it is puts in the way of our freedom and our dreams.]

He follows this theme in Onetti's novels and short stories, highlighting the 'flight into fantasy' that inventing fictions provides for Onetti's frustrated anti-heroes (see *El viaje*, p. 87).

As in his other critical studies, Vargas Llosa analyses the narrative devices that Onetti uses to create the 'clima enigmático, de claroscuro y de sombras, de silencios momentáneos o totales' [enigmatic climate, of twilight and shadows, of momentary or total silences] (p. 88) which characterizes his fiction. He looks at the role of the narrator and the various points of view which produce 'esa atmósfera de relatividad, de inconclusión' [this atmosphere of relativity and inconclusion] (p. 89); he analyses the 'hidden facts' of the narrative, the handling of time, and talks about Onetti's style. Vargas Llosa highlights the influence that Faulkner had on the Uruguayan writer's 'totalizing ambition', since he created a coherence in his oeuvre where individual works can be read in conjunction with others, all set in the fictional world of Santa María. The metafictional element of Onetti's literary cosmos – a world which is in itself invented by a fictional character – fascinates Vargas Llosa more than anything, and he comes to the conclusion: 'Onetti consagró su vida entera de escritor a elaborar una saga en la que la voluntad de fuga hacia lo imaginario fuera la columna vertebral alrededor de la cual girase toda su obra, el eje que la trabara y diera coherencia' [Onetti devoted his entire life as a writer to elaborating a saga in which the desire to escape into fantasy formed the axle around which his whole work spun, the central idea that held it together and gave it coherence] (p. 224).

Here, as in most of Vargas Llosa's critical essays, he not only applies the concepts he has developed for describing his own creative processes to the work of other authors, but his approach also confirms that writing about other writers is part of an overarching, 'total' project. Literary theory as well as criticism, plus (as we will see) the metaliterary elements in Vargas Llosa's fictional work, are three aspects of one single endeavour: the attempt to grasp and put into words the meaning, method and effect of fiction. In one of his most delightful metafictional creations, *La tía Julia y el escribidor* [*Aunt Julia and the Scriptwriter*] (1977), which deals in a light-hearted way with the question of how to create fictions, we find the following epigraph from the text 'El grafógrafo' by Mexican writer Salvador Elizondo, a motto most suited to describe the secret 'communicating vessels' between Vargas Llosa's literary theory, criticism and metafiction:

Escribo. Escribo que escribo. Mentalmente me veo escribir que escribo y también puedo verme ver que escribo. Me recuerdo escribiendo ya y también viéndome que escribía. Y me veo recordando que me veo escribir y me recuerdo viéndome recordar que escribía y escribo viéndome escribir que recuerdo haberme visto escribir que me veía escribir que recordaba haberme visto escribir que escribía y que escribía que escribo que escribía. También puedo imaginarme escribiendo que ya había escrito que me imaginaría escribiendo que había escrito que me imaginaba escribiendo que me veo escribir que escribo.[46]

[I write. I write that I am writing. Mentally I see myself writing that I am writing and I can also see myself seeing that I am writing. I remember writing and also seeing myself writing. And I see myself remembering that I see myself writing and I remember seeing myself remembering that I was writing and I write seeing myself write that I remember having seen myself write that I saw myself writing that I was writing and that I was writing that I was writing that I was writing. I can also imagine myself writing that I had already written that I would imagine myself writing that I had written that I was imagining myself writing that I see myself writing that I am writing.][47]

---

[46] Mario Vargas Llosa, *La tía Julia y el escribidor* (Barcelona: Seix Barral, 1986), p. 9.
[47] Mario Vargas Llosa, *Aunt Julia and the Scriptwriter*, trans. Helen R. Lane (London: Picador, 1984), p. 3.

3

Journalism and Essays: from Art to Politics

Vargas Llosa's literary criticism is complemented by his keen interest in other art forms. In his newspaper column 'Piedra de toque' [Touchstone],[1] which appears in *El País* and is licensed to other newspapers internationally, he regularly discusses cultural issues arising from, for example, attending a theatre production or a concert, watching a film or visiting an art exhibition.[2] Sometimes his curiosity is aroused by an interesting piece of writing, such as Hayden Herrera's biography of the Mexican painter Frida Kahlo which he mentions in an article about an exhibition of the artist's work.[3] It is striking to what extent the notions of Vargas Llosa's literary criticism also shape his approach to art. Discussing Frida Kahlo he highlights the total dedication to painting with which she overcame the extreme difficulties of her life and created a work of great coherence, 'un estremecedor testimonio sobre el sufrimiento, los deseos y los más terribles avatares de la condición humana' [a shattering testimony of the suffering, the desires and most horrendous vicissitudes of the human condition] ('Resistir pintando', p. 451). In an interesting twist he inverses his favourite *antimetabole* about the vital necessity of creating fiction and says about her: 'Ella no vivía para pintar, pintaba para vivir' [she did not live to paint, but painted to live] (p. 453), thus expressing the thought that Frida Kahlo could not have continued living without transforming her agony and her rebellion against that agony into art.

A similar idea is at the heart of an article defending the important role of museums like the Prado: 'the walls are full of myriad examples of how to combat adversity with the arm of fantasy, of how to defeat dissatisfaction by gorging oneself on beauty, of how to overcome the grey mediocrity of

---

[1] While putting the finishing touches to this book, a comprehensive collection of Vargas Llosa's journalistic work for *El País* has appeared as part of an ongoing edition of the complete works in the Círculo de Lectores series: Mario Vargas Llosa, *Obras completas*, vols. IX–XI, *Piedra de toque 1962–2012* (Barcelona: Galaxia Gutenberg/Círculo de Lectores, 2012).

[2] For example, see his polemical review of the Royal Academy of Art's notorious exhibition of the so-called Young British Artists, 'Sensation', in 1997: Mario Vargas Llosa, 'Caca de elefante', in *El lenguaje de la pasión* (Madrid: Ediciones El País, 2000), pp. 199–209.

[3] Mario Vargas Llosa, 'Resistir pintando', in *Sables y utopías. Visiones de América Latina* (Madrid: Aguilar, 2009), pp. 449–53.

existence by turning it into the terrifying or majestic lives depicted there'.[4] Analogue to his concept of the novel as an alternative, oppositional reality Vargas Llosa speaks of the paintings of the old masters as 'wonderful fictions', which 'all had their origins in a defiance of the real world', while at the same time 'subtly contaminating reality with their forms and values' (p. 157).

In a substantial essay on the German artist George Grosz, famous for his grotesque depictions of life in the Weimar Republic after the First World War, Vargas Llosa reiterates that, in the same manner as verbal fictions, he understands his art as 'a creative response to real life' and appreciates the 'parallel and autonomous life found in great artistic fictions' such as his.[5] Grosz is important to him for 'the relationship of art and fiction to history and life, to truth and lies, the type of testimony that fiction offers on the objective world' (p. 158). All the key concepts of Vargas Llosa's literary theory are there, and so are some of his ideas about the creative process. Grosz' 'fiction', he concedes, is 'completely deformed and stripped of all positive aspects' (p. 166), it renders a one-dimensional, distorted image of reality which is nevertheless 'rooted in this common fund of shared experience, and we can recognise in it something that we are *as well*' (pp. 166–7). There are similarities between Vargas Llosa's interpretation of the art of George Grosz and his fascination for the writings of George Bataille and the French writer's concept of Evil. Whether created in words or in pictures, fictional worlds that are represented with a one-dimensional focus on the irrational, dark side of life, but nevertheless instilled with a 'persuasive power that overcomes any reservations we might have about their evil' (p. 167), fulfil the same kind of compensatory function: 'the deceitful world of fiction [is a] creative response to real life. A life without which the other life, the one that we live and not the one we dream, would be much more difficult to endure' (p. 169).

Vargas Llosa finds a completely different kind of fictional counter-world in the work of the contemporary Colombian painter and sculptor Fernando Botero, on whom he has published several essays.[6] Botero's art is instantly recognizable for its distinctive 'blown-up', fattened depiction of people or objects (his portrait of Vargas Llosa is on the cover of the edition of *Making Waves* used here). 'The swelling that his brushes impress on reality', writes

---

[4] Mario Vargas Llosa, 'A Dream Factory', in *Touchstones. Essays on Literature, Art and Politics*, select., trans. and ed. John King (London: Faber and Faber, 2007), pp. 153–7 (p. 157).

[5] Typically for Vargas Llosa, his essays on art have appeared in various forms and languages. The piece on Grosz was first published as a separate essay in German; an English version called 'George Grosz: A Sad and Ferocious Man' is included in *Touchstones*, pp. 158–83 (with the above quotation at p. 158).

[6] The essay on Botero was first published in a French book on the artist; an English version, 'Botero: A Sumptuous Abundance', can be found in Mario Vargas Llosa, *Making Waves*, ed. and trans. John King (London: Faber and Faber, 1996), pp. 254–67. See also Mario Vargas Llosa, 'Botero at the Bullfight', in *Touchstones*, pp. 211–16.

Vargas Llosa, 'has an ontological effect: it empties the people and objects of this world of all sentimental, intellectual and moral content. They are reduced to physical presences, to forms that refer in a sensory way to certain models of real life, but which contradict and disown this real life' ('Botero at the Bullfight', p. 215) – again the same concept as in his literary theory of art as a rebellion against life, establishing a different reality from real life. In addition, Vargas Llosa sees Botero's art as opposing dominant trends in modern art, making 'constant references to the art of the past, its rational balance, its exquisite craft, its benevolent, unified and optimistic vision, devoid of tension or anguish, its sensuality' in a world of sheer 'forms and colours ... not justified according to any moral standard or list of principles', where 'the hunger for beauty is still a legitimate appetite' ('A Sumptuous Abundance', pp. 266–7). This is quite a different evaluation of the distinctive quality of art from that applied to either George Grosz or Frida Kahlo. The common denominator, however, is art seen as a fictional representation of reality, oppositional and rebellious in one way or another: more or less beautiful, more or less violent, more or less cruel, more or less emotional.

The positive evaluation of Botero's striving for beauty through the abundance of form and colour in his work ties in with Vargas Llosa's rejection of the type of modern art, especially conceptual art, that he finds 'fraudulent or laughable, ... divorced from life and its problems, from human needs, a soulless trick'.[7] His opinions concerning the art world reveal parallels with his views on literary criticism. In literature, due to the rise of postmodernism and the 'terrible trinity' of Lacan, Foucault and Derrida,[8] Vargas Llosa fears the further erosion of still existing 'códigos estéticos que permiten identificar la originalidad, la novedad, el talento, la desenvoltura formal o la ramplonería y el fraude' [aesthetic codes which allow originality, novelty, talent, formal boldness, or crudeness and imposture to be identified] ('Caca de elefante', p. 202). The art world, he says, has already totally lost that ability 'to distinguish between what is good, bad and deplorable in art' and is reigned by 'an irresponsible frivolity' ('Degenerate art', p. 273). The criteria for evaluating art have been reduced to its market value, which often depends on nothing more than its ability to shock ('Caca de elefante', pp. 201–2).

This conservative attitude – conservative in the sense of wanting to preserve the concepts of beauty, skill and meaning – does not imply that Vargas Llosa only appreciates figurative art. One of his favourite artists, on whom he has published several texts, is the Peruvian painter Fernando de Szyszlo,[9] a personal friend as well as an ally in the defence of democratic

---

[7] Mario Vargas Llosa, 'Degenerate Art', in *Making Waves*, pp. 271–5 (p. 274).
[8] Mario Vargas Llosa, 'La identidad francesa', in *El lenguaje*, pp. 97–103 (p. 102). See also Mario Vargas Llosa, 'La hora de los charlatanes', in *El lenguaje*, pp. 193–7.
[9] For example, see Mario Vargas Llosa, 'Szyszlo in the Labyrinth', in *Making Waves*,

structures and a free society in Peru. Back in 1983 Vargas Llosa dedicated the first volume of *Contra viento y marea* [Against Wind and Tide][10] to Szyszlo, and one of his non-figurative works is included in the paintings reproduced in the erotic novel *Elogio de la madrastra* [*In Praise of the Stepmother*] (1988)[11] to complement the narrative of events with observations and fantasies engendered by works of art. Szyszlo's work, which is inspired by pre-Colombian Andean cultures, Latin American poetry and painting as well as European and North American modern art, embodies what Vargas Llosa calls a Latin American identity. Having been intrigued for a long time by the question whether such an identity exists or not,[12] Vargas Llosa affirms that this fusion of diverse external and internal factors, turned into something original, 'is Latin America in its highest expression, the best of what we are and what we possess' ('Szyszlo in the Labyrinth', p. 268). Szyszlo's paintings, 'disturbing', 'violent' but beautiful in a mysterious way, 'map out a vast geography, a labyrinth so complicated and diverse, that even the most skilful explorer can become lost' (pp. 268–9). Vargas Llosa appreciates 'su fuerza comunicativa, la suntuosidad y sutileza con que en ellos se combinan los colores' [their communicative power, the sumptuous and subtle way of combining colours] which produce a world of their own, 'un mundo propio' ('Bienvenida', p. 440).

At the same time as the literary notion of a different, fictional world invades Vargas Llosa's writing about art, paintings and artists come to play an important role in some of his fiction: in *Elogio de la madrastra* and its sequel, *Los cuadernos de Don Rigoberto* [*The Notebooks of Don Rigoberto*] (1997)[13] art is a crucial element of the narrative, while one part of the 2003 novel *El Paraíso en la otra esquina* [*The Way to Paradise*][14] revolves around the painter Paul Gauguin. The play *Ojos bonitos, cuadros feos* [Pretty Eyes, Ugly Paintings] (1996)[15] deals with the role of art, the artist and the art critic;

---

pp. 268–70; Mario Vargas Llosa, 'Bienvenida a Fernando de Szyszlo', in *Sables y utopías*, pp. 437–47. The website <http://www.mvargasllosa.com/biblio.htm> also lists contributions to various exhibition catalogues.

[10] Mario Vargas Llosa, *Contra viento y marea, I (1962–1972)* (Barcelona: Seix Barral, 1986).

[11] Mario Vargas Llosa, *Elogio de la madrastra* (Barcelona: Tusquets, 1988); Mario Vargas Llosa, *In Praise of the Stepmother*, trans. Helen Lane (New York: Penguin, 1990).

[12] For example, see Vargas Llosa's latest collection of essays on the topic, *Sueño y realidad de América Latina* (Barcelona: Arcadia, 2010).

[13] Mario Vargas Llosa, *Los cuadernos de Don Rigoberto* (Madrid: Alfaguara, 1997); Mario Vargas Llosa, *The Notebooks of Don Rigoberto*, trans. Edith Grossman (London: Faber and Faber, 1999).

[14] Mario Vargas Llosa, *El Paraíso en la otra esquina* (Madrid: Alfaguara, 2003); Mario Vargas Llosa, *The Way to Paradise* trans. Natasha Wimmer (London: Faber and Faber, 2004).

[15] Mario Vargas Llosa, *Ojos bonitos, cuadros feos* (Lima: PEISA, 1996).

and *El loco de los balcones* [The Madman of the Balconies] (1993)[16] has a main character obsessed with the preservation of architectural features of the past, in a play that confronts life and art.

Other journalistic pieces by Vargas Llosa reflect his wider cultural interests. The helpfully categorized official bibliography on his website reveals that, especially during the 1950s and 1960s, he was a prolific film and theatre critic. In the last twenty years articles about music and festivals such as Salzburg and Bayreuth have become more frequent. One topic that has been a staple of his journalistic writing from the beginning is football, starting in 1952 with an article called 'Aquí habla el Estadio' [This is the Stadium Speaking]. Vargas Llosa reported from the 1982 football World Cup in Spain, and has continued to write about the sport in his regular newspaper columns, again transposing categories from his literary criticism to this area of his cultural commentary. In an article about the Argentinian footballer Maradona he states that, 'as has happened in literature, Argentina has produced a style of football which is the most European expression of being Latin American' and comes to the conclusion that the game provides a harmless outlet for hero worship:

> People need contemporary heroes, beings that they can turn into gods. No country escapes this rule. Cultured or uncultured, rich or poor, capitalist or socialist, every society feels this irrational need to enthrone idols of flesh and blood ... The cult of a football star ... is the least alienating of cults since to admire a footballer is to admire something very close to poetry or abstract painting. It is to admire form for form's sake, without any rationally identifiable content.[17]

More controversial is Vargas Llosa's passionate defence of bullfighting, an example of how he likes to intervene in public debates about hotly disputed issues. A long-time admirer of the sport, he has repeatedly taken a stance in defence of bullfighting since it came under attack for its cruelty: 'los toros representan una forma de alimento espiritual y emotivo tan intenso y enriquecedor como un concierto de Beethoven, una comedia de Shakespeare o un poema de Vallejo' [a bullfight represents a form of spiritual and emotional nourishment which is as intense and enriching as a Beethoven concerto, a Shakespeare play, or a poem by Vallejo].[18] In the same article he goes on to compare the spectacle of a (good) bullfight to an artistic creation, both equally capable of representing the human condition:

---

[16] Mario Vargas Llosa, *El loco de los balcones* (Barcelona: Seix Barral, 1993).
[17] Mario Vargas Llosa, 'Maradona and the Heroes', in *Making Waves*, pp. 168–70 (p. 170).
[18] Mario Vargas Llosa, 'Torear y otras maldades', *El País*, 18 April 2010, <http://www.elpais.com/articulo/opinion/Torear/otras/maldades/elpepiopi/20100418elpepiopi_11/Tes> [accessed 29 October 2012].

la fiesta de los toros es algo más complejo y sutil que un deporte, un espectáculo que tiene algo de danza y de pintura, de teatro y poesía, en el que la valentía, la destreza, la intuición, la gracia, la elegancia y la cercanía de la muerte se combinan para representar la condición humana.

[bullfighting is something more complex and subtle than a sport, a spectacle containing elements of dance and painting, theatre and poetry, in which bravery, skill, intuition, grace, elegance and the closeness of death combine to represent the human condition.]

The element that links Vargas Llosa's concerns in his fiction with the issues he discusses in his contributions to public debate is the human condition. This is what – in his view – literature and art is about, and this is what determines his interest in the wide variety of topics that he deals with in his other areas of intellectual endeavour: the exploration of human nature in its social, cultural and political context. His journalistic work often reveals the perspective of a novelist, for example in the strong visual elements in his reports from conflict zones. On the other hand, his regular columns for newspapers help him to stay in touch with everyday life, as he writes in his prologue to the essay collection *El lenguaje de la pasión* [*The Language of Passion*] (2000): 'El periodismo ha sido la sombra de mi vocación literaria; la ha seguido, alimentado e impedido alejarse de la realidad viva y actual, en un viaje puramente imaginario' [Journalism has always been the shadow of my literary vocation; it has followed it, fed it, and prevented it from moving away from life as it is lived here and now on a purely imaginary journey] (p. 9).[19] The interrelations between fiction and journalism become apparent when tracing the development of Vargas Llosa's ideas through his various essay collections. They document how his reading of fiction, biography, philosophy and economy has always influenced and advanced his way of thinking, making him focus on new issues which then also manifest themselves in his fiction, for example in the choice of Utopian dreamers, fanatics or nationalists as his subject matter.

'The essay is the intellectual genre *par excellence*', writes Vargas Llosa in an article on Jean-Paul Sartre.[20] His first essay collection, *Entre Sartre y Camus* [Between Sartre and Camus],[21] focuses on the question of revolution or reform and the role of the writer in the conflict between utopia and morals that divided the two French authors in their notorious argument of 1952. They famously fell out over the existence of labour camps in the Soviet Union: Camus

---

[19] The English edition of this essay collection is *The Language of Passion*, trans. Natasha Wimmer (New York: Farrar, Straus & Giroux, 2003). However, it is difficult to find in Europe, at least in the printed version, and so all translations of quotations from *El lenguaje de la pasión* are my own.
[20] Mario Vargas Llosa, 'The Mandarin', in *Making Waves*, pp. 131–43 (p. 134).
[21] Mario Vargas Llosa, *Entre Sartre y Camus* (Río Piedras, Puerto Rico: Huracán, 1981).

refused to accept that freedom could be temporarily sacrificed for the establishment of a more just society in the future, whereas Sartre, although critical of the labour camps, stood firm in his absolute commitment to the cause of social justice. This argument, ultimately about the question of whether the end justifies the means, is highly significant for Vargas Llosa's own development from an enthusiastic supporter of the Cuban Revolution in its early years to his disenchantment with the authoritarian tendencies that later emerged, leading to his rupture with Cuba and some of his best friends of the Boom years. He describes the essays in his collection as showing 'el itinerario de un latinoamericano que hizo su aprendizaje intelectual deslumbrado por la inteligencia y los vaivenes dialécticos de Sartre y terminó abrazando el reformismo libertario de Camus'[22] [the itinerary of a Latin American who undertook his intellectual apprenticeship dazzled by the intelligence and dialectical swings of Sartre and ended up embracing the libertarian reformism of Camus].[23]

The influence of both writers on Vargas Llosa's thinking is considerable. Sartre's idea of commitment has never left him: in his Nobel Lecture, Vargas Llosa acknowledged the French philosopher as the source of his conviction that 'words are acts'. When Sartre himself famously rejected the Nobel Prize in 1964, an act which provoked scathing criticism from all sides, he found a sympathetic defender in Vargas Llosa:

> La irritación que suele provocar Sartre a los críticos se debe en parte, sin duda, a la imposibilidad en que se hallan de integrarlo a una institución ideológica establecida, de asimilarlo a cualquier tipo de iglesia. ... Lo que no le perdonan es su condición de francotirador, su independencia de criterio, su disponibilidad alerta, su imprevisibilidad, su inconformismo militante. Ni la derecha ni la izquierda han conseguido 'oficiarlo': por eso lo atacan con tanta virulencia.[24]

> [The irritation that Sartre seems to provoke in critics is, without doubt, at least partly due to the fact that they find it impossible to integrate him into an established ideological institution, to put him in line with any type of church. ... What they cannot forgive him is his rebellious attitude, his independence of judgement, his alertness, his unpredictability, his militant non-conformism. Neither the Right nor the Left have managed to officially make him one of their own: that is why they attack him with such virulence.]

This ideal of Sartre as an independent and somewhat contrary intellectual is one that Vargas Llosa himself has always tried to live up to.

On the other hand, he highlights crucial features of Albert Camus's thinking which are also his own: 'este horror del dogma, de todos los

---

[22] Mario Vargas Llosa, 'Prólogo', in *Entre Sartre y Camus*, pp. 9–14 (p. 9).
[23] Mario Vargas Llosa, 'Foreword', in *Making Waves*, pp. xi–xxi (p. xiv).
[24] Mario Vargas Llosa, 'Sartre y el Nobel', in *Entre Sartre y Camus*, pp. 29–34 (pp. 32–3).

dogmas ... Su convicción de que toda teoría que se presenta como absoluta ... acaba tarde o temprano por justificar el crimen y la mentira' [this horror of dogma, of all dogmas ... His conviction that every theory that presents itself as absolute ... sooner or later ends up justifying crimes and lies].²⁵ Vargas Llosa identifies with Camus's 'morality of limits'; he agrees with him that the writer's function is to 'moderate, correct and counterbalance' the institutions of power, to be the 'voice of reason and moderation, of tolerance and prudence but also of courage, freedom, beauty and pleasure'.²⁶

Entre Sartre y Camus was later absorbed into the much larger three-volume collection *Contra viento y marea* (1983, 1986 and 1990). Its first two volumes progress chronologically, the third widens the scope even more and assembles texts from 1964 to 1988, thematically organized (a selection of essays in English from all three volumes is included in *Making Waves*). Apart from the crucial texts on the writer's role in society already quoted above, the first volume reflects the discussions and the political and intellectual atmosphere of the 1960s and early 1970s amongst the Boom authors. Questions of social justice were in the foreground, and Vargas Llosa's texts clearly show his conviction at the time that the solution to poverty and inequality lies in socialism. In his report 'Crónica de la revolución' [Chronicle of the Cuban Revolution] from a trip to Cuba in 1962 he writes: 'el socialismo cubano es singular, muestra diferencias flagrantes con el resto de los países del bloque soviético y este fenómeno puede tener repercusiones de primer orden en el porvenir del socialismo mundial'²⁷ [Cuban socialism is idiosyncratic, very different from the rest of the countries of the Soviet bloc, a fact that could have very important repercussions for the future of world socialism].²⁸ The crucial difference lay in the absence of censorship that Vargas Llosa noticed during his visit in 1962: 'no existe una censura destinada a preservar la pureza ideológica de las publicaciones' (p. 32) [There is no censorship aimed at maintaining the ideological purity of the publications] (p. 21); differing ideological viewpoints could, *'until now at least*, ... be freely expressed' (p. 22; my italics). Enthusiasm and hope are dominant in this report – even though a certain scepticism is noticeable about the future development of the Cuban revolution 'ante las agresiones abiertas o encubiertas de Estados Unidos' (p. 33) [faced with the open or covert aggression of the United States] (p. 23). This does not prevent Vargas Llosa from predicting a better, socialist future for his own country: he expects to find himself

---

²⁵ Mario Vargas Llosa, 'Albert Camus y la moral de los límites', in *Contra viento I*, pp. 321–42 (p. 332).
²⁶ Quoted from a shortened version of the 1975 essay, 'Albert Camus and the morality of limits', in *Making Waves*, pp. 107–16 (pp. 114–15).
²⁷ Mario Vargas Llosa, 'Crónica de la revolución', in *Contra viento I*, pp. 30–5 (p. 30).
²⁸ Mario Vargas Llosa, 'Chronicle of the Cuban Revolution', in *Making Waves*, pp. 20–4 (p. 20).

'dentro de diez, veinte o cincuenta años, en un Perú distinto, emancipado de la injusticia social' [in ten, twenty or fifty years in a different Peru, free of social injustice].[29] A manifest called 'Toma de posición' [Taking a Stand] that he helped to draft in 1965 openly supports the Peruvian guerrilla movement MRI and states that, to achieve prosperity and dignity for all, 'no queda otro camino que la lucha armada' [there is no other way than armed struggle].[30]

In 1966 he is still convinced that 'el sistema que reemplace al actual sólo puede ser socialista' [the system that replaces the present one can only be socialist],[31] and a year later he famously tells his listeners in the 'La literatura es fuego' speech: 'Yo quiero que ... el socialismo nos libere de nuestro anacronismo y nuestro horror'[32] [I want ... socialism to free us from our anachronism and our horror].[33] But his hope for a new kind of socialism for Latin America, where the project of social justice would not exclude freedom and free speech, was already waning at that time. The growing economic pressure on Cuba, due to the US blockade, forced the country to succumb more and more to Soviet ideological orthodoxy and to adopt its repression of dissident opinion. In 1966 Vargas Llosa wrote an article protesting against the incarceration in the Soviet Union of two writers, Andrei Sinyavsky and Yuli Daniel, in which he postulates creative freedom in all socialist societies:

> Los escritores que creemos en el socialismo y que nos consideramos amigos de la URSS debemos ser los primeros en protestar ... Nosotros debemos luchar porque la sociedad socialista del futuro corte todas las vendas que a lo largo de la historia han inventado los hombres para tapar la boca majadera del creador.[34]
>
> [We writers who believe in socialism and who consider ourselves friends of the USSR must be the first to protest ... We have to fight for the socialist society of the future to cut all bandages that have been invented throughout history to muzzle the loose mouth of the artist.]

The opening words of this statement confirm Vargas Llosa's earnest commitment to socialism during the 1960s. He reported from a visit to Moscow[35] and travelled to Cuba five times, where he was enthusiastically

---

[29] Mario Vargas Llosa, 'En torno a un dictador y al libro de un amigo', in *Contra viento I*, pp. 74–7 (p. 74).

[30] Mario Vargas Llosa, 'Toma de posición', in *Contra viento I*, pp. 91–2 (p. 92).

[31] Mario Vargas Llosa, 'El papel del intelectual en los movimientos de la liberación nacional', in *Contra viento I*, pp. 105–6 (p. 105).

[32] Mario Vargas Llosa, 'La literatura es fuego', in *Contra viento I*, pp. 176–81 (p. 179).

[33] Mario Vargas Llosa, 'Literature is Fire', in *Making Waves*, pp. 70–4 (p. 73).

[34] Mario Vargas Llosa, 'Una insurrección permanente', in *Contra viento I*, pp. 107–10 (pp. 107, 110).

[35] Mario Vargas Llosa, 'Moscú: notas a vuelo de pájaro', in *Contra viento I*, pp. 205–13.

involved in the country's cultural institutions such as the journal *Casa de las Américas* and its various activities. He later admitted that he noted more and more worrying signs of a repressive climate building up, and he was involved in a meeting of intellectuals with Fidel Castro questioning Cuba's attitude towards homosexuals.[36] The issue of censorship remained the all-important benchmark for his support of socialism since, for him as a writer, literature was more important than anything else.[37] In his article about the Sinyavsky/ Daniel case in the Soviet Union he states: 'En el socialismo que nosotros ambicionamos, no sólo se habrá suprimido la explotación del hombre; también se habrán suprimido los últimos obstáculos para que el escritor pueda escribir libremente lo que le dé la gana y comenzando, naturalmente, por su hostilidad al propio socialismo' [The socialism that we strive for will not only have eliminated the exploitation of man; it will also have eliminated the last obstacles for the writer to write freely about whatever he wants to, beginning, of course, with his hostility to socialism itself] ('Una insurrección', p. 110).

One of the crucial events in Vargas Llosa's disillusionment with the possibilities of a free socialist society was the brutal military intervention by Warsaw Pact states which, in 1968, ended the so-called Prague Spring in Czechoslovakia, where Alexander Dubček had introduced liberal reforms and tried to establish a 'socialism with a human face'. Vargas Llosa denounced the intervention as 'una agresión de carácter imperial que constituye una deshonra para la patria de Lenin, una estupidez política de dimensiones vertiginosas y un daño irreparable para la causa del socialismo en el mundo'[38] [an imperialist aggression which is a dishonour to the country of Lenin, a political blunder of dizzying proportions and an irreparable setback for the cause of socialism in the world].[39] Even more devastating of his hopes for a Latin American socialism inspired by the Cuban model was Fidel Castro's explicit justification of this aggressive act by the Soviet Union and its satellite countries against a sovereign state. Vargas Llosa's criticism of Castro, and his insistence on the importance of freedom, provoked hostile reactions from other pro-Cuban intellectuals. In 1970 it sparked an argument with Columbian critic Oscar Collazos, who criticized Vargas Llosa's idea of literature as a subversive and oppositional force in whichever type of society.[40] Collazos

---

36   See Mario Vargas Llosa, 'El gigante y la historia', in *Contra viento y marea, III (1964–1988)* (Barcelona: Seix Barral, 1990), pp. 423–8 (p. 424). See also Ricardo A. Setti, ... *sobre la vida y la política: Diálogo con Vargas Llosa* (México: Kosmos Editorial, 1989), pp. 144–5.
37   For example, see Mario Vargas Llosa, 'Carta al vocero del Partido Comunista Peruano', in *Contra viento I*, pp. 182–3.
38   Mario Vargas Llosa, 'El socialismo y los tanques', in *Contra viento I*, pp. 219–22 (p. 219).
39   Mario Vargas Llosa, 'Socialism and the Tanks', in *Making Waves*, pp. 79–82 (p. 79).
40   The whole argument can be found in book form as Oscar Collazos, Julio Cortázar and Mario Vargas Llosa, *Literatura en la revolución y revolución en la literatura* (México: Siglo

accused Vargas Llosa of forgetting his 'duty as a revolutionary', daring to 'give lessons in international politics' to Fidel Castro 'from a reactionary podium' (i.e. a US university; 'Luzbel', p. 237). Vargas Llosa countered this accusation by saying that Castro could not possibly be 'in possession, once and for all times, of truth': 'Sólo a partir de esta convicción —que es un acto de fe religiosa— es comprensible la afirmación de que criticar a Fidel es un acto de arrogancia' [Only if one shares this conviction – which is an act of religious faith – one can understand the assertion that to criticize Fidel is an arrogant deed] ('Luzbel', p. 237). This episode reveals the beginnings of a polarization that gripped the Latin American intellectual scene over the next few years.

The Padilla Affair of 1971 (see 'Introduction', above) led to Vargas Llosa's final dissociation from Cuba. *Contra viento y marea* reprints a number of open letters, a medium that he has always used to intervene in public debates, register his protest or clarify his position in an argument. Vargas Llosa's letter to Castro protesting against the 'desprecio a la dignidad humana' [disregard for human dignity][41] in the treatment of poet Heberto Padilla was signed by a large number of prominent left-wing intellectuals including Sartre. Castro reacted with invectives against the Latin American writers who live in Europe, calling them 'canallas' [rogues] and banning them from entering Cuba. In April 1971, Vargas Llosa publicly resigned from *Casa de las Américas*. In his letter to its director Haydée Santamaría, he said about the Padilla Affair: 'es la negación de lo que me hizo abrazar desde el primer día la causa de la revolución cubana: su decisión de luchar por la justicia sin perder el respeto a los individuos'[42] [it is the negation of everything that made me embrace, from the first day, the cause of the Cuban revolution: its decision to fight for justice without losing respect for individuals].[43]

Even after his dissociation from Cuba, Vargas Llosa continued for a couple of years to speak out in favour of socialism, albeit without the optimism of previous years.[44] Nevertheless, as he said in 1974, if he were made to choose between capitalism and socialism it would be the latter which he found better equipped to guarantee a degree of social justice for the majority of people: 'aprieto los dientes y sigo diciendo: "con el socialismo"' [I clench my teeth

---

XXI, 1970). See also Mario Vargas Llosa, 'Luzbel, Europa y otras conspiraciones', in *Contra viento I*, pp. 231–40.

[41] Mario Vargas Llosa, 'Carta a Fidel Castro', in *Contra viento I*, pp. 250–2 (p. 251).

[42] Mario Vargas Llosa, 'Carta a Haydée Santamaría', in *Contra viento I*, pp. 248–9 (p. 249).

[43] Mario Vargas Llosa, 'Letter to Haydée Santamaría', in *Making Waves*, pp. 105–6 (p. 105).

[44] See, for example, his 1974 essay on the Chilean Jorge Edwards and on *Persona non grata* (1973), Edwards' account of the Cuban developments: Mario Vargas Llosa, 'Un francotirador tranquilo', in *Contra viento I*, pp. 288–99.

and continue saying: 'with socialism'] ('Un francotirador', p. 299). Such statements were met with great irritation by the pro-Cuban Left who, by then, had placed Vargas Llosa firmly in the enemy camp.[45]

By 1978, however, Vargas Llosa's attitude had changed. In a presentation under the title 'Libertad de información y derecho de crítica' [Freedom of Information and the Right to Criticize][46] he left no doubt about his total disillusionment with the socialist approach to achieving social justice, a goal that he continued to feel strongly committed to. Despite the great achievements of socialist societies in terms of education, health provision and the spread of literacy and culture, he said: 'hoy día creo estar en discrepancia casi total con la visión marxista del hombre y de la sociedad' [today I find myself in almost total disagreement with the Marxist vision of man and of society] (p. 71). Instead he pointed to social democrat societies which he found more efficient in reducing social injustices than socialist ones, without sacrificing freedom. He named Sweden, but also Israel, a country which had impressed him deeply on his travels in 1977.[47] In a lecture to the Latin American Jewish Congress in 1978, Vargas Llosa read out a long passage listing all the evils committed in the name of socialism, paradoxically the doctrine which had raised the hopes of so many people to abolish just these evils: inequalities, exploitation, the lack of freedom and workers' rights, authoritarianism, imperialism and neocolonialism, tyranny, brutality, the spirit of domination, control over cultural and artistic production, the reign of bureaucracy and the existence of a privileged ruling class.[48]

In 'Libertad de información y derecho de crítica' and other texts of the period Vargas Llosa underlined his conviction that censorship is the evil at the root of every unfree society. Only by guaranteeing the free flow of information would citizens be able to make informed choices and build a free and democratic society. Already here he made the connection to free enterprise, a doctrine which would become his main credo in the following decades: 'creo que la libertad de información y de crítica desaparece en los regímenes marxistas en la medida en que en ellos desaparece la empresa privada' [I believe that, under Marxist regimes, freedom of information and criticism disappears at the same rate as private enterprise disappears] ('Libertad de información', p. 73). And he concludes: 'Es la independencia económica la que garantiza la independencia para informar y para criticar' [It is economic

---

[45] Vargas Llosa has on many occasions deplored the 'demonization' and 'vilification' that he received following his criticism of Castro. For example, see Setti, pp. 146–7.

[46] Mario Vargas Llosa, 'Libertad de información y derecho de crítica', in *Contra viento y marea, II (1972–1983)* (Barcelona: Seix Barral, 1986), pp. 67–91.

[47] Mario Vargas Llosa, 'Tres notas sobre Israel', in *Contra viento II*, pp. 30–44.

[48] See Mario Vargas Llosa, 'Ganar batallas, no la guerra', in *Contra viento II*, pp. 92–106 (pp. 96–7).

independence which guarantees the independence to inform and criticize] (p. 75).[49]

The fight against censorship became the defining topic of Vargas Llosa's extraliterary activities during this period. *Contra viento I* contains several letters by him protesting against restrictive measures which targeted journals and other media in Peru under the leftist military regimes of General Velasco Alvarado and General Morales Bermúdez and in Argentina under the right-wing junta of General Videla;[50] with his forceful condemnations of authoritarian tendencies Vargas Llosa upset the Left just as easily as the Right. The letter of protest to General Videla was sent in his function as President of PEN International, the writers' organization devoted to promoting literature and defending freedom of expression around the world, a prestigious post to which he was elected in 1976.

In parallel with his practical work in defending the freedom to write, to disagree and to utter dissident opinions, Vargas Llosa turned his attention to theories of freedom and liberalism, embarking on what he would later call his 'aprendizaje intelectual de la libertad' [intellectual apprenticeship of freedom].[51] He gives credit to liberal thinkers such as Isaiah Berlin and Raymond Aaron, and to 'heterodox' writers such as Jean-François Revel,[52] for shaping his re-evaluation of socialism in the 1970s, and instigating his enthusiasm for liberal ideas. The discovery of Isaiah Berlin's concept of the 'contradictory truths, the irreconcilable ends'[53] was particularly helpful in rationalizing Vargas Llosa's disappointed hopes for a socialist society which would be both just and free. What Berlin holds responsible for 'many of the tragedies that have befallen humanity' is, in Vargas Llosa's words, the illusion that 'the most noble and inspiring ideas – justice, freedom, peace, pleasure, and so on – are compatible with one another'. Berlin vigorously refutes 'the belief that one true answer exists for every human problem, and that once we find this answer, then all others must be rejected as mistaken' ('Isaiah Berlin', p. 139). Vargas Llosa himself had earlier denounced systems which promote a 'single truth', lamenting that in Cuba 'las diversas verdades

---

[49] This is not the place to take issue with Vargas Llosa's political and economic convictions. However, considering his claim that such convictions have to be readjusted in the light of new realities, it is surprising not to find a recent comment by him on the state of freedom of information in the privately owned media empires of a Silvio Berlusconi or a Rupert Murdoch.

[50] Mario Vargas Llosa, 'Protesta por la clausura de dos semanarios', 'Carta abierta al general Juan Velasco Alvarado', 'Protesta por clausura de semanarios y revistas' and 'Carta al General Jorge Rafael Videla', in *Contra viento I*, pp. 309–10, 317–20, 343–4 and 351–3 respectively.

[51] Mario Vargas Llosa, 'Dedicatoria a la vieja usanza', in *Contra viento III*, p. 5.

[52] See Mario Vargas Llosa, *Contra viento II*, Dedication.

[53] Mario Vargas Llosa, 'Isaiah Berlin, A Hero of Our Time', in *Wellsprings*, trans. Kristin Keenan de Cueto, John King and Jonathan Titler (Cambridge, MA and London: Harvard University Press, 2008), pp. 133–59 (p. 139).

particulares que daban a la revolución su rica humanidad eran reemplazadas por esa verdad oficial única que todo lo burocratiza y uniforma' [the different individual truths that made the revolution rich in humanity were replaced by this single official truth which shaped everything in a uniform, bureaucratic manner] ('Un francotirador', p. 298). In Isaiah Berlin's concept of the different kinds of liberty and his division of mankind, and of artists in particular, into 'hedgehogs' and 'foxes' – the first representing a 'central, systematized vision of life', the others accepting 'a vast panoply of different behaviours and moral outlook'[54] – Vargas Llosa finds confirmation for his growing scepticism about Utopian ideas which pursue a 'single truth'. Berlin's ideal of pluralism, tolerance and the freedom of choice, 'not just as moral imperatives but as practical requirements for the survival of humankind' ('Isaiah Berlin', p. 144) ties in with Vargas Llosa's plea to accept human diversity and to build society on tolerance of this diversity, on mutual respect and freedom.

During Vargas Llosa's background research for his 1981 novel *La guerra del fin del mundo* about a millenarian uprising in nineteenth-century Brazil, a project that had been developing since the early 1970s, the concept of utopia and the fanatic as a type had come into view. Vargas Llosa's total disillusionment with socialism led him to the conclusion that every Utopian project bears in it the threat of totalitarianism. He rejected as dangerous any type of ideology – religious, political or otherwise – built on a 'verdad única' [single truth], and warned against fanatic followers of such an ideology, who think themselves in possession of the truth. Unwilling to accept other visions of the world, the single-minded attitude of such fanatics can lead them to defend their dogma by every means possible, including violence: 'la persona que está absolutamente segura de su verdad puede aplicar la violencia con absoluta frialdad' [the person who is absolutely sure of his or her truth can apply violence with absolute cold-bloodedness].[55]

Such violence became a brutal reality in Peru during the 1980s when the Maoist 'Sendero Luminoso' [Shining Path] guerrillas unleashed their atrocious campaign of terror in the Andean region. Counter-insurgency forces fought back with brutality, contributing to a climate of lawlessness in this remote part of the country. Abuses of power by the forces of order were widespread, as was later documented. The massacre of eight journalists from various national newspapers and their guide in the mountain village of Uchuraccay in 1983 was an event that shocked Peru and the wider world, and its reverberations continue to the present day.[56] The Peruvian government

---

[54] This distinction goes back to the Greek poet Archilochus's saying 'The fox knows many things, but the hedgehog knows one, big, thing'. Vargas Llosa, 'Isaiah Berlin', pp. 149–50.

[55] Mario Vargas Llosa, 'Después del informe: conversación sobre Uchuraccay. Entrevista de Alberto Bonilla', in *Contra viento III*, pp. 141–55 (p. 152).

[56] The *Informe Final* [Final Report] of the Comisión de la Verdad y Reconciliación

sent an independent commission to investigate the events and made Vargas Llosa its president. Drafted by him but discussed and approved by the other two members of the commission,[57] the report came to the conclusion that the villagers had killed the journalists because they had mistaken them for members of the terror group. 'Malentendido' [misunderstanding] is one of the key words in this document. Even though the report went into some detail to highlight the complex series of factors that had contributed to the massacre, its findings were bitterly disputed. The document contained a section titled 'La violencia antisubversiva' [Antisubversive Violence], which pointed the finger at abuses by the forces of order as one of the factors contributing to the situation that made the massacre possible. Nevertheless, Vargas Llosa found himself denounced as an 'instrument' of the government of Belaúnde Terry in covering up any responsibility by the authorities, since the report stated that there were no official forces present at the time of the massacre. In a climate of polarization, the commission's appeal for legality, morality, and respect for human rights in the fight against terrorism (see p. 123) went largely unheard. The report is marked by Vargas Llosa's concern about a democracy which, at the time, was only just re-establishing itself after twelve years of military rule. Its appeal to morality in politics is firmly rooted in the context of Vargas Llosa's general ideas:

> La matanza de los periodistas ha venido a recordar dramáticamente al país que un sistema democrático no puede olvidar jamás, ni siquiera cuando lucha por su supervivencia, que su superioridad moral sobre los sistemas autoritarios y totalitarios radica en que, en su caso, como dijo Albert Camus, son los métodos los que justifican los fines. (p. 119)
>
> [The killing of the journalists has come to remind the country in a dramatic way that a democratic system may never forget, not even when it fights for its survival, that its moral superiority over authoritarian and totalitarian systems lies in the fact that in it – as Albert Camus said – the means justify the ends.]

This is a position that appears again in Vargas Llosa's sharp reaction to Peruvian President Alberto Fujimori's dismantling of democratic structures

---

[Truth and Reconciliation Commission], published in 2003, called Uchuraccay 'un referente emblemático de la violencia y el dolor en la memoria colectiva del país' [an emblematic referent of the violence and pain in the country's collective memory] (see *Informe Final*, Tomo V, Capítulo 2: Historias representativas de la violencia, 2.4 El Caso Uchuraccay, p. 121, <http://www.cverdad.org.pe/ifinal/> [accessed 15 September 2013]). But as recently as 2009 there were calls to reopen the investigation, and journalists' organizations continue to mark the anniversary of the massacre to keep its memory alive.

[57] See Mario Vargas Llosa, 'Informe sobre Uchuraccay', in *Contra viento III*, pp. 87–128. The original report as referenced in *Contra viento III* ran to 152 pages.

in his 'autogolpe' [self-coup] of 1992, justified by the fight against Sendero Luminoso.

Apart from the official report of the independent commission, a large part of *Contra viento III* documenting the 'Sangre y mugre de Uchuraccay' [Blood and Filth of Uchuraccay] (pp. 85–226) contains a journalistic account of the events that Vargas Llosa first published in *The New York Times Magazine* as 'Inquest in the Andes'; two interviews in which he elaborates on the findings of the commission; a number of articles; and an open letter to the victims' families defending his role in the investigation and the conclusions the commission had come to. It makes highly interesting reading, especially in conjunction with other texts by Vargas Llosa, including works of fiction such as the novel that preceded his mission in the Andes, *La guerra del fin del mundo* [*The War of the End of the World*] (1981),[58] and the novel that followed it, *Historia de Mayta* [*The Real Life of Alejandro Mayta*] (1984),[59] about a dogmatic revolutionary. His experiences in 1983 also influenced the 1993 novel *Lituma en los Andes* [*Death in the Andes*],[60] set at the time of the Sendero Luminoso violence.

Vargas Llosa's analyses of the events in Uchuraccay carry striking echoes of *La guerra del fin del mundo*. During his intensive research for the novel, about a fanatical religious uprising in the backward region of north-eastern Brazil, Vargas Llosa had come to the conclusion that the orgy of violence which brought Canudos's millenarian movement to an end was caused by a general misunderstanding amongst all sides involved.[61] Parallel with what he had found during his work on the nineteenth-century Brazilian hinterland, twentieth-century Peru confronted him with the same kind of simultaneous existence of cultures totally foreign to each other.[62] He encountered a mutual ignorance and lack of communication between the indigenous population of the mountains, the guerrillas and the counterinsurgents, leading to fear of each other, to violence, cruelty and hatred. As he said in an interview on the eve of the official report's publication: 'Hay una serie de desconocimientos mutuos en toda esta historia, detrás de los cuales aparece una problemática nacional:

---

[58] Mario Vargas Llosa, *La guerra del fin del mundo* (Barcelona: Plaza y Janés, 1982); Mario Vargas Llosa, *The War of the End of the World* (London: Faber and Faber, 1986).

[59] Mario Vargas Llosa, *Historia de Mayta* (Barcelona:Seix Barral, 1984); Mario Vargas Llosa, *The Real Life of Alejandro Mayta*, trans. Alfred MacAdam (London: Faber and Faber, 1986).

[60] Mario Vargas Llosa, *Lituma en los Andes* (Barcelona: Planeta, 1993); Mario Vargas Llosa, *Death in the Andes*, trans. Edith Grossman (London: Faber and Faber, 1997).

[61] For example, see Setti, pp. 46–51; also Mario Vargas Llosa, *A Writer's Reality* (London and Boston: Faber and Faber, 1990), pp. 129–31.

[62] In a 1988 lecture series he said: 'in contemporary Latin America you still have Canudos in many countries. In Peru, for instance, we have a living Canudos in the Andes.' Vargas Llosa, *A Writer's Reality*, p. 133.

las enormes distancias que separan a los peruanos de diferentes regiones, clases sociales y culturales' [In this story there is a whole series of things that the opposing sides did not know about each other. This mutual ignorance reveals a national problem: the enormous gulf that divides Peruvians from different regions, social classes, and cultures].[63] The report highlights the 'actitud atávica' [atavistic attitude] ('Informe sobre Uchuraccay', p. 128) of the indigenous population, and in a later interview Vargas Llosa utters his opinion that the Peruvian state has a responsibility to fight the structural basis of violence by 'sacar al campesinado de ese subdesarrollo profundo en que se encuentra' [pulling the rural population out of this state of deep underdevelopment in which it finds itself] ('Después del informe', p. 150). This was another hotly disputed point in the report, and Vargas Llosa was attacked for attributing part of the blame for the violence to the backwardness of the indigenous population. Since then, the continuing conflict between him and his critics about the indigenous question have included scathing reviews of his book on José María Arguedas with its critical view of *Indigenismo*, his Andean novel *Lituma en los Andes*, and the 1987 novel about an indigenous people in the Amazon region, *El hablador* [*The Storyteller*].[64] Vargas Llosa's fiction – and the reception of it – has always been linked to his extraliterary activities, and vice versa.

The vilification he suffered in parts of the press for his role in the Uchuraccay investigation – he mentions the Marxist *Diario de Marka* in a number of articles – found its way into the Western press in a form that provoked Vargas Llosa's outrage. The most angry text included in 'Sangre y mugre de Uchuraccay' is an attack by him on a journalist from *The Times* for spreading tendentious and false information in a highly respected Western quality newspaper, drawn unquestioningly from extreme left-wing sources. What enraged Vargas Llosa most in this case, and has continued to anger him, is the fact that this kind of reporting reinforces existing prejudices about Latin America which feed the revolutionary dreams of people bored with their uneventful civilized Western democratic societies. Such journalists, researchers or academics, he says,

> contribuyen más que nadie a propagar ese imagen de sociedades salvajes y pintorescas con que muchos nos conocen en Europa, por las distorsiones que llevan a cabo cuando simulan describirnos, investigarnos, estudiarnos. América Latina es, para ellos, una estratagema que les sirve para desfogar sus frustraciones políticas, esas quimeras revolucionarias a las que sus propias sociedades no dan cabida. ¡Pobrecitos! Tienen la desgracia de

---

[63] Mario Vargas Llosa, 'El terrorismo en Ayacucho. Entrevista a Mario Vargas Llosa por Uri Ben Schmuel', in *Contra viento III*, pp. 129–40 (p. 133).

[64] Mario Vargas Llosa, *El hablador* (Barcelona: Seix Barral, 1987); Mario Vargas Llosa, *The Storyteller*, trans. Helen Lane (London: Faber and Faber, 1991).

haber nacido en países donde la vida política se decide en las aburridas ánforas electorales y no en las excitantes montañas, donde lo que pone y depone a los gobiernos son los votos y no las pistolas y las bombas. Como no se conforman con semejante desgracia, vuelven los ojos hacia nosotros. Para ellos, se diría, nuestra razón de ser es consolarnos, proveerlos de esa violencia que añoran, de esos apocalipsis con los que sueña su incurable romanticismo político.[65]

[contribute more than anyone to propagate this image of savage and picturesque societies, that many Europeans know us by, thanks to the distortions [these people] produce when they pretend to describe, research, or study us. For them, Latin America is a stratagem which serves to vent their political frustrations, the revolutionary fantasies their own societies have no room for. Poor things! They suffer the disgrace of having been born in countries where politics is determined in boring ballot boxes and not in the exciting mountains; where the making and unmaking of governments is decided by votes and not by pistols and bombs. Since they don't want to conform to such a disgrace, they turn their eyes on us. For them, you could say, our reason for being is to put up with it and provide them with the violence they crave, with the apocalypse they dream of in their incurable political romanticism.]

The polemical tone of this piece recurs in other articles condemning the European Left for projecting their unfulfilled revolutionary dreams onto far-away countries. The best-known argument of this kind is Vargas Llosa's confrontation with the German writer Günter Grass in the same year, 1983. During a visit to Nicaragua under the Sandinistas, Grass had advised Latin American countries to follow the example of Cuba in order to solve their problems. In an article entitled '¿Libertad para los libres?' [Freedom for the Free?][66] and an even more acerbic follow-up letter, 'Carta a Günter Grass' [Letter to Günter Grass],[67] Vargas Llosa accused Grass of promoting solutions for Latin America that he would never accept in his own country, where he has always supported the social democrats and fought for democratic reform. Vargas Llosa calls it 'una suerte de racismo visceral' ('Libertad', p. 352) [a sort of visceral racism][68] that Western intellectuals and part of the media – he names *Le Monde*, *The New York Times* and *El País* – 'nos ve como bárbaros e inciviles, constitutivamente ineptos para la libertad y condenados a elegir, por eso, entre el modelo Pinochet o el modelo Fidel Castro' (p. 354) [see us as barbarians and uncivilized, essentially incapable of freedom and

---

[65] Mario Vargas Llosa, 'El periodismo como contrabando', in *Contra viento III*, pp. 193–8 (p. 197). Vargas Llosa had already raised this issue in 1979, in a polemic article called 'El intelectual barato', in *Contra viento II*, pp. 143–55 (p. 154).
[66] Mario Vargas Llosa, '¿Libertad para los libres?', in *Contra viento II*, pp. 350–5.
[67] Mario Vargas Llosa, 'Carta a Günter Grass', in *Contra viento II*, pp. 356–60.
[68] Mario Vargas Llosa, 'Freedom for the Free?' in *Making Waves*, pp. 200–4 (p. 202).

condemned, for that reason, always to choose between the Pinochet model and the Fidel Castro model] (p. 203). In the open letter to Grass he attacks the 'curiosa esquizofrenia ideológica y moral' [strange ideological and moral schizophrenia] ('Carta a Günter Grass', p. 356) of Western intellectuals, born out of their 'romanticismo ideológico trasnochado' [hung-over ideological romanticism] (p. 360). His angry conclusion that Latin America has to rely on itself if it wants to establish democracy ties in with his harsh refutation of the thesis that Latin America's underdevelopment is due to its dependency on the West. In a book review, also written in 1983, called 'La falacia del tercermundismo' [The Fallacy of Third-Worldism],[69] he takes up the argument:

> en contra de ese pertinaz complejo que atribuye la responsabilidad de todos nuestros males a Europa y Estados Unidos y que, a la vez que nos exonera de toda culpa en nuestro atraso, nos condena a una suerte de plañidera impotencia, ya que, según aquella tesis, nuestro progreso jamás dependerá de nuestros esfuerzos sino de la destrucción del mítico enemigo exterior que nos saquea y anula. (p. 335)

> [against this persistent complex which attributes responsibility for all our evils to Europe and the United States and which, at the same time as it relieves us from all blame for our backwardness, condemns us to a sort of pathetic impotence, since, according to this thesis, our progress will never depend on our own efforts but on the destruction of this mythical enemy from outside who plunders and annihilates us.]

Vargas Llosa's criticism of Western intellectuals and media goes hand in hand with this attack directed against left-wing intellectuals closer to home who, for various reasons, won't believe that the huge inequalities in Latin American countries could be tackled by a home-grown democracy, in the framework of a parliamentarian system with an independent judiciary and free media:

> Porque la magnitud de las igualdades económicas y de las injusticias sociales lo impacientan, o porque los horrores de las dictaduras militares que hemos sufrido (y que aún sufren países como Chile y Paraguay) lo exasperan, y porque la ineficiencia y la inmoralidad que suelen acompañar a nuestros gobiernos democráticos lo llevan a desesperar de una solución pacífica y gradual para los males del subdesarrollo, el intelectual progresista latinoamericano cree aún en el mito de la revolución marxista-leninista como panacea universal.[70]

---

[69] Mario Vargas Llosa, 'La falacia del tercermundismo', *Contra viento II*, pp. 334–9.
[70] Mario Vargas Llosa, 'Respuesta a Günter Grass', in *Contra viento III*, pp. 394–400 (pp. 395–6).

[Whether it is because the magnitude of economic inequalities and social injustices make him impatient, or because the horrors of military dictatorships that we have suffered (and that countries like Chile and Paraguay are still suffering) exasperate him, and because the inefficiency and immorality which tend to accompany our democratic governments bring him to despair of a peaceful and gradual solution for the evils of underdevelopment, the progressive intellectual in Latin America still believes in the myth of the Marxist-Leninist revolution as a universal cure.]

Vargas Llosa does not mince his words when he attacks 'the progressive intellectual', an expression he always uses in the singular, so as to typecast his left-wing opponents in a sardonic manner. In the polemic article 'El intelectual barato' [The Cut-Price Intellectual] we find a scathing parody and exposure of the hypocrisy of 'the progressive intellectual' who leads his revolutionary battles from the safety and comfort of a visiting scholarship at one of the class enemy's universities in the United States (see p. 147). Vargas Llosa's opponents usually answer with the same kind of vitriol, and it is hard to know who is to blame for the polarization and vilification that he regularly complains about. For example, in a 1984 argument with Mario Benedetti published as 'Entre Tocayos' [Between Namesakes],[71] Vargas Llosa quotes the Uruguayan writer as saying about him: 'Hace tiempo que nos hemos resignado a que no esté con nosotros, en nuestras trincheras, sino con ellos, en la de enfrente' [For some time now we have resigned ourselves to the fact that he is not with us, in our trenches, but with them, in the opposite trench] (p. 414). Vargas Llosa rightly complains about such martial vocabulary which suggests that there is a war with two enemies dug in opposite each other, one fighting for the revolution, the other being the reactionary. In the same piece he names the journalist Mirko Lauer as one of the worst perpetrators of the 'satanización' [demonization] (p. 415) that confronts him. Considering that climate of debate, his controversial status could only become worse once he made the step into actual politics.

Vargas Llosa's conviction that Latin America needed to establish sound democratic structures, applying the same standards of legality and morality as in Western democracies, drew him more and more into his country's politics. Offered several official posts by the government of Belaúnde Terry between 1980 and 1985, he refused each one.[72] But with the election of populist President Alan García in 1985 he saw the renascent democracy in

---

[71] Mario Vargas Llosa, 'Entre Tocayos', in *Contra viento II*, pp. 408–17.

[72] With the exception of his unpaid appointment as head of the commission investigating the Uchuraccay killings, Vargas Llosa refused 'embassies in London and in Washington, the ministries of education and foreign relations and, finally, the office of prime minister.' Mario Vargas Llosa, 'A Fish out of Water', trans. Helen Lane, *Vargas Llosa for President* (*Granta*, 36 (1991)), 15–76 (p. 41).

Peru under renewed threat from authoritarian measures and socialist policies. (Alan García, too, had offered him a post as ambassador.) In 1986 Vargas Llosa tried to intervene by the traditional means of an open letter protesting against the armed forces' brutal crushing of a revolt by Sendero Luminoso prisoners in several jails. But it was his leading role in the nationwide protests against the planned nationalization of the finance sector that propelled him into the centre of politics. *Contra viento III* contains the crucial texts marking his reluctant development from an independent intellectual observer and polemicist to a deeply involved politician: his article from August 1987, 'Hacia el Perú totalitario' [Towards a Totalitarian Peru],[73] protesting against the nationalization of banks, was followed by the manifest 'Frente a la amenaza totalitaria' [Opposing the Totalitarian Threat],[74] a text resonating with Vargas Llosa's long-held conviction that a free press is the basis of a free society: 'La concentración del poder político y económico en el partido gobernante podría significar el fin de la libertad de expresión y, en última instancia, de la democracia' [The concentration of political and economic power in the ruling party could mean an end to freedom of expression and, ultimately, of democracy itself] (p. 421). These texts led up to the demonstration in the Plaza San Martín in Lima on 21 August 1987 where Vargas Llosa, turned political orator, spoke to over a hundred thousand people. *Contra viento III* also includes two speeches broadcast to the Peruvian public in September 1987 – 'En el torbellino de la Historia' [In the Whirlwind of History][75] – and September 1988: 'Por un Perú possible' [Towards a Possible Peru].[76] The latter concentrates on the economy and attacks the economic measures of President Alan García as 'keynesiana en apariencia y socialista en esencia' [Keynesian in appearance but socialist in essence] (p. 454). This was followed up by the newspaper article 'Entre la libertad y el miedo' [Between Freedom and Fear],[77] in which Vargas Llosa once again denounced the widely accepted 'dependency theory' which blames external forces such as the World Bank or the International Monetary Fund for Latin America's desolate economic situation. By contrast, he held the widening of the state sector in almost all Latin American countries responsible for their economic failures. This conviction formed the basis of his free-market election programme once he decided to run for Peru's presidency in the 1990 elections.

Vargas Llosa's interest in economics had developed in the context of his readings about liberalism. In addition to Jean-François Revel, Isaiah Berlin and Karl Popper, whose distinction between closed and open societies he

---

[73] Mario Vargas Llosa, 'Hacia el Perú totalitario', in *Contra viento III*, pp. 417–20.
[74] Mario Vargas Llosa, 'Frente a la amenaza totalitaria', in *Contra viento III*, pp. 421–2.
[75] Mario Vargas Llosa, 'En el torbellino de la Historia', in *Contra viento III*, pp. 429–43.
[76] Mario Vargas Llosa, 'Por un Perú possible', in *Contra viento III*, pp. 453–62.
[77] Mario Vargas Llosa, 'Entre la libertad y el miedo', *Contra viento III*, pp. 477–92.

found very useful,[78] he discovered the anti-collectivist free-market theories of economists Ludwig von Mises and Friedrich Hayek. He had been introduced to Hayek at a conference in Lima in 1979, organized by the Peruvian economist Hernando de Soto, and had studied his work during a stay at the Woodrow Wilson Center in Washington in 1980.[79] In 1986, Vargas Llosa wrote a prologue to de Soto's book *El otro sendero. La revolución informal* [The Other Path. The Informal Revolution] which promoted the informal sector of the Peruvian economy as a model of free enterprise.[80] This preface marked the transition from Vargas Llosa's contributions to public debate about political and economic issues into a concrete statement of a political and economic agenda. 'Libertad' [freedom] is the leitmotif in this text, by which he means above all deregulation. But he insists on the essential link between economic and political freedom, between the free market and democracy:

> La libertad es una sola y ella es obviamente incompatible con regímenes autoritarios o totalitarios. ... La libertad económica es la contrapartida de la libertad política y sólo cuando ellas se funden en una unidad, como el anverso y el reverso de una moneda, son operativas y genuinas. ... La función del poder político es garantizar unas reglas de juego tales que aquellas iniciativas puedan ser tomadas de manera equitativa y libre. Y ello requiere un consenso mayoritario sobre estos principios, anterior a su materialización, que sólo el sistema democrático puede dar. ('La revolución silenciosa', pp. 346–7)
>
> [Freedom is a single, unified concept, and is obviously incompatible with authoritarian or totalitarian regimes. ... Economic freedom is the counterpart of political freedom, and only when the two become one, like the two sides of a coin, are they effective and genuine. ... The function of political power is to guarantee the rules of the game so that such initiatives can be undertaken fairly and freely. And that requires the consensus of a majority about these principles, before they are implemented, which is only achievable in a democratic system.]

This was expressly directed against the libertarian economic measures of the so-called 'Chicago boys' in Chile under Pinochet, which threw that country into a 'crisis without precedent' (p. 346). Vargas Llosa's insistence on the

---

[78] For example, see Vargas Llosa's 1988 article on Revel called 'La sociedad abierta y sus enemigos', in *Contra viento III*, pp. 493–9, and his essay, based on an article of 1988, on 'Updating Karl Popper', in *Wellsprings*, pp. 160–200.

[79] See Mario Vargas Llosa, 'Una cabeza fría en el incendio', in *Contra viento III*, pp. 356–64.

[80] Mario Vargas Llosa, 'Prólogo', in Hernando de Soto, *El otro sendero. La revolución informal* (Lima: El Barranco, 1986), pp. XVII–XXIX, included in *Contra viento III*, pp. 333–48 as 'La revolución silenciosa' [The Silent Revolution]. The subsequent English version of de Soto's book does not include Vargas Llosa's prologue.

indivisible link between economic liberty and political freedom has been a constant ever since. He mentions this notion in his preface to the essay collection *Desafíos a la libertad* [Challenges to Freedom] (1994).[81] And he repeats it again in 'Confessions of a Liberal', his acceptance speech for the 2005 Irving Kristol Award, in front of the American Enterprise Institute, a bastion of US neo-conservatism.[82]

After losing the presidential elections in 1990 to Alberto Fujimori, Vargas Llosa left for Europe where he started work on his memoirs, which appeared three years later as *El pez en el agua* [*A Fish in the Water*].[83] But he had already published an account of his political adventure in the British journal *Granta* in 1991, under the title 'A Fish out of Water'. The interesting reversal of the title reveals the differing focus of the two accounts: written shortly after his defeat, the 1991 essay concentrates on his experiences as a writer in the unfamiliar field of politics and ends with the resigned statement: 'No, finally, I don't believe that I succeeded in putting across what I wanted to. Peruvians did not vote for *ideas* in the elections' ('A Fish out of Water', p. 74). The memoirs, by contrast, combine the story of his candidacy with a second layer of narrative about his early development into a writer. In this hybrid work both narrative strands end with his departure from Peru to pursue his true, literary vocation in Europe. (*El pez en el agua* will be discussed in chapter 8 below.)

Once elected President, the victorious Alberto Fujimori took over large parts of his opponent's economic programme, even adopting the economist Hernando de Soto as his special adviser. Despite Vargas Llosa's resolution not to get drawn into political quarrels in Peru again, he felt compelled to protest against Fujimori's suspension of the democratic institutions in his 1992 'autogolpe' and his subsequent governing by decrees. In an article called '¿Regreso a la barbarie?' [Return to Barbarity?][84] Vargas Llosa appealed to the Western world to enforce economic sanctions against the authoritarian regime, a move that nearly cost him his Peruvian citizenship.

Desafíos a la libertad is a collection of essays published in Vargas Llosa's column 'Piedra de toque' between 1990 and 1994. Nationalism in all its forms had become his main focus at this time, whether in the most brutal form of ethnic cleansing in the Balkans, in the shape of regional autonomy movements, in the attempts to build a nation state on religious or ideological

---

[81] Mario Vargas Llosa, *Desafíos a la libertad* (Madrid: El País/Aguilar, 1994).

[82] Mario Vargas Llosa, 'Confessions of a Liberal', 2005 Irving Kristol Lecture AEI Annual Dinner, <http://www.aei.org/speech/22053> [accessed 27 October 2012].

[83] Mario Vargas Llosa, *El pez en el agua. Memorias* (Barcelona: Seix Barral, 1993); Mario Vargas Llosa, *A Fish in the Water. A Memoir*, trans. Helen Lane (London: Faber and Faber, 1995).

[84] Mario Vargas Llosa, '¿Regreso a la barbarie?', in *Sables y utopías*, pp. 71–5.

fanaticism, in reawakening racist movements, or xenophobia. Inspired by Isaiah Berlin's warnings against the dangers of nationalism[85] he writes:

> El verdadero adversario que tiene por delante la cultura de la libertad en este fin de milenio engloba a todos aquellos extremismos, brutalidades y excentricidades sectarias, y, si no es atajado a tiempo, podría crecer, metabolizarlos y conferirles una suerte de terrible respetabilidad. Es el nacionalismo.'[86]
>
> [The true enemy that the culture of freedom is facing at the end of the millennium is an accumulation of all those forms of extremism, brutalities and sectarian eccentricities which, if not stopped in time, could grow, turn into something else and end up with a terrible sort of respectability: I am talking about nationalism.]

Almost every single essay in this collection mentions nationalism as the biggest obstacle to a free society which, as Vargas Llosa elaborates in many of these texts, is built on openness, mutual respect, tolerance, democratic consensus, free markets, individualism, and cultural, religious and ethnic diversity.

> El miedo y la violencia son componentes inevitables de todo nacionalismo. Miedo al otro, a lo diferente y a lo nuevo, a cambiar y a innovar, al movimiento de la historia y a la plena soberanía del individuo que es incompatible con toda reducción colectivista, miedo al mestizaje, al pluralismo, a la coexistencia en la diversidad que es principio básico de la cultura democrática.[87]
>
> [Fear and violence are the unavoidable components of every form of nationalism. Fear of the other, of the different and the new; fear of change and innovation, of the progress of history, and of the full sovereignty of the individual which is incompatible with any collectivist reduction; fear of racial mixture, of pluralism, and of coexistence in diversity which is the basic principle of democratic culture.]

Desafíos a la libertad also revisits Vargas Llosa's free market ideas, for example in an obituary for Friedrich Hayek.[88] Hayek, 'el más radical de los pensadores liberales de nuestro tiempo' [the most radical liberal thinker of our time],[89] and Isaiah Berlin are mentioned in many of the texts. Vargas Llosa draws on their ideas to strengthen his 'defensa del internacionalismo,

---

[85] See Mario Vargas Llosa, 'El nacionalismo y la utopía', in *Desafíos*, pp. 49–54 (p. 49).
[86] Mario Vargas Llosa, 'Los nuevos retos', in *Desafíos*, pp. 205–10 (p. 210).
[87] Mario Vargas Llosa, 'Cuestión de fondo', in *Desafíos*, pp. 247–51 (pp. 248–9).
[88] Mario Vargas Llosa, 'Muerte y resurrección de Hayek', in *Desafíos*, pp. 103–7.
[89] Mario Vargas Llosa, 'Bienvenido, caos', in *Desafíos*, pp. 73–7 (p. 75).

camino de civilización, y de la opción liberal como una alianza simultánea e indivisible de democracia política y libertad económica' [defence of internationalism – the path of civilization – and of the liberal option as a simultaneous and indivisable alliance of political democracy and economic liberty], as he says in his preface (p. 9).

Fidel Castro, 'ese maestro supremo de la hechicería y el cinismo políticos' [this supreme master of political trickery and cynicism],[90] continues to be a constant in these texts from the early 1990s, but Vargas Llosa also condemns the Mexican PRI, the Party of the Institutionalized Revolution, as the 'perfect dictatorship'.[91] Defending himself against criticism from various sides about his intransigence in holding up democracy as an absolute value he states: 'un régimen civil y representativo, sustentado en elecciones libres, amparado por la ley y fiscalizado por la libertad de prensa, no importa cuán corrupto e ineficiente sea, será siempre preferible a una dictadura' (however corrupt or inefficient, a civilian, representative regime, sustained by free elections, protected by the law and held accountable by a free press, will always be preferable to a dictatorship).[92] He makes this statement in an article on Hugo Chavez's 1992 coup attempt in Venezuela. The Venezuelan populist leader would later become the frequent target of Vargas Llosa's attacks on the return of Latin America's tradition of the authoritarian and populist 'strong man', and remained so until the President's death in 2013.[93]

El lenguaje de la pasión (2000), the subsequent collection of articles from 'Piedra de toque' and covering the years 1992 to 2000, presents an eclectic selection touching on art, literature, the media and social, political and cultural developments. Two topics become more prominent in these years: the role of religion in society, and the trivialization of culture. In an article on birth control Vargas Llosa makes this sweeping statement about all religions:

> Desde el punto de vista de los orígenes, la doctrina y la tradición no hay religiones modernas y primitivas, flexibles o inflexibles, democráticas y autoritarias. Todas, incluido el benigno budismo, que parece la más gaseosa de todas las creencias, son dogmáticas y autosuficientes, convencidas de poseer una verdad absoluta y la autoridad moral necesaria para imponerla a los demás, aunque sea mediante baños de sangre.[94]

> [Looking at their origins, their doctrine and tradition, there are no religions that are either modern or primitive, flexible or inflexible, democratic or authoritarian. All of them – benign Buddhism, which seems the most airy of

---

[90] Mario Vargas Llosa, 'Desbarajuste con samba', in *Desafíos*, pp. 241–6 (p. 242).
[91] Mario Vargas Llosa, 'La dictadura perfecta', in *Desafíos*, pp. 121–6 (p. 121).
[92] Mario Vargas Llosa, 'La OEA y los golpistas', in *Desafíos*, pp. 175–9 (p. 175).
[93] For example, see Mario Vargas Llosa, 'El suicidio de una nación', in *El lenguaje*, pp. 299–304, and his '¡Fuera el loco!' in *Sables y utopías*, pp. 211–15.
[94] Mario Vargas Llosa, 'Dios los cría', in *El lenguaje*, pp. 45–56 (p. 45).

all creeds, included – are dogmatic and self-sufficient, convinced that they are in possession of absolute truth and have the necessary moral authority to force this truth onto others, even if it has to be through bloodbaths.]

A vigorous defender of the separation between state and religious authority, in an article from 1998 he speaks out in favour of the right to abortion, linking the Taliban and the Catholic church when it comes to women's rights: 'Pero, sin llegar, claro está, a los extremos talibanes, es seguro que la mujer retrocedería del lugar que ha conquistado en las sociedades libres a ese segundo plano, de apéndice, de hija de Eva, en que la Iglesia, institución machista si las hay, la ha tenido siempre confinada' [But, obviously without reaching the extremes of the Taliban, it is certain that women would retreat from the place they have conquered in our free societies into the background, which is where the Church, a macho institution if ever there was one, has always kept them confined, as an appendix, as the daughter of Eve].[95] Such statements show how Vargas Llosa's political and social attitudes do not easily fit into the Right/Left or conservative/progressive categories. He infuriates people from all sides with his opinions which are presented with great verve, often in a very provocative and polemical manner, as above. It requires a portion of self-irony to state in his preface to *El lenguaje*: 'La verdad es que siempre trato de escribir de la manera más desapasionada posible' [In truth, I always try to write in the most dispassionate way possible] (p. 7). The essays assembled here have a particularly acerbic tone, and many of them contain *ad hominem* invectives (such as one of Vargas Llosa's favourites, the untranslatable 'cacaseno').[96]

Postmodernism is another target for his vitriol. The notions of ethics, responsibility and a recognizable value system that he believes in are incompatible with postmodern arbitrariness and the dissolution of values. The mind games of postmodern thinkers such as Lacan and Derrida – he calls them 'frivolous'[97] – have little in common with his project of exploring the human condition. In 'La hora de los charlatanes' [The Hour of the Charlatans] he exposes their undermining of the concepts of 'truth' and 'reality'. In conjunction with these challenges to meaningfulness, he names media obsession and the cult of celebrity as having turned culture into a 'feria de impostura, de la confusión y de las vanidades' [carnival of imposture, confusion and vanities].[98] In the same vein he condemns the sensationalism of the media when it comes to exposing scandals in the private lives of public

---

[95] Mario Vargas Llosa, 'El "nasciturus"', in *El lenguaje*, pp. 247–52 (p. 252).
[96] The word derives from the name Cacasenno, a character in early modern Italian literature, who could be described in modern terms as a twit or a twerp.
[97] See Mario Vargas Llosa, 'Posmodernismo y frivolidad', in *El lenguaje*, pp. 33–8.
[98] Mario Vargas Llosa, 'Las profecías de Casandra', in *El lenguaje*, pp. 139–44 (p. 144).

figures such as politicians, a practice typical of the 'frivolity that reigns our postmodern civilization' which has spread from tabloid journalism to serious newspapers and television channels. But, he says in a 1998 article, 'el periodismo escandaloso, amarillo, es un perverso hijastro de la cultura de la libertad. No se lo puede suprimir sin infligir a esta una herida acaso mortal' [sensational tabloid journalism is the perverse illegitimate child of the culture of freedom. One cannot suppress the former without inflicting a near-fatal injury to the latter].[99] This becomes the paradox of the new millennium: the achievement of more and more freedom in the most developed parts of the world has brought about a devaluation of culture as Vargas Llosa has always understood it.

But it is not only culture where the 'frivolous' has taken hold. Vargas Llosa even detects a vain pretence and masterful manipulation of the media in the revolutionary movement which sprang up in Mexico in 1994, the 'Ejército Zapatista de Liberación Nacional' [Zapatist National Liberation Army] and its telegenic leader, Subcomandante Marcos with his trademark mask and pipe. He cites Carlos Fuentes's characterization of the insurgency in Chiapas as 'la primera revolución posmoderna' [the first postmodern revolution] and exposes 'la facilidad con que un bufón del Tercer Mundo, a condición de dominar las técnicas de la publicidad y los estereotipos políticos de moda, puede competir con Madonna y las Spice Girls en seducir multitudes' [the ease with which a Third World buffoon, with a firm grip on the mechanisms of publicity and fashionable political stereotypes, is able to compete with Madonna and the Spice Girls in seducing multitudes].[100] The fact that Subcomandante Marcos became a media sensation and raised sympathies for the revolutionary movement's 'vague and confused' goals was due to the 'frenesí sensacionalista, ávido de exotismo, de los medios de comunicación y la irresponsable frivolidad de cierto progresismo occidental' [sensationalist frenzy, avid for exoticism, of the communication media and the irresponsible frivolity of certain Western progressives] (p. 220).

In the age of postmodernism, political and cultural phenomena become more and more intertwined, hence the subdivision of *Touchstones*, the 2002 collection of essays in English translation, into 'Literature', 'Art' and 'Culture and Politics'. This last, new category reflects the fact that Vargas Llosa's political writing becomes increasingly embedded into the context of his cultural concerns. His warnings about nationalism, that 'culture of the uncultured',[101] is extended to 'cultural nationalism', the attempt to preserve a cultural identity by fighting globalization. In 'Culture and the New

---

[99] Mario Vargas Llosa, 'Nuevas inquisiciones', in *El lenguaje*, pp. 253–8 (p. 257).
[100] Mario Vargas Llosa, 'La otra cara del Paraíso', in *El lenguaje*, pp. 219–25 (p. 220).
[101] Mario Vargas Llosa, 'Nationalism and Utopia', in *Touchstones*, pp. 219–24 (p. 223).

International Order' (2002),[102] he reiterates his deep suspicion of any kind of collective identity and expresses his optimism about a free and open world, where 'globalization is not primarily economic' but also cultural. 'Culture can flourish only if it is closely interdependent with other cultures', he would later write in 'The Challenge of Nationalism', published in the 2008 collection *Wellsprings*.[103]

But in parallel with Vargas Llosa's optimism about the possibilities of a globalized world, especially for underdeveloped countries, he has become more and more disheartened about the rise, in the developed world, of a superficial, banal and trivial worldwide culture of light entertainment and frivolous voyeurism, emptied of substance, devoid of form and meaning, 'una cultura que ha hecho de la diversión el valor supremo de la existencia, al cual todos los viejos valores, la decencia, el cuidado de las formas, la ética, los derechos individuales, pueden ser sacrificados sin el menor cargo de conciencia' [a culture that has made entertainment the most important goal in life, to which all the old values – decency, care of form, ethics, individual rights – can be sacrificed without the slightest qualms of conscience].[104] In fact, Vargas Llosa's recent essays reveal a deep cultural pessimism about the 'total confusion of values' within what he calls 'la civilización del espectáculo' [the civilization of entertainment]: 'Los iconos o modelos sociales —las figuras ejemplares— lo son, ahora, básicamente, por razones mediáticas, pues la apariencia ha reemplazado a la sustancia en la apreciación pública. ... Frivolidad, banalidad, estupidización acelerada del promedio es uno de los inesperados resultados de ser, hoy, más libres que nunca en le pasado' [The icons or social role models of today are exemplary figures for reasons to do with the media, since appearance has replaced substance in the public's valuation. ... Frivolity, banality and the accelerated dumbing down of the norm is one of the unexpected results of the fact that we now have more freedom than ever before in the past] ('La civilización'). Media obsession, the loss of hierarchies of knowledge through excessive specialization, and the consequent loss of value judgements have opened the doors to the 'charlatans' of postmodernism dominating the intellectual scene with their theoretical waffle ('palabrería'), as he puts it in his 2010 essay 'Breve discurso sobre la cultura' [Short Discourse on Culture]: 'Es otra de las razones de la pérdida de "autoridad" de los pensadores de nuestro tiempo:

---

[102] Mario Vargas Llosa, 'Culture and the New International Order', in *Touchstones*, pp. 242–55.

[103] Mario Vargas Llosa, 'The Challenge of Nationalism', in *Wellsprings*, pp. 70–108 (pp. 101–2).

[104] Mario Vargas Llosa, 'La civilización del espectáculo', *El País*, 3 June 2007, <http://elpais.com/diario/2007/06/03/opinion/1180821605_850215.html> [accessed 29 October 2012]. This was the original version of what has now become part of the eponymous essay collection *La civilización del espectáculo* (Madrid: Alfaguara, 2012).

no eran serios, jugaban con las ideas y las teorías como los malabaristas de los circos con los pañuelos y palitroques, que divierten y hasta maravillan pero no convencen' [This is another reason for the loss of 'authority' of the thinkers of our time: they were not serious, they played around with ideas and theories like circus jugglers with their handkerchiefs and clubs, entertaining and even dazzling, but not convincing].[105] Whereas culture in the past had to do with posing questions about – and providing possible answers to – our existence, the human condition and the reality we live in, culture nowadays is expected to provide nothing more than an opportunity to escape reality: 'Ahora, más bien, lo que llamamos cultura es un mecanismo que permite ignorar los asuntos problemáticos, distraernos de lo que es serio, sumergirnos en un momentáneo "paraíso artificial", poco menos que el sucedáneo de una calada de marihuana o un jalón de coca, es decir, una pequeña vacación de irrealidad' [Today, however, what we call culture is a mechanism allowing us to ignore problematic issues, distract us from anything serious, submerge ourselves for a moment in an 'artificial paradise', almost like the surrogate for a joint of marihuana or a line of cocaine, that is to say, a little holiday away from reality].[106]

Even freedom of information, an issue which has always been closest to Vargas Llosa's heart, has become the playing field for vanities and irresponsible sensationalism. In 2011, Julian Assange, the Wikileaks founder who claims to fight secrecy and expose official lies by making information available to all via the Internet, has become 'el símbolo emblemático de una cultura donde el valor supremo de la información ha pasado a ser la de divertir a un público frívolo y superficial, ávido de escándalos' [the emblematic symbol of a culture in which the supreme value of information has become that of entertaining a frivolous and superficial public eager for scandal].[107] By going too far in its quest for transparency, Wikileaks has broken down the border between the public and the private, destroying the notion of confidentiality and trust, with potentially terrible consequences: 'podría significar, no una hazaña libertaria sino pura y simplemente un liberticidio que, además de socavar los cimientos de la democracia, infligiría un rudo golpe a la civilización' [it could mean, not a libertarian feat, but purely and simply the killing off of freedom, which would not only undermine the foundations of democracy but inflict a heavy blow on civilization]. Vargas

[105] Mario Vargas Llosa, 'Breve discurso sobre la cultura', *Letras Libres*, July 2010, <http://www.letraslibres.com/revista/convivio/breve-discurso-sobre-la-cultura> [accessed 29 October 2012].

[106] Mario Vargas Llosa, 'La civilización del espectáculo', *El País*, 22 January 2011, <http://elpais.com/diario/2011/01/22/babelia/1295658733_850215.html> [accessed 29 October 2012].

[107] Mario Vargas Llosa, 'Lo privado y lo público', *El País*, 16 January 2011, <http://www.elpais.com/articulo/opinion/privado/publico/elpepiopi/20110116elpepiopi_10/Tes> [accessed 27 October 2012]; now in *La civilización del espectáculo*, pp. 152–6.

Llosa deplores the unrestrained indulgence of a 'universal voyeurism' which he detects in 'the great farce that public life is' today. The fact that this 'manifestation of barbarity' has appalled him so much in recent years might have to do with the public's eagerness to satisfy their transgressive impulses in real life rather than in literature. But it is literature whose purpose Vargas Llosa defines as providing a counter-world which can fulfil our desire for transgression. As he states again in a recent review, 'las obras logradas nos civilizan y humanizan, alejándonos del bruto que llevamos dentro, ese que fuimos antes de que los buenos libros, las buenas historias, la buena poesía y la buena prosa, lo domesticaran y enjaularan' [accomplished works of fiction civilize and humanize us, distancing us from the monster that we all carry inside, the brute that we were before good books, stories, poetry and prose tamed and caged it].[108]

Vargas Llosa has always upheld the notion that literature provides a realm where the dark, evil impulses and desires that belong to humankind can be realized without harm to anyone, and where the wish for a better, Utopian world, a 'total' reality, can be fulfilled. The 2009 collection of essays *Sables y utopías. Visiones de América Latina* [Sabres and Utopias. Visions of Latin America], which takes stock of the big topics of Vargas Llosa's life, reflects this idea in the way it is organized, beginning with the dangers facing Latin American reality, and ending with the area where illusions, dreams and fantasies have their place: literature. These essays, which have all appeared elsewhere between 1967 and 2006, are arranged thematically under the chapter headings 'La peste del autoritarismo' [The Pest of Authoritarianism], 'Auge y declive de las revoluciones' [The Rise and Fall of Revolutions], 'Obstáculos al desarrollo: nacionalismo, populismo, indigenismo, corrupción' [Obstacles to Development: Nationalism, Populism, Indigenism, Corruption], 'Defensa de la democracia y del liberalismo' [In Defence of Democracy and Liberalism] and, finally 'Los beneficios de la irrealidad: arte y literatura latinoamericana' [The Benefits of Unreality: Latin American Art and Literature]. This was followed in 2012 by *La civilización del espectáculo* [The Civilization of Entertainment] which brings together articles of the past fifteen years denouncing the trivialization of culture (most of them already mentioned above), the disappearance of eroticism, the loss of values and the rise of religious fanaticism. When published individually over a period of time, they expressed protest, irritation and anger; assembled in one volume, they give the impression of a writer who looks at contemporary society with a deep cultural pessimism, still rebellious, but also nostalgic for a world that has irrevocably changed.

On the other hand, one has to acknowledge that Vargas Llosa, now in

---

[108] Mario Vargas Llosa, 'Los ensayos de Luis Loayza', *El País*, 10 April 2011, <http://elpais.com/diario/2011/04/10/opinion/1302386412_850215.html> [accessed 29 October 2012].

his mid-seventies and a Nobel Laureate, has an undiminished capacity to surprise his readers with the unexpected and to provoke further controversy. The international prestige that the Nobel Prize has brought him did not prevent an Argentinian group of intellectuals from opposing his invitation to open the 2011 Book Fair in Buenos Aires. Under the leadership of none other than the director of the National Library, the 'Carta Abierta' [Open Letter] group appealed to the organizers to withdraw this invitation because, as a foreigner, the 'reactionary' Vargas Llosa had dared to criticize the populist policies of Argentina's President Cristina Kirchner. The President herself opposed this intolerant attempt to silence Vargas Llosa. In his retort to the protest group, Vargas Llosa pointed out the absurdity of such nationalistic arguments in a country from where the liberator José de San Martín, as well as the revolutionary Che Guevara, had set out on their missions across the national boundaries. He wrote:

> El nacionalismo es una ideología que ha servido siempre a los sectores más cerriles de la derecha y la izquierda para justificar su vocación autoritaria, su prejuicios racistas, sus matonerías, y para disimular su orfandad de ideas tras un fuego de artificio de esloganes patrioteros. Está visceralmente reñido con la cultura, que es diálogo, coexistencia en la diversidad, respeto del otro.[109]

> [Nationalism is an ideology that has always served the crudest sectors of the Right and the Left to justify their authoritarian inclination, their racist prejudices, their bullying, and to hide their lack of ideas behind a fireworks display of patriotic slogans. Nationalism stands in total opposition to culture, which is dialogue, coexistence in diversity, respect for the other.]

In the end, Vargas Llosa did not actually open the book fair in Buenos Aires, but gave his 'inaugural' lecture a day later, defending freedom of speech and praising reading as a path to tolerance and mutual understanding.

In his own country Vargas Llosa has recently intervened – successfully – in the elections of June 2011 to prevent the daughter of dictator Alberto Fujimori from becoming President. This meant advising the public to vote against the country returning to authoritarianism and to choose, in the second-round run-off between Keiko Fujimori and the leftist candidate Ollanta Humala, the populist Humala (whom he had vigorously criticized in the previous election). An open letter by 107 Peruvian writers headed by Vargas Llosa, 'Escritores contra el fujimorismo' [Writers Against Fujimorism],[110] was followed by

---

[109] Mario Vargas Llosa, 'Piqueteros intelectuales', *El País*, 13 March 2011, <http://elpais.com/diario/2011/03/13/opinion/1299970811_850215.html> [accessed 29 October 2012].

[110] Mario Vargas Llosa, Alfredo Bryce Echenique, Fernando Iwasaki 'y 104 escritores peruanos más', 'Escritores contra el fujimorismo', *El País*, 26 May 2011, <http://elpais.com/diario/2011/05/26/opinion/1306360807_850215.html> [accessed 29 October 2012].

Vargas Llosa withdrawing his 'Piedra de toque' column from the newspaper *El Comercio* in protest, since it had turned into a 'propaganda machine' for Keiko Fujimori.[111] Vargas Llosa's appeal to vote for Humala was a hotly disputed pragmatic recommendation which lost him political friends on the Right and made him clash publicly with the leader of the Roman Catholic Church in Peru, Cardinal Cipriani, who preached against him from the pulpit of Lima's cathedral. Vargas Llosa's battle against authoritarian tendencies and the political manipulation of the media was, in this case, successful, and he used strong – and surprising – words to point this out: in 'La derrota del fascismo' [The Rout of Fascism][112] he expressed his hopes that, with a 'genuinely democratic and liberal Left', Peru will no longer run the risk of falling back into the barbarity of dictatorship.

Vargas Llosa's liberal stance has always included the possibility of error and a revision of his opinions in the light of new information or new developments: 'Creo que la posibilidad del error es, básicamente, lo que define a un intelectual liberal, un intelectual que reconoce la posibilidad de equivocarse en aquello que defiende' [I believe that the possibility of error is basically what defines a liberal intellectual, an intellectual who recognizes that he might be wrong in what he defends].[113] He has also never shied away from the opportunity to back up his opinions with some first-hand experience, to verify or modify his ideas about an event or a situation, by travelling to regions in turmoil (such as the Andes), visiting revolutionary countries (such as Nicaragua in 1985), or spending time in zones of war (Iraq in 2003) or conflict (Israel/Palestine in 2005). The reportages from these visits bridge the gap between his journalism and his narrative work. They use literary devices such as individualizing an issue, visually depicting a person or a scene, filling out the background to a person by giving details about their past or family life, and ascribing emotions to them. This becomes clear, for example, in the contrast between the official Uchuraccay report and Vargas Llosa's reportage for *The New York Times Magazine*.[114] Atmospheric descriptions of the moments before the journalists set off on their fateful mission and sentences such as 'His heart must have been beating fast that morning' ('Story of a Massacre', p. 171), expressing anxious expectation, and 'That

---

[111] Jaime Cordero, 'La elección más reñida de la historia de Perú polariza a toda la sociedad', *El País*, 2 June 2011, <http://elpais.com/diario/2011/06/02/internacional/1306965607_850215.html> [accessed 29 October 2012].

[112] Mario Vargas Llosa, 'La derrota del fascismo', *El País*, 19 June 2011, <http://elpais.com/diario/2011/06/19/opinion/1308434411_850215.html> [accessed 29 October 2012].

[113] *Semana de autor: Mario Vargas Llosa* (Madrid: Ediciones Cultura Hispánica, 1985), p. 67.

[114] Mario Vargas Llosa, 'Inquest in the Andes', trans. Edith Grossman, *The New York Times Magazine*, 31 July 1983, pp. 18–23, 33, 36–7, 42, 48–51 and 56, later extended to 'The Story of a Massacre', in *Making Waves*, pp. 171–99.

night, in Chacabamba, Doña Rosa, Juana Lidia and Julia Aguilar waited in vain for Juan Argumendo to return' (p. 191), conveying the pain of one victim's family, emotionally engage the reader.

The same goes for Vargas Llosa's text on Nicaragua where he spent a whole month in 1985 to report on the country's development under the revolutionary Sandinistas, again for *The New York Times Magazine*.[115] 'Nicaragua at the Crossroads', as the later version in *Making Waves* is called, is not a one-sided condemnation of a Marxist attempt to revolutionize a country as one might imagine from Vargas Llosa's bitterly disillusioned attitude to socialism at the time. It is instead a well-balanced piece of reportage on the achievements, difficulties and contradictions (such as the implementation of Marxism in a catholic context) of a country in transformation, benefiting from a novelist's eye for detail, and written with sympathy (see the section 'Is the Virgin anti-Sandinista?', which does not show any of the vitriol against the Church known from Vargas Llosa's polemics). The ability to portray individuals and render conversations with a diverse range of people make this report informative and engaging, and Vargas Llosa's feistiness allows him to throw light on all kinds of controversial issues, from different angles.

In June and July 2003, he spent twelve days in Iraq to witness for himself the effect of the invasion by US and British forces and the ousting of Saddam Hussein's regime, a war which he had opposed as illegal for its lack of backing from the UN. His reportage from his travels to Baghdad and other parts of the country was first published in eight instalments in *El País* before coming out as a book, *Diario de Irak* [Iraq Diary].[116] His narration of the impressions he gained from conversations with officials, religious leaders, civilians, militants and victims of torture are complemented by photos taken by his daughter Morgana, a professional photographer who accompanied him. The reports convey many different sides of the country, speaking of the friendliness and hospitality with which some people received him, and the threatening atmosphere of hostility that greeted him elsewhere. Vargas Llosa vividly puts in front of our eyes the devastation caused by the looting in Baghdad following the invasion, where people mindlessly 'chipped and broke and gutted and smashed everything' ('Iraq Diary', p. 276) – the rhetorical repetition of the connective 'and' graphically evoking the orgy of destruction that happened under the gaze of the occupying forces who did nothing to combat it. Vargas Llosa explains the destructive behaviour with notions

---

[115] Mario Vargas Llosa, 'In Nicaragua', trans. Edith Grossman, *The New York Times Magazine*, 28 April 1985, pp. 36–46, 76–7, 81–3 and 92–4, reproduced as 'Nicaragua en la encrucijada' in *Contra viento III*, pp. 247–304; an edited English version with the title 'Nicaragua at the Crossroads' can be found in *Making Waves*, pp. 205–24.

[116] Mario Vargas Llosa, *Diario de Irak*, photos Morgana Vargas Llosa (Madrid: Aguilar, 2003), included in English as 'Iraq Diary' in *Touchstones*, pp. 266–319.

familiar from his essays: 'Finding themselves free and uncensored, in a world without any checks or laws, some gave vent to the unbridled, savage thirst for violence that we all carry within us. ... a people humiliated, maltreated, terrorised and alienated by thirty-five years of authoritarianism wallowed in a bath of purifying brutality and licentiousness' (p. 289). Concerning the future of Iraq, Vargas Llosa asks more questions than can be answered, but the personal experience of the situation in the country has changed his opinion about the war: 'now, with what I have seen and heard in this short stay, I would have supported the intervention, without hesitation ... if the argument to intervene had been, clearly and explicitly, to put an end to an execrable and genocidal tyranny' (p. 318).

In the summer of 2005 Vargas Llosa waded into an even greater minefield, travelling to the Middle East to write a reportage on the Israeli–Palestinian conflict. *Israel/Palestina: Paz o guerra santa* [Israel/Palestine: Peace or Holy War] appeared in seven instalments between 18 September and 8 October 2005 in *El País*, followed by its publication in book form, with photographs again by Morgana Vargas Llosa.[117] The conversations he had during this trip take in very different points of view: he reports talking to Israeli settlers as well as to peace activists, to Palestinians in Gaza and Hebron as well as to Israeli victims of terror; he writes about the separation wall dividing Palestinian communities and experiences for himself the difficulties of travelling to the occupied territories. The technique of multiple points of view which, taken together, form a picture of the whole, mirrors the multiperspectivism of many of his novels. Here – as well as in his fiction – it helps to give the reader an idea of the complex situation and the many factors that play a role in this conflict, seen from the perspective of individuals who are all affected by it. Vargas Llosa's criticism of Israel as a 'potencia colonizadora' [colonizing power] whose actions 'maculan moralmente el formidable progreso material y social' [morally stain the formidable material and social progress] (p. 18) of the state necessarily provoked controversy (see the preface, pp. 10–11). On the other hand, he praised Israel as the country where he still feels great sympathy and respect for the Left – a surprising admission from the staunch anti-socialist liberal: 'Allí, la izquierda ... todavía actuaba movida por razones más morales que ideológicas, era profundamente democrática —tolerante, pluralista, anti autoritaria ...— había conservado aquel idealismo libertario y el sentido ético de la política que a mí, de joven, me habían seducido tanto' [There, the Left, ... still moved to act for moral rather than ideological reasons, was profoundly democratic – tolerant, pluralistic, anti-authoritarian ... – it had conserved this libertarian idealism and the moral dimension of politics that had seduced me so much when I was young] (pp. 108–9). This is

---

[117] Mario Vargas Llosa, *Israel/Palestina: Paz o guerra santa*, photos Morgana Vargas Llosa (Madrid: Aguilar, 2006).

another example of Vargas Llosa's readiness to revise (some of) his convictions in the light of new experiences or research.

The *in situ* research that Vargas Llosa has undertaken for his journalistic reportages is matched by the extensive trips he has undertaken to research some of his novelistic projects. Over the years he has embarked on several trips to the Amazon region; he travelled to the Sertão in the north-east of Brazil; made a trip to the South Seas tracing Gauguin's last years for *El Paraíso en la otra esquina*, and, more recently, has travelled to the Congo to see the region for himself and gain information for his latest novel *El sueño del celta* [*The Dream of the Celt*].[118] In Vargas Llosa's case, journalism and fiction are two sides of the same coin: both rely on thorough research and first-hand experience. This is what he means when he says that 'la literatura debe hundirse hasta el cuello en la vida de la calle, en la experiencia común, en la historia haciéndose' [literature has to immerse itself deep in life on the streets, in common experiences, in history in the making].[119] He has never shied away from that.

---

[118] Mario Vargas Llosa, *El sueño del celta* (Doral, FL: Alfaguara, 2010); Mario Vargas Llosa, *The Dream of the Celt*, trans. Edith Grossman (London: Faber and Faber, 2012). Documented in Mario Vargas Llosa, 'Viaje al corazón de las tinieblas', *El País*, 11 January 2009, <http://elpais.com/diario/2009/01/11/eps/1231658814_850215.html> [accessed 29 October 2012].

[119] Mario Vargas Llosa, 'Dinosaurios en tiempos difíciles', in *Friedenspreis des deutschen Buchhandels 1996. Mario Vargas Llosa. Ansprachen aus Anlass der Verleihung*, ed. Börsenverein des Deutschen Buchhandels (Frankfurt am Main: Verlag der Buchhändler-Vereinigung, 1996), pp. 35–48 (p. 39); also in *La civilización del espectáculo*, pp. 212–26.

PART 2:
THE NARRATIVE WORK

4

Prelude: *Los jefes* (1959)

The collection of short stories, published in 1959 under the title *Los jefes* [The Leaders],[1] was Mario Vargas Llosa's first literary publication in book form. English versions of *Los jefes* are usually published in conjunction with his only other piece of short narrative, *Los cachorros* [The Cubs] (1967),[2] under the title *The Cubs and Other Stories*.[3] But while he regards *Los cachorros* as a mature piece of writing, Vargas Llosa characterizes the stories that make up *Los jefes* as 'youthful transgressions' inspired by Hemingway's 'stylistic abstinence and objectivity', a 'handful of survivors out of the many I wrote and tore up between 1953 and 1957, while I was still a student in Lima'.[4] Despite the author's retrospective self-critical attitude to those 'adolescent and *machista* stories' ('Author's Preface', p. xv) the book won a Spanish literary prize in 1959, the Premio Leopoldo Alas. Since he was the first of the future Boom authors to publish his work in Spain, this was an important step towards the success of Latin American fiction in Europe. But already in 1957 one of the stories, 'El desafío', had won first prize in a competition for Peruvian short fiction organized by the French art and travel magazine *La Revue Française*. It gained Vargas Llosa a two-week stay in Paris, a trip that would enable him to look beyond the confines of his native country and

---

[1] According to Oviedo the early editions varied in title and number of the individual stories: the first edition contained only five stories; one story was substituted by another in the second; and only from the third edition onwards are the titles, number and sequence of stories as follows: 'Los jefes' [The Leaders], 'El desafío' [The Challenge], 'El hermano menor' [The Younger Brother], 'Día domingo' [On Sunday], 'Un visitante' [A Visitor] and 'El abuelo' [The Grandfather]. See José Miguel Oviedo, *Mario Vargas Llosa: la invención de una realidad* (Barcelona: Seix Barral, 1982), p. 86. The edition used here is Mario Vargas Llosa, *Los jefes* (Barcelona: Bruguera, 1983).
[2] Mario Vargas Llosa, *Los cachorros* (Madrid: Cátedra, 1990).
[3] Mario Vargas Llosa, *The Cubs and Other Stories*, trans. Gregory Kolovakos and Ronald Christ (London: Faber and Faber, 1991). This edition, with a preface by the author, has reordered the stories.
[4] Mario Vargas Llosa, 'Author's Preface', in *The Cubs and Other Stories*, pp. xiii–xviii (pp. xvii, xiii); we will encounter a writer-protagonist who produces and throws away stories à la Hemingway and others in the young Varguitas of *La tía Julia y el escribidor* [*Aunt Julia and the Scriptwriter*].

overcome the limited possibilities for writers in Peru that he later denounced so strongly in his 'La literatura es fuego' [Literature is Fire] speech.

Like a musical prelude, the stories brought together in *Los jefes* can be seen as an introduction to a large-scale work to follow, setting up themes which will subsequently be developed and reworked in numerous variations. But, as some preludes, these short stories are also able to stand alone, as manifestations of a young writer trying to find his literary individuality. Seen for themselves, the stories explore different modes of writing: there is the urban character of 'Día Domingo' and 'Los jefes', the indigenist or 'telluric' mould recognizable in 'El hermano menor', the suspense and mystery created in 'Un visitante', and the elements of Gothic fiction in 'El abuelo'. Various genres and art forms have been absorbed into the stories: the visual descriptions in 'El hermano menor' and 'Un visitante' and the fight scene in 'El desafío' owe a great deal to cinema. In his preface Vargas Llosa mentions the imagery of Hollywood westerns as one of the genres that influenced him at the time. He also indicates the importance of his 'voracious' reading habit, with an eclectic mix of authors such as Dostoyevsky, Faulkner, Henry Miller, Hemingway, Paul Bowles and André Malraux all leaving a mark on his writing (pp. xiii–xv). But what makes the stories truly remarkable is the way in which they anticipate so many of the defining features of Vargas Llosa's later work: in rudimentary form these juvenile pieces announce themes, characters, structural patterns and technical devices that will become the individual hallmark of the mature writer.

The title story 'Los jefes' is set in a school where an inner circle of pupils organizes a revolt against the school authorities' refusal to announce an exam timetable. Defiance of rules set by the institution and power struggles within the circle of leaders of the rebellion anticipate motives that will be developed in *La ciudad y los perros* [*The Time of the Hero*] (1963),[5] but also point forward to the internal frictions of the clandestine Communist cell in *Conversación en la catedral* [*Conversation in the Cathedral*] (1969).[6] In his memoirs Vargas Llosa says about 'Los jefes':

> Ese cuento prefigura mucho de lo que hice después como novelista: usar una experiencia personal como punto de partida para la fantasía; emplear una forma que finge el realismo mediante precisiones geográficas y urbanas; una objetividad lograda a través de diálogos y descripciones hechas desde un punto de vista impersonal, borrando las huellas de autor y, por último,

---

[5] Mario Vargas Llosa, *La ciudad y los perros* (Barcelona: Seix Barral, 1983); Mario Vargas Llosa, *The Time of the Hero* (London: Picador, 1986).

[6] Mario Vargas Llosa, *Conversación en la catedral* (Barcelona: Seix Barral, 1985); Mario Vargas Llosa, *Conversation in the Cathedral*, trans. Gregory Rabassa (New York: HarperCollins, 2005).

una actitud crítica de cierta problemática que es el contexto u horizonte de la anécdota.⁷

[That short story prefigures much of my later practice as a novelist: using a personal experience as a point of departure for the imaginary; employing a form that pretends to be realistic by virtue of its precise geographical and urban details; an objectivity arrived at through dialogues and descriptions observed from an impersonal point of view, effacing the author's tracks; and finally, a politically committed, critical attitude toward a certain set of problems that is the context or horizon of the story line.]⁸

At the centre of another story, 'El desafío', is a knife fight between two young men. The reason for this violent confrontation remains totally unexplained. The fighters are closely observed and encouraged by their mates and by an older man, who only at the very end is revealed to be the father of the youth who gets killed. The unquestioned value system of a male-dominated society where violence and physical dominance rule will become a recurring subject matter in Vargas Llosa's work. The story 'El hermano menor' rehearses a whole range of important themes: honour and revenge, truth and lies, racism, and injustice. Two brothers set out to kill an indigenous worker who has fled their ranch having been accused of raping their sister, an allegation which turns out to be false. The narrative develops the moral conflict in which the younger brother finds himself. He is part of the landowning class and belongs to the family running the farm, but he ends up being disgusted by the proprietorial and racist attitude of his family and social class towards their employees. 'Día Domingo', on the other hand, portrays the rituals of a group of adolescents in Lima's well-off middle-class 'barrio' [neighbourhood] Miraflores, the setting of a number of Vargas Llosa's works. The rivalry between two boys leads to a dangerous swimming competition in rough seas in which, for a moment, authentic camaraderie prevails over inauthentic posing. But, back on shore amongst their peers, the role-play which characterizes the group's behaviour – a prominent topic in Vargas Llosa's fiction – takes over again. 'Un visitante' introduces a type of protagonist who will have a prominent place in a number of his novels throughout the years: the traitor. In exchange for his release from prison a criminal helps the police set up an ambush for a wanted man. The police – amongst them Sergeant Lituma, a character who will appear in various incarnations throughout Vargas Llosa's work – arrest the man they are after, but abandon the informer helpless and exposed to the revenge of the arrested man's friends who are already waiting in the

---

⁷ Mario Vargas Llosa, *El pez en el agua. Memorias* (Barcelona: Seix Barral, 1993), p. 291.
⁸ Mario Vargas Llosa, *A Fish in the Water. A Memoir*, trans. Helen Lane (London: Faber and Faber, 1995), p. 288.

undergrowth. The traitor ends up being betrayed, mutual trust is overruled by power. The story 'El abuelo' is the odd one out in these tales of machismo. However, it is an interesting addition to the emerging pattern of leaders and followers, father and son, older and younger brother. Here the grandfather, a figure of the establishment but no longer at the centre of either family or social group, commits a malicious transgression by terrifying his grandson with a human skull engulfed in flames. The old man, no longer the authoritative father but outside the current power structures, takes his resentment out on the young boy who is still an underdog in family and society, but soon growing up to be at the top of the hierarchy. The story plays with the unexpected maliciousness of the grandfather, a figure usually regarded as a benevolent member within a family, in a way that is later mirrored in the undermining of the innocence associated with a child in *Elogio de la madrastra* [*In Praise of the Stepmother*] (1988)[9] and *Los cuadernos de Don Rigoberto* [*The Notebooks of Don Rigoberto*] (1997).[10]

The stories in 'Los jefes' establish realism as the dominant mode of Vargas Llosa's writing. Reflecting 1950s Peruvian society, they are concerned with the individual and his position in a social context (females are only present in these stories as catalysts for male conflicts). The depiction of groups, their power structures, their collective rituals and their way of communicating anticipates Vargas Llosa's future exploration of closed circles within wider social collectives: the gang within a school, the friendship group within a particular neighbourhood, the family within a social class, the urban middle class within the wider society. The tensions between outsiders and insiders, already important in these short stories, will form the basis for plot lines in later narrative works. The group leading the school strike in 'Los jefes' called the 'Coyotes' is an early version of 'el Círculo' [the Circle] in *La ciudad y los perros*. Their challenge of the social order ends in conformity, since it has more to do with posing and role-play than with an authentic rebellion. Ultimately, as one of the protagonists expresses, it comes down to a personal rivalry between two boys, a struggle for leadership. In 'Día Domingo' the inner circle of 'los pajarracos' [the Hawks] who engage in drinking competitions anticipate the group of rogues calling themselves 'los Inconquistables' [the Unconquerables] who appear in *La casa verde* [*The Green House*] (1966)[11] and other later works. The false exhibition of machismo by the 'Hawks' (the animal imagery is another important narrative

[9] Mario Vargas Llosa, *Elogio de la madrastra* (Barcelona: Tusquets, 1988); Mario Vargas Llosa, *In Praise of the Stepmother*, trans. Helen Lane (New York: Penguin, 1990).
[10] Mario Vargas Llosa, *Los cuadernos de Don Rigoberto* (Madrid: Alfaguara, 1997); Mario Vargas Llosa, *The Notebooks of Don Rigoberto*, trans. Edith Grossman (London: Faber and Faber, 1999).
[11] Mario Vargas Llosa, *La casa verde* (Barcelona: Argos Vergara, 1980); Mario Vargas Llosa, *The Green House* (London: Picador, 1986).

element that Vargas Llosa is going to develop further) is not just a common feature of adolescent behaviour, it also reflects the codes of the society they live in. This becomes clear in 'El desafío', where Leonidas, the father of one of the fighters, urges his son to 'carry himself like a man' – only to see him die in the brutal confrontation he encouraged. Father and son, leader and follower, insider and outsider, traitor and loyal friend – such pairings will come to dominate Vargas Llosa's fiction. Within the closed circles portrayed in these stories strong antagonisms arise: between two rivals for leadership, or for a girl; between the two brothers in 'El hermano menor'; between police and informant in 'Un visitante'. The pattern of dual categories embedded in circular structures, which will evolve as one of the most important features of Vargas Llosa's narrative, is already taking shape here.

Apart from the defining themes that emerge from these early pieces of narrative, and the first signs of narrative structures which will characterize Vargas Llosa's fiction right up to the present day, the short stories also experiment with techniques that he will come to define as crucial for his fiction writing: the choice of different narrators, perspectives and levels of time, and the 'dato escondido' [hidden fact] of a person's true identity. In 'El desafío' Vargas Llosa even rehearses the narrative device of the 'vasos comunicantes' or telescopic dialogues, as Oviedo has pointed out (see Oviedo, *Invención*, p. 92), where a conversation between two people contains another dialogue on a different level of time, between different people, in order to create a sense of immediacy (see *Los jefes*, p. 39).[12] And finally *Los jefes* announces Vargas Llosa's interest in exploring different codes of language. His attention to the characteristic linguistic patterns of youth dialogue and his recreation of its oral quality, already present in the exchanges between the adolescent protagonists in these stories, will be developed further in *La ciudad*, but especially in *Los cachorros*. The collection *Los jefes* must be regarded as an important prelude to more than fifty years of narrative creation.

---

[12] In the English version used here, the strange decision was made to italicize the exchange that is embedded within the main dialogue; see Vargas Llosa, *The Cubs and Other Stories*, p. 113.

5

Experimenting with Form and Language: Narratives of the 1960s and 1970s

Vargas Llosa wrote his debut novel while living in Europe with his first wife Julia, whom he had married in 1955 when he was still a teenager. After spending the year 1959 at the Complutense University in Madrid, where he held a bursary for a doctoral research project on modernism, the grant ran out and the couple moved to Paris.[1] Despite holding several jobs simultaneously in order to keep himself afloat, he found time to work on his first novel which had the working titles 'La morada del héroe' [The House of the Hero] and 'Los impostores' [The Impostors]. In 1962 he entered the finished manuscript into the competition for the Biblioteca Breve award, organized by the Spanish publishing house Seix Barral, and became the first Latin American author to win this literary prize. The following year he published the novel under the title *La ciudad y los perros* [*The Time of the Hero*][2] with Seix Barral. It became an instant success with readers and won the Spanish Critics' prize as well as coming second in the Prix Formentor, a competition organized by the publisher Carlos Barral who became his friend and mentor.

The novel is based on Vargas Llosa's experiences at the Leoncio Prado military school in Lima where he was a pupil from 1950 to 1951, sent there by his father to eradicate his literary inclinations and make a man out of him, as he has reiterated in many interviews. The duality of the Spanish title, which translates as 'The City and the Dogs', refers to the two poles of the narrative: the world outside the academy in the city of Lima and the barracks where the first year students, the 'dogs', are submitted to a humiliating ritual of initiation by the older years, an introduction to the brutal dog-eat-dog mentality that reigns inside the school. As Alberto, one of the main protagonists, says at the beginning of the novel to the boy nicknamed 'the Slave': 'aquí eres militar aunque no quieras. Y lo que importa en el Ejército es ser bien macho. ... O comes o te comen' (*La ciudad*, p. 26) [you're a soldier here whether you like it or not. And the big thing in the army is to be real

---

[1] Vargas Llosa obtained his PhD years later, in 1971, for his study *García Márquez. Historia de un deicidio* (Barcelona: Barral Editores, 1971).

[2] Mario Vargas Llosa, *La ciudad y los perros* (Barcelona: Seix Barral, 1983); Mario Vargas Llosa, *The Time of the Hero* (London: Picador, 1986).

tough. ... Screw them first before they screw you] (*Hero*, p. 23). The polarity suggested by the title, between the closed world of the academy and the outside world of the city into which the cadets escape from time to time, is undermined by the novel exposing how violence and corruption reign inside as well as outside the military school. The Leoncio Prado Military Academy appears under its real name, which caused a scandal in Peru, especially since it became known that a considerable number of copies of the book were burnt in protest on the academy's parade ground – an act which can only have had the effect of further promoting the novel and arousing even more curiosity about its content rumoured to be semi-pornographic.[3]

The fact that *La ciudad y los perros* became equally popular with critics and readers, as well as being highly regarded in academic criticism, is due to its combination of a simple, engaging story and a complex literary structure. As the first novel by a twenty-seven-year-old Latin American author, the expert use of narrative techniques derived from Faulkner has attracted much critical attention, possibly more than any other single work in Vargas Llosa's oeuvre. Many articles, chapters in books, special symposia and monographs have dealt with the intricacies of *La ciudad*.[4] And yet the simplicity of the underlying plot makes the novel accessible to a wide readership despite its fragmented narration, complex time structure, and the puzzle of a number of not instantly identifiable narrative voices. The formal features actually

---

[3] The notorious book-burning episode has become common knowledge. I can't help wondering whether the military actually *bought* the one thousand copies that some critics speak of, in order to destroy them by fire. When Vargas Llosa was awarded the Nobel Prize forty-seven years later, the leadership of the Leoncio Prado joined the country in celebrating a writer who for many years had been a highly controversial figure. The Peruvian military honoured Vargas Llosa in a ceremony at the Leoncio Prado Academy, and a photo documents the proud military leaders posing with the famous author wearing his school kepi: Jaime Cordero, 'El Ejército "rehabilita" a Vargas Llosa', *El País*, 19 March 2011, <http://elpais.com/diario/2011/03/19/cultura/1300489206_850215.html> [accessed 29 October 2012].

[4] Monographs specially dedicated to *La ciudad* have appeared in a number of languages. The English study by Peter Standish, *Vargas Llosa. La ciudad y los perros* (London: Grant & Cutler, 1982) remains a useful introduction to the work. See also Miguel Angel Zapata (ed.), *Mario Vargas Llosa and the persistence of memory: celebrating the 40th anniversary of 'La ciudad y los perros' ('The Time of the Hero') and other works* (Lima: Universidad Nacional de San Marcos, 2006). In Spanish, amongst many excellent articles such as José Miguel Oviedo's chapter in *Mario Vargas Llosa: la invención de una realidad* (Barcelona: Seix Barral, 1982), and the relevant articles in José Miguel Oviedo (ed.), *Mario Vargas Llosa* (Madrid: Taurus, 1981), there is the book by Carmen Rodríguez Moncada, *La ciudad y los perros. Mario Vargas Llosa. Estudio literario* (Bogotá: Panamericana, 2001). The majority of articles in the following French publication are also in Spanish: Françoise Aubès et al. (ed.), *Lectures d'une oeuvre. 'La ciudad y los perros'. Mario Vargas Llosa* (Paris: Éditions du Temps, 1999). Most recently, a special edition commemorating fifty years of *La ciudad y los perros* has been published under the auspices of the Real Academia Española (Madrid: Alfaguara, 2012), including extensive notes, several critical essays, bibliography, glossary and index.

enhance the suspense that the narrative creates and contribute to the mystery at the centre of it, the death of the cadet Ricardo Arana during a field exercise.

La ciudad y los perros starts *in medias res*, with an act of transgression by a group of cadets known as 'the Circle' who decide to steal the upcoming chemistry exam. The draw to execute this theft falls on Cava, a boy from the Andes. He obtains the papers but breaks a window in the act. As a consequence of the break-in, the school authorities cancel the cadets' leave indefinitely. Ricardo Arana, an outsider known as 'the Slave' for his weakness, has observed the theft. Since he is desperate to visit his girlfriend Teresa he reveals the identity of the thief to the school authorities. Cava gets expelled, and weekend leave is reinstated. Shortly afterwards the Slave dies of a shotgun wound received during a military field exercise. Alberto Fernandez, called 'the Poet', an outsider himself and the only friend the Slave had in school, is convinced that Arana was deliberately shot in the back of his head by Jaguar, the ruthless leader of the Circle, as an act of revenge for betraying Cava. Alberto takes a moral stance and reports Jaguar to Lieutenant Gamboa, also revealing the many illegal activities that the cadets engage in: gambling, smoking, drinking, secret visits to prostitutes, bestialities, and masturbation competitions. Gamboa detains Jaguar and approaches his superiors in order to initiate a formal investigation into the death of Ricardo Arana. But the leaders of the Leoncio Prado Military Academy decide to hush things up so as to avoid damage to the institution. Alberto is blackmailed into silence with the pornographic stories he used to write for his friends, and Lieutenant Gamboa, who had a brilliant career as an officer in front of him, gets a transfer to a remote part of the country. When the school puts an end to the secret activities in the dormitories and punishes the culprits, the boys accuse Jaguar, up to then their respected and feared leader, of squealing. When Jaguar finds out that he has totally lost the respect of his friends who suspect him of being the one thing that he dislikes most, a traitor, he approaches Gamboa and confesses to the murder of Arana. But by then the authorities have decided to draw a veil over the whole affair to keep up appearances. Whether Ricardo Arana was actually murdered by the Jaguar or not remains unclear since Jaguar's confession seems to be motivated by his bitter disappointment: 'Eran como mi familia', he says about the others (p. 373) [they were like a family to me] (p. 385). The new experience of being a victim – 'Yo no sabía lo que era vivir aplastado' (p. 373) [I didn't know what it was like to have everybody against you] (p. 386) – makes him want to re-establish his image as a tough leader. This is the first of several cases in Vargas Llosa's work where a crime remains unsolved and the expected sequence of crime and punishment is unfulfilled.[5]

---

[5] On a number of occasions during 2012, for example at the book launch for the English translation of *El sueño del celta* [*The Dream of the Celt*] in London organized by the British

In terms of structure, *La ciudad y los perros* is divided into two main parts and a short but crucial epilogue. Part 1 leads up to the death of the Slave, an event that happens right in the centre of the book; part 2 deals with the aftermath of this death. Each of these parts has eight numbered chapters. Within each chapter there are a number of short, untitled sections characterized by different narrative voices. The main events of the plot are told by an impersonal narrator who remains outside the story. Other sections dealing with events in the military academy are told by an omniscient narrator who adopts the perspective of Alberto Fernández. A third type of narration is a stream of consciousness by one of the cadets, a rough boy only known by his nickname 'Boa'. In an unstructured, colloquial way, past and present events in the academy are mirrored in his consciousness, sometimes as if he related them to his pet dog, 'La Malpapeada' ('Skimpy' in the English version). Interwoven into the main story of the Slave's death are flashbacks to the lives of some of the protagonists before they entered the military school. These sections about life in the city reveal the background to why Ricardo Arana, Alberto Fernández and a first-person narrator who only at the very end of the novel is identifiable as the Jaguar, were sent to the Leoncio Prado academy in the first place. The crosscutting between events in the school and the prehistory to these events, a technique adopted from cinema, corresponds to the polarity between city and military academy which is suggested in the title. It also shows how the expectations with which the adolescents entered the school end in disappointment. The only student aspiring to a military career, Cava, gets expelled. The Jaguar, who expected to establish himself as the undisputed leader of his surrogate family of friends and teach them 'how to be men', ends being despised as a coward and a traitor. Alberto, who was sent to the academy to make him work harder and teach him discipline, gains a reputation as 'the Poet' providing pornographic stories for his classmates. Ricardo, wanting to escape his bullying father, ends up being bullied and brutalized as 'the Slave' by his whole year. The pattern of expectation and disillusionment also affects Lieutenant Gamboa, a model officer: 'Él amaba la vida militar precisamente por lo que otros la odiaban: la disciplina, la jerarquía, las campañas' (p. 174) [Gamboa loved the military life for exactly the same reasons that the others hated it: discipline, rank, field exercises] (p. 180). He is respected by the boys for his strong sense of justice, but ends in total disillusionment.

Academy on 6 June, Vargas Llosa revealed with great self-irony that for him it was always clear that the Jaguar had killed the Slave, but that the French translator of *La ciudad* told him this could not possibly be true, since it would mean that he had written a mediocre book; only the ambiguity made it a brilliant novel. 'Mario Vargas Llosa in conversation with Professor Efraín Kristal (UCLA) and Professor Michael Wood FBA (Princeton University)', video, British Academy, <http://www.britac.ac.uk/events/2012/MarioVargasLlosa.cfm> [accessed 15 September 2013].

The brief epilogue has three sections which bring to a close the stories of Gamboa, Jaguar and Alberto. In the first section Jaguar confesses to Gamboa that he murdered the Slave. This happens after the final exams, just before the cadets end their schooling in the Leoncio Prado, and just before Gamboa's departure for his new post. The Jaguar shows some self-questioning of his code of behaviour but, in the end, sticks to his dual world-view that there are only friends and foes: the ones require total loyalty, the others need to be fought. He thinks he understands the Slave's betrayal of his schoolmates since they must have seemed like 'enemies' to him. And while he hates Alberto for his denunciation, he respects that he did it to avenge his friend the Slave. Despite his world having been turned upside down, Jaguar has not changed his thinking. Lieutenant Gamboa, resigned to the fact that there is no justice in the military, tells Jaguar it is too late to open the case of Arana's death again, and then leaves Lima and the Leoncio Prado for good. The following two sections of the epilogue relate the reintegration of Alberto and Jaguar into Lima's society as adults, thus closing the circular movement of the protagonists' history before, during and after their period at Leoncio Prado Military Academy. The epilogue rounds off their development from vulnerable youngsters to rebellious adolescents and finally to conforming adults, after what Alberto regards in retrospect as 'el oscuro paréntesis de tres años, que lo había arrebatado a las cosas hermosas' (p. 378) [the three-year parenthesis in which he had been separated from everything that was pleasant and good] (p. 391). Despite the distorted sequence of time and narrative voices there is a recognizable linear development throughout the novel which, in the end, reconnects to the beginning of the story.

Much has been said about the military academy as a microcosm reflecting the macrocosm of Peruvian society. Boys from all social classes, ethnicities and geographical regions attend the regimented school, some to achieve a higher social status than their families have, such as Cava; others from middle-class families are sent there as a correctional measure (Jaguar, Alberto); and then there are those who enrol as a way to escape an unhappy family situation like Ricardo Arana. Their different narrative styles reflect their different social backgrounds: Alberto Fernández belongs to the well-off middle classes of Lima's wealthier areas and is intelligent, articulate and confident enough to talk his way through life. The third-person narrations from his perspective are shrewd and observant, his view of the other cadets is credible. Since 'the Poet' is gifted with language, he also conveys atmospheric descriptions of places. The sections by the unnamed first-person narrator who, surprisingly, turns out to be Jaguar, show him to be from a humble background. He delivers a straightforward and honest account of how, as an adolescent in love with his neighbour Tere, his unhappy circumstances turned him into a petty criminal. This credible account from his own perspective makes it so difficult to identify the unassuming voice with the brutal and ruthless Jaguar in the military academy. The sections relating the background to Ricardo Arana's entry into the military school depict him as a not very confident boy from a modest middle-class background with a seriously dysfunctional family. Almost all of his sections start with the leitmotif-like 'Ha olvidado ...' [He has forgotten ...], thus signifying that Ricardo desperately wants to escape his past. But the section preceding the military exercise during which he gets killed states: 'pero no ha olvidado el desánimo, la amargura, el rencor, el miedo que reinaban en su corazón' (p. 170) [but he had not forgotten the discouragement, the bitterness, the resentment and the fear with which his heart was filled] (p. 176). This play with parallels and contrasts on the level of language, structure and content characterizes the whole novel. Boa's disturbing, unreflected monologue with its free-floating reminiscences identify him as a member of an uneducated underclass, even though the novel does not give him an identity outside school. The more unsavoury details of the cadets' secret activities in the barracks, such as the rape of animals as well as of younger boys, are seen through the perspective of 'the brute Boa', as Alberto describes him. This narrative trick makes it possible to represent the most abominable acts in a way that is free of moral judgement. The brutal frankness of Boa's inner monologue also reveals social attitudes common in the academy: racism, homophobia, misogyny. Boa is an extreme case: his most human side comes out in his relationship with the academy's dog Skimpy whom he treats like a woman – including sexually. He talks to her, strokes her, calls her tender names and finds comfort in her: 'uno piensa que es una muchachita. Algo así debe ser cuando uno se casa' (p. 308) [I think of her as a girl. It must be something like that when you're married] (p. 316). But when she annoys him he breaks her leg, a shocking reflection of the abuse that women outside the academy are shown to suffer from their husbands.

The military academy is a parallel world with its own rules, yet in its brutality, corruption and hypocrisy it mirrors society as a whole. The snapshots of family life in various segments of society show a world ruled by machismo, double standards and violence, where betrayal and abuse are rife. Jaguar's mother feels sorry for herself, neglects her son, but takes the money from his criminal activities. Alberto's father is a ruthless womanizer who forces the mother 'to keep up appearances' and put up with his betrayals. Ricardo had been led to believe that his father was dead, until one day he brutally enters his life, beating his mother and reproaching her for spoiling Ricardo and bringing him up like a girl. (The theme of the abusive father will run through Vargas Llosa's whole work, in various incarnations, but this is the first and clearest allusion to Vargas Llosa's own traumatic experience.) The novel describes a sort of *scène originaire* when the boy hears the parents quarrelling and tries to prevent his mother from being beaten:

> Pensó: 'está desnudo' y sintió terror. Su padre lo golpeó con la mano abierta y él se desplomó sin gritar. Pero se levantó de inmediato: todo se había puesto a girar suavemente. Iba a decir que a él no le habían pegado nunca, que no era posible, pero antes que lo hiciera, su padre lo volvió a golpear. … lo vio dar media vuelta y venir hacia él, vociferando, y se sintió en el aire, y de pronto estaba en su cuarto, a oscuras, y el hombre cuyo cuerpo resaltaba en la negrura le volvió a pegar en la cara, y todavía alcanzó a ver que el hombre se interponía entre él y su madre que cruzaba la puerta, la cogía de un brazo y la arrastraba como si fuera de trapo y luego la puerta se cerró. (p. 82)
>
> [He's naked, he thought, and he was terrified again. His father hit him with his open hand and he fell down without uttering a sound. He got up again immediately but everything was spinning around him. He wanted to say that nobody had ever hit him before, he wouldn't be hit, but before he could say it his father hit him again. … he saw him coming toward him, still bellowing, and he felt himself hoisted in the air and he was back in his own room, his own bed, and the man who looked white in the darkness hit him in the face again, and he could see how the man got himself between himself and his mother when she came to the door, and how he dragged her away as if she were a rag doll, slamming the door behind him.] (p. 84)

This terrifying scene of domestic violence is seen from the child's perspective. The third-person narrator gets close to the feelings of Ricardo: the multitude of short, breathless clauses convey the child's fear and outrage at being beaten by 'the man'. The violence Ricardo suffers from his father parallels the brutalizing he later has to endure in the military school which, ironically, he sought out as a refuge from his family situation, and he is equally unable to withstand it. The link between sex and violence (the father is naked when he beats the mother) also repeats itself in the school. Power structures amongst the pupils in the Leoncio Prado academy mirror those of the family: the strong ones at the top beat and violate the younger, weaker or dependent ones. The city and the dogs suffer the same fate. The Circle, established to prevent the first-year students from being humiliated, ends up reproducing the gratuitous violence that rules the wider circle of the academy and the overall hierarchy of society.

The law of the jungle in the dormitories is highlighted by the frequent use of animal imagery. Boys have nicknames that relate them to the aspect and behaviour of beasts: the Jaguar is strong, fast and a predator; Boa's nickname refers to his sex; other frequent references are to monkeys, reptiles, birds, insects and, of course, dogs. During the initiation ritual Ricardo Arana is made to act like a dog in a vicious fight with another dog/cadet, foaming at the mouth while he bites him. Officers are given names such as 'Piranha' and 'Rat'. In general, nicknames denote the existence of a separate identity which defines a role within the academy. A number of these names are given by

Jaguar, a fact that shows his power over the others: he chooses the name 'el Círculo' [the Circle] for the defence group, and he assigns a name and therefore a role to Ricardo Arana: 'Me das asco —dijo el Jaguar—. No tienes dignidad ni nada. Eres un esclavo' (p. 61) ['You make me sick,' the Jaguar said. 'You haven't got any guts or anything else. You're just a slave'] (p. 61). The Jaguar also names himself: 'me llamo Jaguar. Cuidado con decirme perro' (p. 56) [They call me the Jaguar. Watch out when you call me a Dog] (p. 56).[6] The cadets collectively decide to label Alberto 'el Poeta' [the Poet] since his gift for language and his imagination enable him to write the pornographic stories for the amusement of his friends; he also earns money by writing love letters for them. Alberto is capable of inventing sexual episodes with a prostitute, although he is the one who has least sexual experience. By lying and playing roles he manages to stay out of their power struggles, as he tells the Slave: '—¿Tú vas a ser un poeta? —dice el Esclavo.— ¿Estás cojudo? Voy a ser ingeniero. Mi padre me mandará a estudiar a Estados Unidos. Escribo cartas y novelitas para comprarme cigarrillos. Pero eso no quiere decir nada' (p. 26) ['Are you going to be a poet?' the Slave asked. 'Are you kidding? I'm going to be an engineer. My father's going to send me to the United States to study. I just write letters and stories so I can buy my cigarettes. But that doesn't mean a thing'] (p. 24). Writing and inventing stories is the Poet's method of survival in the animal world of the academy, but it is not an authentic activity, as he finds out when he falls in love with Teresa, the Slave's girlfriend, and wants to express his true feelings for her in a letter. His words fail him, they seem stale and false. The role of Poet is just another imposture. This crucial aspect of role-play, alluded to in the temporary title that Vargas Llosa gave his novel, 'Los impostores', is highlighted in the epigraph preceding part 1 of *La ciudad y los perros*, a quotation from Sartre's *Kean*:[7] 'We play the part of heroes because we're cowards, the part of saints because we're wicked: we play the killer's role because we're dying to murder our fellow man: we play ... because we're liars from the moment we're born'.

For a moment after the Slave's death Alberto shows real feeling ('el poeta está llorando' [the Poet's crying], p. 257/p. 265), but his decision to act in an authentic, ethical manner is suppressed by the authorities who opt for a corrupt cover-up. Both Alberto and Lieutenant Gamboa fail in their attempt to act morally. The Colonel does not even understand why the cadets in his military academy feel disturbed after the death of one of their number. Instead, he wants to make provisions so that, during the funeral involving Ricardo's family, they act as if they were 'deeply affected by the death of

---

[6] The English translation does not reflect that. It should say: 'I am called Jaguar'.
[7] The epigraph in the Spanish version is in French. Vargas Llosa's choice of epigraphs containing a motto or a clue for interpreting a work will become a recurring feature of his fiction.

this cadet. It might help us out a good deal' (p. 248): 'Quiero que el quinto año dé la impresión de sentir mucho la muerte del cadete. Eso constituye siempre una nota positiva' (p. 241). The military leadership is concerned with appearances and therefore encourages imposture. They even condone the irregularities that have been going on under their noses, in the dormitories, because these are within the code of machismo that rules their world:

> —Usted exagera, Gamboa —dijo el capitán ... Yo no digo echar tierra a todo. Lo de los exámenes y lo del licor hay que castigarlo, naturalmente. Pero no olvide tampoco que lo primero que se aprende en el Ejército es a ser hombres. Los hombres fuman, se emborrachan, tiran contra, culean. Los cadetes saben que si son descubiertos se les expulsa. Ya han salido varios. Los que no se dejan pescar son los vivos. Para hacerse hombres, hay que correr riesgos, hay que ser audaz. Eso es el Ejército, Gamboa, no sólo la disciplina. También es osadía, ingenio. (p. 301)

> ['You're exaggerating, Gamboa', the captain said. ... 'I don't say we should cover up everything. We'll have to punish them for the liquor and the exams. But remember, the first thing you learn in the army is to be a man. And what do men do? They smoke, they drink, they gamble, they fuck. The cadets all know they get expelled if they're discovered. *If*, Gamboa. We've already expelled quite a few. But the smart ones don't get caught. If they're going to be men, they have to take chances, they have to use their wits. That's the way the army is, Gamboa. Discipline isn't enough. You've got to have guts, and you've also got to have brains.'] (p. 310)

La ciudad y los perros paints a devastating picture of the army reproducing corrupt and machista values in their cadets, who then go back and integrate into a corrupt and male-dominated society. This is what happens to Alberto, who follows in the footsteps of his father: he drops Teresa, the girl he was in love with, and denies ever having had any real desire for her, because she was socially inappropriate for him. Instead, he takes a girl from his own class and intends to treat her like his father treats his mother: 'Me casaré con Marcela, y seré un don Juan' (p. 385) [I'll marry Marcela and be a Don Juan] (p. 399). Society has perpetuated itself, with all its corruption and false values.

The most surprising outcome of the novel is Jaguar's reintegration into society. The protagonist who seemed most adept to the dog-eat-dog mentality while in the military school ends up marrying Tere, the love of his youth, and becomes a bank employee. The plot involving Tere/Teresa, desired by three of the main protagonists who seem to ignore each other's acquaintance with the same girl, has been criticized as unlikely and artificial. It might be one of the less successful instances of a 'dato escondido' (the reader only gradually finds out that Tere is identical with the girl Ricardo is in love with, who also becomes Alberto's girlfriend). But the main 'hidden fact' that the timid first-person narrator and the ruthless leader of the Circle are identical advances the dominant theme of role-play. It also anticipates a subject matter that will become more prominent in Vargas Llosa's later work: the fact that a person is not one-dimensional. Jaguar's ambiguity is a first sign of Vargas Llosa's exploration of human nature where good and evil characteristics coexist. The contrast between the two sides of Jaguar is already hinted at in chapter 7 of part 1: the innocent first-person narrator admires Tere's neatness and cleanliness and gives her a piece of chalk as a present so that she can tidy up her only pair of shoes. The next section starts with Boa's crass statement: 'No creo que exista el diablo pero el Jaguar me hace dudar a veces' (p. 159) [I don't believe in the devil but sometimes the Jaguar makes me wonder] (p. 164). This clever juxtaposition can only be grasped fully in a second reading of the novel, but already before then it establishes a secret, associative link in the reader's mind, one of the functions that Vargas Llosa's ascribes to the 'dato escondido' technique.

Some of the narrative strategies introduced in *La ciudad* point ahead to future works by Vargas Llosa: the simultaneous representation of Alberto's phone call denouncing Jaguar to Lieutenant Gamboa and the voices of other people around him in the pub is an early attempt to recreate the famous 'comices agricoles' scene in Flaubert's *Madame Bovary*.[8] Flaubert juxtaposes a delicate declaration of love and a profane agricultural meeting that goes on in the background by intermingling the two levels of narration. Vargas Llosa uses this technique to contrast the weight of the moral choice that Alberto makes and the banality of drunken talk around him. The speakers in the following excerpt from the much longer passage are Alberto, Lieutenant Gamboa, a punter in the pub commenting on the quality of different drinks, and a man who declares his intention to get married:

> 'Sí, dice el teniente Gamboa. ¿Quién es?' 'Se acabó la jarana para siempre, muchachos. En adelante, hombre serio a más no poder. Y a trabajar duro para hacer dinero y tener contenta a la chola.' '¿Teniente Gamboa?', pregunta Alberto. 'Pisco de Montesierpe, afirma la sombra, mal pisco. Pisco Motocachi, buen pisco.' 'Yo soy. ¿Quién habla?' 'Un cadete, responde Alberto. Un cadete de quinto año.' 'Viva mi chola y vivan mis amigos' '¿Que quiere?' 'El mejor pisco del mundo, a mi entender, asegura la sombra. Pero rectifica: O uno de los mejores, señor. Pisco Motocachi.' 'Su nombre', dice Gamboa. 'Tendré diez hijos. Todos hombres. Para ponerles el nombre de cada uno de mis amigos, muchachos. El mío a ninguno, sólo los nombres de ustedes.' 'A Arana lo mataron, dice Alberto. Yo sé quién fue. ¿Puedo ir a su casa?' (p. 274)

---

[8] Vargas Llosa discusses this scene in *La orgía perpetua. Flaubert y 'Madame Bovary'* (Barcelona: Seix Barral, 1975), pp. 227–8.

['Hello', Lt Gamboa said, 'who's calling?' 'I'm off the booze for good. I've got to behave myself from now on. Got to earn lots of money to keep my half-breed happy.' 'Lt. Gamboa?' Alberto asked. 'Montesierpe pisco', the shadow said, 'that's bad pisco. Motocachi pisco, that's good pisco.' 'Yes, speaking. Who is it?' 'So here's to my half-breed and here's to my friends.' 'A cadet', Alberto said, 'a cadet from the fifth Year.' 'In my personal opinion', the shadow said, 'it's the best pisco in the world', but then he qualified his statement: 'Or one of the best, gentlemen, one of the best. Motocachi.' 'Your name', Gamboa said. 'We'll have ten kids, all of them boys, and I'll name every one of them after my friends. Not one of them after myself, just after my friends.' 'They killed Arana', Alberto said. 'I know who it was. Can I come to your house?'] (p. 282)

The clash of voices recreates the extreme tension of the moment when Alberto betrays one of his peers out of a sense of moral responsibility towards his friend. It highlights the contrast, but also brings out surprising parallels between the different levels of simultaneous narration: while one of the drinkers praises friendship, Alberto on the phone takes a stand for his friend. Another function of this simultaneity of voices is to create suspense: the fragmented narration underlines Alberto's hesitation and Gamboa's anticipation of bad news. In his next novels Vargas Llosa will take the narrative technique of simultaneity a step further.

***

Not quite in the chronological sequence of works, but very much in the continuation of *Los jefes* [The Leaders][9] and *La ciudad y los perros*, the short novel *Los cachorros*[10] [The Cubs],[11] published in 1967, is a coming-of-age story in which male adolescents, their rituals and their cult of machismo take centre stage again. The setting is the 'barrio' [neighbourhood] of Miraflores, previously the social background to protagonist Alberto Fernández as well as the setting of the short story 'Día Domingo' [On Sunday] in *Los jefes*. The religious school Colegio Champagnat, where an important part of the action takes place, follows on from the Leoncio Prado and the school setting in 'Los jefes'. As an experiment in form and language *Los cachorros* builds on the recreation of youth-specific oral speech patterns in Vargas Llosa's first novel, especially on Boa's inner monologue with its abundance of expletives and onomatopoeic exclamations.

[9] Mario Vargas Llosa, *Los jefes* (Barcelona: Bruguera, 1983).
[10] Mario Vargas Llosa, *Los cachorros* (Madrid: Cátedra, 1990). This is an annotated edition with a useful introduction by Guadelupe Fernández Ariza. The most insightful article on the novel is by Roslyn M. Frank: 'El estudio de "Los cachorros"', in Oviedo, *Mario Vargas Llosa*, pp. 156–75.
[11] Mario Vargas Llosa, 'The Cubs', in *The Cubs and Other Stories*, trans. Gregory Kolovakos and Ronald Christ (London: Faber and Faber, 1991), pp. 1–43.

The title, once more associating young pupils with animals, refers to the group of four friends in a college run by clerics. They are joined by a new boy, Cuéllar, who quickly integrates into the group. After football practice Cuéllar is attacked in the shower by the school's dog, a Great Dane called Judas, who emasculates him. At first, this accident does not make him an outsider, his friends stick by him. But eventually they, too, start calling him 'Pichula' (a rude Peruvian term for penis; the English translation turns it into the less offensive 'P.P.'). Cuéllar starts to exploit the fact that, since the accident, he can get away with anything at home and in school, and he enjoys being envied for having all sorts of privileges. When the boys turn into adolescents and become interested in girls, Pichula Cuéllar (this was supposed to be the title of the novel) becomes an outsider. He shies away from girls and, instead, starts playing up, engaging in rude, annoying and dangerous behaviour. This changes temporarily when he falls in love with Teresita, a capricious, coquettish girl who plays with his feelings. But she ends up with another young man who comes to the neighbourhood. Cuéllar goes back to being a show-off, driving fast cars and trying to impress other young people with his outrageous behaviour, even as an adult. While his friends grow up to start families and become part of the Miraflores bourgeoisie, Cuéllar hangs out with a dubious crowd and eventually gets killed in a car accident.

The story is told in six chapters, following the chronology of events: Cuéllar's entry into the school and his accident as a pre-teen is the subject of chapter 1, followed by his development into 'Pichula', the boy with the defining nickname, in chapter 2. Adolescence with its pastimes and love interests is the main focus of the work, with narrated time stretched out over two chapters (3–4). The subsequent account of the group's development to young adulthood in chapter 5 is much less extensive, and the novel ends in chapter 6 with a chronologically condensed report of the friends in middle age, now sending their own children to the Colegio Champagnat, and a very brief and laconic mention of Cuéllar's death. The impression created by this time structure is that of a story covering about thirty years told in one big sweep (of only forty-odd pages), as if speeded up towards the end, after the most important formative years of adolescence have left their indelible mark on the protagonists.

For Cuéllar, who is the only individualized protagonist in the group – the others have no more than a group identity and are not physically described – events after his emasculation take their fatal course towards his premature death. This impression is underpinned by the fact that the story seems to move forward without the help of a narrator. The narrative voice frequently switches from a third-person narration with shifting perspectives to the first-person-plural voice of the group, creating a kind of simultaneity of objective and subjective reality within a single phrase, as in the novel's opening paragraph: 'Todavía llevaban pantalón corto ese año, aún no fumábamos, entre todos los deportes preferían el fútbol y estábamos aprendiendo a correr olas, a zambullirnos desde el segundo trampolín del 'Terrazas', y eran traviesos, lampiños, curiosos, muy ágiles, voraces' (*Los cachorros*, p. 55) [They were still wearing short pants that year, we weren't smoking yet, they preferred soccer to all the other sports and we were learning to surf, to dive from the high board at the Terraces Club, and they were devilish, smooth-cheeked, curious, agile, voracious] ('The Cubs', p. 1). There are frequent switches from a more distant, reflective point of view to the immediacy of experienced action. Reported speech becomes direct speech, without the use of quotation marks or reporting phrases (so-called *inquit formulae*, such as 'he said'):

> Hermano Leoncio, ¿cierto que viene uno nuevo?, ¿para el 'Tercero A', Hermano? Sí, el Hermano Leoncio apartaba de un manotón el moño que le cubría la cara, ahora a callar. Apareció una mañana, a la hora de la formación, de la mano de su papá, ... y en la clase el Hermano Leoncio lo sentó atrás, con nosotros, en esa carpeta vacía, jovencito. ¿Cómo se llamaba? Cuéllar, ¿y tú? Choto, ¿y tú? Chingolo, ¿y tú? Mañuco, ¿y tú? Lalo. (p. 56)

> [Brother Leoncio, is it true a new boy's coming? into 3A, Brother? Yes, with his fist Brother Leoncio pushed back the forelock hanging in his face, now let's have some quiet. He appeared one morning at inspection time, holding his father's hand ... and in class Brother Leoncio sat him in the back with us, at that vacant desk, young man. What's your name? Cuéllar, and yours? Choto, and yours? Chingolo, and yours? Manny, and yours? Lalo.] (p. 1)

The protagonists are introduced here without the obvious interference of a narrator. They form a sort of choral voice, a collective narrator, sometimes dividing into individual voices, only to then rejoin the chorus. Vargas Llosa says in his preface that he intended to write the story as if the 'barrio' itself narrated it. In the following quotation each member of the group contributes an element to the overall depiction of what happened in the washrooms. Lalo was present, but the other boys witnessed the aftermath of the accident. Frequent elliptical contractions and distorted word order imitate oral speech; visual and aural impressions convey the excitement and terror of the moment; the *verbum dicendi* is mostly dropped and only the name indicates who is speaking (a technique already used in Boa's monologue to create immediacy):

> Ahí, encogido, losetas blancas, azulejos y chorritos de agua, temblando, oyó los ladridos de Judas, el llanto de Cuéllar, sus gritos, y oyó aullidos, saltos, choques, rebalones y después sólo ladridos, y un montón de tiempo después, les juro (pero cuánto, decía Chingolo, ¿dos minutos?, más hermano, y Choto ¿cinco?, más mucho más), el vozarrón del Hermano Lucio, las lisuras de Leoncio (¿en español, Lalo?, sí, también en francés, ¿le entendías?, no, pero se imaginaba las carambas, Dios mío, fueras, sapes, largo largo, la desesperación de los Hermanos, su terrible susto.

Abrió la puerta y ya se lo llevaban cargado, lo vio apenas entre las sotanas negras, ¿desmayado?, sí, ¿calato, Lalo? sí y sangrando, hermano, palabra, qué horrible. (pp. 65–6)

[There, shrunk back, white tiles and trickles of water, trembling, he heard Judas's barking, Cuéllar's sobbing and only barking and a lot later, I swear to you (but how much later, asked Chingolo, two minutes? longer man, and Choto five? longer much longer), Brother Luke's booming voice, Brother Leoncio's curses (in Spanish, Lalo? yeah, and in French too, did you understand him? no, but you could tell they were curses, stupid, from the anger in his voice), the shits, the my Gods, the get outs, the scrams, the get losts, the get goings, the brothers' desperation, their terrible fright. He opened the door and already they were carrying him out, wrapped up, you could hardly see him between the black robes, passed out? yeah, naked, Lalo? yeah, and bleeding, man, I swear, it was horrible.] (pp. 5–6)

Another feature already present in Boa's monologue is the onomatopoeic use of language, applied here to frightening effect in the threatening growls of Judas which grow stronger. The onomatopoeic representation of the dog's bark appears twice, both times combined with a gradual amplification by repetition: 'y en su jaula Judas se volvía loco, guau, paraba el rabo, guau guau, les mostraba los colmillos, guau guau guau, tiraba saltos mortales, guau, guau, guau, guau, sacudía los alambres. Pucha diablo si se escapa un día' (pp. 59–60) [in his cage Judas went crazy, gr-r-r, his tail stood straight up, gr-r-r gr-r-r, he bared his fangs, gr-r-r gr-r-r gr-r-r, he jumped in somersaults, gr-r-r gr-r-r gr-r-r gr-r-r, he shook the wire fence. Jeez, if he escapes one day] (p. 3). Onomatopoeic language is more frequent in the early chapters, as it matches the speech patterns of youngsters which resemble those of comic books. The later use of word painting is limited to the stutter that Cuéllar develops when he feels under pressure and embarrassed about his relationship with girls.

Exclamations add to the oral quality of the language in *Los cachorros*, as do the many local expressions (see the abundance of notes on Peruvianisms in Fernández Ariza's edition) and the frequent use of diminutives, a distinctive linguistic feature of Miraflores that Vargas Llosa has commented on elsewhere.[12] There is an abundance of diminutives (a feature not easily translatable into English) in the chapters dealing with the adolescents' gatherings and their love interests: 'El amor hace milagros, decía Pusy, qué formalito se ha puesto, qué caballerito' (p. 100) [Love works miracles, said Kitty, how serious he's gotten, what a regular gentleman] (p. 28). The language becomes extremely affected and mannered when it refers to Teresita, the girl Cuéllar falls in love with (another boy who falls for a Tere/Teresa/Teresita): '¿no se

---

[12] See his article '¿Un champancito hermanito?', in *Contra viento y marea, II (1972–1983)* (Barcelona: Seix Barral, 1986), pp. 345–9.

daba cuenta cómo la miraba? Y ella ay, ay, ay, palmoteando, manitas, dientes, zapatitos, que miráramos, ¡una mariposa!, que corriéramos, la cogiéramos … y ella aj, aj, arruguitas, frentecita, la mataron y la pachurraron, un hoyito en los cachetes, pestañitas, cejas, ¿a quién?' (pp. 101–2) [didn't she realize how he looked at her? And she oh, oh, oh, clapping, little hands, teeth, tiny shoes, we should look, a butterfly! we should run catch it … and she ahh, ahh. little wrinkles, little forehead, they killed it and mangled it, little dimples on her cheeks, little eyelashes, eyebrows, who?] (p. 30). The juxtaposition of Teresita's pretence not to know about Cuéllar's love for her and her capricious interest in the butterfly instead, together with the overuse of diminutives, paints her as a spoilt and superficial flirt.

The whole novel is narrated in a paratactical manner. Phrases are not ordered or organized in hierarchical structures, but all seem to exist on the same level, mostly connected with 'y' [and]. This polysyndetic construction generally has the effect of making the narration more spontaneous. But in the final chapter, this technique combined with the condensed chronology gives an impression of superficiality, of events happening on the same level, without much emphasis on any of them. This includes Cuéllar's death, which is mentioned in passing (the switch between 'they' and 'we' is still there, but it now excludes Cuéllar):

> Cuéllar ya se había ido a la montaña, a Tingo María, a sembrar café, decían, y cuando venía a Lima y lo encontraban en la calle, apenas nos saludábamos, qué hay cholo, cómo estás Pichulita, qué te cuentas viejo, ahí vamos, chau, y ya había vuelta a Miraflores, más loco que nunca, y ya se había matado, yendo al Norte, ¿cómo?, en un choque, ¿dónde?, en las traicioneras curvas de Pasamayo, pobre, decíamos en el entierro, cuánto sufrió, qué vida tuvo, pero este final es un hecho que se lo buscó. (pp. 120–1)

> [Cuéllar had already gone up into the mountains, to Tingo María, to grow coffee, they said, and whenever he came down into Lima and they met him on the street, we hardly said hello, what's new kid, how are you P.P., what's up old boy, so-so, ciao, and he had already come back to Miraflores, crazier than ever, and he had already killed himself, going up north, How? in a crack-up, where? on those treacherous curves at Pasamayo, poor guy, we said at the funeral, how much he suffered, what a life he had, but this finish is something he had in store for him.] (p. 43)

In this final chapter the linguistic and narrative technique represents the detached attitude of the former 'cubs' towards their friend. The 'little cubs' of the Colegio Champagnat, who were affected by what the big dog, Judas, had done to one of them, end up as grown-up 'Judases' betraying their former friend by their indifference.

***

In 1966, Vargas Llosa published his second big novel, *La casa verde* [*The Green House*],[13] a work that famously won the Rómulo Gallegos Prize for International Fiction in the following year, an opportunity for Vargas Llosa to consolidate his dual reputation as a great novelist as well as a political firebrand with his notorious acceptance speech 'La literatura es fuego' [Literature is Fire]. The scope of this new novel goes well beyond the world of adolescents in Lima, extending its focus on Peru as a geographically, socially and ethnically divided country. The military which was the dominant institution in the world of *La ciudad y los perros* is now complemented by the Church and the political administration as the other factors in the country's power structure. *La casa verde* is organized around two very different centres: Piura, a town surrounded by desert in the coastal area of northern Peru, and Santa María de Nieva, a small settlement with a Catholic mission in the rainforest region along the upper part of the river Marañon. Vargas Llosa himself elaborated on the novel's dual setting in a lecture given at Washington State University in 1968, published in 1971 as *Historia secreta de una novela* [Secret Story of a Novel]: 'Piura es el desierto, el color amarillo, el algodón, el Perú español, la "civilización". Santa María de Nieva es la selva, la exuberancia vegetal, el color verde, tribus que aún no han entrado a la historia, instituciones y costumbres que parecen supervivencias medievales' [Piura is the desert, the colour yellow, cotton, it is Spanish Peru, 'civilization'. Santa María de Nieva is the jungle, exuberant vegetation, the colour green, tribes that have not yet entered into history, institutions and customs that seem to have survived from medieval times].[14] The two different colours that Vargas Llosa associates with the two regions point to the importance of the visual element in this novel. They also hint at the fact that these two settings will not stay apart, since the green house of the title is located in the desert zone of Piura. As so often in Vargas Llosa's work, the two opposites seemingly defining a novel turn out to be connected by a number of links which only become apparent in the course of the narration.

The narrative technique of 'communicating vessels' linking different geographical zones as well as events on different levels of time is the main organizing principle of this novel. It is combined with the device of withholding important pieces of information ('datos escondidos'), in some cases until the epilogue. In terms of structure *La casa verde* is the most complex work of fiction Vargas Llosa has ever produced where, in seventy-two non-linear narrative sequences, time and space seem to dissolve. The demands on the reader during a first reading are substantial: the impression of an unordered muddle of narrative voices, times, spaces and levels of reality

[13] Mario Vargas Llosa, *La casa verde* (Barcelona: Argos Vergara, 1980); Mario Vargas Llosa, *The Green House* (London: Picador, 1986).
[14] Mario Vargas Llosa, *Historia secreta de una novela* (Barcelona: Tusquets, 1971), p. 9.

remains confusing throughout most of the novel. Yet the immediacy of the visual and aural depiction of scenes is captivating and helps the reader through the apparent chaos behind which there is, all the same, a regular structure. Four books plus an epilogue are each divided into four (1, 3 and epilogue) or three numbered chapters (books 2 and 4), all preceded by a prologue. Each of the chapters contains a regular sequence of five or four segments following a certain narrative strand (these will be summarized below): 1. Bonifacia and the Santa María mission, 2. Fushía, 3. Anselmo and the Green House, 4. Jum, 5. the 'Unconquerables'. In books 3 and 4 and in the novel's epilogue the narrative segment covering Jum is absent, since his story is integrated into other plot lines in the prologue of each of these.[15] The existing, but not obvious, lattice supporting the novel in the background makes it possible to follow a narrative which, according to Vargas Llosa, was originally planned as two separate novels.

In *Historia secreta de una novela* Vargas Llosa gives an account of how, in the creative process, he was unable to keep the two centres of narration, Piura and the Amazon jungle, apart. This little booklet telling the 'secret story' of *La casa verde* is one example of Vargas Llosa's frequent exercises in self-exegesis (together with, for example, *A Writer's Reality* and the interviews with Cano Gaviria and Setti),[16] whereby he explains the personal background to a novel – the 'demons' which contributed to its genesis – and provides guidelines for its understanding. In this case he describes the one year he spent as a ten-year-old boy in Piura as one of the most important periods of his life, when he discovered the sexual nature of human relationships. This loss of innocence was connected to the mysterious 'casa verde', a brothel on the outskirts of town, with its forbidden and unspeakable secrets that spawned the child's imagination. He also tells of his second encounter with Piura and its green house, when he briefly returned to the town in his adolescence to finish college. This time he actually visited the brothel and found the reality disillusioning in comparison to the fantasies of his childhood. The clash between the mythical place of his early youth and the reality of the cheap brothel of his adolescence is reflected in the two green houses that exist in the novel on different time planes and, possibly, different levels of reality.

The other autobiographical experience that has gone into the novel is a journey to the Alto Marañon in 1958 (followed by another trip to the Amazon region in 1964) where Vargas Llosa discovered that a different Peru existed

---

[15] The best visualization of the order that lies behind the apparent arbitrariness of *La casa verde* can be found in Oviedo, *Invención*, p. 165.

[16] Mario Vargas Llosa, *A Writer's Reality* (London and Boston: Faber and Faber, 1990); Ricardo Cano Gaviria, *El buitre y el ave Fénix. Conversaciones con Mario Vargas Llosa* (Barcelona: Anagrama, 1972); Ricardo A. Setti, ... *sobre la vida y la política: Diálogo con Vargas Llosa* (México: Kosmos Editorial, 1989).

alongside the modern, urban world he knew: 'el Perú era también la Edad Media y la Edad de Piedra' [Peru was also the Dark Ages and the Stone Age] (*Historia secreta*, p. 25). He learned how violence and injustice dominated life in this remote region of the country, and he heard stories of deceit, brutality and exploitation which would form the raw material for his novel. When he speaks of Peru's rainforest region as a place civilization has not yet reached, whereas Piura represents the 'civilized' Hispanic Peru, he seems to suggest that there is an opposition between civilization and barbarism, a topos in Latin American thought since the Argentine writer Sarmiento's influential book *Facundo*.[17] But, in a move that will become typical for Vargas Llosa's writing, he undermines this dual model for explaining Latin American reality: into the archaic world of the rainforest he introduces representatives of civilization – traders, nuns, soldiers, political officials – who, each in their own way, commit acts of crude barbarism. By contrast, the 'civilized' town of Piura is transformed by a stranger, Anselmo, who, much later, turns out to be from the jungle, founding the brothel 'la casa verde'. This brings out the hypocrisy, corruption and secret longing for uninhibited pleasure and excess in the good townspeople. Piura also has at its margins a poor neighbourhood which plays an important part in the novel as a counterweight to the 'civilized' town: la Mangachería, a destitute but vibrant shanty town full of music, dancing and all sorts of amusements which Vargas Llosa describes as representing 'la antigua, colorida y rechinante vida bárbara de la ciudad' [the ancient barbaric life of the town, colourful and noisy] (*Historia secreta*, p. 16). The dual categories of civilization and barbarism contaminate each other, just like the two contrasting settings of the novel become intertwined.

This happens, for example, in one of the main plot lines involving Bonifacia, a girl from the jungle raised by the nuns of the Santa María de Nieva mission, who marries a sergeant stationed in the jungle and follows him to his home town of Piura, where he gets involved again with his rogue friends from the Mangachería, 'los Inconquistables' [the Unconquerables] ('the champs' in the English version of this novel). Lituma, as he is called on his home ground, gets into trouble after a game of Russian roulette and goes to jail. His old friend Josefino takes advantage of Bonifacia, and she ends up in the Green House as the prostitute 'la Selvática' [the jungle girl] ('Wildflower' in the English version). Structurally, this plot line develops in two different strands of the narration, and for a long time it remains a 'hidden fact' that Lituma in Piura is identical with 'the Sergeant' in the jungle, and that Bonifacia from the 'selva' becomes 'la Selvática' in the city. The novel needs to be read to the end to discover the full extent of developments and links between events

---

[17] Domingo Faustino Sarmiento, *Facundo. Civilización y barbárie* (Santiago: Progreso, 1945). Translated into English as *Facundo: Civilization and Barbarism* (Berkeley, CA: University of California Press, 2003).

and protagonists on multiple, disjointed narrative strands which unfold on different levels of time, of which the Lituma/Bonifacia story is but one.

There are two other plot lines involving couples: Anselmo and Antonia/Toñita, and Fushía and Lalita. Anselmo is a mysterious stranger who arrives in Piura – very much in the manner of a Hollywood western – and builds a brothel on the desert sands which he paints green, the same colour as his harp. (Only at the very end does Anselmo's predilection for the colour green become clear, when it emerges that he is actually from the Amazon region. He is thus another protagonist who moves from one centre of the novel to the other.) To the dismay of the local priest, Father García, the Green House becomes a great success. Anselmo abducts and hides in his tower the blind and mute orphan Antonia and makes her his lover. The scandalous relationship results in Antonia giving birth to a girl. Antonia dies during childbirth in the brothel, and shortly afterwards a fire destroys the Green House, started by an angry mob incited by Father García. Years later, their daughter Chunga runs the second Green House which, ironically, rises up 'singular and central like a cathedral', where Anselmo, old and by now also blind, plays the harp in an orchestra. By then the existence of the first Green House and its destruction in a fire has become the stuff of legends and nobody is sure anymore whether it actually existed. Anselmo himself gives ambiguous answers when asked, and so does Father García. But in his dying soliloquy, recognizable by the form of address 'you',[18] Anselmo recalls the tragic story of his love for Toñita. The mythical quality of this plot line is evoked in the first narrative segment that mentions Piura: 'La noche piurana está llena de historias. … historias de desafíos, adulterios y catástrofes, de mujeres que vieron llorar a la Virgen de la Catedral, levantar la mano al Cristo, sonreír furtivamente al niño Dios' (*La casa verde*, pp. 32–3) [The night is full of stories in Piura. … stories of duels, adultery, and catastrophe, of women who saw the Virgin in the cathedral weep, raise her hand to Christ, smile furtively at the Infant Jesus] (*The Green House*, pp. 25–6). The Piurans' imagination and their appetite for stories blurs the borders between fiction and reality and takes the story of Anselmo and the Green House, which stretches over sixty years, to a mythical level.

Another plot line ends with its protagonist Fushía left to die lonely and sad in a leper colony, after a life dominated by ambition and greed. Fushía is an adventurer of Japanese descent who has built himself an empire on

---

[18] This is possibly a homage to the French 'nouveau roman' which was in vogue at the time when Vargas Llosa was writing *La casa verde* in Paris. For example, see Michel Butor's *La modification* (1957), narrated entirely in the second person. Vargas Llosa has spoken about the difficulties of narrating this episode in a way that would leave it ambiguous, by using a narrative voice very close to Anselmo but also representing the collective consciousness of the town and its imagination of what happened. See *Historia secreta*, p. 56.

a remote island, where he acquires wealth by robbing indigenous tribes of their caoutchouc harvest with the help of the warrior tribe of the Huambisas, and surrounds himself by a harem of women. He used to work for Julio Reátegui, the wealthy landowner and corrupt governor of Santa María de Nieva, also involved in shady dealings in the rubber business, who is now pursuing Fushía. In his thirst for wealth, power and women Fushía acquires the young Lalita as the only non-native woman in his harem and makes her his favourite. His ambitions – and his relationship with Lalita – come to an end when he develops leprosy and is forced to abandon his island, making his way by boat to a leper colony. During this journey, the miserable and sick Fushía tells his life story to the boatman Aquilino who takes him slowly down the river Santiago. The river itself becomes an important feature of the novel, representing the journey of life through the dense jungle towards death. There is no way back against the current, as Aquilino tells him. This strand of the narrative is also a story about storytelling. It is organized largely in 'Chinese boxes', with an abundance of stories within stories, often in the form of telescopic dialogues opening up from the conversation between Aquilino and Fushía. The second segment in book 1, chapter 3, for example, starts with Aquilina asking Fushía how he met Lalita, a question in direct speech which is answered in a different dialogue in the past between the lawyer Dr Portillo and Lalita's mother, also in direct speech, in which the mother remembers – in reported speech – how her daughter asked her who that elegant man was.

This technique of nestling bits of conversation within other conversations is continued all the way through that narrative segment. It also contains a further dialogue between Dr Portillo and Julio Reátegui, chronologically after the lawyer's conversation with the mother. In this indirect manner important information is revealed about Fushía illegally selling rubber to the enemy during the Second World War, which also helps to date the period when Fushía and Lalita ran away together. The telescopic dialogues often work with indicators such as a question being asked on one level of the conversation (here: Lalita's mother and the lawyer) but answered on another level by different speakers (here: Fushía and the 'old man' Aquilino): '—¿Y en qué la hizo trabajar a su hija, señora? —dijo el doctor Portillo. En un trabajo estúpido, viejo, que lo habría hecho rico para siempre' (p. 70) ['And what kind of work did he have your daughter, do, Madam?' Dr Portillo asked. Stupid work, old man, which would have made him rich for the rest of his life] (p. 60). This gives the reader simultaneously two different perspectives on the same thing. In other cases, the montage technique informs about connections between events that the speakers are not (yet) aware of, such as in the dialogue between the lawyer and Reátegui, which is indirectly answered by crosscutting to the conversation between Aquilino and Fushía:

> Me llaman de urgencia de Uchamala. Vino un peón, no sé qué diablos pasa ...
> —¿Y dónde te fuiste a esconder con la Lalita? —dijo Aquilino.
> —A Uchamala —dijo Fushía—. Un fundo en el Marañon de ese perro de Reátegui. Vamos a pasar cerca, viejo. (p. 74)

> [I got an urgent message from Uchamala. A worker came with it, I don't know what the devil is going on ...
> 'And where did you go to hide with Lalita?' Aquilino asked.
> 'To Uchamala,' Fushía said. 'Some property on the Marañon that belongs to that bastard Reátegui. We're going to pass right by it, old man.'] (p. 64)

That last sentence, which also ends this particular narrative segment, brings the many intercalated and superimposed conversations back to the main level of dialogue, time and space.

The plot line involving the caoutchouc boom in the Amazon region touches on the story of Jum, the chief of an Aguaruna tribe, who tries to organize a producers' cooperative in order to avoid the exploitation of indigenous workers by the big players in the rubber trade, such as Julio Reátegui. The theme of inequality, corruption and injustice in the exploitation of Amazonia's natural resources will gain prominence again in Vargas Llosa's 2010 novel *El sueño del celta* [*The Dream of the Celt*].[19] The brutal abuse of indigenous tribes depicted in that novel is already exposed in one of the narrative strands of *La casa verde* forty-four years earlier: under the eyes of the corrupt governor, Jum is brutally tortured and humiliated by having his head shaved, which robs him of his position of respect in his community. Lost and confused, Jum ends up working for Fushía, the biggest exploiter of native communities – a bitter sort of irony.

As Vargas Llosa describes in *Historia secreta*, all these plot lines derive from real-life events that inspired him – the mysterious green house in Piura, the popular life in the Mangachería, the dubious practices of the Catholic mission in the jungle – and stories he heard about real-life people, such as the *cacique* Jum, the Japanese adventurer Tushía (Fushía) and a girl who was the model for Bonifacia. The way he elaborates this raw material and interlinks the different life stories creates a dense atmosphere and unifies the diverse content. This is best exemplified by Bonifacia, the most interesting female protagonist in the novel: she is expelled from the mission for liberating some indigenous girls who were captured by the nuns with the help of Sergeant Lituma's men and brought to the convent to 'civilize' them (her name means 'benefactress'). Abandoned by the nuns, Bonifacia is picked up by Lalita who suggests her marrying the sergeant. There are also signs that Bonifacia could

---

[19] Mario Vargas Llosa, *El sueño del celta* (Doral, FL: Alfaguara, 2010); Mario Vargas Llosa, *The Dream of the Celt*, trans. Edith Grossman (London: Faber and Faber, 2012).

be the daughter of the indigenous chief Jum. Her journey thus leads her from a native community to a Catholic convent in the jungle, and from there to marriage with a military man which transplants her to Piura, where she ends up in a brothel in the middle of the desert which is painted in the colour of the jungle. In the end she has to support her husband and his rogue friends from the shanty town by prostituting herself as the 'jungle girl', while she also looks after the dying Anselmo who turns out to be from the jungle himself. Bonifacia best represents the clash but also the convergence of jungle and desert, country and town. At various points in the novel, the striking green colour of her eyes is highlighted. In an episode in Piura, Bonifacia's eyes are repeatedly described as 'two little animals' when Lituma castigates her for not being able to walk on high heels, to him a sign of her 'savage' nature (even though his friend Monk concedes that Mangache women are not used to high heels either). Bonifacia's untameable nature clashes with Lituma's wish to domesticate her and make her adapt to his *machista* expectations:

> —Lo distinto es que Piura es una ciudad con edificios, autos y cinemas —explicó Lituma, bostenzando—. Y Santa María de Nieva, un pueblucho con calatos, mosquitos y lluvias que lo pudren todo, comenzando por las gentes.
> Dos bestiecillas se agazaparon tras unas mechas de cabellos sueltos y, verdes, hostiles, atisbaron. El pie izquierdo de Bonifacia, medio salido del zapato, forcejeaba por entrar de nuevo. ...
> —No te acostumbras a la civilización —suspiró, por fin—. Espérate un tiempito y verás las diferencias. Ni querrás oír hablar de la montaña y te dará vergüenza decir soy selvática. ...
> —Nunca me dará vergüenza —dijo Bonifacia—. A nadie puede darle vergüenza su tierra.
> —Todos somos peruanos —dijo el Mono—.
> ... las humilladas bestiecillas observaban desde lo alto con desconfianza.
> ... las bestiecillas se sosegaron y, de pronto, silenciosos, rebeldes, rapidísimos, ayudándose uno al otro, sus pies se libraron de los zapatos.
> ... En Piura no se puede portar como una salvaje. (pp. 315–16)

['What's different is that Piura is a city with buildings, cars, and movies', Lituma explained, yawning. 'And Santa María de Nieva is a miserable little village with naked savages, mosquitoes, and rain that rots everything, starting with the people.'
Two little animals crouched behind the strands of loose hair, and, green, hostile, they peeped out. Bonifacia's left foot, halfway out of her shoe, was struggling to get back in. ...
'You're not used to civilization', he said finally, with a sigh. 'Wait a little while and you'll see the difference. And you won't want to hear about the jungle any more and you'll be ashamed to say "I'm from the jungle"'. ...
'I'll never be ashamed', Bonifacia said. 'No one should ever be ashamed where they come from'.

'We're all Peruvians', Monk said.
... the humiliated little animals were observing from up above with mistrust
... the little animals became calm, and suddenly, silently, very quick, helping each other, her feet freed themselves of the shoes.
... 'In Piura she can't go around like a savage.'] (pp. 305–6)

The irony of this scene derives from the fact that the 'civilized' champs are a bunch of work-shy, violent, wife-beating good-for-nothings who spend their time drinking, gambling and whoring, as they proudly declare in their hymn. The crude machismo of the 'Unconquerables' is another instance in the novel where the dual concept of civilization and barbarism is being undermined. The same goes for the animal metaphors which abound in *La casa verde*. They not only denote life in the jungle but also characterize inhabitants of urban Piura: in the sequence quoted above Josefino, who tries to seduce Bonifacia after Lituma beats her, is described as 'hombre-lombriz' (p. 317) [worm-man] (p. 307) and 'serpiente' (p. 317) [serpent] (p. 307).

One of the 'datos escondidos', the elements left out of *La casa verde*, is an answer to the unresolved question whether Bonifacia is actually the daughter of Jum, the girl he pleads to be returned to him. In a sequence of the epilogue which deals with events going back to the time of Bonifacia's childhood, the nameless little girl who is brought to the mission from Urakusa by Julio Reátegui after his expedition to catch Jum has green eyes: 'La chiquilla los mira de soslayo, entre sus pelos brillan sus ojos, asustadizos, verdes y salvajes' (p. 366) [the girl is looking at them furtively, her eyes are shining through her hair, frightened, green, and savage] (p. 358). The striking parallel description of eyes looking out, scared and green, from underneath hair in this episode and the one quoted above points to the identity of Bonifacia with Jum's daughter. In another sequence which refers to an encounter some years later, but which is narrated earlier in the novel, Bonifacia refuses to join Reátegui whom she seems to recognize, staying on in the mission instead: 'Bonifacia abre los ojos verdes, húmedas, desafiantes' (p. 117) [Bonifacia opens her green, wet, challenging eyes] (p. 107). What is even more remarkable is the fact that Jum's eyes are repeatedly described as of a striking yellow: 'Su expresión es tranquila pero en sus ojos amarillos hay vibraciones indóciles, medio fanáticas' (p. 192) [His expression is peaceful, but in his yellow eyes there are restless vibrations, half fanatical] (p. 180); 'sus ojos, amarillos revolotean maliciosamente' (p. 196) [his yellow eyes turn malicious] (p. 184). Yellow is the colour that Bonifacia insists on wearing for her wedding to the sergeant, possibly a reminder of her lost father, possibly an anticipation of her life in the desert zone of Piura.

This kind of colour symbolism could be followed through the whole novel. It is part of the strong visual quality of *La casa verde*, its play with

EXPERIMENTING WITH FORM AND LANGUAGE 109

light and shadow, complemented by the atmospheric evocation of sounds. One recognizes Vargas Llosa's love for the cinema, but also his gift for visual observation which will later become apparent in the integration of paintings and their descriptions into his narratives. In places, this evocation of vision and sound is so intense – and always perceived from the outside – that it takes on the quality of a film script. In the following episode the reader gains the impression of being the spectator of a scene in the distance where one can just make out the white trousers of a man called Pantacha and slowly realizes that what one sees emerging from the huts are indigenous women:

> Y una explosión de voces sacude la mañana: aullantes, súbitos, desnudos, emergen de la lengua de bosque y corren hacia el poblado, gesticulando ascienden la ladera y entre los veloces cuerpos distantes se divisan los calzoncillos blancos de Pantacha, se oyen sus gritos que recuerdan la sarcástica risa de la chicua y ahora ladran muchos perros y las cabañas expulsan sombras, chillidos y una tenaz agitación, una especie de hervor conmueve la ladera por donde huyen tropenzando, rebotando, chocando unas con otras, figuras que vienen hacia el bosque y se distinguen, por fin, nítidamente: son mujeres. (p. 292)

> [And an explosion of shouting shakes the morning: howling, sudden, naked, they emerge from the tongue of woods and run toward the village, gesticulating, they go up the rise, and among the fast, distant bodies, Pantacha's white shorts can be seen, his shouts can be heard, reminding one of the sarcastic laugh of the chicua bird, and now a lot of dogs are barking, and the huts are ejecting shadows, shrieks, and a tenacious agitation, a kind of boiling, moves along the slope as they flee, tripping, rebounding, bumping against each other, figures that come toward the woods and can finally be distinguished clearly: they are women.] (p. 282)

The prologue to each of the novel's parts sets the scene in the manner of the opening sequence of a film. The use of the present tense in all of these sequences underlines the immediacy of a visual impression, seen from a particular angle or perspective. In the following phrases which open the epilogue we follow Reátegui into the mission and through a dark corridor as if a camera recording the scene were looking over his shoulder:

> El Gobernador da tres suaves toques con los nudillos, la puerta de la Residencia se abre: el rostro rosado de la Madre Griselda porfía por sonreír a Julio Reátegui, pero sus ojos se desvía llenos de azoro hacia la Plaza de Santa María de Nieva y su boca tiembla. El Gobernador entra, la chiquilla lo sigue dócilmente. Avanazan por un sombreado pasadizo hacia el despacho de la Superiora y el vocerío del pueblo es ahora pagado y lejano. (p. 365)

> [The Governor gives three soft raps with his knuckles, the door of the Residence opens: Sister Griselda's ruddy face tries hard to smile at Julio

Reátegui, but her eyes turn away, very restless, toward the square of Santa María de Nieva and her mouth trembles. The Governor enters, the little girl follows him docilely. They advance along a dark passageway to the Mother Superior's study, and the shouting in the village is now muffled and distant.] (p. 357)

The short descriptive phrases sound like instructions to a film director. In the following sequence which opens book 2, the reader creates in his mind the setting with the main action in the foreground – Julio Reátegui's energetic arrival – and scenes of everyday life filling out the background, such as the guard playing with a dog:

> Una lancha se detiene roncando junto al embarcadero y Julio Reátegui salta a tierra. Sube hasta la Plaza de Santa María de Nieva —un guardia civil echa al aire una madera, un perro la atrapa al vuelo y se la trae— y cuando llega a la altura de los troncos de capirona un grupo de personas sale de la cabaña de la Gobernación. El alza la mana y saluda: lo observan, se animan, se precipitan a su encuentro. (p. 109)

> [A boat roars up to the dock and Julio Reátegui jumps out. He goes up to the square of Santa María de Nieva – a Civil Guard is throwing a stick into the air, a dog catches it in flight and brings it back – and when he reaches the level of the capirona poles, a group of people come out of the Governor's building. He raises his hand in greeting: they watch him, become excited, run to meet him.] (p. 99)

What follows then are dialogue fragments in reported speech, in quick succession and without speech marks or reporting phrases, drawing the reader closer into the frame. This mixture of cinematographic techniques and narrative devices is particularly striking at the very beginning of the novel, with its action-packed chase sequence. We see the nuns, aided by guards, going into the jungle to capture and abduct girls from an indigenous tribe in order to take them to the mission. The initial calm rhythm of the narration recreates the inertia of the wait at the beginning of the scene, until a sudden sighting of Aguarunas causes hectic activity, conveyed in the polisyndetic use of 'and' and the frequent repetition of the affirmative 'sí'. The perspective is that of the Sergeant:

> los guardias volvían corriendo. ¿Una canoa?, y el Oscuro sí, ¿con aguarunas?, y el Rubio mi Sargento sí, y el Chiquito sí, y el Pesado y las Madres sí, sí, van y preguntan y vienen sin rumbo y el Sargento que el Rubio volviera al barranco y avisara si subían, que los demás se escondieran y el práctico Nieves recoge las polainas del suelo, los fusiles. (p. 12)

> [the soldiers come back on the run. A canoe?, and Blacky yes, with Aguarunas?, and Blondy, yes Sergeant, and Shorty yes, and Fats and the

nuns yes, yes, they come and ask questions and go off in all directions, and the Sergeant has Blondy go back to the top of the hill and tell him if they are coming up, the others should hide, and Nieves the pilot picks the leggings up off the ground and the rifles.] (p. 6)

The sudden burst of action when the children are torn from their families is narrated in short breathless phrases, intercalated with fragments of the rosary that one of the nuns is reciting, creating an intense clash between praying and cruel action which highlights the contrast between the sisters' good intentions and the ruthless way they go about achieving their goal (I have highlighted the fragments of the Hail Mary prayer in italics):

> muchachos, nada de brutalidades: *Santa María, Madre de Dios.* Todos contemplan los labios exangües de la Madre Patrocinio, y ella *Ruega por nosotros*, tritura con sus dedos las bolitas negras ... y hay carreras ahora, chillidos, y *en la hora*, pisotones, el varoncito se tapa la cara, *de nuestra muerte*, y los dos aguarunas han quedado rígidos *amén*, sus dientes castañean y sus ojos perplejamente miran los fusiles que los apuntan. (pp. 18–19)

> [boys, no brutalities: *Holy Mary, Mother of God.* All of them look at the bloodless lips of Sister Patrocinio, and she, *Pray for us*, is shedding the little black balls in her fingers, ... there is running, screams and *at the hour*, trampling, the little boy covers his face, *of our death*, and the two Aguarunas stay rigid, *amen*, their teeth chatter and their eyes look perplexedly at the rifles that are pointed at them.] (p. 12)

Narrative techniques of juxtaposition and simultaneity are used to convey meaning. Criticism of the Church's attitude to 'saving' children by taking them away from their families is not made explicit, but it is all the more poignant for coming across in this subliminal, emotional manner. (The arguments for or against wanting to 'civilize' indigenous children is later discussed between the members of the civil guard involved in the abductions, in the first segment of book 2, chapter 1. This relates to Vargas Llosa's discussion of the subject matter in texts such as *La utopía arcaica* [The Archaic Utopia][20] (see chapter 2 above), but also in his later novel *El hablador* [*The Storyteller*].)[21] At the most brutal moment when the Aguaruna mother is physically restrained while her daughters are carried off, the clash between good intentions and evil means, between words and deeds, becomes most acute in the juxtaposition of a heartbroken mother and the part of the prayer which says 'blessed was the fruit of her womb': 'El Chiquito y el Oscuro sujetan a la vieja de los

---

[20] Mario Vargas Llosa, *La utopía arcaica. José María Arguedas y las ficciones del indigenismo* (México: Fondo de Cultura Económica, 1996).
[21] Mario Vargas Llosa, *El hablador* (Barcelona: Seix Barral, 1987); Mario Vargas Llosa, *The Storyteller*, trans. Helen Lane (London: Faber and Faber, 1991).

hombros y los pelos y ella está sentada chillando, ... y bendito era el fruto, Madre, Madre, de su vientre' (pp. 19–20) [Shorty and Blacky are holding the old woman by the shoulders and the hair and she sits down shrieking ... and blessed was the fruit, Mother, Mother, of her womb] (p. 13).

Vargas Llosa's virtuoso handling of diverse techniques encompasses traditions as far apart as the cinema and classical rhetoric. But classical rhetoricians already knew the importance of visualization, of 'creating a vivid mental picture'[22] to produce a lasting effect on an audience. In Cicero we read: 'the most complete pictures are formed in our minds of the things that have been conveyed to them and imprinted on them by the senses, but ... the keenest of all our senses is the sense of sight'.[23] What Cicero called *evidentia*, Quintilian named *enargeia*, a process 'which makes us seem not so much to narrate as to exhibit the actual scene'.[24] A last example from *La casa verde* confirms how Vargas Llosa specifically uses rhetorical figures to create an emotional – and visual – effect:[25] 'se le zafaban, ahorita se le zafaban y ellas no grita pero tironean y sus cabezas, hombros, pies y piernas luchan y golpean y vibran' (p. 19) [they were getting away from him, they were getting away from him and they are not shouting but they are pulling, and their heads, shoulders, feet, and legs struggle and kick and vibrate] (p. 13). The repetition of an exact phrase (*ploke*) signals the agitation of the speaker while a combination of *asyndeton* (the absence of connecting particles: 'cabezas, hombros, pies') and *polysyndeton* (the profusion of connecting particles: 'luchan y golpean y vibran') recreate the chaotic and unequal fight that is going on between the guards and the children.

A lot more could be said about narrative technique and linguistic invention in *La casa verde*, and the many levels of meaning this creates. But it is difficult to dissect this *Gesamtkunstwerk* of multiple plots, techniques, language, colour, sound and vision into analytical units and do justice to the whole. I have tried to concentrate on a number of narrative devices and focus on themes such as machismo, corrupt government, the Church, inequality, exploitation of the indigenous population and the divided country, all of which play a role in the continuity of Vargas Llosa's work. His creation of a highly complex novel that combines romance and adventure story with a critical view of Latin American reality points forward to his masterpiece,

---

[22] *Rhetorica ad Herennium* (Cambridge, MA: Harvard University Press, The Loeb Classical Library, 1954), 4.34.45.

[23] Cicero, *De oratore* (Cambridge MA: Harvard University Press, The Loeb Classical Library, 1959), 2.87.357.

[24] Quintilian, *The Orator's Education* (Cambridge, MA and London: Harvard University Press, The Loeb Classical Library, 1963), 6.2.32.

[25] See also my forthcoming article 'Mistrust and mastery – Goethe, Victor Hugo, Mario Vargas Llosa and the art of rhetoric', *Rhetorica*, 2014.

La guerra del fin del mundo [*The War of the End of the World*].[26] But *La casa verde* has a unique place in Vargas Llosa's fictional universe due to the combination of its broad thematic scope with an unprecedented technical wizardry and strong visual quality.

***

Conversación en la catedral [*Conversation in the Cathedral*],[27] a monumental work of over 650 pages, was first published in two volumes in 1969. It is often regarded as the culmination and end point of Vargas Llosa's early work. This first phase in his fictional creation, so the argument goes, is defined by two parallel characteristics: technical complexity and experimentation on the formal level go hand in hand with social criticism on the level of contents, informed by Vargas Llosa's political commitment to socialism at the time. Some critics see a direct link between his fiction writing and his political convictions and argue that his disillusionment with Cuba in the 1970s ended the period of 'socialist' novels and initiated a new phase in his writing, with lighter, humorous novels replacing the works which explored Peruvian society and its injustices. *Conversación en la catedral* is definitely the work in which Vargas Llosa has driven the technical complexity of a novel and its vast expanse to a new limit, but it does not mark the end point of his experimentation with form and language, as we will see. Neither does his concern with Peruvian society and its institutions end here: the military and the brothel, two focal points of his early novels, continue to play a role in the following novel, *Pantaleón y las visitadoras* [*Captain Pantoja and the Special Service*] (1973),[28] and so does journalism, a topic that is introduced for the first time in *Conversación*. What changes after the 1969 work is the tone of utter devastation and defeat that characterizes *Conversación*, a mood that is set in the very first lines of the novel:

> Desde la puerta de 'La Crónica' Santiago mira la avenida Tacna, sin amor: automóviles, edificios desiguales y descoloridos, esqueletos de avisos luminosos flotando en la neblina, el mediodía gris. ¿En qué momento se había jodido el Perú? ... Las manos en los bolsillos, cabizbajo, va escoltado por transeúntes que avanazan, también, hacia la Plaza San Martín. Él era como el Perú, Zavalita, se había jodido en algún momento. Piensa: ¿en

---

[26] Mario Vargas Llosa, *La guerra del fin del mundo* (Barcelona: Plaza y Janés, 1982); Mario Vargas Llosa, *The War of the End of the World* (London: Faber and Faber, 1986).

[27] Mario Vargas Llosa, *Conversación en la catedral* (Barcelona: Seix Barral, 1985); Mario Vargas Llosa, *Conversation in the Cathedral*, trans. Gregory Rabassa (New York: HarperCollins, 2005).

[28] Mario Vargas Llosa, *Pantaleón y las visitadoras* (Barcelona: Seix Barral, 1986); Mario Vargas Llosa, *Captain Pantoja and the Special Service* (London: Faber and Faber, 1987).

cuál? ... El Perú jodido, piensa, Carlitos jodido, todos jodidos. Piensa: no hay solución. (*Conversación*, p. 9)

[From the doorway of *La Crónica* Santiago looks at the Avenida Tacna without love: cars, uneven and faded buildings, the gaudy skeletons of posters floating in the mist, the gray midday. At what precise moment had Peru fucked itself up? ... His hands in his pockets, head down, he goes along escorted by people who are also going in the direction of the Plaza San Martín. He was like Peru, Zavalita ... he'd fucked himself up somewhere along the line. He thinks: when? ... Peru all fucked up, Carlitos all fucked up, everybody all fucked. He thinks: there's no solution.] (*Conversation*, p. 3)

This opening sequence introduces an atmosphere of decay, depression and hopelessness that will pervade the whole novel, which consists of four books with an irregular number of chapters. The leitmotif-like question of when exactly it was that Peru 'had fucked itself up' is posed in these first few sentences, and the link between the protagonist's personal state and that of the country is firmly established. Santiago's self-questioning of when it all went wrong for him will reappear obsessively in little fragments such as '¿Ahí? ¿Fue ahí?' [Here? Was it here?] throughout the novel. The fact that the narrative opens with his resigned declaration 'there is no solution' is particularly poignant when it becomes clear that this opening chapter already marks the beginning and the end of the novel. It delivers the time frame of half a day during which Santiago Zavala, son of a wealthy family turned local news reporter for a Lima paper, living in humble circumstances with his wife Ana, has a chance meeting with Ambrosio Pardo, former chauffeur of his father, who now has a miserable job as a dog-catcher. They go for a drink in the squalid bar 'La Catedral', talk for four hours, and part again, returning to their frustrated existences. This main dialogue between Santiago and Ambrosio in the present opens a window onto other dialogues and events of the past, in a manner reminiscent of the telescopic dialogues in the Fushía chapters of *La casa verde*. The past is partly narrated in an explicit manner by Santiago and Ambrosio during their meeting, partly reflected in their minds during the conversation, in the mode of two parallel streams of consciousness evoking other dialogues of the past and memories of certain events.

The period covered by the novel stretches over fifteen years, recognizable by the political history mentioned.[29] The present in which the conversation in 'La Catedral' takes place is set during the government of Fernando Belaúnde Terry who came to power in 1963 following on from Manuel

---

[29] For an excellent analysis see Claudio Eugenio Cifuentes Aldunate, '*Conversación en la catedral'. Poética de un fracaso. Análisis texto-estructural* (Odense: Odense University Press, 1983).

Prado, whose regime ended the eight-year dictatorship of Manuel Odría, the so-called 'ochenio', from 1948 to 1956. This is the period in which Vargas Llosa grew up, a time which he has often commented on as oppressive, with a political and social climate that suffocated the ambitions of many young aspiring writers and nonconformists.[30] The novel had to deal with the problem of how to integrate this personal background, as well as a particular historical period and its politics that Vargas Llosa felt strongly about, into an autonomous work of fiction, without letting personal resentment or political opinions contaminate the illusion of a story narrating itself. The absence of a central narrative perspective seemed essential, and the overwhelming proliferation of voices results from that. This becomes clear in the way the single recognizably historical event in the novel, the general strike in Arequipa directed against Odría's rule, is narrated: here, in chapter 4 of book 3, we find the biggest proliferation of dialogue fragments in the whole novel (in this cacophony of voices Oviedo has identified sixteen different conversations going on simultaneously).[31] It represents the first of many attempts to turn history into fiction.

Out of a multitude of intermingled dialogues in *Conversación*, set on different levels of time and space and covering the whole range of Peruvian society, emerge individual life stories which reflect the state of the country, the political and social atmosphere of the time, and the political mechanisms that create this atmosphere. Vargas Llosa's choice of epigraph for the novel alludes to his intention of creating a panorama of Peru under the Odría dictatorship by showing how it affected the lives of a great variety of individuals. He quotes from a novel by Honoré de Balzac: 'Il faut avoir fouillé toute la vie sociale pour être un vrai romancier, vu que le roman est l'histoire privée des nations' [One has to have explored every sphere of social life to be a true novelist, since novels are the private history of nations]. This is an appropriate motto for a novel with an obvious 'totalizing' ambition, trying to concentrate a vast number of stories and topics into a single narrative work, which itself tries to bring together a multitude of different narrative strands in the framework of this first chapter which opens a brief view onto the present and closes it again. The structural composition underlines the lack of an outlook for the future, but highlights the retrospective search for what went wrong in the past.

The primary conversation in 'La Catedral', which is narrated in the present tense, opens up onto four subordinate dialogues. A point of orientation in

---

[30] Vargas Llosa's speech, 'La literatura es fuego', was a potent denunciation of the unsupportive, anti-liberal climate that he and his artist friends endured. Mario Vargas Llosa, 'La literatura es fuego', in *Contra viento y marea, I (1962–1972)* (Barcelona: Seix Barral, 1986), pp. 176–81.

[31] Oviedo, *Invención*, p. 252.

this confusing labyrinth of conversations is the form of address used in the fragmented and intermingled dialogues. Santiago who is addressed as 'niño' [son] by Ambrosio calls himself 'Zavalita' in his inner monologue during their talk. (The use of his first name and the verb form 'piensa' [he thinks] in the present tense indicates the voice of an impersonal narrator.) Typical for the telescopic structure of Santiago's inner monologue is a phrase repeating the same verb in two different tenses and conjugations: 'Piensa: pensabas no, Zavalita' (p. 114) [He thinks: you thought not, Zavalita] (p. 100). His ongoing inner monologue reveals Santiago's self-doubts, recognizable by a multitude of question marks, and the feeling of failure that haunts him. The second conversation arising out of his exchange with Ambrosio is a series of dialogues in the near past between Santiago and his friend and journalistic colleague Carlitos, who also addresses him as Zavalita. Its place is the bohemian bar 'El Negro-Negro', and its subject matter is the loss of ideals, the frustration of their literary ambitions and their work at the newspaper *La Crónica*. On Ambrosio's side there are also two conversations that arise out of the main dialogue: one between him and his former boss, Santiago's father Fermín Zavala, taking place in Zavala's weekend house in Ancón in the past, when Ambrosio was still working for him. The form Ambrosio uses to address his boss is 'don' [sir]. He talks to him about his life and the past when he used to work for Cayo Bermúdez, the – fictitious – strong man in the background of the dictatorial regime. The second dialogue reflected in Ambrosio's mind while talking to Santiago is his conversation with the call-girl Queta, who asks him about his relationship to Fermín Zavala. It is situated on about the same time level as the dialogue between Ambrosio and his boss. Fragments of the main conversation and these four subordinate ones are rendered throughout the novel, creating a confusing simultaneity of voices from different periods of time, relating to different people, places and contexts. Leaps forwards and backwards in time put actions into perspective, for instance when during a conversation Santiago's adolescent friend Popeye utters his interest in Santiago's sister Teté and the dialogue suddenly jumps forward to Santiago telling Ambrosio in 'La Catedral' that they had married, thus underlining that a union between two children from rich and influential families was totally predictable. The same chapter 2 of book 1 narrates Santiago and Popeye forcing themselves on the maid Amalia who consequently gets fired. The excited conversation between the two adolescents planning their assault frequently cuts across to Santiago guiltily visiting Amalia after she has lost her job because of him, in order to apologize and hand over some of his savings to her. This creates an interesting simultaneity between transgression and atonement.

In addition to this 'pyramid of voices' (see Oviedo, *Invención*, p. 253) the novel contains a number of ongoing dialogues which evolve neither out of the primary nor the secondary conversations. The maid Amalia has various conversations about her life which, over the course of time, has brought her into contact with all the main characters of the novel: Santiago, Fermín Zavala, Ambrosio, the prostitutes Queta and Hortensia (also called 'La Musa' [the Muse]) and, through them, Cayo Bermúdez. She provides insights into their lives from a different perspective, as an observer from a low social status. Amalia is another example of those women in Vargas Llosa's novels who touch the life of all the important protagonists, establishing a secret link between them without ever being an active agent themselves. Previous examples were Teresa in *La ciudad* and Lalita in *La casa verde*. The narration of Amalia's death from her own perspective is the first example of a number of instances in Vargas Llosa's fiction where he tries to imagine the process of dying from the inside of a character, an obsession which might go back to his fascination with Emma Bovary's suicide and the cathartic effect it had on him (see *La orgía*, p. 25).

The most important conversation which does not evolve out of any of the other dialogues is the talk between Cayo Bermúdez, the novel's main political character, and his confidant Paredes, in which Bermúdez reveals the political mechanisms by which a dictatorial regime secures power. The workings of a corrupt regime are thus dissected from an inside perspective, by the man who actually orchestrates the corruption and violence that keep Odría in power. The formal and stylistic elaboration of these various dialogues is adapted to the speaker's personality and situation: Cayo Bermúdez's account of his political manoeuvres is rendered in a straightforward, explicit and unfragmented manner, reflecting his totally cold and dispassionate way of looking at politics, whereas the fragments of Santiago's inner monologue are full of self-doubting questions without answers; Ambrosio's utterings appear unreflected and submissive, whereas the commentaries of Queta and Carlitos are cynical and judgemental.

This complicated network of disjointed conversations, where different plot lines are confronted and act in a complementary manner – the technique described as 'vasos comunicantes' [communicating vessels] – reveals surprising parallels and contrasts on the various levels of narration that would remain invisible in a linear version. The disruption of chronological, geographical and causal structures has an important function for the meaning of the novel. The narrative device, for instance, of mentioning events under the democratically elected government of Manuel Prado *before* incidents that actually occurred earlier, under the dictatorial regime of Odría, highlights the long-lasting damage that a dictatorship inflicts on a country. The fact that there is no obvious difference in the political and social climate between the period of authoritarianism and the legitimate government that follows shows that corruption and authoritarianism affect society on a much deeper level and stay virulent despite a change in the form of government.

As in the previous novels, only on a much larger scale, *Conversación* plays with ambiguities by sudden jumps in time and space, or by abrupt changes of interlocutors, without any warning or indicator, thus creating a temporary disorientation of the reader. For example, this happens in a highly confusing manner in book 2, chapter 7 where, integrated into various other dialogues and narrative fragments, Ambrosio's account of his father Trifulcio is directed alternately to Zavala father and son, in conversations which actually lie years apart. And in the same way Ambrosio notices that, when he talks to Fermín Zavala about Cayo Bermúdez's conflict with his father, Fermín's answers actually relate to himself and his conflict with Santiago. The father–son conflict, an important subject matter in *Conversación*, thus reveals surprising parallels between fathers and their sons on totally different levels of society: Santiago's rejection of his father's social status and his resulting condition of a *déclassé*, reinforced by his marrying below his social class, is comparable to Cayo Bermúdez being disinherited by his father, the ambitious pawnbroker 'El Buitre' [The Vulture], because he marries a socially unsuitable woman; and these two unhappy father–son relationships offer comparisons with Ambrosio and his unfeeling father Trifulcio.

A number of 'datos escondidos' [hidden facts] contribute to the challenge that the novel's complexity offers. The ominous question that overshadows Santiago's conversation with Ambrosio in the opening pages alludes to some dark secret in the past. He asks his father's former chauffeur, 'Que hablemos con franqueza de la Musa, de mi papá. ¿El te mandó? Ya no importa, quiero saber. ¿Fue mi papá?' (p. 25) [to talk frankly about the muse, about my father. Did he order you? It doesn't matter anymore, I just want to know. Was it my father?] (p. 17). The reader only understands much later that Santiago tries and fails to discover his father's role in the murder of 'la Musa', a nightclub singer who blackmailed Fermín Zavala with her knowledge of his homosexual relationship with his chauffeur. Throughout the conversation in 'La Catedral' one feels the presence of some traumatic event hanging over Santiago: 'No debiste venir, no debiste hablarle, Zavalita, no estás jodido sino loco. Piensa: la pesadilla va a volver. Será tu culpa, Zavalita, pobre papá, pobre viejo' (p. 20) [You shouldn't have come, you shouldn't have spoken to him Zavalita, you're not fucked up, you're crazy. He thinks: the nightmare will come back. It'll be your fault, Zavalita, poor papa, poor old man] (p. 13). The fact that 'La Musa' (or Hortensia as she is called) was murdered is not mentioned until the beginning of book 3, in the second volume of the original edition. Ambrosio's confession of the crime, narrated in several fragments of a conversation with his former colleague Ludovico in book 3, chapter 4 (p. 506), goes almost unnoticed. Here, the reader also learns that Fermín Zavala was not involved, a fact that will remain obscured from his son. The introduction of this important 'hidden fact' in the opening chapter makes it possible to anticipate the ending without destroying suspense. Despite the tone of frustration and hopelessness established in the opening pages, the beginning of the novel engages the reader in the search for what it is that oppresses Santiago.

The murder case in *Conversación* is comparable to the mysterious death of the Slave in *La ciudad* in its function as a catalyst which brings to the surface dark secrets, lies and a system of corruption that covers up the deed. The murder victim Hortensia, 'La Musa', used to be the companion of Cayo Bermúdez at the height of his power. But the newly elected regime has no interest in involving him nor in making public Fermín Zavala's connection to the murder case. Not even the newspapers are willing to investigate and expose these links, so that Santiago ends up asking himself:

> ¿Había sido la dejadez, la abulia limeña, la estupidez de los soplones, Zavalita? Piensa: que nadie exigiera, insistiera, que nadie se moviera por ti. ¿Olvídense o te olvidaron de verdad, piensa, échenle tierra al asunto o la echaron de por sí? ¿Te mataron los mismos de nuevo, Musa, o esta segunda vez te mató todo el Perú? (p. 406)

> [Had it been the sloppiness, Lima and its moping ways, the stupidity of the detectives, Zavalita? He thinks: that no one demanded anything, insisted, that no one made a move on your behalf. Forget about it or did they really forget you, he thinks, bury the matter, or did they really bury it on their own? Did the same people kill you again, Muse, or did all Peru kill you this second time?] (p. 370)

The link between the individual and the country relates to Santiago's question of when it was that 'Peru had fucked itself up', since 'He was like Peru, Zavalita'. The general climate of corruption and inertia renders the individual powerless. By the time Hortensia's murderer Ambrosio leaves Lima and goes into hiding with the help of his policeman friend Ludovico (who, ironically, was the officer investigating her murder), Cayo Bermúdez is on his way out of the country having been forced to hand over his post as head of security to his protégé Paredes, a nephew of Odría. These two developments are narrated in a densely intercalated way, establishing a parallel between events on different levels, between the private and the public, which underlines the general atmosphere of corruption during this historical period.

The representative of the corrupt regime in the novel is Cayo Bermúdez, the strong man in charge of organizing a network of intrigues and dirty manoeuvres that have the single political purpose of keeping Odría in power. But his attitude towards the dictator is totally indifferent and cynical: 'Aquí cambian las personas', he says, 'nunca las cosas' (p. 56) [People change here ... never things] (p. 45). Lacking any political convictions and moral standards, and known by the nickname 'Cayo Mierda' [Cayo shithead], Bermúdez succeeds very well in Peruvian politics. He pursues his goals in an unscrupulous manner, aware that his power will not last forever, and openly reveals in his conversations with Paredes how he manipulates power and maintains a system of repression. He justifies his deeds by a cynical view of Peru as an uncivilized country that cannot be governed by civilized methods: '—Este no es un país civilizado, sino bárbaro e ignorante' (p. 135) [This isn't a civilized country, it's barbarian and ignorant] (p. 119). This gives him the justification for applying the whole range of repressive measures: suppressing freedom of speech, manipulating public opinion, infiltrating the trade unions, rigging elections, making oppositional candidates disappear, and organizing demonstrations of support for the government by intimidation while dissolving the opposition's demonstrations by force. The novel exposes these workings of an authoritarian government in the words of the manipulator himself, whose illegal practices include bribing, spying, blackmailing, arbitrary arrests and torture. Under Cayo's watch, his subordinates create a real hierarchy of repression and corruption. Lozano, his immediate collaborator, cashes in protection money from brothels, while his helpers take over the really dirty work: marking and threatening adversaries, provoking fights amongst them and torturing them. This perverse hierarchy stretches from Cayo's subtle, almost playful manipulations (anticipating Trujillo in *La Fiesta del Chivo* [*The Feast of the Goat*])[32] to the cruder methods of repression that he delegates to his subordinates, down to the lowest level of security forces, where the pervert Hipólito gets sexual gratification out of torturing his victims. This all-encompassing system of repression, not invented by Cayo Bermúdez but conducted by him in the most sovereign manner, produces the climate of corruption and paralysis affecting the whole country and everybody in it.

Bermúdez's lack of interest in politics allows him to suggest that the regime should broker an agreement with its declared ideological enemy, the APRA, in order to overcome a crisis of power. With this suggestion he is well ahead of his time and shows more political understanding than anybody else, since years later, at the time of the conversation between Santiago and Ambrosio in 'La Catedral', his then outrageous idea has become reality. The distorted chronology of the narration shows that Bermúdez is the most negative, but simultaneously the cleverest figure in the political scenery of *Conversación*. The ambivalence in his characterization turns this representative of the darkest side of power – almost against the reader's will – into the most fascinating figure of the novel. His controlled handling of public affairs stands in strong contrast to the perverse fantasies in which he releases his class resentment. These fantasies appear when he is made to feel an outsider, for instance during a visit to the exclusive Club Cajamarca where Bermúdez tries to raise the members' support for a public meeting with Odría. This

---

[32] Mario Vargas Llosa, *La Fiesta del Chivo* (Madrid: Alfaguara, 2000); Mario Vargas Llosa, *The Feast of the Goat*, trans. Edith Grossman (New York: Farrar, Straus and Giroux, 2001).

scene is narrated from Cayo's perspective who, as a dark-skinned 'cholo', feels very foreign to this milieu, a technique that turns the readers into secret accomplices of Cayo's disparaging view of Peru's leading class, a world that seems arrogant, racist, hypocritical and only concerned with its own interests. Bermúdez's social resentment releases itself in pornographic fantasies concerning the wife of senator Heredia and Cayo's mistress Queta, imagining a sexual encounter across social and racial boundaries, with him present as a voyeur. His secret revenge undermines the social structure by joining, in his imagination, a white upper-class woman with a dark-skinned prostitute, thus humiliating the former. The encounter of those two different women in his mind shows the collision of opposites that Cayo enjoys to the full: 'Las manos blancos y las morenas, la boca de labios gruesos y la de labios tan finos, los pezones ásperos inflados y los pequeños y cristalinos y suaves, los muslos curtidos y los transparentes de venas azules' (p. 326) [the dark hands and the white ones, the thick-lipped mouth and the thin-lipped one, the rough, inflated nipples and the small, crystalline, soft ones, the tanned thighs and the transparent ones with blue veins] (p. 296). The scene at the Club Cajamarca is developed in a way that intermingles Cayo's calculated business behaviour with his voyeuristic fantasies. The novel does not mark the transitions from the outer level of official negotiations to the inner level of his imaginations and back. With both levels merging, the fantasies can be distinguished merely by the use of the conditional. This long sequence in Cajamarca is another attempt by Vargas Llosa to recreate the famous 'comices agricoles' scene in *Madame Bovary*. Where Flaubert's novel elaborates the contrast between profane agricultural meeting and delicate love scene by simultaneous narration, *Conversación* shows Don Remigio Saldívar, a representative of agriculture, giving a long-winded speech while the erotic scene in Cayo's fantasy (which I have highlighted in italics) reaches its climax:

> Me van a perdonar y sobre todo usted, señor Bermúdez, carraspeó don Remigio Saldívar, él era un hombre de acción y no de discursos, es decir que no hablo tan bien como el Pulga Heredia y el senador lanzó una carcajada y hubo un estrépito de risas. El abrió la boca, arrugó la cara, *y ahí estaría, blanca, desnuda, seria, elegante, inmóvil, mientras Quetita delicadamente le quitaría las medias arrodillada a sus pies,* y todos celebraban con sonrisas las proezas de oratoria de don Remigio Saldívar sobre su falta de oratoria, y oía al grano Remigio, eso es Cajamarca don Remigio: *las enrollaría en cámara lenta y él vería las manos de la sirvienta tan grandes, tan morenas, tan toscas, bajando, bajando, por las piernas tan blancas, tan blancas,* y don Remigio Saldívar adoptó una expresión hierática: entrando en materia quería decirle que no se preocupara, señor Bermúdez ... los agricultores del departamento habían colaborado magníficamente en los preparativos, y también los comerciantes y profesionales, oígalo bien. *Y él saldría de detrás del biombo y se acercaría, su cuerpo sería una antorcha, llegaría hasta los tules, vería*

y su corazón agonizaría: sepa que le pondremos cuarenta mil hombres en la Plaza, si es que no más. *Ahí estarían bajo sus ojos abrazándose, oliéndose, transpirándose, anundándose* y don Remigio Saldívar hizo una pausa para sacar un cigarrillo y buscar los fósforos. (pp. 325–6)

[You'll have to excuse me, all of you and especially you, Mr Bermúdez, Don Remigio Saldívar cleared his throat, he was a man of action, not speeches, that is, I can't speak as well as Fleafoot Heredia and the senator gave a chuckle and there was an outburst of laughter. He opened his mouth, wrinkled his face, *and there she would be, white, naked, serious, elegant, motionless, while Quetita would delicately take off her stockings, kneeling at her feet*, and with laughter they all celebrated Don Remigio Saldívar's oratorical prowess concerning his lack of oratory, and he heard come to the point Remigio, that's Cajamarca Don Remigio: *she would roll them in slow motion and he would see the maid's hands, so large, so dark, so rough, lowering, lowering them over the legs that were so white, so white*, and Don Remigio Saldívar assumed a hieratic expression: getting down to the matter at hand he wanted to tell them that he shouldn't worry, Mr Bermúdez ... the agricultural community had collaborated magnificently in the preparations, and the business and professional men too, keep that in mind. *And he would come out from behind the screen and get closer, his body would be like a torch, he would go up to the curtains, he would look and his heart would be in agony*: keep in mind that we'll have forty thousand men in the square, if not more. *There they would be under his eyes, embracing, smelling each other, perspiring on each other, getting all knotted together* and Don Remigio Saldívar paused to take out a cigarette and look for matches.] (pp. 294–5)

The invented or real humiliations that Bermúdez uses to release his deep resentments become more and more sadistic as he himself is exposed to political pressure. When he is finally forced to resign, the cycle of injustice, repression and nepotism continues without him.

Peruvian politics as represented in *Conversación en la catedral* is all about power. The businessman Fermín Zavala embodies the political opportunism of the oligarchy (although he himself is a social climber), supporting anyone who promotes their interests. In his arrogant and snobbish attitude, he despises 'cholos' as much as 'gringos'; his chauffeur whom he abuses for his homosexual needs is only a 'poor nigger'. Nevertheless, he continues to be friendly with Bermúdez as long as he needs him, and fosters his good relations with the United States. The moment Bermúdez withdraws his support, that is, his orders for Zavala's business, Fermín Zavala joins the rebellion of general Espina and the coalition's attempt to overthrow the government. Again in this situation, he keeps in contact with the US Embassy and secures North American support for their plans, for the benefit of his business interests. His image of Peruvian politics is cynical: 'Con diez millones de soles no hay golpe de estado que falle en el Perú' (p. 417) [With ten million soles behind it, no coup d'état in Peru can possibly fail] (p. 380). On this level, *Conversación* seems to correspond to Vargas Llosa's socialist convictions of the time. The portrayal of Peruvian politics in this novel matches the political reality which Vargas Llosa the intellectual criticized in various non-fictional texts of the 1960s, for instance in a manifesto of 1965, signed by eight Peruvian intellectuals: '150 años de vida republicana nos han enseñado que el poder lo han detentado alternativamente dictaduras militares o representantes civiles de la oligarquía, que no se han preocupado de otra cosa que de acrecentar sus privilegios o de crear otros nuevos, a expensas de la mayoría del pueblo peruano' [150 years of republican life have shown us that power has been held alternately by military dictatorships or civilian representatives of the oligarchy, preoccupied with nothing else but to increase their privileges or create new ones, at the expense of the majority of the Peruvian people].[33]

But the novel has another political dimension, which is not quite in tune with Vargas Llosa's very public support for socialism at the time. In Santiago Zavala, the son who rejects his father and his social class out of a deep concern for social injustices, who then goes to study at the radical San Marcos University, joins a clandestine communist cell called Cahuide, but ends up totally disillusioned with left-wing political commitment, Vargas Llosa has created a protagonist who goes through many of the developments that he has gone through in his youth. But he makes him unsuccessful in all of them and lets him end in mediocrity and resignation – as if to exorcize the demons of his youthful illusions. Santiago is a failed writer, shamed and made fun of by his siblings when they discover that he secretly writes poems. Before entering university, Santiago understands his love for literature as part of a subversive, rebellious attitude and describes himself as 'un tipo puro': 'Me cagaba en la plata y me creía capaz de grandes cosas' (p. 71) [I said to hell with money and I thought I was capable of great things ... Pure in that sense] (p. 60). His idea of 'pureza', meaning moral purity, includes the activity of writing and reading. In his imagination Santiago sees himself consulting 'explosive books' which he then discusses with a clandestine circle of friends. Culture is part of his romantic image of revolutionary politics: 'La revolución, los libros, los museos' (p. 84) [Revolution, books, museums] (p. 72) all belong to his idea of 'breaking with the bourgeoisie':

> Libros prohibidos, revistas prohibidas y Santiago vio estantes rebalsando de folletos que no se vendían en las librerías, de volúmenes que la policía había retirado de las Bibliotecas. A la sombra de paredes roídas por la humedad, entre telarañas y hollín, ellos consultaban los libros explosivos, discutían y tomaban notas, en noches como boca de lobo, a la luz de improvisados candeleros, hacían resúmenes, cambiaban ideas, leían, se

---

[33] Mario Vargas Llosa, 'Toma de posición', in *Contra viento I*, pp. 91–2 (p. 91).

> instruían, rompían con la burguesía, se armaban con la ideología de la clase obrera. (p. 84)

> [Forbidden books, forbidden magazines and Santiago could see shelves overflowing with pamphlets that weren't sold in bookstores, volumes that the police had taken out of libraries. In the shadow of walls gnawed by dampness, through cobwebs and mildew, they consulted the explosive books, argued and took notes, on nights which were as dark as the mouth of a wolf, in the lights of improvised candelabras they made résumés, exchanged ideas, read, taught each other, broke with the bourgeoisie, armed themselves with the ideology of the working class.] (p. 72)

At San Marcos University his idealized, romantic concept of revolution is confronted by the tedious reality of a clandestine group he forms with other students, who are from the working-class background he dreams of. He falls in love with the Communist student Aída, fascinated to discover a woman who has more to offer than 'the pretty little idiots from Miraflores'. But he soon finds out that he actually does not know anything about party politics: 'decidió no soy bustamantista, no soy aprista, soy comunista. ¿Pero cuál era la diferencia?' (p. 73) [he decided I'm not a Bustamantist, I'm not an Aprista, I'm a Communist. But what was the difference?] (p. 62). And he is appalled by the censure that his co-conspirators want to impose on his readings: instead of Kafka's *The Castle*, which he liked, they want him to appreciate the socialist work by Ostrovski, *The Making of a Hero*, which he found utterly boring. Santiago finds himself unable to submit to the rules and rituals of the group's meetings:

> Siempre te olvidabas de tu seudónimo, Zavalita, siempre que eras secretario de actas y que debías resumir la sesión anterior. Lo hizo rápidamente, sin ponerse de pie, en voz baja. ... Los informes, piensa, los largos monólogos donde era difícil distinguir al objeto del sujeto, los hechos de las interpretaciones y las interpretaciones de las frases hechas. (p. 191)

> [You were always forgetting your pseudonym, Zavalita, forgetting you were recording secretary and were to give the minutes of the last meeting. He did it rapidly, without standing up, in a low voice. ... The reports, he thinks, the long monologues where it was hard to distinguish object from subject, facts from interpretations, and interpretations from clichés.] (pp. 170–1)

He soon realizes that his intellectual scepticism – a typically bourgeois feature, as his rival for Aída, Jacobo, points out – makes him just as much of an outsider in this circle as in his family surroundings. He is unable to adopt Marxist ideology without questioning, and feels ashamed not to believe in its absolute truth:

Cerrar los ojos, el marxismo se apoya en la ciencia, apretar los puños, la religión en la ignorancia, hundir los pies en la tierra, Dios no existía, hacer crujir los dientes, el motor de la historia era la lucha de clases, endurecer los músculos, al liberarse de la explotación burguesa, respirar hondo, el proletariado liberaría a la humanidad, y embestir: e instauraría un mundo sin clases. No pudiste, Zavalita, piensa. (p. 114)

[Closing your eyes, Marxism rests on science, clenching your fists, religion on ignorance, sinking your feet into the earth, God doesn't exist, grinding your teeth, the motive force of history was the class struggle, hardening your muscles, when it freed itself of bourgeois exploitation, breathing deeply, the proletariat would free humanity, and attacking: and set up a world without classes. You couldn't, Zavalita, he thinks.] (pp. 100–1)

When the students finally make contact with the forbidden Communist Party, the others become party members without hesitation. Only Santiago refuses to commit himself totally and asks to work for the party without having to join. The doubts and scepticism depicted in Santiago Zavala's inability to subscribe to a political doctrine reflect a problem that is not yet explicitly discussed in Vargas Llosa's essays of the late 1960s. Later on, however, it becomes a recurring issue in his fictional as well as his non-fictional writing. The questioning of an ideology as a 'single truth' anticipates a major topic of Vargas Llosa's later novels *La guerra del fin del mundo* and *Historia de Mayta* [*The Real Life of Alejandro Mayta*],[34] suggesting that Santiago's inner conflict echoes Vargas Llosa's own growing doubts about ideologies and their truth claims at a time when he still pronounced himself to be a socialist and firm supporter of Cuban politics. Under the surface of *Conversación* and its critical depiction of a politically corrupt society, there is therefore a sense of disillusionment with ideology that does not appear openly in Vargas Llosa's non-fictional texts until much later.

Santiago's naive kind of idealism does not survive the confrontation with political reality. But his disillusionment goes deeper when he realizes that his father, whom he had turned into his negative role model, in reality does not fit into his simple categories of good and bad. Fermín Zavala is not only corrupt, but also takes part in a conspiracy against the government. And he is not only the smooth businessman and father of a family, but also a sad closet homosexual who abuses his chauffeur. Santiago's schematic thinking is shattered by these ambiguities while, at the same time, he finds himself unable to live up to his own expectations. Reality turns out to be far more complicated than he had thought. Santiago's ideal of 'purity' collapses and

---

[34] Mario Vargas Llosa, *Historia de Mayta* (Barcelona:Seix Barral, 1984); Mario Vargas Llosa, *The Real Life of Alejandro Mayta*, trans. Alfred MacAdam (London: Faber and Faber, 1986).

gives way to a perception of reality as 'una montaña de mierda' (p. 377) [a whole mountain of shit] (p. 344), of 'excrementos, charcas pestilentes' (p. 16) [excrement, stinking puddles] (p. 9), in which an amoral manipulator like the aptly named Cayo Mierda is able to thrive. The prevailing filth – literally and metaphorically – makes it impossible to remain pure. The situation in Peru now appears as an inscrutable squalor of corruption, evil, filth and depravity affecting everybody and everything: 'ni tú ni yo teníamos razón papá', Santiago says in his inner monologue at the beginning – and the chronological end – of the novel, 'es el olor de la derrota papá' (p. 23) [neither you nor I was right, papa, it's the smell of defeat, papa] (p. 15). The colour symbolism and strong visual descriptions of *La casa verde* are continued in *Conversación*, with additional sensory elements: the bar where Santiago and Ambrosio talk 'huele a sudor, ají y cebolla, a orines y basura acumulada, y la música de la radiola se mezcla a la voz plural, a rugidos de motores y bocinazos, y llega a los oídos deformada y espesa' (p. 21) [smells of sweat, chili and onions, urine and accumulated garbage and the music from the jukebox mingles with the collective voice, the growl of motors and horns, and it comes to one's ears deformed and thick] (p. 14). Images of dilapidation, dirt and wretchedness are combined with disgusting smells, noises and repulsive colours, excrement being the main point of comparison: 'Un gran canchón rodeado de un muro ruin de adobes color caca —el color de Lima, piensa, el color del Perú' (p. 15) [A broad yard surrounded by a run-down, shit-coloured adobe wall – the color of Lima, he thinks, the color of Peru] (p. 8).

Totally disillusioned, Santiago settles for a mediocre existence as a news reporter, thus sacrificing his literary as well as his political ideals, since journalism is 'the grave of poetry', in the words of his friend Carlitos, himself a failed writer. Unauthentic writing without conviction marks the collapse of Santiago's ideals, and the corruption of his standards: 'Vengo temprano, me dan mi tema, me tapo la nariz y en dos o tres horas, listo, jalo la cadena y ya está' (p. 10) [I get in early, they give me my topic, I hold my nose, and in two or three hours all set I [pull the chain] and that's it] (p. 4).[35] The promising adolescent 'supersabio' [Superbrain] has turned into Zavalita, the thirty-year-old 'cacógrafo' [cackographer]. *Conversación en la catedral* is a novel of lost illusions, depicting the disappointment and lack of orientation caused by the loss of juvenile ideals and expectations, the slowly dissolving certainty of what is good and bad, and the gradual loss of a firm belief in a positive model for a just, egalitarian society. It is a perspective for the future that has been lost in Lima's eternal misty rain: 'Miraflores, Lima, la

---

[35] I've revised the published translation because the English translator seems to have missed the metaphor of defecation – of pulling the toilet's chain – which is part of the novel's metaphors of excrement.

miserable garúa de siempre' (p. 28) [Miraflores, Lima, the same miserable drizzle as always] (p. 20).

***

The bleakness of Vargas Llosa's portrayal of Peruvian society in the 1950s, with its protagonist Santiago Zavala who, by choice, had manoeuvred himself into a dead end, could not be developed much further. *Conversación* had to be the culmination of the depressive and pessimistic tone that had characterized Vargas Llosa's fictional work so far, where a corrupt society leaves its mark on the individual and quashes every attempt to rebel or be different. Perhaps the writer himself had to break out of this circle of novels describing a stagnant world of injustices and violence from which there is no escape. The development in the late 1960s of his literary theory of the writer's demons which are exorcized in fiction coincided with the banishment of the worst experiences and fears of his youth into literature. (The sheer amount of traumatizing personal experiences that have gone into Vargas Llosa's first novels becomes clear in his memoirs, *El pez en el agua* [*A Fish in the Water*],[36] which will be discussed later.) For the time being, *Conversación* had helped to exorcize the personal demons of lost illusions in Santiago's exemplary failure. The degree of structural complexity of Vargas Llosa's novels had also reached a peak from which it would have been difficult to continue without a change in direction. His study of Gabriel García Márquez's work, the 1971 *Historia de un deicidio* [History of a Deicide], made him analyse the workings of humour in fiction, possibly an important factor in his change of mind regarding its inclusion in realist fiction: talking about his novels of the 1970s, Vargas Llosa suggested that a useful criterion for dividing his work into different phases other than by their political commitment or their technical complexity would be his discovery of humour.[37] In a lecture at Syracuse University in 1988 he described how he tried to write a serious novel using a story he had heard in the Amazon jungle about a mobile brothel organized by the military to serve their men in remote posts (*A Writer's Reality*, pp. 85–6). But he discovered that a serious treatment of this topic would have made it incredible, and that humour and parody were needed to provide the necessary power of persuasion to the narrative, which appeared in 1973 as *Pantaleón y las visitadoras*. Unlike his other novels, which he says cost him enormous

[36] Mario Vargas Llosa, *El pez en el agua. Memorias* (Barcelona: Seix Barral, 1993); Mario Vargas Llosa, *A Fish in the Water. A Memoir*, trans. Helen Lane (London: Faber and Faber, 1995).

[37] Roland Forgues, 'La especie humana no puede soportar demasiado la realidad', in Michel Moner, *Les avatars de la première personne et le moi balbutiant de 'La tía Julia y el escribidor', suivi de 'La especie humana no puede soportar demasiado la realidad': entrevista a Mario Vargas Llosa por Roland Forgues* (Toulouse: Institut d' Études Hispaniques et Hispano-Americaines, 1983), pp. 67–80 (p. 67).

efforts to write, *Pantaleón* gave him great pleasure and flowed out of his pen with ease, a completely new experience in his creative life. Once he had discovered humour in writing, he was as excited and inspired as a child with a new toy.[38] Nevertheless he is disappointed with critics who see his humorous novels of the 1970s as 'lighter' works of entertainment, written in a popular vein for a broader market. Instead, he says, *Pantaleón* is 'probably the book in which I have been most conscious of form, of the purely technical aspects of the creation of the novel' (*A Writer's Reality*, p. 104), which is plausible since his interest in literary theory and criticism had intensified in the years leading up to its publication. We will see how this novel, instead of abandoning the experimentation with form and language as is often said, takes it to a new dimension.

After the excruciating self-questioning and existential doubts of Santiago Zavala with his lack of conviction in all areas of life, the protagonist of the new novel represents the complete opposite: Pantaleón Pantoja, captain in the administration of the Peruvian army, is born to receive orders, as he says himself, which he fulfils with total conviction, making whatever task he is entrusted with his own – in a way that borders on fanaticism: 'Un sentido de la obligación malsano, igualito a una enfermedad. Porque no es moral sino biológico' (*Pantaleón*, p. 217) [A sense of the unhealthy obligation, same as a sickness. Because it's not moral but biological] (*Captain Pantoja*, p. 168). His assignments literally get into his system: in the past, he had become obsessed with food when he was responsible for rations, and with tailoring and clothes when put in charge of uniforms. His new assignment is a secret mission to set up a Special Service of 'Visitadoras' [visiting 'Specialists'] based in Iquitos, a mobile unit of prostitutes who would provide their services in an orderly manner so that the soldiers in the jungle would no longer attack local women. 'Un oficial sin vicios' (p. 13) [An officer without vices] (p. 3), Captian Pantoja is entrusted with organizing vice – one of the many contrasts and clashes of the irreconcilable that the novel uses to comic effect. His sense of duty is absolute, and he believes to the letter what he learnt at cadet school, 'que no hay misión que no ofrezca dificultades y que no hay dificultad que no pueda ser vencida con energía, voluntad y trabajo' (pp. 50–1) [that there is no mission without its difficulties and that there are no difficulties that cannot be conquered by energy, will power and work] (p. 33). Without questioning the unusual order, the chameleon-like Captain Pantoja accepts his new role which he has to conceal from his wife and mother, who move to Iquitos with him believing that he is working for the intelligence service and therefore has to keep his affiliation to the army a secret.

The action of the novel unfolds in the 'selva', the Amazon jungle that was already the setting of *La casa verde*. The time frame is indicated in

---

[38] See Forgues, p. 67.

the dispatches that Pantoja sends to his superiors in Lima: his assignment lasts three years, from 1956 to 1959. The political background of the time, however, is not mentioned, apart from references to the corrupt police in Iquitos. The military world with its hierarchy and its machismo once more comes into focus in this novel, but the criticism of this institution does not happen by exposing its malfunctioning or abuse of power, but by irony: the sheer efficiency of Captain Pantoja erodes the system from the inside. Without wanting to, his sense of duty and his absolute obligation to serve end up subverting the system. In a methodical manner, he acquaints himself with his new field of work by visiting brothels and making contact with pimps and madams, doing exhaustive research into sexual needs and habits by devising questionnaires, analysing statistical data and drawing up charts, trying to establish 'desired normal mean times' of service duration, setting up a 'logistics centre' and organizing the facilitation of 'utilization activities'. Doing everything in his power to fulfil his order rationally and systematically, he succeeds in turning the Special Service into 'el organismo más eficiente de las Fuerzas Armadas' (p. 225) [the most efficient unit of the armed forces] (p. 174), as his superiors state with astonishment – which then causes more problems than it set out to solve. Demand for its services grows and grows, and so does the envy of civilians and military personnel not entitled to use the Special Service. This in turn causes violent incidents. The success of Pantoja's mission has produced a dynamic of its own, also in his private life: his identification with his 'corps' of prostitutes becomes so great that he falls for one of the new 'recruits', the beautiful 'Brazilian'. His overcorrect bureaucratic behaviour becomes eroded by human weakness: the attempt to exert control over physical needs and irrational desires by military organization is put into question, and the realm of the instinctive starts to contaminate the sphere of discipline. The quasi-'biological' sense of obligation that Captain Pantoja develops in his tasks leads, in this case, to his wife leaving him with their newborn daughter.

In his absolute devotion to the armed forces, Pantoja is comparable to Lieutenant Gamboa of *La ciudad*. Both men's unquestioning belief in the military code of conduct collides with their superiors' corrupt manoeuvres, and both soldiers end up being punished for sticking to their principles. But whereas Gamboa's failure is tragic because it represents a moral defeat, Pantoja's is comic since he becomes hopelessly entangled in a moral maze. He feels a deep sense of responsibility for his prostitute 'recruits', and when the Brazilian gets killed in an ambush by envious civilians he appears at her funeral in full uniform, paying tribute to her as a soldier fallen in action, serving her country. He does not understand why his superiors advise him to request his discharge from the Army after this incident. An example of the bureaucratic 'deformation of the mind' (*A Writer's Reality*, p. 91), Pantoja has lost any sense of judgement. This protagonist is an early manifestation

– and an extreme, grotesque case – of the specialization and fragmentation of knowledge, the lack of insight into the bigger picture, that Vargas Llosa will go on to criticize in many non-fictional texts, including his Nobel Lecture. Captain Pantoja refuses to leave the army and also declines the offer by his collaborators to turn the immensely successful Special Service into a private enterprise: 'esto lo organicé por orden superior, como negocio no me interesa. Además, yo necesito tener jefes. Si no tuviera, no sabría qué hacer, el mundo se me vendría abajo', p. 294; 'I organized this at the orders of my superiors; as a business it doesn't interest me. Besides, I need to have bosses. If I didn't, I wouldn't know what to do, the world would fall out from under my feet', p. 231). The irony arises from the contrast between the initiative and shrewd sense of business he shows in executing an almost impossible task, and the total dependency on his superiors for giving him a specific order upon which he can focus his single-mindedness. Punished for the overzealous execution of this particular assignment, he accepts a transfer to a remote post in the Andes (just like Gamboa). The end of the novel hints to the fact that he pursues his new orders there with the same kind of fanatical attitude. His wife with whom he is reunited complains: 'No sé por qué tienes que ir tú mismo a ver los desayunos de los soldados, maniático' (p. 309) [I don't know why you have to go yourself to see the soldiers' breakfast, you maniac] (p. 244). With its last words – 'son las cinco. Despierta, Panta' (p. 309) [it's five o'clock already. Wake up, Panta] (p. 244) – the novel refers back to the very first words at the beginning: '—Despierta, Panta ... Ya son las ocho' (p. 11) [Wake up, Panta! ... It's eight o'clock already] (p. 1), a circular structure which, in this case, has a comic effect since it underlines that Pantaleón Pantoja is incorrigible in his Quixotic zeal.

Set against this military fanatic and the hilarious story of his Special Service is the serious but no less outrageous, over-the-top story of the religious fanatic Brother Francisco, founder of the Brotherhood of the Ark, whose obsession with crucifixions attracts a large following and equally spins out of control. Religion and sex, the Church and the brothel set against each other, is a motif developed from *La casa verde* and its antagonism between Anselmo and Father García, between the Green House and the Catholic nuns of the mission. But here it takes on the form of a parallel crescendo of fanatical behaviour which leads both prostitution service and religious movement towards excess and inevitable cataclysm. Just like Pantaleón Pantoja, Brother Francisco is obsessed with a single idea, redemption through death on the cross, taken out of context and followed through with an absurd determination that completely goes against common sense and morality. His preachings do not really have a message, but his imagery is powerful which guarantees him a large following amongst the uneducated inhabitants of the Amazon region: he addresses his followers while suspended from a cross, with torches lighting the scene, and asks them to kneel down at his feet. He blends Christ's suffering on the cross with pagan rituals of sacrifice and incites his followers to crucify animals. What starts with insects, mice and other small animals soon turns to human beings: a child is crucified and becomes a saint in the popular imagination. The sect grows, and the rituals become more and more gruesome, with the so-called Brothers and Sisters drinking and bathing in the blood of the 'martyrs'. In the end Brother Francisco, hunted down by the authorities, dies on a cross he has erected for himself in the jungle. The report of his death, soon turned into legend, is intercalated with Pantoja's departure from Iquitos, thus establishing a comic parallel between the two contrasting protagonists, both fanatics in their own way, both inspirational to their disciples and a threat to public order for the authorities. The following dialogue fragments juxtapose different prostitutes reporting the religious leader's death with some of Pantoja's collaborators reporting the prostitutes' regret about Pantaleón's departure, the captain's own words, and those of his mother (the words of the Chinese Porfirio are transcribed with the customary parodistic exchange of the letters *r* and *l*):

—Y a las 'hermanas' que se revolcaban llorando, les decía pónganse contentas, más bien, allá he de seguir con ustedes, 'hermanitas'.
—Las chicas siempre lo repiten, señor Pantoja —abre la portezuela del camión, sube y se sienta Chuchupe—. Nos hace sentir útiles, orgullosas del oficio.
—Las dejó mueltas cuando les anunció que se iba —se pone la camisa, se instala en el volante, calienta el motor el Chino Porfirio—. Ojalá en el nuevo negocio podamos enchufales ese optimismo, ese espílitu. Es lo fundamental ¿no? ...
—Adiós Pantilandia, hasta la vista río Itaya. Arranca, Chino.
—Y dicen que en el mismo momento que murió se apagó el cielo, eran sólo las cuatro, todo se puso tiniebla, comenzó a llover, la gente estaba ciega con los rayos y sorda con los truenos ... Los animales del monte se pusieron a gruñir, a rugir, y los peces se salían del agua para despedir al Hermano Francisco que subía.
—Ya tengo hecho el equipaje, hijito —sortea bultos, paquetes, camas deshechas, hace el inventario, entrega la casa la señora Leonor—. (pp. 296–7)

['And to the "sisters" who were rolling around and crying, he said be happy, because up there I shall be with you, my little sisters.'
'The girls say it over and over, Mr Pantoja,' Chuchupe opens the truck door, gets in, sits down. '"He makes us feel useful, proud of our work."'
'It really killed them when you said you wele going,' Chino Porfirio puts on his shirt, gets behind the wheel, warms up the motor. 'I hope we can give 'em that optimism, that spilit, in new business. ...'
'Goodbye, Pantiland, so long, Itaya River. Step on it, Chino.'
'And they say the same moment he died the light went out of the sky, it was only four o'clock, everything got dark, it began to rain, the people

were blinded by the lightning and deafened by the thunder ... The animals on the mountain began to grunt, to bellow, and the fish came out of the water to bid farewell to Brother Francisco, who was ascending.'

'I've already packed the suitcases, son,' Mother Leonor shuffles bundles, packages, unmade beds, takes inventory, gives up the house.] (pp. 233–4)

The prostitutes are as devoted to Pantoja as they are to their religious leader: 'Usted es un genio,' Chino Porfirio tells him, 'Todas las chicas lo dicen: encima del señol Pantoja, sólo el Hemano Fancisco' (p. 293) [You ale a genius ... All the gils say so: only Blothel Flancisco above Mistel Pantoja] (p. 231). The irony created by this juxtaposition becomes even greater when some of the women who used to work in the Special Service become 'Sisters of the Ark' and vow chastity. The intermingling of the two opposite poles of religion and brothel reaches its climax when, in the final chapter, Father Beltrán, the military chaplain who vigorously opposed the 'carnal commerce' sanctioned by the military and resigned from the army due to his moral outrage, is seen enjoying the services of one of the former Specialists ('No olvides las bolitas, Peludita' [Don't forget my balls, Peludita], p. 305/p. 241). The hypocrisy exposed here is a recurring theme in Vargas Llosa's work, but it has never been caricatured in such a subversive way. The same prostitute turns out to be servicing General Scavino, the army commander of the Amazon region, while he is declaring his relief that:

> —En fin, en fin, las dos pesadillas de la Amazonía terminaron de una vez por todas —se desabotona la bragueta el general Scavino—. Pantoja mutado, el profeta muerto, las visitadoras hechas humo, el Arca disolviéndose. Esto va a ser otra vez la tierra tranquila de los buenos tiempos. Unos cariñitos en premio, Peludita. (p. 304)

> ['At last, at last, the two nightmares of the Amazon ended once and for all,' General Scavino unbuttons his fly. 'Pantoja silenced, the prophet dead, the specialists up in smoke, the Ark dissolving. This will be the peaceful country of the good old days once again. A little affection as a prize, Peludita.'] (p. 240)

The fact that both general and priest talk about going back to the good times before the crisis caused by the Special Service and the Ark, and then reveal in the last sentence that their words are addressed to the ex-Specialist whose services they use – obviously not for the first time – is a scathing attack on military and church, disguised by humour.

Situational humour is one of the facets of comedy that Vargas Llosa uses to great effect in *Pantaleón*. The military leadership, for instance, seems ridiculous in their various attempts to control their soldiers' libido. Before devising the Special Service, they had asked a Swiss doctor to introduce a diet that would weaken the men's sex drive – with catastrophic results for their health: soldiers fainted and died of tuberculosis and hunger. Exaggeration, as in this case, is one of the most frequent strategies in creating the novel's humoristic tone. Another comic situation arises when Pantaleón and his wife, unaware of freelance prostitutes going around Iquitos offering their services as 'washerwomen', misunderstand this offer and invite one of them into their bedroom. Pantaleón's thorough research into his new area of work allows for other comic situations such as when he times the duration of his own lovemaking at home. Pantoja's need to recruit suitable prostitutes calls for a military inspection of a troupe of women, who have to take off their clothes and present themselves in formation. The clash of two completely incongruous worlds produces hilarity. In another situation it is Pantoja's total loss of reality that makes him suggest armed protection for the Special Service which increasingly comes under threat from attackers, a suggestion which is perfectly logical in his partial way of thinking, but provokes the comment by one of his superiors: 'La compañia entra en zafarrancho de combate para que los números cachen en paz, puta qué cómico' (p. 221) [The base gets into combat condition, so the soldiers can screw in peace. Hell, how funny it all is!] (p. 171). But Pantoja does not see the funny side because, as he says himself, 'No tengo sentido del humor' (p. 134) [I don't have a sense of humor] (p. 103). That he takes himself so seriously makes him particularly funny.

Captain Pantoja goes so far as to suggest a 'risk bonus' for the Specialists, an example of the novel's verbal humour created through the use of bureaucratic terms in a totally unsuited context; this kind of wordplay abounds in the novel. Military or bureaucratic terms have a comic effect when referring to sexual activities: after a successful 'pilot project', 'convoys' of Specialists go out to 'utilization centres' in the jungle. Pantoja undertakes a 'market estimate' and an 'efficiency analysis' to predict a prostitute's 'operational capacity'. He instils pride in his employees as 'civilian functionaries' of the Army, not traffickers in sex. And he adopts a hymn for the Special Service, a caricature of an upbeat song that soldiers sing when they march off into battle: 'En la tierra, en la hamaca, en la hierba/Del cuartel, campamento o solar/Damos besos, abrazos y afines/Cuando lo ordena el superior' (p. 157) [On the cots, in the dirt or the grasses/Of the campsites and the field grounds deploying/When our Captain says 'Now, girls, start serving!'/Ticket-holders get serviced in mass (*sic*)] (p. 119), not quite so funny in the English translation.

Verbal humour also manifests itself in names. The captain's first name, Pantaleón, evokes the figure of Pantalone in the Italian *commedia dell'arte*. Various people modify this name: for his wife and his mother he is Panta or Pantita, as if he were a little boy (four chapters start with the captain being woken by either his wife or his mother, who treat him like a child). His troupe of women soon call him affectionately 'señor Pan-Pan', and what he labels his 'logistics centre' acquires the popular name Pantilandia. The Brazilian makes a mockery of his vain attempts to keep private and professional life separate by calling him 'señor Pantita'. Apart from Pantaleón Pantoja there are more names that show a playful use of alliteration or repeated sound, such as Chuchupe and Chichi, the generals Sarmiento Segovia and López López, and the 'Cuerpo de Capellanes Castrenses (CCC)' [Corps of Military Chaplains], the alliteration being lost in English. The excessive use of acronyms by the military is another source of humour. The Special Service, 'Servicio de Visitadoras para Guarniciones, Puestos de Frontera y Afines', is referred to in documents as 'SVGPFA' – not exactly memorable in the way that acronyms should be.

Other instances of verbal humour derive from the different uses of language in the novel's ten chapters, divided into dialogue and documents. Chapters consisting entirely of dialogue (numbers 1, 5, 8 and 10) are combined with others containing radio broadcasts or documents such as military dispatches, a number of private letters, newspaper articles, and the transcription of dream sequences. This patchwork of voices, using different levels of language, forms part of Vargas Llosa's attempts to make the narrator of his novels disappear. Having the story tell itself through documents also allows him to parody the style of these different texts. The reports that Pantoja sends to his superiors create hilarity by the contrast between their use of the formalistic, bureaucratic language of military dispatches and their content, his progress in finding a solution for the sexual needs of the soldiers stationed in the jungle. The clash between form and content is particularly funny in a dispatch marked 'Top Secret', which deals with the experiments the captain undertook on himself, testing locally known aphrodisiacs that might have contributed to the problem of increased libido. He reports:

> Que a partir del segundo día el suscrito experimentó un aumento brusco del apetito sexual, acentuándose la anomalía en los días sucesivos al punto de que en los dos últimos de la semana, los malos tocamientos y el acto viril fueron las únicas reflexiones que ocuparon su mente, tanto de día como de noche (sueños, pesadillas), con grave perjuicio de su poder de concentración, sistema nervioso en general y efectividad en el trabajo. (p. 89)

> [That starting with the second day the undersigned experienced a sudden increase in sexual appetite, the abnormality accentuating itself on the following days to the point that on the last two days of the week dirty thoughts and the virile act were the only ideas occupying his mind, as much during the day as at night (dreams, nightmares), with serious detriment to his power of concentration, his nervous system in general and his effectiveness at work.] (p. 66)

He signs off this dispatch, as all the others concerned with sexual matters, with the totally inappropriate 'Dios guarde a Ud.' [God bless you] and never forgets to include receipts (for drinks he had to consume, pornographic material he had to buy, etc.).

A different perspective on Pantoja's sexual self-experimentation can be found in the letter that his wife Pocha writes to her sister Chichi (chapter 3), a parody of 'girls' talk', colloquial and intimate, full of gossip and allusions to things that she cannot possibly mention – only to do so in the next sentence (the rhetorical figure *paralipse*): 'me parece haber cambiado de marido y no sólo por eso (uy, qué vergüenza, Chichi, eso sí que no me atrevo a contártelo)' (p. 67) [it seems to me I've switched husbands and not just because of that. (Oh, I'm so embarrassed, Chichi, so much I really wouldn't dare tell you)] (p. 47). Pocha's long letter represents an uninterrupted flow of language, and with its unreflected and immediate quality it blurs the border between oral and written communication.

The dream sequences included in chapters 2, 3 and 7 are a parody of Freudian dream interpretation and take the sexual imagery of the novel to a grotesque level. They contain the nightmares that Pantoja mentions in the dialogue-based chapters, induced by the rising tension in his life to keep his private and his professional world apart. Although narrated in the third person, perhaps by Pantaleón who observes himself in these dreams from the outside, as a different person, they render emotions and sensations from the inside. In these nightmares people from one sphere of Pantoja's life invade the other sphere, and different events merge into one (illustrating Freud's concepts of condensation and displacement): the 'madam' Chuchupe turns into his mother in one dream, his wife Pocha turns out to be one of the prostitutes in another. Well-known motifs from Freud's writings are alluded to: the wolfhound turns up in a troupe parade, the fear of wetting (humiliating) himself and being found out is there, the figure of the mother looms large, people have doubles, there are any amount of metamorphoses, and there is a whole nightmare about haemorrhoids where the anal theme is grotesquely exaggerated. Asked about the role of Freudian psychoanalysis in his writing, Vargas Llosa has stated that he read Freud with great pleasure, despite having grave reservations about psychoanalysis as a system: 'Algunos de los casos clínicos descritos por Freud son para mí piezas literarias extraordinarias más que trabajos científicos, unos piezas de una extraordinaria imaginación' [Some of the clinical cases described by Freud are for me extraordinary literary pieces rather than scientific works, pieces of an extraordinary imagination].[39] In the dream sequences, the already grotesque assignment obliging Pantoja to lead a double life turns into an even more surreal nightmare, where all the spheres of his existence merge into one horrible fantasy, culminating in the gong that beats deafeningly in his ears in the last sequence – which,

---

[39] Vargas Llosa in his interview with Forgues, p. 73.

ironically, turns out to be his mother waking her 'hijito' [little son], urging him to rise and get on with his life.

Another sort of text parodied in the novel is radio journalism. Throughout the book we find broadcasts by the local radio station's popular commentator 'el Sinchi', a hypocritical and corrupt journalist who pompously declares himself to be the voice of 'Truth and Justice'. But he changes his opinions several times in the course of the novel, depending on who bribes him for his public support. His programmes are full of hyperbolic rhetoric and false patriotism: he denounces the Special Service as 'peruanicidio' (p. 191) [Peruvicide] (p. 147) and does not miss an opportunity to praise Iquitos, 'our beloved city', as the pearl of the Amazon region, 'esta progresista ciudad' (p. 189) [this progressive city] (p. 146). His stereotypical language includes clichés such as 'el llanto es a una dama lo que el rocío a las flores' (p. 203) [Weeping is to a lady what dew is to flowers] (p. 157). But what he excels at is finding epithets that work on his hearers' emotions: in his false outrage he calls Pantoja 'el Gran Macró de la Amazonía' [the Great Pimp of the Amazon], 'el Califa de Pantilandia ... con toda su caravana de odaliscas en subasta' (p. 191) [the Caliph of Pantiland ... with his entire caravan of odalisques sold at auction] (p. 147), and denounces 'las escabrosas actividades del Barba Azul del río Itaya' (p. 201) [the scabrous activities of the Bluebeard of the Itaya River] (p. 155). Having whipped up public opinion against Pantoja, he changes his tone after the Brazilian's funeral, adapting to the popular mood: '—Entre el contento de unos y las lágrimas de otros, odiado y querido por la ciudadanía dividida ... partió a Lima, por vía aérea, el discutido capitán Pantaleón Pantoja. Lo acompañaban su señora madre y las emociones controvertidas de la población loretana' (p. 300) [Amidst the rejoicing of some and the tears of others, hated and beloved by a divided citizenry ... the much-discussed Captain Pantoja left for Lima by air. He was accompanied by his mother and the conflicting emotions of the people of Loreto] (p. 236). The emotionally effective use of antitheses, a popular rhetorical device, is combined with a laughable *zeugma*, where one verb serves two objects which are not quite on the same level (the mother and the conflicting emotions).

A different form of journalism is parodied in chapter 9. The whole story of the Brazilian's death is narrated through the documents and comments published in a special edition of the daily newspaper *El Oriente*. These texts use all the clichés of journalistic writing: flowery language, sensationalist headlines ('El crimen de la Quebrada del Cacique Cocama, minuto a minuto: su cortejo de sangre, pasión, sadismo necrofílico e instintos desbocados' [Blow-by-blow Account of the Crime at Cacique Cocama Bend: Its Cortege of Blood, Passion, Necrophiliac Sadism and Base Instincts], p. 255/p. 198) and exaggerations, for example when the editor-in-chief of this small, provincial newspaper becomes 'el conocido periodista de prestigio internacional'

(p. 273) [the well-known journalist of international reputation] (p. 215). His questioning by police 'viniera a engrosar la adiposa lista de víctimas de la libertad de prensa' (p. 273) [swell[s] the list of martyrs for freedom of the press] (p. 215). The newspaper also prints the speech that Captain Pantoja delivered at the murdered prostitute's burial, a parody of a funeral oration, full of pathos, where every paragraph starts with the refrain-like 'Llorada [lamented] Olga Arellano Rosaura'. Highlighting the prostitute's generous services to the courageous soldiers of Peru, Pantoja's speech finishes with a totally out-of-place personal note: 'déjame darte las gracias más profundas, poniendo el corazón en la mano ... por tantas enseñanzas íntimas que nunca olvidaré' (p. 254) [allow me, laying bare my heart, to thank you profoundly ... for so many intimate lessons that I shall never forget] (p. 198). Such a loss of decorum, which produced the comic effect in the dispatches where Pantoja divulged all kinds of personal details in bureaucratic tone, also accounts for the tragicomedy that turns this funeral oration into the 'most widely read speech in the history of this country', as one general remarks: 'La gente recita párrafos de memoria, se hacen chistes sobre él en las calles' (p. 304) [The people are reciting paragraphs by heart, they make jokes about it on the street] (p. 240).

The most interesting technical experimentation of this innovative novel is the way that background information is not actually narrated but condensed into the so-called 'acotaciones', the reporting phrases that accompany dialogue and qualify what is said in direct speech. This happens in chapters 1, 5, 8 and 10 which are made up of multiple dialogues intermingled in a technique of montage that here, unlike in other Vargas Llosa novels, is not so much telescopic but continuous. The montage used in these chapters creates a broad tapestry of voices, without a sense of transition between the different dialogues. Conversations between different people blend in and out in a smooth manner, without the abrupt crosscutting known from previous works, and create a 'plural dialogue', as Vargas Llosa has described his intention (*A Writer's Reality*, p. 93). The effect is not one of disturbing fragmentation or a clash of opposites, but of a continuum of multiple voices complementing each other, sometimes explaining causal connections in a very condensed manner. At other times, this technique has a comic effect: an intimate scene between Pantoja and his wife is juxtaposed with a dialogue between the captain and general Scavino: '—Pellízcame en la orejita. Así, asisito. Ay, ya siento que me muero, chola, ya no sé quién soy. —Sé muy bien quién es usted y a qué viene a Iquitos —murmura el general Roger Scavino' (p. 22) ['Nibble my ear. Like that, just like that. Ahh, I already feel like I'm coming. Oh, babe, I can't tell who I am.' 'I know very well who you are and why you've come to Iquitos, mutters General Roger Scavino'] (p. 10).

The effect of a continuum is supported by extended reporting phrases which condense all the essential circumstantial information that the reader needs into a couple of words between dialogue, thus avoiding what Vargas Llosa calls the 'dead language' of explanations (*A Writer's Reality*, p. 95). Developed in *Pantaleón* to include background information without interrupting the dynamics of the novel, this strategy works in various ways. It enhances the immediacy of the situation: '—Estoy de acuerdo con usted, tiene que creerme —suda, ve empaparse los brazos de su uniforme, implora el capitán Pantoja—' (p. 23) ['I agree with you, you have to believe me,' Captain Pantoja sweats, sees the sleeves of his uniform getting wet, implores] (p. 11).[40] In other instances, this strategy condenses time, describing a series of actions in one small fragment of a conversation, such as Mother Leonor arranging the new house in Iquitos: '—Qué secreto militar ni qué ocho cuartos —ordena roperos, cose visillos, desempolva pantallas, enchufa lámparas la señora Leonor—. ¿Secretos con tu mamacita? Cuenta, cuenta' (p. 29) ['I don't give a damn about military secrets,' Mother Leonor puts closets in order, sews curtains, dusts screens, plugs in lamps. 'Secrets from your mother? Tell me, tell me'] (p. 16). A further example of this condensing effect is at the end of the novel, where Pantoja gets increasingly obsessed with his feverish activities: '—Podríamos comenzar con un equipo seleccionado de diez visitadoras para oficiales, mi general —habla solo por la calle, se queda dormido en su escritorio, fantasea, aterra a la señora Leonor con su flacura el capitán Pantoja—' (p. 245) ['We could begin with a corps of ten specialists for officers, General, sir,' Captain Pantoja talks to himself on the street, falls asleep at his desk, fantasizes, terrifies Mother Leonor with his thinness] (p. 189). Other 'acotaciones' function as a supplement to dialogue in the manner of stage directions:

> —Le juro que mis sentimientos personales por esa visitadora no han influido en lo más mínimo en este asunto —enrojece, siente brasas en las mejillas, tartamudea, se hunde las uñas en la palma de las manos el capitán Pantoja—. Si en vez de ella la víctima hubiera sido otra, habría procedido igual. Era mi obligación.
> —¿Su obligación? —chilla con alegría, se levanta, pasea, se detiene ante la ventana, ve que llueve a cántaros, que la bruma oculta el río el general Scavino—. (p. 285)

['I swear to you that my personal feelings for that specialist did not have the least bearing on the matter,' Captain Pantoja reddens, feels flames in his cheeks, stammers, digs his fingernails into his palms. 'If instead of her the victim had been some other specialist, I would have proceeded in the same way. It was my duty.'

---

[40] What we see here applies to all the quotations that follow: the effect in Spanish is produced by placing the subject of the reporting phrase at the very end, something that the English translation cannot render.

'Your duty?' General Scavino screeches out with joy, stands, paces, stops in front of the window, sees that it's raining cats and dogs, that the fog hides the river.] (p. 224)

This versatile technique is able to produce visualization, perspectivization, exaggeration, and even a telescopic condensation of past events, for instance when one of the Specialists gives an account of Brother Francisco's death while the reporting phrase – in the present tense! – goes back to the scene when she had taken her baby to the preacher while he was still alive: '—Y dicen que no dio ni un grito, ni soltó una lágrima ni sentía dolor ni nada —lleva al Arca a su hijo recién nacido, pide al apóstol que lo bautice, ve al niño lamer las gotitas de sangre que vierte el padriño Iris' (p. 295) ['And they say he didn't even cry out, didn't shed one tear, didn't feel pain or nothing,' Iris carries her recently born son to the Ark, asks the apostle to baptize him, sees the boy lick up the droplets of blood his godfather spills] (p. 232). This innovative use of time contributes to the impression of a continuum in which events on different levels of time and space blend into each other.

Pantaleón shows many continuities in themes and techniques from earlier novels which Vargas Llosa will develop further in later works. A religious preacher and a fanatic military leader will become the central figures of *La guerra del fin del mundo* (1981). In *Pantaleón*, Vargas Llosa's experiments with form and language take some interesting new turns, and the discovery of humour and parody distinguish this 1973 novel in the large body of his work. His next novel will continue a number of elements introduced here, above all the parody of journalistic writing, especially radio broadcasts, and the light-hearted, humorous tone of the narrative which will be extended to include self-irony.

***

La tía Julia y el escribidor [*Aunt Julia and the Scriptwriter*][41] appeared in 1977, two years after Vargas Llosa's work on Flaubert, *La orgía perpetua* [*The Perpetual Orgy*], where he states: 'Una novela ha sido más seductora para mí en la medida en que en ella aparecían, combinadas con pericia en una historia compacta, la rebeldía, la violencia, el melodrama y el sexo' (*Orgía*, p. 20) [The greater the role that rebellion, violence, melodrama, and sex, expertly combined in a compact plot, have played in a novel, the greater its appeal has been to me].[42] Vargas Llosa would now turn the characteristics

---

[41] Mario Vargas Llosa, *La tía Julia y el escribidor* (Barcelona: Seix Barral, 1986); Mario Vargas Llosa, *Aunt Julia and the Scriptwriter*, trans. Helen R. Lane (London: Picador, 1984).
[42] Mario Vargas Llosa, *The Perpetual Orgy. Flaubert and 'Madame Bovary'*, trans. Helen Lane (London: Faber and Faber, 1987), pp. 11–12.

that made *Madame Bovary* so fascinating for him into an integral part of his own novel.

He tells the story of how the young aspiring writer Varguitas works as a news bulletin writer in Radio Panamericana, while at the same time aspiring to become a serious writer of fiction. Trying to find his own style, he composes but then dismisses any number of short stories. During this period he becomes acquainted with Pedro Camacho, writer of popular radio soap operas for the neighbouring Radio Central, who has no such doubts or hesitations about his own writing, inventing episodes for different serials at an incredible rate. Varguitas is intrigued by Camacho's prolific imagination and the way he is totally committed to his fiction-writing – until it transpires that the scriptwriter can no longer keep his different story-lines separate. His frantic way of work causes him to lose the plot, literally and metaphorically, at which point Varguitas has to step in and take over.

Varguitas's double process of learning – in the field of love and of literature, hence the duality of the title – is set against the backdrop of 1950s Lima, but this time seen from the ironic distance of a first-person narrator with the connotation 'Mario Vargas Llosa' (Varguitas is called Marito by his family), whom we learn in the final chapter is a mature and successful writer of fiction. It is the first of Vargas Llosa's metafictional works, where writer-protagonists and the process of writing itself become the main subject matter of the novel. It is also the first time he uses undisguised autobiographical material: the novel is dedicated to his first wife Julia Urquidi Illanes, the sister-in-law of his uncle and ten years older than him, whom Vargas Llosa married when he was eighteen (although the age difference between the two is exaggerated to underline the scandalous nature of the liaison, and Marito never ceases to refer to her as 'aunt Julia' to playfully imply an incestuous nature to their relationship).[43]

In *La orgía perpetua* Vargas Llosa had highlighted duality as the main organizing principle of Flaubert's novel. The underlying dual patterns of his own previous fictions – military and city life in *La ciudad y los perros*, Piura and the jungle in *La casa verde*, army and religion in *Pantaleón* – develop into the main organizing structure of *La tía Julia*: apart from the last, epilogue-like chapter, the novel's twenty chapters alternate between a first-person narration of events surrounding the two radio stations and Varguitas's relationship with Julia and Pedro Camacho (in the odd-numbered chapters),

---

[43] Humour, self-referentiality, pastiche of popular fiction, and the playful use of autobiography have engendered a large number of studies focusing on this novel. For example, see *Actes du colloque Manuel Puig/Mario Vargas Llosa. Les Cahiers de Fontenay* (Paris: ENS Éditions, 1982), Moner, *Les avatars de la première personne*, and Liliana Tiffert Wendorff, *Camacho, c'est moi: parodia social y géneros literarios en 'La tía Julia y el escribidor'* (Lima: Editorial San Marcos, 2006).

and a narrated, synoptic version of the scriptwriter's radio episodes (in the even-numbered ones). This structure of alternating chapters will become a recurring feature of Vargas Llosa's fiction. Here it establishes a regular interchange between 'reality' and 'fiction' (as two levels within the novel), between the 'true' world of a protagonist who resembles the author, and the 'lies' that his fellow writer Pedro Camacho invents for mass entertainment. This set-up includes a switch between two different styles: the realistic, ironic mode of the narrative about Varguitas's double apprenticeship in matters of love and literature alternates with the comically elaborated, stereotypical style in which the radio episodes are rendered. But once the dual principle is established and the reader has come to expect a continuous switch between the two levels of narration and the two styles, the borders between these distinctly different elements of the narrative begin to blur. An amusing game of parallels and contrasts develops in which events on the realistic level take on the quality of melodramatic fiction, and the style of the radio broadcasts invades communication in 'real' life. The difference between the two contrasting writer-protagonists also diminishes when Varguitas takes Camacho's way of immersing himself in writing as a model for himself. The dividing line between realistic literature and melodrama, between reality and fiction becomes undermined. This even stretches so far as to trivialize the dictator Odría whose oppressive regime cast such a paralysing shadow over Santiago Zavala, the writer-protagonist in *Conversación*. Here we find the authoritarian President turned into a fan of Pedro Camacho's radio serials: 'El General, como las cuestiones de gobierno no le daban tiempo para oírlos durante el día, se los hacía grabar y los escuchaba cada noche, uno tras otro, antes de dormir. La Presidenta en persona se lo había contado a muchas señoras de Lima' (*La tía Julia*, pp. 202–3) [Since affairs of state didn't allow him time to hear them during the day, the General had tape recordings made and listened to them, one after another, each night before he went to sleep. The President's wife herself had personally reported this to a great many ladies in Lima] (*Aunt Julia*, pp. 167–8).

With *La tía Julia* Vargas Llosa introduces self-irony into his writing: the literary concepts that he developed in his works on García Márquez and Flaubert are simultaneously exemplified and parodied, and the seriousness with which the young writer-protagonist tries to live up to his role as writer and intellectual is gently mocked. The derision of 1950s Peruvian society for the profession of writer, which was hinted at in the sarcasm of the generals towards Alberto's 'novelitas' in *La ciudad*, and which prevented Santiago Zavala in *Conversación* from becoming the writer that he wanted to be, is turned into mild, inconsequential mockery here: '—El no piensa en faldas ni en jaranas —le explicó mi tío Lucho—. Es un intelectual. Ha publicado un cuento en el Dominical de "El Comercio" —Cuidado que el hijo de Dorita nos vaya a salir del otro lado —se rió la tía Julia y yo sentí un arrebato de solidaridad con su ex-marido' (p. 17) ['He's not thinking about skirts or about sprees,' my Uncle Lucho explained to her. 'He's an intellectual. He's had a short story published in the Sunday edition of *El Comercio*.' 'We'll have to watch out that Dorita's boy doesn't turn out to be a queer, in that case.' Aunt Julia laughed, and I suddenly felt a wave of fellow feeling for her ex-husband] (p. 8).

The short stories that the aspiring writer produces are overly influenced by his 'cultural demons'. He tries to emulate the style of the great masters, sometimes attempting 'algo ligero y risueño, a la manera de Somerset Maugham, o de un erotismo malicioso, como en Maupassant' (p. 63) [something light and entertaining, in the manner of Somerset Maugham, or perversely erotic, as in Maupassant] (p. 47). Other times he envisages 'un relato espartano, preciso como un cronómetro, al estilo de Hemingway' (p. 203) [a Spartan story, as precise as a chronometer, in the manner of Hemingway] (p. 168), whereas another anecdote calls for something 'frío, intelectual, condensado e irónico como un cuento de Borges' (p. 59) [as coldly objective, intellectual, terse, and ironic as one of Borges's stories] (p. 44). Varguitas's excessive self-criticism, however, is a reminder of Flaubert's perfectionist attitude: 'Escribía y rompía, o, mejor dicho, apenas había escrito una frase me parecía horrible y recomenzaba' (p. 59) [I wrote and then tore up what I wrote, or rather, the moment I'd written a sentence it struck me as absolutely dreadful and I began all over again] (p. 44). As subject matter of his stories he uses anecdotes that he reads or hears about, turns them into texts which he then reads to his friend Javier, a sort of alter ego, or to Julia. These are stories within the story of Marito, Julia and Pedro Camacho – in addition to the melodramatic stories of the radio episodes which are intercalated with the 'realistic' level of the narration – and illustrate Vargas Llosa's favourite technique of 'Chinese boxes'. Literature and life become intertwined, but also literature and love. Marito tells his future wife the story of how he will one day be a writer living in Paris:

> Le conté toda mi vida, no la pasada, sino la que tendría en el futuro, cuando viviera en París y fuera escritor. Le dije que quería escribir desde que había leído por primera vez a Alejandro Dumas, y que desde entonces soñaba con viajar a Francia y vivir en una buhardilla en el barrio de los artistas, entregado totalmente a la literatura, la cosa más formidable del mundo. (pp. 108–9)

> [I told her the whole story of my life – not my past life, but the one I was going to have in the future, when I lived in Paris and was a writer. I told her I'd wanted to write ever since I'd first read Alexandre Dumas, that since that moment I'd dreamed of going off to France and living in a garret, in the artists' *quartier*, dedicating my heart and soul to literature, the most marvelous thing in the world.] (p. 87)

This is a dazzling game of mirrors and reflections, in which the author makes the first-person narrator of the 'autobiographical' chapters narrate how, in the past, he told Julia his future life as a writer in Paris, that he had envisaged ever since his first encounter with literature in the remote past, and which, for the grown-up narrator, as well as the author, is already a past fact of his life – a fitting illustration of the novel's epigraph taken from Salvador Elizondo's 'El grafógrafo' (quoted in full at the end of chapter 1 above): 'Escribo. Escribo que escribo. ... Y me veo recordando que me veo escribir y ... puedo imaginarme escribiendo que ya había escrito que me imaginaría escribiendo' etc. etc. [I write. I write that I am writing. ... And I see myself remembering that I see myself writing and ... I can also imagine myself writing that I had already written that I would imagine myself writing].

The game of mirrors continues on many levels: one of Varguitas's stories illustrates the blurring of reality and fiction and has the title 'El salto cualitativo', 'qualitative leap' being one of the main literary devices that Vargas Llosa defines as crucial for fiction writing. Another of the author's theoretical concepts which are exemplified and parodied at the same time are the 'elementos añadidos', the elements added to an anecdote that turn it into literature. Varguitas reads Julia a literary text based on a story she told him:

> La experiencia fue catastrófica para la suceptibilidad [*sic*] del futuro escritor. A medida que progresaba en la lectura, la tía Julia me iba interrumpiendo:
> —Pero si no fue así, pero si lo has puesto todo patas arriba —me decía, sorprendida y hasta enojada—, pero si no fue eso lo que dijo, pero si ...
> Yo, angustiadísimo, hacía un alto para informarle que lo que escuchaba no era la relación fiel de la anécdota que me había contado, sino *un cuento, un cuento*, y que todas las cosas añadidas o suprimidas eran recursos para conseguir ciertos efectos:
> —Efectos *cómicos* —subrayé, a ver si entendía y, aunque fuera por conmiseración, sonreía.
> —Pero, al contrario —protestó la tía Julia, impertérrita y feroz—, con las cosas que has cambiado le quitaste toda la gracia. (pp. 151–2)

[The experience had a devastating effect on the susceptibility of the future writer.
As I read on, Aunt Julia kept interrupting me.
'But it wasn't like that at all, you've turned the whole thing topsy-turvy, that wasn't what I told you, that's not what happened at all ...' she kept saying, surprised and even angry.
I couldn't have been more upset, and broke off my reading to inform her that what she was listening to was not a faithful, word-for-word recounting of the incident she'd told me about, but *a story, a story*, and that all the things that I'd either added or left out were a way of achieving certain effects: '*Comic* effects,' I emphasized, hoping she'd see what I was getting at. She smiled at me, if only out of pity for my misery.

'But that's precisely the point,' she protested vehemently, not giving an inch. 'With all the changes you've made, it's not a funny story at all any more.'] (p. 123)

Even though Julia accepts all kinds of improbable developments in the soap operas she loves, she protests against the fictionalization of her story through literary techniques such as the dilation of time: 'Quién se va a creer que pasa tanto rato desde que la cruz comienza a moverse hasta que se cae' (p. 152) [What reader is going to believe that such a long time goes by between the moment the cross begins to teeter and the moment it comes crashing down?] (p. 123) – at which point Varguitas passionately defends 'los derechos de la imaginación literaria a transgredir la realidad' (p. 152) [the rights of literary imagination to transgress reality] (p. 124). These discussions function as an ironic illustration of Vargas Llosa's ideas about narrative techniques and literature's special kind of 'truth' which he had established in his non-fictional texts of the early 1970s.[44]

His concept of a deep-rooted rebelliousness at the bottom of any literary vocation also plays a role in *La tía Julia*. Varguitas's opposition to his parents and especially to his father in wanting to marry the divorcee Julia at the age of eighteen and become a professional writer goes against the expectations and pressures of his family: 'la familia se hacía ilusiones, ... yo era la esperanza de la tribu. Era verdad: mi cancerosa parentela esperaba de mí que fuera algún día millonario, o, en el peor de los casos, Presidente de la República' (pp. 204–5) [the family had great expectations for me ... I was the hope of the tribe. It was true: that cancerous family of mine had every expectation that I'd be a millionaire someday, or at the very least President of the Republic] (p. 169), a very amusing anticipation of what would happen to Vargas Llosa in real life, and an unintentional instance of the novel's play with reality and fiction. Varguitas's desire to become a serious writer is hampered by his various day jobs, but he realizes that 'la única manera de serlo era entregándose a la literatura en cuerpo y alma. ... Lo más cercano a ese escritor a tiempo completo, obsesionado y apasionado con su vocación, que conocía, era el radionovelista boliviano' (p. 236) [the only way to be one was to devote oneself heart and soul to literature. ... The person I'd met who

---

[44] In an astonishing continuation of the novel's game with reality and fiction, the real Julia Urquidi Illanes was not amused by the publication of *La tía Julia y el escribidor*. She complained about the distortions of their story – just as the Julia of the novel protests against the literary version of the story she told Marito for not representing the truth – and published her own, 'true' version of events: Julia Urquidi Illanes, *Lo que Varguitas no dijo* (La Paz: Khana Cruz, 1983), translated into English by Catherine R. Perricone as *My Life with Mario Vargas Llosa* (New York: Peter Lang, 1988). She was particularly upset that a Bolivian TV company gained the rights to turn the novel into a 'telenovela' [TV soap opera], where the incestuous element of their relationship was much more emphasized, and less ironic, than in the book.

came closest to being this full-time writer, obsessed and impassioned by his vocation, was the Bolivian author of radio serials] (p. 195).

In his attitude to work Pedro Camacho incarnates Varguitas's (and Vargas Llosa's) ideal: 'Vivir era, para él, escribir' (p. 159) [For him, to live was to write] (p. 130). He spends nine or ten hours a day writing his trivial melodramas, unaffected by what is going on around him, and unhindered by doubts or self-criticism. In complete contrast to Varguitas he does not read at all in order to keep his style 'authentic'. He sees himself as a true artist, even though his radio episodes represent a schematic and oversimplified world-view: 'Me gustan el sí o el no, los hombres masculinos y las mujeres femeninas, la noche o el día. En mis obras siempre hay aristócratas o plebe, prostitutas o madonas. La mesocracia no me inspira y tampoco a mi público' (p. 65) [I like a straightforward yes or no, masculine men and feminine women, night or day. In my works there are always blue bloods or the hoi polloi, prostitutes or madonnas. [Mediocrity] doesn't inspire me or interest me – or my public, either] (pp. 49–50). Varguitas notices that the scriptwriter's interest in the extremes – 'millonarios y mendigos, blancos y negros, santos y criminales' (p. 65) [millionaires or beggars, blacks and whites, saints and criminals] (p. 49) – links him to the Romantics, but in his self-satisfied and sententious way Camacho rejects that idea: '—En todo caso, ellos se parecen a mí. ... Nunca he plagiado a nadie' (p. 65) [In point of fact, *they're* like *me* ... I've never plagiarized anybody] (p. 50). His total lack of humour makes him a worthy successor to Pantaleón Pantoja, protagonist of the previous novel, with whom he also shares the fanatical dedication to his 'mission'. Varguitas observes with 'mystical rapture' how Camacho inspires the actors who interpret his soap operas with his zeal, 'con la voz fanática del hombre que está en posesión de una verdad urgente y tiene que propagarla, compartirla, imponerla' (pp. 122–3) [he spoke in the fanatical voice of a man in possession of an urgent truth that he must disseminate, share, drive home] (p. 99). The absolute conviction that Camacho feels for his work has a transfixing, bewitching effect on the people he works with. Like Pantoja he is extremely methodical in fulfilling his task at hand: in order to ensure the truthfulness of his radio dramas he has drawn up a map of Lima classifying various districts according to their social status, using acronyms such as 'MPA (Mesocracia Profesionales Amas de casa)' for Jesús María, or 'VMMH (Vagos Maricones Maleantes Hetairos)' for La Victoria (p. 64) [MCLPH (Middle Classes Liberal Professions Housewives) ... BFHH (Bums Fairies Hoodlums Hetaerae)] (p. 49). His reasoning for this 'artistic, not scientific' classification is that he wants to represent reality the way it is: 'mis obras se aferran a la realidad como la cepa a la vid ... Lo más importante es la verdad, que siempre es arte y en cambio la mentira no, o sólo rara vez' (p. 64) [my writings are firmly rooted in reality, as the grapevine is rooted in vinestock ... What is most important is the truth, which is always art, as lies, on the other hand, never are, or only very rarely] (p. 48). Considering Vargas Llosa's insistence on the 'truth of lies' which is always different from referential truth, this makes Pedro Camacho the caricature of a realist writer.

The parody of this literal understanding of realism and the concept of mimesis becomes grotesque when Varguitas finds Camacho at work wearing disguises that allow him to identify with his characters while writing. He takes the idea of role-play (one of the recurring themes in Vargas Llosa's fiction with its many impostors) to the extreme, not unlike Pantaleón Pantoja and his 'biological' identification with his job: '¿Que mejor manera de hacer arte realista que identificarse materialmente con la realidad?' (p. 164) [What better way is there of creating realistic art than by materially identifying oneself with reality?] (p. 135). And so Pedro Camacho transforms himself into a sailor, a judge, an old lady, a beggar, a cardinal, etc. – the whole personnel of his soap operas. This total commitment to his 'art' translates into the soap operas and makes them totally compelling for his public. His own fanaticism is mirrored in the fanatical protagonists of his melodramas, such as the preacher who threatens to castrate himself to prove that he is innocent of rape (chapter 6), or the vermin catcher in chapter 8 who becomes completely obsessed with extinguishing rats. The even-numbered chapters, each containing a different melodrama, all end with a 'cliffhanger', an unresolved, open end creating suspense.

Pedro Camacho's imaginative plots turn out to be rooted in his own experiences and obsessions, a parody of Vargas Llosa's theory of the 'personal demons' as material for fiction. The rat episode derives from his fear of rodents in his own apartment; his dislike of children echoes in his melodramas; and his xenophobic remarks about Argentinians, in his soap operas as well as in his everyday life, turn out to be a reaction to his unhappy marriage with a woman from that country. By process of exaggeration and augmentation Camacho turns his own 'demons' into fiction. The abundance of fifty-year-old protagonists, each one of them introduced as having reached 'la flor de la edad, la cincuenta' [the prime of life, his fifties] and distinguished-looking in a stereotypical way – 'frente ancha, nariz aguileña, mirada penetrante, rectitud y bondad en el espíritu' [broad forehead, aquiline nose, a penetrating gaze, the very soul of rectitude and goodness] – reflect his fear of ageing: 'el artista había dogmatizado, con fuego, sobre los cincuenta años del hombre. La edad del apogeo cerebral y de la fuerza sensual, decía, de la experiencia digerida. La edad en que se era más deseado por las mujeres y más temido por los hombres' (p. 73) [Camacho had held forth, dogmatically and eloquently, on the subject of the man in his fifties. The age at which his intellectual powers and his sensuality are at their peak, he had said, the age at which he has assimilated all his experiences. That age at which one is most desired by women and most feared by men] (p. 56). Camacho's categorical statements and grand gestures show that he is unable to tell reality and fiction apart.

Despite being minute, he challenges big men to a fight, and when asked about his love life he claims it is very rich and rewarding, but that he has never actually loved a woman of flesh and blood.

The scriptwriter's delusions and his obsessive work habits take their toll. The already quite ludicrous plots of his melodramas involving incest, murder, phobias and other extreme behaviour start to become confused (from chapter 10 onwards). Protagonists from one radio serial pop up in another; they change names, professions and even their gender: ironically it is a character called Lituma – like the protagonist of various Vargas Llosa novels – who goes through the most outrageous metamorphoses, ending as Madre Lituma, before being killed off several times, in a number of the different catastrophes that Pedro Camacho invents to finish off the radio serials that he can no longer keep under control. These mixed-up stories represent a nightmare scenario that Vargas Llosa had already described in *Historia secreta de una novela*, when he was writing *La casa verde* and tried to keep the two different story lines separate. But while he found a way of creatively interconnecting the stories of Piura's Green House and the jungle, the scriptwriter-protagonist's creations take on a destructive life of their own. An additional ironic twist that Vargas Llosa gives to Pedro Camacho's intermingling of his melodramas is the reaction of some of the listeners who interpret the mix-ups as clever 'modernist' or 'existentialist' ploys, 'a stroke of genius'.

In parallel with the increasingly catastrophic developments in Camacho's radio episodes, the love story between Julia and Varguitas becomes more and more melodramatic. The couple's attempts to find a mayor or priest who would marry them despite the missing consent of Marito's parents takes on the quality of an episodic drama. The language in which they talk about their relationship is also that of the radio melodramas: 'En vista de lo ambiguo y extravagante de nuestro romance, jugábamos a bautizarlo: "noviazgo inglés", "romance sueco", "drama turco"' (p. 112) [Realizing how ambiguous and offbeat our relationship was, we made a game of thinking up amusing names for it and called it our English engagement, our Swedish romance, our Turkish drama] (p. 90). Varguitas finds himself on an emotional roller-coaster ride, 'poseído de sentimientos encontrados: desasosiego, cólera, tristeza, ganas de abofetear a la tía Julia y de besarla' (p. 325) [overcome by contrary emotions: anxiety, anger, sadness, a desire to slap Aunt Julia's face, and a desire to kiss her] (p. 269). His mother reacts to their elopement with a melodramatic outburst of crying: 'Hijito, cholito, amor mío, qué te han hecho, qué ha hecho contigo esa mujer' (p. 408) [My baby, my little darling, my treasure, what have they done to you, what has that woman done to you?] (p. 339) and Varguitas tries to calm her down by saying: 'Mamacita, no empieces otra vez con tus radioteatros' (p. 423) [Mama dearest, don't begin another of your radio serials] (p. 353). Meanwhile his father threatens to shoot him 'like a dog'. The only plot line that is missing from Pedro Camacho's soap operas, that of a melodramatic love story, is covered by the narrative of Julia and Marito on the 'realistic' level of the book. Realism and melodrama not only exist side by side, they influence each other and are mutually dependent. Popular fiction in all its forms, including the melodramatic Mexican films that Julia and Marito love to watch, turns out to be part of reality. Qualifications such as 'le ocurrió algo de película' (p. 316) [like a double take in a film] (p. 262) and 'como en una buena película de suspenso' (p. 240) [as in a good suspense film] (p. 199) show that fiction is part of life. (When Marito first meets the much older Julia they go and see a Mexican melodrama called *'Madre y amante'* [Mother and Lover], alluding to their possibly ambiguous relationship.)[45]

Varguitas, the well-read and ambitious apprentice writer, has to take over the job as scriptwriter of trivial, clichéd melodramas with their mass appeal, since the public demands a continuation of the radio serials which are so much part of their lives. As one of the actors puts it: '¿qué haría la gente sin nosotros? ... ¿Quienes les dan las ilusiones y las emociones que los ayudan a vivir?' (p. 281) [what would people do without us? ... Who else gives them the illusions and emotions that help them to go on living?] (p. 233). This is of course exactly the function that Vargas Llosa ascribes to literature in his theoretical texts. In the novel, Varguitas has to make the symbolic move from his own office at the top of the building to Camacho's workplace which the scriptwriter insisted be at street level – a move from the heights of highbrow fiction to the level of the people on the streets. Varguitas's new challenge represents the fusion of serious and popular literature that Vargas Llosa finds so appealing in some of his favourite nineteenth-century writers:

> From a cultural point of view the richest moments in civilization, in history, have occurred when the boundaries separating popular and creative literature disappear, and literature becomes simultaneously both things – something that enriches all audiences, something that can satisfy all kinds of mentalities and knowledge and education, and at the same time is creative and artistic and popular: Dickens, Hugo, and Dumas are extraordinary cases in point. (*A Writer's Reality*, p. 116)

---

[45] In *La orgía perpetua* Vargas Llosa admits: 'no soporto el melodrama literario en estado puro —el cinematográfico sí, y es posible que esa debilidad mía haya sido forjada por el melodrama mexicano de los años cuarenta y cincuenta que frecuenté viciosamente y que todavía añoro; en cambio, cuando una novela es capaz de usar materiales melodramáticos dentro de un contexto más rico y con talento artístico, como en *Madame Bovary*, mi felicidad no tiene límites' (p. 26) [I cannot bear literary melodrama in its pure state (though I am a devotee of melodramatic movies, and it may well be that this weakness of mine stems from the Mexican films to which I was addicted in the forties and fifties, and for which I still feel a keen nostalgia). When a novel is capable of using melodramatic materials within a broader context and with artistic talent, as is the case in *Madame Bovary*, my joy knows no bounds] (*Orgy*, p. 17.)

La tía Julia y el escribidor is an example of such a creative and at the same time popular novel which is enjoyable on many different levels. The novel's metafictional layer complements Vargas Llosa's writings on literary theory and criticism in a humorous and illustrative manner. The playful use of a number of genres – melodrama, autobiography, radio serials, *Bildungsroman*, metafiction – points ahead to Vargas Llosa's experimentation with different genres in the works of the 1980s.[46] But it is the following novel that takes his ambition to combine popular and creative, artistic fiction to a new level.

---

[46] Other critics draw parallels with the chivalric novel (Raymond Leslie Williams, *Mario Vargas Llosa* [New York: Ungar, 1986]) and the picaresque novel (Rosemary Geisdorfer Feal, *Novel lives: The fictional Autobiographies of Guillermo Cabrera Infante and Mario Vargas Llosa*, Chapel Hill: University of North Carolina, 1988). In an interview with José Miguel Oviedo in Charles Rossman and Alan Warren Friedman (eds.), *Mario Vargas Llosa. A Collection of Critical Essays* (Austin: University of Texas Press, 1978), pp. 152–65 (p. 164), Vargas Llosa has revealed that he considered the picaresque title 'Vida y milagros de Pedro Camacho' [Life and Wonders of Pedro Camacho]. The novel also parodies Freudian psychoanalytical writings: the incest motif, for example, plays a prominent role, on the 'realistic' level as well as in the radio dramas, whose protagonist Richard from chapter 2 ends up, through confusion of the various episodes, having incestuous relationships with his sister, daughter and mother. The radio episode in chapter 10 contains a caricature of psychiatric treatment. On the 'realistic' level, Varguitas declares his intention to compose one of his short stories as 'una fantasía freudiana' (*La tía Julia*, p. 71) [a Freudian fantasy] (*Aunt Julia*, p. 55). Roy C. Boland, whose study of Vargas Llosa is based on Freudian concepts, insists: 'such references to Freud, although patently burlesque, may also be interpreted as an invitation to the reader to once again play the role of mock-psychologist and attempt to decipher and interpret the Freudian symbolism in which Marito's two-fold dilemma is couched: to wield his penis like a man and to brandish his pen like a writer'. Roy Charles Boland, *Mario Vargas Llosa: Oedipus and the 'Papa' State. A Study of Individual and Social Psychology in Mario Vargas Llosa's Novels of Peruvian Reality. From 'La ciudad y los perros' to 'Historia de Mayta'* (Madrid: Editorial Voz, 1990), p. 108.

6

Towards the Total Novel:
La guerra del fin del mundo (1981)

Published in 1981, *La guerra del fin del mundo* [*The War of the End of the World*][1] is in many regards the central work of Vargas Llosa's oeuvre. The novel shows important continuities of motif and technique with the works published so far, but combines them with major new concerns that have evolved out of Vargas Llosa's intellectual, artistic and political development during the 1970s, concerns which will remain important in all of his later fiction. The 'demons' that have shaped his writing since the beginning of his career are present in *La guerra* in the form of religion and the military, the two main antagonistic forces in the war between a millenarian movement and the newly established republic in late nineteenth-century Brazil; journalism and the question of truth and lies in writing once more play an important part in this novel; and the relationship between idealism and fanaticism, a developing theme in the early work, becomes a central issue in *La guerra*. As in other works, the novel's structure supports its meaning: a system of parallels and contrasts plays a vital role in illustrating the similarity between opponents in the conflict at the centre of *La guerra*. Important narrative devices further underpin this interplay between form and meaning: perspectivization through multiple points of view becomes the crucial technique to emphasize mutual misunderstandings between all sides involved. Although *La guerra* is a much less experimental novel with an omniscient narrator, in some important cases free indirect style is used to give the reader an insight into a protagonist's mind. In addition to these features familiar from Vargas Llosa's previous work, the new novel is informed by his critical attitude towards ideologies since his rupture with the political Left after the Padilla Affair in Cuba in 1971. It also incorporates his thoughts on the nature of fiction, developed in his works of the 1970s on literary criticism and theory. Vargas Llosa's exploration of the ambiguous relationship between truth and lies in literature (or, in this case, historiography) and his concerns about the truths and lies of ideologies are the two major themes in *La guerra*. Following

---

[1] Mario Vargas Llosa, *La guerra del fin del mundo* (Barcelona: Plaza y Janés, 1982); Mario Vargas Llosa, *The War of the End of the World* (London: Faber and Faber, 1986).

on from this novel, metafictional and anti-ideological elements will recur in almost all of Vargas Llosa's fiction right up to the present day.

La guerra del fin del mundo is a novel on a grand scale that approaches the ideal Vargas Llosa had set for himself at the beginning of his career: the total novel, able to integrate questions of myth, history, religion, politics, military, sociology, ethics, love and sexuality into a story full of action and adventure. He regards *La guerra* as coming closest to this ideal: 'la sociedad que aparece es mucho más diversa y compleja que en cualquiera de mis otras novelas' [the society represented here is a lot more diverse and complex than in any of my other novels].[2] The novel best represents Vargas Llosa's ambition to bridge the gap between fiction that is entertaining, and thus able to reach a wide and diverse audience, and literature that is creative and innovative in expressing human experience in a historical and socio-political context. The work reflects his love for the nineteenth-century novel, which started in his childhood with Alexandre Dumas's *The Three Musketeers*, but Vargas Llosa had not yet found an opportunity to write his own great adventure story because his work had always been closely linked to his immediate concerns. *La guerra* is the first novel that is not set in his own country nor directly informed by his own experience of contemporary reality. It started as a project for the cinema: in 1972, the film director Ruy Guerra asked Vargas Llosa to write a script about the Canudos war in Brazil at the end of the nineteenth century, the historical rebellion of a socio-religious movement in the country's inhospitable north-east, the Sertão. Lead by the charismatic preacher Antônio Conselheiro, this movement provoked the young Brazilian Republic by rejecting its progressive reforms: the followers of the Consejero [Counselor], as he is called in *La guerra*, opposed civil marriage and the metric system, they refused to pay taxes or take part in a census since they were unable to understand these measures, and misinterpreted the Republic as the work of the Antichrist. Settling in the remote hamlet of Canudos, the growing number of supporters became a threat to the Republic who sent out troops to suppress the rebellious movement. The powerful resistance encountered by the forces of state convinced the Republic that it was confronted by a reactionary, monarchist conspiracy, aided by British agents and weapons. The two sides were thus equally blinded by their prejudices and fought each other with a hatred based on a complete lack of understanding. After a total of four military campaigns during the years 1896 to 1897, the rebellion was suppressed and Canudos and its inhabitants were annihilated.

Vargas Llosa discovered this extraordinary story at a time when he had been going through a deep crisis of his political beliefs and had come to experience the distortions that ideologies can impose on reality. This attracted

---

[2] Ricardo A. Setti, *... sobre la vida y la política: Diálogo con Vargas Llosa* (México: Kosmos Editorial, 1989), p. 55.

him to the story of Canudos which he perceived as an example of the dangers of Utopian and ideological world-views. But there was an additional factor for his fascination with the historical events, a famous work of Brazilian literature that he read for his initial information: *Os sertões* [*Rebellion in the Backlands*] (1902),³ written by Euclides da Cunha who had been an eyewitness of the final campaign against Canudos, became one of Vargas Llosa's great reading experiences,⁴ inspiring him to write his own novel when the film project was eventually dropped. *Os sertões* is not so much a novel as a hybrid form of essay, eyewitness report, chronicle of the military campaigns and scientific treatise, written in the spirit of positivism. As war correspondent, da Cunha discovered that the prejudices, half-truths and lies which he had previously helped to reproduce by his journalistic writing had nothing in common with the reality of Canudos: the religious fanatics were not conspirators wanting to re-establish monarchy, as he had believed, but destitute people of the backlands who had fallen under the spell of the charismatic Conselheiro. By writing *Os sertões* da Cunha tried to set the record straight and find an explanation for the violent clash between religious community and state. His deterministic explanatory model, influenced by the racial theories of his time, is based on a broad positivist account of nature and life in the Brazilian north-east and their influence on the mentality of its inhabitants, which made them prone to 'absorb the collective psychosis'⁵ that reigned Canudos. The case of da Cunha, a progressive intellectual whose firm convictions were shattered when he witnessed the crushing of the hopelessly outnumbered adversary by the Republic's united military forces, seemed to Vargas Llosa like a typical example of intellectuals in Latin America who 'have been responsible so many times for the conflicts and troubles Latin America has faced in its history ... promoting a kind of zealous and dogmatic interpretation of our society and our reality'.⁶ Vargas Llosa's reception of the Canudos story as a clash of ideological world-views, unable to understand or communicate with each other, makes it a subject matter in the line of his previous works where a microcosm (such as school, army, circle of friends) represented the macrocosm of the country: in this case Canudos becomes a paradigm of Latin America's past and present conflicts rooted in a mutual misunderstanding, as a consequence of fanaticized, ideologically distorted views of reality.⁷

---

³   Euclides da Cunha, *Os sertões* (Rio de Janeiro: Francisco Alves, 1982); translated in 1944 by Samuel Putnam as *Rebellion in the Backlands* (Chicago: University of Chicago Press, 1992).
⁴   See Setti, p. 41.
⁵   da Cunha, *Rebellion*, p. 148.
⁶   Mario Vargas Llosa, *A Writer's Reality* (London and Boston: Faber and Faber, 1990), pp. 124–5.
⁷   Vargas Llosa has always regarded Latin America as a unity, in which the shared

The fact that there is a literary model for *La guerra* makes it possible to see how Vargas Llosa's fictional version of the Canudos story differs from da Cunha's book which was intended to be a scientific explanation of the events. It becomes clear that Vargas Llosa's different evaluation of facts and people, his introduction of a fictional European character next to the historical ones, and the shifts in characteristics of certain historical personalities to others[8] is intended to create an autonomous fictional world, based on the historical events, but able to convey his strong anti-ideological convictions. Above all, he invents a whole layer of reality that is almost completely absent from the sources, that of the *yagunzos*,[9] the followers of the Consejero.

Vargas Llosa faced the challenge of adapting his language to a novel set in nineteenth-century Brazil, and of inventing dialogue which would actually have taken place in Portuguese. Dialogue is important between the educated protagonists, whose way of speaking he could more convincingly imitate than that of the religious fanatics. In the case of the *yagunzos*, by contrast, direct speech is rare, and Antonio Consejero's words are only ever related by an impersonal narrator, with an abundance of figures of repetition and enumeration mimicking the recurring patterns of his counsels and his ambulant lifestyle:

> Hablaba de cosas sencillas e importantes. ... Cosas que se entendían porque eran oscuramente sabidas desde tiempos inmemoriales y que uno aprendía con la leche que mamaba. Cosas actuales, tangibles, cotidianas, inevitables, como el fin del mundo y el Juicio Final, que podían ocurrir tal vez antes de lo que tardase el poblado en poner derecha la capilla alicaída. ... cosas prácticas, cotidianas, familiares, como la muerte, que conduce a la felicidad si se entra en ella con el alma limpia, como a una fiesta. (*La guerra*, p. 16)
>
> [He spoke of simple and important things. ... Things that were understandable because they had been vaguely known since time immemorial,

---

historical, social, political and cultural features are more important than national differences. In *A Writer's Reality* (p. 133) he points out that 'in contemporary Latin America you still have Canudos in many countries. In Peru, for instance, you still have Canudos in the Andes', referring to the conflict between state and Maoist guerrilla forces in the 1980s. In his 1976 inaugural speech as president of PEN International, Vargas Llosa had characterized the present as 'esta época de división e incomunicación' [this epoch of division and incommunication] (Mario Vargas Llosa, 'Mensaje al PEN Internacional', in *Contra viento y marea, I (1962–1972)* [Barcelona: Seix Barral, 1986], pp. 349–50 [p. 349]), using the same concepts as those used to characterize Canudos.

[8] For an excellent study of Vargas Llosa's use of the sources see Leopoldo M. Bernucci, *Historia de un Malentendido. Un Estudio Transtextual de 'La Guerra del Fin del Mundo' de Mario Vargas Llosa* (New York: Peter Lang, 1989).

[9] The English translation of Vargas Llosa's novel uses the Portuguese form 'jagunço'. For a discussion of the term see Robert M. Levine, *Vale of Tears: Revisiting the Canudos Massacre in Northeastern Brazil, 1893–1897* (Berkeley: University of California Press, 1992), pp. 62–70.

things taken in along with the milk of one's mother's breast. Present, tangible, everyday, inevitable things, such as the end of the world and the Last Judgment, which might well occur before the time it would take for the town to set the chapel with drooping wings upright again.] (*The War*, p. 4)

Inspired by da Cunha's role as a war correspondent, Vargas Llosa introduces an intellectual protagonist into his novel who in some respects represents the Brazilian writer: the nameless 'periodista miope' [short-sighted journalist] writes for a progressive newspaper and joins the third expedition against Canudos. Unlike da Cunha who accompanied the military during the final fourth campaign, Vargas Llosa makes his writer-protagonist witness the shocking defeat of the third expedition. But, lost in the general confusion following the crushing of the state forces, the journalist ends up inside Canudos, where he experiences life amongst the followers of Antonio Consejero during the final siege of the 'holy city'. In this respect he also represents Vargas Llosa himself who, in his imagined version of events, narrates partly from the point of view of the *yagunzos*. By inventing the rebels' perspective on the conflict, their motivations for following Antonio Consejero and their everyday life in the city under siege, *La guerra* complements the existing historiography about Canudos with an aspect of reality that is not documented anywhere (what Vargas Llosa calls 'La visión de los vencidos' [the view of the defeated]).[10] Where the sources present the conflict from the point of view of the victorious adversaries of Canudos, the impersonal, omniscient narrator in *La guerra* tells the story not only from the differing perspectives of the political parties, the military, the Church, the press and the general public, but also from inside the rebel city. This perspective exposes the attitudes of the various parties fighting against the rebellion as being based on lies and fantasies.

The short-sighted journalist survives his time in Canudos and returns to tell the truth about the *yagunzos*. He wants to write a book in which he intends to clear up all the misunderstandings that led to the war, and in this intention he resembles the author of *Os sertões* on whom he is modelled. But since the writer-protagonist is in the unique position of combining his perspective of an outsider with a view from inside Canudos, he even more represents Vargas Llosa himself who renders a 'total' picture of the conflict from all different perspectives to compensate for the one-sidedness of the historical version. Unlike da Cunha's attempt to explain the truth about Canudos, Vargas Llosa's aim is to question the notion of a single historical truth and uncover the many different truths and lies about the events: 'A mí eso es lo

---

[10] See Vargas Llosa's interview with José Miguel Oviedo, 'Historia de la historia de la historia: conversación en Lima', *Escandalar*, 3 (1980), 82–7.

que me apasionó más, y lo fui descubriendo a medida que estaba haciendo la investigación, que iba reuniendo la documentación: ver cómo Canudos era cosas tan distintas según la perspectiva desde la cual se contaba' [What was most exciting for me to discover during my research and documentation work was to see how Canudos meant so many different things depending on the perspective from which it was told].[11] Vargas Llosa turns this into one of the main subject matters of the novel: how historical reality can be interpreted or, most important, misinterpreted by looking at events from one angle only.

The use of multiple perspectives in *La guerra* has a relativizing effect: by seeing events from a multitude of points of view the reader realizes how distorted each of these views is. This is particularly striking in two instances where an event is told twice, from opposing perspectives: the defeat of the first expedition against Canudos in Uauá is narrated first from the military's point of view (in book 1, chapter 2, second section), and later on from the perspective of the *yagunzos* (book 1, chapter 5, first section). The second instance of this narrative technique concerns one of the most dramatic scenes in the novel, the fatal shooting of the leader of the third expedition, Moreira César, in book 3. In the first section of chapter 7, the reader perceives the events through the eyes of the short-sighted journalist, who looks down onto the scene of battle from the post of command on top of a hill. The journalist, totally ignorant of military strategy, observes the confusing battle in the town of Canudos down below as if looking onto a stage and becomes only gradually aware of the grave situation he is witnessing. In the following section the scene is narrated from the perspective of another neutral and inexperienced observer, Jurema, who finds herself in the trenches with the fiercest *yagunzo* Pajeú, and witnesses him shooting Moreira César. The strong visual element of this perspectivization is clearly linked to the original film project.

The novel's pluriperspectivism serves to reveal the fact that ideas about the rebellion are either distorted by an ideological perspective such as that of the Jacobin military leader Moreira César, the religious fanatic Antonio Consejero, or the Scottish anarchist and atheist Galileo Gall who sees Canudos as a realization of his anarchist dreams; or they are manipulated for a specific purpose, for example by ruthless politicians such as Epaminondas Gonçalves, whose hunger for power does not even stop at plotting to kill the red-haired Gall as a 'cadaver inglés', a body that would prove the presence of British spies working with the Monarchists. The press plays its own role in the manipulation of public opinion about Canudos. As the short-sighted

---

[11] Roland Forgues, 'La especie humana no puede soportar demasiado la realidad', in Michel Moner, *Les avatars de la première personne et le moi balbutiant de 'La tía Julia y el escribidor'*, suivi de *'La especie humana no puede soportar demasiado la realidad': entrevista a Mario Vargas Llosa por Roland Forgues* (Toulouse: Institut d'Études Hispaniques et Hispano-Americaines, 1983), pp. 67–80 (p. 79).

journalist explains: 'Lo importante en esas crónicas son los sobrentendidos. ... No lo que dicen, sino lo que queda librado a la imaginación' (p. 395) [The important thing in these dispatches are the intimations. ... Not what they say but what they suggest, what's left to the reader's imagination] (p. 416).

There are many different factions in this conflict which seems, on the surface at least, to be between the state and a religious sect. Canudos goes beyond the obvious dichotomy of a modern, central, secular Republic opposed to a traditional, regional community assembled around a charismatic religious leader: 'La guerra que ellos libraban era sólo en apariencia la del mundo exterior, la de uniformados contra andrajosos, la del litoral contra el interior, la del nuevo Brasil contra el Brasil tradicional' (p. 114) [The war that they were waging was only apparently that of the outside world, that of men in uniform against men in rags, that of the seacoast against the interior, that of the new Brazil against traditional Brazil] (p. 109). As in *La casa verde* [*The Green House*],[12] the interpretative model of civilization and barbarism is undermined. Within each of the two enemy camps there are many different interest groups. On the side of the state we find republicans as well as monarchist and autonomist politicians, but also supporters of the Jacobin ideology of a Dictatorial Republic. Meanwhile, the defenders of Canudos consist of the Sertão's poor population, fighting side by side with notorious bandits, the much-feared *cangaceiros*. The religious backland community also gains surprising support from the cosmopolitan Gall. Opposites dissolve: while the *yagunzos* anticipate twentieth-century tactics of warfare and manage to produce modern weapons such as explosive bullets with the primitive means at their disposal, the modern army falls back into barbaric rituals like cutting their enemies' throats.

The opponents themselves think in dualistic patterns. But despite their antagonism they actually resemble each other when it comes to fanaticism and intransigence. The religious community's reasoning is explained by the journalist: 'El Perro o el Padre, el Anticristo o el Buen Jesús. Sabían al instante qué hecho procedía de uno u de otro, si era benéfico o maléfico. ... Todo resulta fácil si uno es capaz de identificar el mal o el bien detrás de cada cosa que ocurre' (p. 361) [The Dog or the Father, the Antichrist or the Blessed Jesus. They knew immediately which of the two was responsible for any given event, whether it was a blessing or a curse. ... Everything becomes easy if one is capable of identifying the good or the evil behind each and every thing that happens] (p. 379). While the *yagunzos* feel they are part of an eternal struggle between good and bad, their adversaries understand the conflict as one based on recent political developments, viewing Canudos as a foreign-influenced attempt to destroy the newly established Republic and restore monarchy with

---

[12] Mario Vargas Llosa, *La casa verde* (Barcelona: Argos Vergara, 1980); Mario Vargas Llosa, *The Green House* (London: Picador, 1986).

the support of Britain. In manner equivalent to Antonio Consejero's simplifying dichotomy of a fight between God and the Devil, they see themselves defending the Brazilian Republic against a presumed British-led monarchist conspiracy. The war cry of the religious zealots 'muera la república, muera el Anticristo' [death to the Republic, death to the Antichrist] is answered by a similarly absurd 'muera Inglaterra' [death to England] from the military's side. Colonel Moreira César's point of view is different again, but it is no less reductive. For him his country can either achieve progress by establishing a military-led Dictatorial Republic without political parties, or else relapse into monarchy. The categories of European anarchist Galileo Gall are equally simplistic. He interprets everything in terms of the struggle against injustice and oppression, as serving either revolution or a class-based society. He supports the religious community because he thinks in Canudos his dream of a classless society has come true. His idea that Antonio Consejero uses a more 'primitive' religious code of God and the Devil in order to talk about oppression and class society exposes the arrogance of a European towards the inhabitants of the backlands as well as the delusions of a fanatic. Gall is convinced: 'En última instancia, los nombres no importaban, eran envolturas, y si servían para que las gentes sin instrucción identificaran más fácilmente los contenidos, era indiferente que en vez de decir justicia e injusticia, libertad y opresión, sociedad emancipada y sociedad clasista, se hablara de Dios y del Diablo' (p. 256) [In the last analysis, names did not matter; they were wrappings, and if they helped uneducated people to identify the contents more easily, it was of little moment that instead of speaking of justice and injustice, freedom and oppression, classless society and class society, they talked in terms of God and the Devil] (p. 264). Galileo Gall embodies a type that Vargas Llosa frequently criticizes in his non-fictional texts, the European intellectual who projects his hopes onto Latin America, unaware that his categories are inappropriate for understanding its reality.

The contradictory, simplistic world-views of all parties involved make it impossible to understand or communicate with each other. Each side sees only what it wants to see, so that the conflict turns into a battle between violently opposed fanatics who are nevertheless very similar in their reduction of reality to a single truth. The political meaning of the novel as criticism of ideologies grows out of this artfully created symmetry between the different distorting world-views. The worst fanatics in the novel, Gall, Moreira César and the Counselor himself, have in common not only that their motivations are idealistic, but also that they are prepared to use every means to pursue their goal: to bring change to people suffering from poverty and injustice. Gall wants to achieve this by abolishing private property, the army colonel by sacrificing freedom and establishing military rule; both of them are equally opposed to politicians, the landowning classes and the Church. The Counselor's method of alleviating the suffering of the poor is by giving meaning and dignity to their lives of deprivation, and making sense of the world for them: 'Les decía cosas que podían entender, verdades en las que podían creer' (p. 28) [He told them things that they could understand, truths that they could believe in] (p. 17). All three of these fanatics are 'puros', pure idealists in the sense that Vargas Llosa has given to that term: uninterested in money or other advantages for themselves, they live frugal and disciplined lives, exerting extreme self-control over their own physical needs all the better to pursue their goal. Antonio Consejero impresses the people of the Sertão with his ascetic looks, his seriousness and his capacity to exist on very little food and sleep. Even the snakes seem to respect him during his hours of praying, lying on the hard ground, so that his myth rapidly grows: 'Cuando el hombre partía, se hablaba de él: que era santo, que había hecho milagros' (p. 17) [When the man left, there was a great deal of talk about him: that he was a saint, that he had worked miracles] (p. 6). His antagonist Moreira César is equally admired and feared for his extreme determination, his inexhaustible energy despite a frail constitution, and his physical discipline: 'No transpira, pese al calor' (p. 171) [Despite the heat, he is not sweating] (p. 172). He, too, needs less sleep than anyone around him. Like Consejero, the military leader appears controlled and emotionless, but is prone to violent outbreaks of indignation. They are both described as having a penetrating gaze, with a dangerous fire of fanaticism burning in their eyes. In the same way, Galileo Gall's harmless appearance clashes with the turbulence of his eyes. His fanatical adherence to the 'Idea', his anarchist ideology, has made him abstain from sex for ten years, another facet of the fanatical 'purity' that links Gall, Consejero and Moreira César.

On the other hand, each of these fanatics cares deeply for the people who suffer. Antonio Consejero is shown to feel their pain: 'A veces lloraba y en el llanto el fuego negro de sus ojos recrudecía con destellos terribles' (p. 15) [Sometimes he would weep, and as he did so the black fire in his eyes would flare up in awesome flashes] (p. 1). His greatest sympathies are with the weak and fallen; those are the ones he chooses to be his apostles. The Counselor appears to sum up the feelings of the people in the Sertão towards their misery and create a solidarity amongst them, expressing their desperation and directing their anger against the new form of state whose measures they cannot understand. The burning of an official state announcement about new tax laws, a historical event and the first instance of a political manifestation by Antonio Consejero becomes, in Vargas Llosa's novel, a manifestation of his ambiguous character in which aloof solemnity clashes with fanatical zeal:

> él, serio y mirando a través de ellos, apenas pareció escuchar. Y, sin embargo, instantes después, al tiempo que una suerte de explosión interior ponía sus ojos ígneos, echó a andar, a correr, entre la muchedumbre que se abría a su paso, hacia las tablas con los edictos. Llegó hasta ellos y sin

molestarse en leerlas las echó abajo, con la cara descompuesta por una indignación que parecía resumir la de todos. (p. 32)

[he scarcely seemed to have heard them. And yet, only seconds later, just time enough for a sort of inner explosion to set his eyes afire, he began to walk, to run through the crowd that stepped aside to let him through, toward the billboard where the decrees had been posted. He reached them and without even bothering to read them tore them down, his face distorted by an indignation that seemed to sum up that of all of them.] (p. 21)

Whereas da Cunha characterizes the Counselor as a dangerous and insane demagogue, a calculating 'monster' with a 'strange power of hypnotism',[13] Vargas Llosa's ambiguous portrayal is that of a distant and mysterious figure, whose confused preachings about the end of the world are never given in direct speech. Instead, the impersonal narrator describes the mesmerizing effect of his enigmatic counsels:

Alguna vez alguien —pero rara vez porque su seriedad, su voz cavernosa o su sabiduría los intimidaba— lo interrumpía para despejar una duda. ¿Terminaría el siglo? ¿Llegaría el mundo a 1900? Él contestaba sin mirar, con una seguridad tranquila y, a menudo, con enigmas. En 1900 se apagarían las luces y llovería estrellas. Pero, antes, ocurrirían hechos extraordinarios. ... En 1898 aumentarían los sombreros y disminuirían las cabezas y en 1899 los ríos se tornarían rojos y un planeta nuevo cruzaría el espacio. Había, pues, que prepararse. Había que restaurar la iglesia y el cementerio. (p. 17)

[Occasionally someone interrupted him – though this occurred rarely, since his gravity, his cavernous voice, or his wisdom intimidated them – in order to dispel a doubt. Was the world about to end? Would it last till 1900? He would answer immediately, with no need to reflect, with quiet assurance, and very often with enigmatic prophecies. In 1900 the sources of light would be extinguished and stars would rain down. But, before that, extraordinary things would happen. ... In 1898 hats would increase in size and heads grow smaller, and in 1899 the rivers would turn red and a new planet would circle through space. It was necessary, therefore, to be prepared. The church must be restored, and the cemetery as well.] (p. 5)

The Counselor's simple explanations of what is good and bad and his charismatic personality bring about astonishing conversions of notorious bandits and violent thugs into martyrs for the Blessed Jesus. He directs their violent behaviour against a clearly identifiable enemy: the Republic, the work of the Devil. While within Canudos solidarity and charity enable the *yagunzos* to live a frugal but dignified life, the fanaticism that their leader sparks incites

---

[13] da Cunha, *Rebellion*, pp. 127, 134.

them to devastate the surrounding region by destroying wells, burning estates and fighting their adversaries with unbelievable cruelty, decapitating and castrating their bodies. The consequences of Consejero's preachings, the brutal fight against the army of the 'Antichrist' in a war in which tens of thousands of people are killed, stand in stark contrast to his goal of leading the poor to a better life.

The same discrepancy between an idealistic goal and the utter brutality of the means to achieve it is highlighted in the behaviour of Moreira César. The 'Cortapescuezos' [throat-slitter], as he is known for his cruel methods of dealing with his enemies, is nonetheless driven by a strong sense of social justice. He is visibly moved by the sight of poverty and human misery: at a banquet organized in his honour he invites the hungry onlookers to feed themselves, which they do avidly. In another encounter with people who strike him as 'the very image of helplessness' he shows compassion and respect for the deprived, reacting with emotions that resemble those of the religious leader: 'Su cara se contrae en una expresión en la que se mezclan la tristeza, la cólera, el rencor' (p. 172) [His face contorts in an expression in which sadness, anger, and rancor are commingled] (p. 173). To the amazement of his entourage the colonel pays the highest military respect to these humble human beings:

> Hay una vibración en su voz y sus ojos relampaguean. En un gesto intempestivo saca la espada del cinto y se la lleva a la cara, como si fuera a besarla. Los corresponsales ven entonces, alargando las cabezas, que el jefe del Séptimo Regimiento, antes de reanudar la marcha, hace con su espada ese saludo que se hace en los desfiles a la bandera y a la máxima autoridad, a los tres miserables pobladores de Pau Seco. (p. 172)

> [His voice trembles and his eyes flash. In an impetuous gesture, he draws his sword from its scabbard and raises it to his face, as though he were about to kiss it. Craning their necks, the press correspondents then see the commanding officer of the Seventh Regiment give, before riding off again, that ceremonial sword salute reserved at parades for the national flag and the highest authority, here addressed to the three miserable inhabitants of Pau Seco.] (p. 174).

Comparable to his antagonist the religious leader, the idealism which instils Moreira César with the sense of a mission has turned into a dangerous kind of fanaticism which distorts his understanding of reality and affects his judgements. Whereas da Cunha's book ascribes the misjudgements causing the army's defeat to the colonel's imbalanced character, rooted in an epileptic condition, Vargas Llosa's version stresses the fanaticism of an extreme idealist, ready to sacrifice the present for the future. In accordance with essays from the 1970s in which Vargas Llosa denounces the 'idolatría de la historia' [the idolatry of History],[14] *La guerra* characterizes Moreira César as someone who acts in view of an abstract future goal, Progress, while disregarding the lives of his subordinates in the present. Obsessed with the idea that the enemy could run away before he is able to defeat him, the leader of the third expedition drives his famished and exhausted soldiers towards Canudos, where the *yagunzos* are expecting them with the same fanatical zeal. Moreira César gives the fatal order of a cavalry attack in the narrow lanes of Canudos and, following an irrational impulse, jumps on his white horse – an emblem of the apocalypse – and charges downhill, with his sabre drawn, shouting: 'Los muchachos necesitan un estímulo' (p. 304) [The boys need to have an example set them] (p. 317). He becomes an easy target for the invisible enemy in the trenches and is mortally wounded. Before his death he insists on dictating a note of protest against the retreat of his hopelessly beaten regiment, a decision taken by 'subalternos que no están a la altura de su responsabilidad histórica' (p. 307) [subordinates who are not capable of assuming their responsibility in the face of history] (p. 321). The fact that Vargas Llosa turns this episode, which in *Os sertões* is only a marginal note, into a crucial scene within *La guerra*'s central chapter shows how he organizes his material to highlight the fanatical adherence to an abstract ideal which moves some of the most important characters in his novel.

The idolatry of History connects the military leader with an ideologue of a totally different kind, the Scottish anarchist Galileo Gall. Like Moreira César, he believes in science as a factor of progress – only in his case it is the pseudo-science of phrenology.[15] In Gall's view, the aim of History is to establish an egalitarian, libertarian society by means of abolishing private property, the cause of poverty and injustice. In pursuing this goal, Gall is prepared to use every possible means, including violence: 'Estamos en guerra y todas las armas valen', he says (p. 242) [We're at war, and every weapon [is permitted]] (p. 250). He firmly believes a division between ethics and politics is justified when it serves a good cause: '¿Era ético para un revolucionario conjurarse con un politicastro burgués? Sí, si la conjura ayudaba a los *yagunzos*' (p. 74) [Was it ethical for a revolutionary to conspire with a petty-bourgeois politician? Yes, if the conspiracy aided the *jagunços*] (p. 67). Gall has an abstract collective in view, he deeply cares for the proletariat, for humanity, but he disregards the individual. Comparable to the Jacobin fanatic Moreira César, his compassion for the masses stands in sharp contrast to his actual behaviour towards a concrete person. In a moment of uncontrolled,

---

[14] For example, see Mario Vargas Llosa, 'Albert Camus y la moral de los límites', in *Contra viento I*, pp. 321–42 (p. 324).

[15] His name refers on the one hand to Galileo Galilei, on the other to Franz Joseph Gall, the founder of phrenology, popular in the eighteenth and nineteenth century, who believed that a person's character traits are palpable in the shape of the skull.

instinctive behaviour following a failed attempt to murder him, he breaks his ten-year vow of abstention and rapes Jurema, wife of the pathfinder Rufino. Despite his egalitarian ideas about the role of women in society, pronounced in the letters he writes to a French anarchist journal, he shows contempt for Jurema's dignity and her place in the society she lives in. The clash between Gall's humanitarian ideal and his actual behaviour is even more striking because the reader gains insight into the protagonist's thoughts, both through his letters and the narrative technique of free indirect style. While Moreira César's ambiguity is always seen from the outside, the contradictions in Gall's character evolve out of the contrast between his own perspective and that of others, an irony that arises, for instance, when he blames a cleric's 'intellectual blindness' in misrepresenting Canudos as a religious movement, whereas the reader clearly sees Gall's own blind fanaticism in misunderstanding the rebellion as a political revolution.

In his fanatical sense of a mission, Gall also resembles Antonio Consejero. His pronouncements about a coming society which will be built on the ashes of the old social order mirror the apocalyptic character of the Counselor's predictions: 'una vez destruido el viejo orden gracias a la acción revolucionaria, la nueva sociedad florecerá espontáneamente, libre y justa' (p. 26) [once the old order was destroyed through revolutionary action, the new society, free and just, would flower spontaneously] (p. 16). The anarchist's public speeches, meant to rouse his listeners to revolutionary action, are full of prophetic and millenarian elements, depicting the nature of the promised new order of society: 'Un día desaparecerá la palabra patria. ... La gente mirará hacia atrás, hacia nosotros, encerrados en fronteras, entrematándonos por rayas en los mapas, y dirán: qué estupidos fueron' (p. 223) [Someday the word 'fatherland' is going to disappear. ... People will look back on us, shut up within frontiers, killing each other over lines on a map, and they'll say: How stupid they were] (p. 229). His missionary zeal is comparable to that of the Counselor, only the effect he has on his listeners is quite the opposite: initial curiosity soon turns into indignation and hostility. Gall's European concepts do not strike a chord with the inhabitants of the Sertão, so that he begins to wonder: '¿Era su acento extranjero lo que hacía brotar la desconfianza en esta gente? ¿O era una incomunicación más profundo, de manera de sentir y de pensar?' (p. 253) [Was it his foreign accent that immediately aroused these people's mistrust? Or was it an even more profound lack of communication, between his entire way of feeling and thinking and theirs?] (p. 262). 'Incomunicación', the inability to communicate due to a lack of understanding for people holding different beliefs, is the key concept of the whole novel, as we have seen. In Galileo Gall's case it leads to his death at the hands of Jurema's husband Rufino, a revenge for Gall's violation of his honour which the Scotsman with his abstract categories of freedom from exploitation is unable to understand.

The symmetry that *La guerra del fin del mundo* establishes between the fanatical opponents is supported by the novel's symmetrical structure. Divided into four books, books 1, 3 and 4 each have six/seven chapters which are subdivided into four/five sections, marked only by a typographical space on the page. These sections are thematically ordered and follow a recurring pattern, creating a regular rhythm of narration.[16] In book 1, for example, all seven chapters begin with a section dealing with Antonio Consejero, followed by a section on Galileo Gall (except chapter 2); each third section within a chapter tells the story of the conversion of one of Consejero's apostles, while the last section concentrates on Gall again. The symmetry of these sequences, which follow protagonists who all set off on their way to Canudos, creates the expectation of a confluence of these diverging life stories. It also establishes the parallel between the different people following the Counselor in order to become members of his fanatical movement, and Gall wanting to join the fanatics for his own reasons. Book 2 is exceptional in its brevity, having a mere three chapters without any further subdivisions. It introduces and characterizes the journalist as one of the main protagonists of the novel who, as both an observer and commentator, is himself exceptional within the symmetry of fanaticisms established throughout the novel. Book 3 brings the many different life stories together. It is at the centre of the novel, where most narrative lines cross and the narration reaches its greatest density. The important protagonist Barón de Cañabrava appears for the first time, and he will be the focus of each of the last sections. Analogous to the first book's composition, book 3 establishes a regular juxtaposition between the sections dealing with the antagonists Moreira César (first segment), who represents modernity, and Consejero and his followers (third segment), who embody a traditional, religious way of life. In sections two and four the final confrontation between Gall and Rufino, who hunts him down to avenge the rape of his wife, is played out. Book 3 ends with Gall's and Rufino's death, in parallel with the fatal clash of Moreira César and the military leader of the *yagunzos*, Pajeú. Up to that point, the novel follows a more or less linear time structure, with few instances of a disrupted sequence of events, and only a couple of 'hidden facts' to create suspense. This changes with book 4, where the narration of the final campaign against Canudos is juxtaposed with a retrospective account and evaluation of the events in a conversation between the journalist and the baron (in each first section of the book's six chapters). A number of sudden narrative switches from the relation of events in retrospect to the immediate action in Canudos have the effect of juxtaposing action and reflection. The more disrupted narration also mirrors the

---

[16] For a schematic depiction of *La guerra*'s symmetrical structure, see my study *Vargas Llosa's Fiction & the Demons of Politics* (Oxford: Peter Lang, 2002), p. 157.

general disintegration brought about by the cataclysmic destruction of the focal point, Canudos.

The violent bloodbath of the city's last days is counterbalanced by an attempt to rationalize the events in a discussion about the meaning of history. Barón de Cañabrava and the short-sighted journalist are two protagonists exempt from the general fanaticism on all sides, and thus well placed to reflect on the meaning of events. The character of the baron, a traditionalist landowner and autonomist politician, has been the subject of much discussion amongst critics, since he is – up to a certain point – Vargas Llosa's mouthpiece in the novel. He is the only protagonist who recognizes the fact that Moreira César, as well as Galileo Gall and the *yagunzos*, are idealists, visionaries and dreamers, and he detects the dogmatism common to these fanatical idealists: 'El tono de la seguridad absoluta, pensó, el de los que nunca dudan. ... Era tan vano tratar de razonar con [Pajeú] como con Moreira César o con Gall. ... era como si el mundo hubiera perdido la razón y sólo creencias ciegas, irracionales, gobernaran la vida' (pp. 237–8) [The tone of absolute certainty, he thought, the tone of those who are never assailed by doubts. ... It was useless to try to reason with [Pajeú] as it was to argue with Moreira César or Gall. ... it was as if the world had taken leave of its reason and blind, irrational beliefs had taken over] (pp. 245–6). The protagonist thus confirms explicitly what the novel implies by characterization and narration of events. It is in the baron's house where, by chance, all these fanatics meet, making it possible to set the baron's sensible opinions against those of the dogmatics. Gall, for instance, is astonished that the baron judges Moreira César – 'Un hombre del que se dicen tantas atrocidades' (p. 240) [A man reputed to have committed so many atrocities] (p. 247) – to be an idealist, but the baron insists: 'Lo mueven cosas abstractas ... Como ocurre con muchos idealistas, es implacable cuando quiere materializar sus sueños' (p. 240) [It's abstract things that motivate him to act ... As is the case with many idealists, he is implacable when it comes to realizing his dreams] (pp. 247–8). But the baron's moderate, pragmatic position outside the general fanaticism does not save him from becoming a victim of the *yagunzos* who burn down his mansion, causing his wife Estela to sink into a deep depression. Appalled by the 'general madness', he retires from public life and wants to forget everything to do with Canudos.

At that point he is visited by the journalist who has escaped Canudos and is looking for work. His attitude is quite the opposite to the baron's: he intends to write a book about the events to keep the memory of this history alive, 'De la única manera que se conservan las cosas. ... Escribiéndolas' (p. 341) [In the only way in which things are preserved. ... By writing of them] (p. 357). The conversation that develops between the two is rendered from the perspective of the baron who does not want to be reminded of what happened, and yet keeps asking the journalist about his experiences inside Canudos. This contradictory attitude points to the fact that his strategy of repressing painful memories is not viable. He wants to hear the journalist's insights about Canudos – a sign that the public needs the book that the journalist intends to write. It is thus the writer who has the last word, and he has the better arguments in explaining Canudos since he has experienced it from the inside. It is significant that the short-sighted journalist, the caricature of an urban intellectual with his thick glasses, violent allergic attacks, and his old-fashioned writing kit which he takes into the wilderness of the Sertão, loses his spectacles and is not able to see what is going on in Canudos. He has to rely on sensorial and emotional perception, intuition and imagination, and on the help and solidarity of Jurema and the midget from the circus with whom he has formed a bond. He has to adopt a perspective other than his own – which also represents a metafictional comment. This experience changes him deeply: from his previous indifference and adaptability to write for whoever paid him, he has become committed to writing an account of Canudos which would clear up the existing misconceptions. The baron's development, by contrast, leads him from an active commitment to public life to a passive withdrawal into privacy, a consequence of his understanding of Canudos as 'locura' [madness]. The journalist, however, has learnt: 'Más que de locos es una historia de malentendidos' (p. 434) [It's not so much a story of madmen as a story of misunderstandings] (p. 461), and misunderstandings can be clarified. He has come to understand that the *yagunzos* were not the monarchist conspirators that they were thought to be, but that they actually believed the monarchy had fallen because it abolished slavery, and that the Republic intended to reintroduce it. The journalist has learnt some 'contradictory truths', to use the Isaiah Berlin concept that Vargas Llosa discovered during his work on *La guerra*, for example concerning the question of whether Canudos was a revolution: 'No lo era y sin embargo lo era. ... Era el reino del oscurantismo y, a la vez, un mundo fraterno, de una libertad muy particular' (p. 433) [It wasn't, and yet it was. ... It was the realm of obscurantism, and at the same time a world of brotherhood, of a very special freedom] (p. 460). His blindness has opened his mind to some essential truths about the religious movement whereas, before, he was one of those reporters who had helped to spread the lies: 'podían ver pero sin embargo no veían; sólo vieron lo que fueron a ver' (p. 394) [They could see and yet they didn't see. All they saw was what they'd come to see] (p. 415).

The spirit of solidarity that the journalist has found in Canudos has changed him. In his accidental union with Jurema and the midget he experiences, for the first time in his life, love, happiness and physical pleasure. This unlikely love triangle that forms in the middle of the last bitter fighting in Canudos is seen from the perspective of all three participants, which underlines the consent on all sides. This stands in stark contrast to another triangular relationship which is seen solely from the baron's male perspective:

after his disturbing conversation with the journalist Barón de Cañabrava intrudes into the bedroom where his wife and her servant are sleeping and forces himself onto the servant, with the baroness looking on. Some critics have understood this as a kind of conclusion to the novel. But the strange encounter, which is actually a rape by the baron who exerts his power over the servant, liberates him only temporarily from the feeling of frustration and absurdity in the face of what he sees as collective madness. The baron's escape into pleasure remains ephemeral, he leaves the two women to their tender and mutually trusting relationship from which he is excluded. As he looks out of the window across the bay, he sees people praying and scattering flowers onto the sea, at the place where the authorities have disposed of the remains of Consejero. Canudos remains alive, the baron's attempt to forget it has failed.

All this points to the privileged position of the writer-protagonist in the novel, who supersedes the baron as Vargas Llosa's mouthpiece. Writing against oblivion is the lasting outcome of the novel. The journalist's intention represents, within the novel, what the two real-life authors of great books about Canudos, Euclides da Cunha and Vargas Llosa, have achieved. Apart from this *mise en abyme* the novel highlights another significant outcome: the short-sighted journalist has joined forces with the midget who, in the itinerant circus, fulfilled the function of storyteller, entertaining his listeners with medieval legends and timeless stories about good and evil. This gift secured their survival amongst the *yagunzos*. By telling the stories of Charlemagne, the Twelve Peers of France, Robert the Devil and other medieval romances preserved in the oral tradition of the backlands, the midget 'los mantenía absortos, fuera del tiempo y de Canudos' (p. 350) [held them spellbound, outside of time and outside of Canudos] (p. 367). The union between this popular storyteller and the intellectual writer-protagonist who used to admire Victor Hugo, write poetry and predict that, one day, he 'would be the Oscar Wilde of Brazil', symbolizes the fusion of intellectual writing and popular fiction that had already been the subject matter of Vargas Llosa's previous novel, *La tía Julia y el escribidor* [*Aunt Julia and the Scriptwriter*].[17] *La guerra* itself represents the synthesis of realist historical fiction using sophisticated narrative techniques with popular literary forms such as the adventure story or, in the sections on Consejero's apostles, the Saints' lives.

The novel's interplay between story and history, form and content, metafictional and anti-ideological dimensions, earns it a unique place at the centre of Vargas Llosa's work. It is a point of confluence where fiction and extra-literary concerns come together in a 'novela total': *La guerra*'s multiperspectivism is in tune with Vargas Llosa's anti-ideological stance and his belief

---

[17] Mario Vargas Llosa, *La tía Julia y el escribidor* (Barcelona: Seix Barral, 1986); Mario Vargas Llosa, *Aunt Julia and the Scriptwriter*, trans. Helen R. Lane (London: Picador, 1984).

that pluralism in politics, art and other areas of public life is preferable to the single truths, the 'verdades únicas' of ideologies. Vargas Llosa's ambitious undertaking to write the 'total novel' about Canudos, taking in all aspects of reality and all points of view, confirms his conviction that literature is able to express a particular kind of truth. In creating a plausible and convincing 'mentira verdadera', a 'lie that tells the truth' as he calls it in the preface to his play *La señorita de Tacna* [*The Young Lady from Tacna*][18] which appeared in the same year as the novel, Vargas Llosa's fictional recreation exceeds the partial truth of historiography. The story of 'the war of the end of the world' highlights the ambiguous relationship that can exist between history and fiction, between truth and lies. As the writer-protagonist in the novel explains: 'Las mentiras machacadas día y noche se vuelven verdades. ... Estaba escrito, era verdad' (p. 362) [The lies that have been harped on night and day have turned into truths. ... It appeared in print, so it was true] (pp. 380–1). Whereas the 'true' history of Canudos turns out to be close to the lies of the imagination, fiction is able to shed light on history. Vargas Llosa further develops this idea in 'La verdad de la mentiras' [The Truth of Lies] where he states:

> La recomposición del pasado que opera la literatura es casi siempre falaz juzgada en términos de objetividad histórica. La verdad literaria es una y otra la verdad histórica. Pero, aunque esté repleta de mentiras —o, más bien, por ello mismo— la literatura cuenta la historia que la historia que escriben los historiadores no sabe ni puede contar.[19]

> [The reconstruction of the past in literature is almost always false in terms of historical objectivity. Literary truth is one thing, historical truth another. But although it is full of lies – or rather, because of this fact – literature recounts the history that the history written by the historians would not know how, or be able, to write.][20]

This view of historical fiction becomes important again in later historical novels such as *La Fiesta del Chivo* [*The Feast of the Goat*] (2000)[21] and,

---

[18] Mario Vargas Llosa, 'Las mentiras verdaderas', in *La señorita de Tacna* (Barcelona: Seix Barral, 1981), pp. 9–12 (p. 9); Mario Vargas Llosa, 'Lies That Tell the Truth', in *Three plays. The Young Lady from Tacna. Kathie y el Hippopotamus. La Chunga*, trans. David Graham-Young (London: Faber and Faber, 1990), pp. 5–7 (p. 5).

[19] Mario Vargas Llosa, 'La verdad de la mentiras', in *La verdad de las mentiras. Ensayos sobre literatura* (Barcelona: Seix Barral, 1990), pp. 5–20 (p. 14).

[20] Mario Vargas Llosa, 'The Truth of Lies', in *Making Waves*, ed. and trans. John King (London: Faber and Faber, 1996), pp. 320–30 (p. 326).

[21] Mario Vargas Llosa, *La Fiesta del Chivo* (Madrid: Alfaguara, 2000); Mario Vargas Llosa, *The Feast of the Goat*, trans. Edith Grossman (New York: Farrar, Straus and Giroux, 2001).

above all, in the 2010 novel *El sueño del celta* [*The Dream of the Celt*],[22] with its historically unresolved questions. But it is in the novel immediately following on from *La guerra* that Vargas Llosa turns the actual process of a writer fictionalizing historical reality into his main subject matter.

---

[22] Mario Vargas Llosa, *El sueño del celta* (Doral, FL: Alfaguara, 2010); Mario Vargas Llosa, *The Dream of the Celt*, trans. Edith Grossman (London: Faber and Faber, 2012).

7

Experimenting with Genres: Novels of the 1980s and After

In 1984 Vargas Llosa published *Historia de Mayta*,[1] a novel whose title alludes to the ambiguous relationship between story and history that was a crucial theme in *La guerra del fin del mundo*. The English translation appeared under the title *The Real Life of Alejandro Mayta*,[2] for lack of an equivalent of the dual meaning of the Spanish 'historia'. Vargas Llosa put it on record that he was unhappy with the English title, and unhappy with the reception of his book as a political novel. Although he initially commented widely on the political meaning of the novel in his interviews following the publication of *Historia de Mayta*, he later insisted that its primary concern was the metafictional aspect of a writer-protagonist seen at work, converting history into fiction, stating that the work 'stands as a metaphor for my vocation as a writer'.[3] A considerable number of his critics, however, focused on the novel's harsh representation of the Peruvian Left as illusionary, irresponsible and hypocritical, accusing Vargas Llosa of misrepresenting historical left-wing revolutionary movements and caricaturing recognizable contemporary leftist personalities.[4] This critical reception was not least influenced by Vargas Llosa's highly controversial political position in Peru after his role in the report on the murders of journalists in Uchuraccay in 1983 (see chapter 3 above), a year before *Historia de Mayta* appeared. The fact that political violence, past and present, plays a pivotal role in this novel makes it difficult to see it solely as an exercise in metafiction.

Historia de Mayta is the account of a novelist wanting to tell the story of a failed revolutionary coup, based on a historical incident which took place in

---

[1]   Mario Vargas Llosa, *Historia de Mayta* (Barcelona:Seix Barral, 1984).
[2]   Mario Vargas Llosa, *The Real Life of Alejandro Mayta*, trans. Alfred MacAdam (London: Faber and Faber, 1986).
[3]   Mario Vargas Llosa, *A Writer's Reality* (London and Boston: Faber and Faber, 1990), p. 155.
[4]   For example, see José Miguel Oviedo, '*Historia de Mayta*: Una reflexión política en forma de novela', *Antípodas*, 1 (1988), 142–59 (p. 151). Even for a reader not familiar with the political scene in Peru, some protagonists of the novel show a clear resemblance to real-life personalities described in Vargas Llosa's memoirs.

Jauja, a town in the Peruvian Andes. In the novel, the rebellion is organized by the Trotskyite Mayta, a former school friend of the writer-protagonist, and the young enthusiast Vallejos, a member of the armed forces. Naively conceived and badly executed, the coup failed because it gained very little support. The writer-protagonist and first-person narrator has the clear connotation 'Mario Vargas Llosa', identifiable by his status as a well-known and successful contemporary author, by his residence in Barranco, his habits (the early morning run) and his political and literary concerns. His motivations for wanting to write about Mayta's story establish a clear link to the real-life author Vargas Llosa and his preferred ingredients of an intriguing story (the often quoted key words from *La orgía perpetua* [*The Perpetual Orgy*][5] are all there, in this quotation from the novel): 'es posible que ... el elemento oscuramente sugestivo en ella, para mí, sean los ingredientes de truculencia, marginalidad, rebeldía, delirio, exceso, que confluyen en aquel episodio' (*Historia de Mayta*, p. 53) [it's also possible that ... the obscurely suggestive element I see in it consists of the truculence, marginality, rebelliousness, delirium, and excess which all came together in that episode] (*The Real Life*, p. 44). From the beginning, *Historia de Mayta* creates the illusion that the novel we are reading is the work that the implied author sets out to write in chapter 1, and that it contains not only a reconstruction of the history of the Jauja rebellion, but also the story of how the writer-protagonist turns the contradictory information he gains from various interviews into a coherent fiction: 'lo que uso no es la veracidad de los testimonios sino su poder de sugestión y de invención, su color, su fuerza dramática' (p. 114) [What I use is not the truth of the testimonies but their power to suggest, their power as inventions, their color, their dramatic strength] (p. 101).

The illusion of seeing a novelist at work is supported by how the first-person narrator explains his intentions and methods to his interviewees. He says that he does not want to recreate the true history but a 'versión muy pálida, remota y, si quieres, falsa' (p. 77) [faint, remote, and, if you like, false version] (p. 66). The only way to achieve this is by doing thorough research of the facts, and then fantasizing: 'Le explico una vez más que no pretendo escribir la "verdadera historia" de Mayta. Sólo recopilar la mayor cantidad de datos y opiniones sobre él, para, luego, añadiendo copiosas dosis de invención a esos materiales, construir algo que será una versión irreconocible de lo sucedido' (p. 93) [I explain once again that I'm not trying to write the 'true story' of Alejandro Mayta. I only want to garner as much information, as many opinions about him as I can, so that later I can add a large dose of fancy to all that data, so I can create something that will

---

[5] Mario Vargas Llosa, *La orgía perpetua. Flaubert y 'Madame Bovary'* (Barcelona: Seix Barral, 1975), p. 20; Mario Vargas Llosa, *The Perpetual Orgy. Flaubert and 'Madame Bovary'*, trans. Helen Lane (London: Faber and Faber, 1987), p. 12.

be an unrecognizable version of what actually happened] (p. 81). These are explicit metafictional comments which mirror statements that the real-life author Vargas Llosa has made about the relationship between history and fiction. The implied author with the connotation 'Mario Vargas Llosa' travels to the locations where his novel is set, just like the extraliterary author who undertakes extensive journeys for his research. When the implied author is being asked why he does not simply make up the story since, in any case, he wants to write fiction, he answers with a formula that has since been quoted many times as the summary of the extraliterary author Vargas Llosa's method of work: 'Porque soy realista, en mis novelas trato siempre de mentir con conocimiento de causa ... Es mi método de trabajo. Y, creo, la única manera de escribir historias a partir de la historia con mayúsculas' (p. 77) [Since I am a realist, in my novels I always try to lie knowing what I lie about. This is my method of work. And, I believe, the only way to write stories about History with a capital H].[6]

This illusion of witnessing, in a novel, the genesis of a novel is built on a dual structure, with two protagonists (the writer-protagonist and the professional revolutionary Mayta), two levels of time (the 'present' of the 1980s in Peru in which the writer researches the events of 1958 on which he wants to base his novel) and two levels of reality (that of the writer at work and that of his invented version of past events which derives from his research). Frequent alternation between these two levels of narration occurs within each individual chapter, in the manner of the 'communicating vessels' familiar from Vargas Llosa's work: a key word or phrase from the 'realistic' level is repeated on the 'fictional' level, or a question posed on the one is answered on the other. In the following example the writer-protagonist's conversation with two nuns about the reason for the rise of liberation theology is answered by Mayta in the past – even though Mayta actually talks about the reason for his loss of faith:

> [María:] Se han dicho tantas cosas sobre los curas revolucionarios, sobre la infiltración marxista de la Iglesia. ... Y, sin embargo, a nadie se le ocurre la explicación más simple.
> [writer]: —¿Cuál es?
> —La desesperación y la cólera que puede dar codearse día y noche con el hambre y con la enfermedad, la sensación de impotencia frente a tanta injusticia —dijo Mayta. (pp. 77–8)

---

[6] This translation is mine. In *A Writer's Reality* (p. 151) Vargas Llosa expresses his dissatisfaction with the English translation of this crucial passage in *The Real Life*, which reads: 'Because I'm a realist, in my novels I always try to lie knowing why I do it. ... That's how I work. And I think the only way to write stories is to start with History – with a capital H' (p. 67).

[[María:] 'So much has been said about revolutionary priests, about Marxist infiltration in the Church. ... But no one comes up with the obvious answer.'
[writer:] 'Which is?'
'The despair and anger you feel at having to see hunger and sickness day and night, the feeling of impotence in the face of so much injustice', said Mayta.] (p. 67)

This pseudo-dialogical juxtaposition of two different conversations about social injustice creates a direct link between past and present, a connection that is very important for the novel's meaning, as we will see.

The intermingling of the novel's two levels suggests that we are participating in the experience of the writer inventing the story out of the information that he collects during his interviews with witnesses of the past events. This impression is sustained until we reach the final chapter 10 which undermines it again. But, to start with, each of the chapters 1 to 7 focuses on one particular person who was an important influence on Mayta or his revolutionary activities. Narrated in the first person by the implied author, the 'Mario Vargas Llosa' within the text, the interviews bring out Mayta's indignation about social injustice, his early signs of fanaticism, and his contrariness and inability to conform to any political party doctrine. This makes him a typical character in the fictional world of Vargas Llosa (the extraliterary author), related to Santiago Zavala of *Conversación en la catedral* [*Conversation in the Cathedral*],[7] or Moreira César and Galileo Gall of *La guerra del fin del mundo* [*The War of the End of the World*].[8] The implied author also describes Mayta in terms reminiscent of Antonio Consejero, the protagonist of *La guerra*. In this literary game of mirrors the implied author claims that what he remembers most about his former school friend Mayta is 'la frugalidad que emanaba de su persona, de su atuendo, de sus gestos. ... había en él algo ascético. Era eso lo que daba autoridad, una aureola respetable, a sus afirmaciones políticas, por delirantes que pudieran parecerme' (p. 29) [the frugality that emanated from his person, from his appearance, from his gestures. ... there was something ascetic [about him]. That was what gave authority, a respectable aura, to his political theories, no matter how wild they may have seemed to me] (p. 22). Moral integrity and a selfless attitude characterize Mayta as being a 'pure' idealist: already as a child he went on a hunger strike out of solidarity with the poor. In his youth he was a devout Catholic, 'un creyente a machamartillo, convencido de que se debía actuar rectilíneamente en todo momento. No aceptaba compromisos.

---

[7] Mario Vargas Llosa, *Conversación en la catedral* (Barcelona: Seix Barral, 1985); Mario Vargas Llosa, *Conversation in the Cathedral*, trans. Gregory Rabassa (New York: HarperCollins, 2005).
[8] Mario Vargas Llosa, *La guerra del fin del mundo* (Barcelona: Plaza y Janés, 1982); Mario Vargas Llosa, *The War of the End of the World* (London: Faber and Faber, 1986).

Nada lo irritaba tanto como que alguien creyera una cosa e hiciera otra' (p. 225) [an unwavering believer, convinced that you had to toe the line at every instant. He would make no compromises. Nothing bothered him more than someone who believed one thing and did something else] (p. 202). Later on, he gave up religion for communism, belonging at one point or another to every possible splinter group, unable to fully accept a single one: 'La búsqueda de la perfección, de lo impoluto' (p. 52) [The search for perfection, for the pure] (p. 43), as one of his former comrades calls it. This leads Mayta from frustration to frustration and explains the appeal of a concrete plan for revolutionary action that the young and bold Vallejos comes up with – at least that is the reasoning developed by the implied author during the research for his novel, a reasoning that he then transposes into an imagined situation in the past. Mayta says in direct speech to the seven members of his splinter party:

> Nos hemos vuelto demasiado teóricos, demasiado serios, un poco politicastros. No sé. ... Oyendo a ese muchacho desbarrar sobre la revolución socialista me dio envidia. Es inevitable que la lucha lo endurezca a uno. Pero es malo perder las ilusiones. Es malo que los métodos nos hagan olvidar los fines, camaradas. (p. 57)
>
> [We're too wound up in theory, too serious, too politicizing. I don't know. ... Listening to that kid spout off about the socialist revolution made me envy him. Being involved in the struggle for so long hardens you, sure, but it's bad to lose your illusions. It's bad that the methods we use make us forget our goals, comrades.] (p. 47)

Here again, Santiago Zavala and his lost illusions come to mind, as well as Galileo Gall's conviction that the goal determines the means to achieve it. Mayta is one of those uncompromising people whom Vargas Llosa calls 'puros' – in his novels as well as in his essays – and for whom he feels a particular fascination. The fact that Mayta is a homosexual fits into the pattern of Vargas Llosa's other fanatical characters, who are all outsiders, in one way or another marginalized and unaccepted by society, which plays a part in their rebelliousness.

The actual coup in Jauja and its aftermath are the subject of chapters 8 and 9. These events are reconstructed out of conversations with multiple witnesses and turned into fiction by the writer-protagonist before our eyes. We see him approach his character Mayta's inner musings through questions that Mayta asks himself, and we see how the writer attributes to him a defiance in the face of the complete failure of his rebellion:

> ¿Te arrepentías, Mayta? ¿Habías actuado con precipitación? ¿Habías sido un irresponsable? No, no, no. Al contrario. A pesar del fracaso, los errores,

las imprudencias, se enorgullecía. Por primera vez tenía la sensación de haber hecho algo que valía la pena, de haber empujado, aunque de manera infinitesimal, la revolución. (p. 305)

[Are you sorry, Mayta? Did you act too quickly? Did you act irresponsibly? No, no, no. On the contrary. Despite the failure, the mistakes, the foolishness, he was proud. For the first time, he had the feeling he'd done something worthwhile, he'd brought the revolution forward, even if only in a minuscule way.] (p. 275)

This use of the free indirect style, familiar to readers of the real-life author Vargas Llosa, is shown here to be part of the process of identification of the implied author 'Mario Vargas Llosa' with his character. This is a clever metafictional ploy which seems to reveal how 'reality' is turned into 'fiction' – but this 'reality' is already part of a wider fiction: that of the novel *Historia de Mayta* that we are reading.

In one of the key sequences of the work, in chapter 4, the writer-protagonist walks into the Museum of the Inquisition after his visit to Senator Anatolio Campos, the former comrade whom Mayta seduced into being his homosexual lover. Seen from the perspective of the writer-protagonist, Senator Campos appears hypocritical, unsympathetic and untrustworthy during the interview. That lasting impression accompanies the novelist on his walk through the exhibition. The writer's first-person narration in the present tense ('I am visiting') switches several times to Mayta's inner perspective in the past, as if it were him walking through the exhibition and thinking about the role of denunciators during the Inquisition: 'Pensó: "¿Cuántos homosexuales quemarían?"' (p. 121) [He thought: how many homosexuals could they have burned?] (p. 106). The identification of the writer with his character Mayta is strongest during this visit to the museum whose subject matter is close to the subject matter of the novel – the use of violence in pursuit of an ideological truth:

> Condensada en unas cuantas imágenes y objetos efectistas, hay en él un ingrediente esencial, invariable, de la historia de este país, desde sus tiempos más remotos: la violencia. La moral y la física, la nacida del fanatismo y la intransigencia, de la ideología, de la corrupción y de la estupidez que han acompañado siempre al poder entre nosotros. (pp. 123–4)

> [Condensed in a few striking images and objects, there is an essential ingredient, always present in the history of this country, from the most remote time: violence. Violence of all kinds: moral, physical, fanatical, intransigent, ideological, corrupt, stupid – all of which have gone hand in hand with power here.] (p. 109)

The narrator puts the violence that emanates from power on a par with the violence that derives from opportunists who are willing to denounce their friends for their own profit: 'esa violencia sucia, menuda, canalla, vengativa, interesada, parásita de la otra' (p. 124) [And that other violence – dirty, petty, low, vengeful, vested, and selfish – which lives off the other kinds] (p. 109) – this is the unspoken link to Senator Anatolio Campos who said in the interview that Mayta might have been an agent of the secret service, while the writer-protagonist suspects him of having denounced Mayta in the past for being a homosexual. The first-person narrator explicitly draws a connection between the country's past and present at the end of the visit to the museum, when on leaving he is immediately confronted by the poverty and social desolation that reigns the country: 'La violencia detrás mío y delante el hambre. Aquí, tocándose, las dos caras de la historia peruana. Y entiendo por qué Mayta me ha acompañado obsesivamente en el recorrido del Museo' (p. 124) [Violence behind me and hunger in front of me. Here, on these stairs, my country summarized. Here, touching each other, the two sides of Peruvian history. And I understand why Mayta accompanied me obsessively on my tour of the museum] (pp. 109–10).

The linking of past and present plays a crucial role for the meaning of *Historia de Mayta*. The present in which the writer-protagonist conducts his interviews is marked by escalating political violence: the country is devastated by a civil war between an extreme leftist terrorist movement (the Maoist 'Sendero Luminoso' [Shining Path] is never mentioned by name, but easily recognizable) and counter-insurgency forces, provoking foreign intervention by communist troupes from Cuba and Columbia, answered by the landing of US marines. The social situation is characterized by a climate of fear and mistrust: food is rationed and hunger is becoming a problem, civilians arm themselves for their own protection, and rubbish is invading even the wealthiest parts of town. Reports of apocalyptic scenes of civil war in Cuzco reach the capital. This characterization of the 'present' is based on existing facts, but exaggerated and dramatized. In addition, recognizable historical elements such as the Soviet invasion of Afghanistan and the Polish 'Solidarity' movement are thrown into the mix, contributing to the illusion of an authentic portrait of the 1980s. The effect is a credible scenario of how the extraliterary situation in contemporary Peru could escalate, a narrative technique that conveys a clear political warning.

This 'present' situation, so the novel suggests, has developed out of a 'past' that is equally made up of history and fiction. The attempted rebellion of a cosmopolitan intellectual and member of the armed forces called Vallejos in the Andes is a historical event which happened in 1962. Led by Jorge Rentería, the model for Mayta, it was the first violent attempt at a left-wing coup in Peru. *Historia de Mayta* predates this relatively obscure event to 1958, before the Cuban Revolution, so that it becomes a precursor of much bigger things to come: 'Vino Cuba y, en 1963, lo de Javier Heraud.

El 65, las guerrillas del MIR y del FLN' (p. 102) [Then came Cuba and in 1963 the Javier Heraud business. In '65, the guerrillas from the Radical Left Movement and the National Liberation Front] (pp. 89–90). The novel puts the Jauja rebellion in a historically incorrect place in an otherwise historically correct time line of leftist revolutionary events, which gives it symbolic importance: 'Cierto simbolismo de lo que vino después, un anuncio de algo que nadie pudo sospechar entonces que vendría' (p. 53) [A certain symbolism of what came later, an announcement of something that nobody could guess was going to happen].[9] The attribution of special importance to the Jauja rebellion frames the narration of events, from chapter 1 to chapter 9. At the beginning the writer-protagonist asks himself why he is attracted to this particular case: '¿Porque su caso fue el primero de una serie que marcaría una época? ... ¿Porque, en su absurdidad y tragedia, fue premonitorio?' [Because his case was the first in a series that would mark out a period? ... Because, in its absurd and tragic character, it was like a premonition?] (p. 21). And at the end he reiterates the special meaning of this forgotten episode in Peruvian history: 'ningún periódico recordó que el primer antecedente de esos intentos de levantar en armas al pueblo para establecer el socialismo en el Perú había sido ese episodio ínfimo' (p. 307) [no newspaper remembered that the forerunner of those attempts to raise up the people in armed struggle to establish socialism in Peru had been that minor episode] (p. 276).

But the novel goes further than ascribing a precursory character to the revolution that Mayta tried to set in motion. It also adds an element of blame. Mayta's attempt to establish a better society by force is made responsible for initiating the violent ideological confrontations that mark the 'present': 'Fue la primera [revolución] de muchas. Inició la historia que ha terminado en esto que ahora vivimos' [It was the first revolution of many. It initiated the process that has ended in what we are living through now] (p. 68). This insistence on a causal link between the 'present' and the 'past', both made up of historical and fictional elements, constructs a political message which hides behind the metafictional games, a message that has provoked harsh criticism by a number of prominent literary critics.[10] Mayta's revolutionary attempt, as the writer-protagonist imagines it, is born out of personal frustration with the institutionalized Left and influenced by the attraction of the irresponsible adventurer Vallejos. This version of events does not mention the social context

---

[9] The translations of this quotation and some of those that follow are mine because, curiously, there is no equivalent for some of these phrases in the English version.

[10] For example, see Antonio Cornejo Polar, *La novela peruana* (Lima: Editorial Horizonte, 1989), pp. 243–56; Roger A. Zapata, 'Las trampas de la ficción en *Historia de Mayta*', in *La historia en la literatura iberoamericana: Textos del XXVI Congreso del Instituto Internacional de Literatura Iberoamericana*, ed. Raquel Chang-Rodríguez and Gabriella de Beer (New York: Ediciones del Norte, 1989), pp. 189–97; James Dunkerley, *Political Suicide in Latin America and Other Essays* (London: Verso, 1992), pp. 139–52.

of the 1950s, for example the corrupting influence of the Odría dictatorship on society. Mayta's outrage at social injustice, which has accompanied him since his hunger strike as a child, is not the actual motivation for the revolutionary coup. That is shown to be the selfish desire for action – 'purifying, redemptive, absolute action' – of a frustrated and marginalized middle-aged dissenter with a 'castrating life'. Nor is Mayta's experience of poverty in the Andes the basis of his planned revolution in Jauja; it only helps him to justify his actions retrospectively, once he has set the armed revolt in motion: '¿No bastaba abrir un poco los ojos para justificar lo que habían hecho, lo que iban a hacer?' (p. 282) [Just looking around here justified what they had done and what they were going to do, didn't it?] (p. 254).

The narrator constantly draws parallels between Mayta's past adventure and the devastating violence of the present, thus cementing the impression that the illusions of a professional revolutionary and his handful of child supporters (who ignore the 'Internationale' and, instead, sing their school hymn during the armed revolt) are to blame for the extreme violence ravaging the country in the 1980s: 'Después, los chicos juraron que era teatro, que jamás me hubieran disparado', says one of the eyewitnesses. 'Pero ahora sabemos que los niños también matan con hachas, piedras y cuchillos, ¿no?' (p. 254) [Afterwards, the kids swore it was only playacting, that they would never have shot me. But now we know that even kids kill, with hatchets, stones, and knives, right?] (p. 228). The practices of the present-day Sendero Luminoso are associatively linked with Mayta's coup. There are frequent comparisons between 'then' and 'now' – 'En ese tiempo se tomaban prisioneros. Ahora, mejor morir peleando' (p. 293) [In those days, the winners took prisoners. Nowadays, it's better to die fighting] (p. 263) – so that it seems justified to extract a strong political message from *Historia de Mayta*: the readiness of a handful of deluded revolutionaries to use violence in order to establish socialism has caused the widespread political violence of the present. In another narrative trick, the intellectual writer-protagonist makes this message explicit by ascribing it to the uneducated indigenous eyewitnesses whom he interviews about the past events. He claims that they intuitively recognize the connection between past and present that he himself has difficulty realizing:

> Me cuesta seguir el hilo, en ese laberinto en el que el quechua se mezcla con el español y en el que el episodio de hace veinticinco años se confunde de pronto con el bombardeo de hace días o semanas —tampoco está claro— y con los 'ajusticiamientios' de la guerrilla. En las mentes de estos campesinos se produce, naturalmente, una asociación que a mí me ha costado trabajo establecer y que muy pocos de mis compatriotas ven (p. 284)

> [It's hard for me to follow the thread in this labyrinth where Quechua mixes with Spanish, where the events of twenty-five years ago suddenly

get confused with the air strike of a few days or weeks ago – when it took place, in fact, is also unclear – and with the guerrilla trials. In the minds of the peasants there is, naturally, an association that it's cost me a lot of work to make and that very few of my compatriots see.] (pp. 255–6)

The political message of *Historia de Mayta* is thus hidden behind various smokescreens of which the dual structure, with its 'past' and 'present', 'fiction' and 'reality', is the most important. But the final chapter 10 destroys this illusion: the writer-protagonist and implied author goes to find the 'real' Mayta who turns out to have nothing in common with the Mayta of the writer's imagination. He has spent many years in Lurigancho prison for various crimes, is married with four children and works as an ice-cream vendor. The writer-protagonist's fictionalization of Mayta's life was thus a complete lie; it was not, as he kept saying, based on a mixture of research and invention, and on his own memories of his classmate and lifelong friend: Mayta is actually a generation older than the writer-protagonist. He is also appalled when the writer explains to him that he imagined him as a homosexual, 'Para acentuar su marginalidad, su condición de hombre lleno de contradicciones. También para mostrar los prejuicios que existen sobre este asunto entre quienes, supuestamente, quieren liberar a la sociedad de sus taras' (p. 336) [To accentuate his marginality, his being a man full of contradictions. Also to show the prejudices that exist with regard to this subject among those who supposedly want to liberate society from its defects] (p. 301). This is a topic close to the extraliterary author Vargas Llosa's heart, since his doubts about Cuban socialism started with reports about the discrimination of homosexuals.[11] The writer-protagonist's version of Mayta's story is thus determined by his 'demons' which are also the 'demons' of the author of *Historia de Mayta*: the idealist in search of 'purity', deeply contrary and unable to conform, marginalized by his sexual orientation like the writer is marginalized by his literary inclination.

The writer-protagonist also reveals to Mayta the fictional character of the 'present' in which he conducted the interviews: 'Además, inventé un Perú de apocalipsis, devastado por la guerra, el terrorismo y las intervenciones extranjeras. Por supuesto que nadie reconocerá nada y que todos creerán

---

[11] This is why the attacks on Vargas Llosa for promoting a supposed homophobic attitude in *Historia de Mayta* are completely unjustified. The latest example of that strand of criticism is the essay by Paul Allatson, 'Mario Vargas Llosa, the Fabulist of Queer Cleansing', in *Vargas Llosa and Latin American Politics*, ed. Juan E. De Castro and Nicholas Birns (New York: Palgrave Macmillan, 2010), pp. 85–102. However, in the scenes where Mayta is expelled from his party for being homosexual (chapter 6), anti-gay sentiment is exposed as hypocritical and the writer-protagonist identifies with Mayta and narrates in the first person. The same happens in chapter 7, which invents the confrontation between Mayta and his wife Adelaida, who wants him 'cured'. Mayta's claim for the right to be what he is is told in the first person singular.

que es pura fantasía' (p. 321) [Besides, I've invented an apocalyptic Peru, devastated by war, terrorism, and foreign intervention. Of course, no one will recognize anything, and everyone will think it's pure fantasy] (p. 288). The supposedly 'real' interviews in the present thus turn out to be part of the fictionalization by this new, second implied author so that we are faced with another 'Mario Vargas Llosa', another alter ego of the real-life author, who has invented his own alter ego conducting the interviews and imagining a Mayta totally different from the one we encounter in chapter 10. The Chinese box technique is used here not only to tell stories within stories within stories, but also to present an author created by an author created by an author.

The invention of an apocalyptic present offers Vargas Llosa and his alter ego in the novel a chance to discuss an issue that has concerned him since the 1960s, when his then role model Sartre declared in an interview that literature had no worth in a situation where children are dying of hunger.[12] Confronted with extreme poverty, the implied author in *Historia de Mayta* finds it difficult to concentrate on his novelistic work and asks himself what sense his project makes under such circumstances. But, he says, 'Si ... yo también me dejo ganar por la desesperación, no escribiré esta novela. Eso no habrá ayudado a nadie; por efímera que sea, una novela es algo, en tanto que la desesperación no es nada' (p. 91) [If ... I also succumb to despair, I won't write this novel. That won't help anyone. No matter how ephemeral it is, a novel is something, while despair is nothing] (p. 79).

In this metafictional game with author personalities, and correspondences and differences between the various levels of 'reality', the final chapter seems to reveal the 'elementos añadidos', the elements that the 'Mario Vargas Llosa' of chapter 10 has added to Mayta's 'reality' in order to turn it into 'fiction': his homosexuality, their personal friendship and the apocalyptic 'present' of the interviews. However, the crucial 'added element' of predating the Jauja revolution to a period before the Cuban Revolution is not revealed as fiction. But it is precisely this deviation from history that adds a contentious political meaning to an otherwise postmodern, ambiguous narrative.

Historia de Mayta is a distinctly postmodern metafictional novel which plays games with the author-personality, blurs the borders between reality and fiction, and questions the distinction between story and history. Nonetheless it is also a deeply political novel which expresses strong opinions about the Left and is thus part of Vargas Llosa's polemical discourse. Moreover,

---

[12] See Mario Vargas Llosa, 'Los otros contra Sartre', in *Contra viento y marea, I (1962–1972)* (Barcelona: Seix Barral, 1986), pp. 44–8. Vargas Llosa stated how he felt betrayed by Sartre's disillusioned and bitter attitude, making the concept of 'littérature engagée' [committed literature] seem worthless. Vargas Llosa's response in 1964 was defiant: 'el único compromiso lícito del escritor es con la materia que trabaja: el lenguaje' [the only commitment possible for a writer is with the material that he uses: language] (p. 45).

hidden behind the metafictional confusions, it presents an alternative to the Utopian model for changing society. In the extremely polarized situation of the fictionalized 'present', the writer-protagonist meets one of Mayta's former Communist comrades, now a well-known figure of the moderate Left who successfully runs a cultural institute. Moisés Barbi Leyva is presented as a positive figure, contradictory in himself, but someone who manages to manoeuvre between all sides and stay independent by adopting a pragmatic attitude. Able to raise support from communist as well as capitalist bodies, he is described in terms that carry a positive meaning in Vargas Llosa's fictional and non-fictional texts: 'su habilidad combinatoria, ciencia antihegeliana que consiste en *conciliar los contrarios*' (p. 34; my italics) [his ability to negotiate, an anti-Hegelian science that consists in *reconciling opposites*] (p. 27; my italics). He thus represents a counter-image to both Mayta's purism and Senator Campos's morally corrupt opportunism, and a model of how to survive and do good in a society characterized by violent ideological clashes.

The other protagonist who stands for positive pragmatism is the 'real' Mayta of chapter 10 who turns out to have led a proper, effective revolution, fighting for hygiene in the horrendous surroundings of Lurigancho prison. During his years there he established a kiosk selling clean water and fought for basic hygienic procedures in preparing food, thus counteracting the all-invading filth that is one of the novel's leitmotifs. He even established a just system of payment with credit coupons, a sort of reliable banking system for the inmates (quite an ironic achievement for someone sentenced to prison for bank robbery). This is the kind of small grass-roots enterprise that Vargas Llosa promoted in the 1980s when he wrote the preface to *El otro sendero* [The Other Path] by economist Hernando de Soto.[13] Despite its metafictional ambiguities, *Historia de Mayta* turns out to be part of Vargas Llosa's battle against Utopian models for change in a future society, and a *plaidoyer* for the politics of small steps in the present.

***

Two years after *Historia de Mayta*, Vargas Llosa published *¿Quién mató a Palomino Molero?* [*Who killed Palomino Molero?*] (1986),[14] a short detective novel narrated from the point of view of Lituma, the character already known from *La casa verde* [*The Green House*][15] and the story 'Un visitante' [A

---

[13] See chapter 3 above, and also the chapter 'Pragmatismus statt Ideologie: das Überleben in einer polarisierten Gesellschaft', in my study *Literatur und Politik – Mario Vargas Llosa* (Bern: Peter Lang, 1996), pp. 257–64.

[14] Mario Vargas Llosa, *¿Quién mató a Palomino Molero?* (Barcelona: Seix Barral, 1986); Mario Vargas Llosa, *Who killed Palomino Molero?*, trans. Alfred MacAdam (London: Faber and Faber, 1989).

[15] Mario Vargas Llosa, *La casa verde* (Barcelona: Argos Vergara, 1980); Mario Vargas Llosa, *The Green House* (London: Picador, 1986).

Visitor] in *Los jefes* [The Leaders].[16] In this thriller, set in the 1950s in the small town of Talara near Piura, Lituma is at the beginning of his career as a policeman in the Guardia Civil. Also making an appearance are his friends the 'Inconquistables' [Unconquerables] ('Unstoppables' in MacAdam's translation), as well as the Green House and La Chunga, daughter of the Green House's founder Anselmo, and title character of a 1986 play[17] in which Lituma also plays a role (his infatuation with Meche, girlfriend of one of the other Inconquistables, is also mentioned in *¿Quién mató a Palomino Molero?*). As unspectacular as it may seem, this short novel is thus deeply embedded in Vargas Llosa's work, not only by its protagonist but also by the themes that run through it: the search for truth and the ambiguous relationship between truth and lies; racism, social inequality and institutional corruption; human evil, sexual obsession and machismo.

Lituma and his superior, Lieutenant Silva, investigate the gruesome murder of Palomino Molero, a young 'cholo' (a man of mixed race and humble background) who had voluntarily joined the air force out of love for the airbase commander's daughter Alicia Mindreau; Molero wanted to be close to her so that he could serenade her by night with his guitar.[18] She had fallen in love with him despite the racial and social divide between them, and they had eloped together in order to get married. But Alicia's father sent his men after them, and they abducted the two lovers and killed Palomino Molero in a bestial manner. To begin with, the military closes ranks to hinder the murder investigation, but the detectives soon establish the background to the crime and identify both the killer and the motive: sent by Alicia's father, her official fiancé committed the sadistic killing in a rage of jealousy, mixed with racial hatred and a feeling of humiliation. The question of who was responsible for a violent death had already played a role in *La ciudad y los perros* [*The Time of the Hero*][19] (was it Jaguar who killed the Slave?) and *Conversación en la catedral* (who was behind the murder of La Musa?), but in both these cases the answer to the murder mystery remained ambiguous. By contrast, the question of who killed Palomino Molero is solved about halfway through

---

[16] Mario Vargas Llosa, 'Un visitante', in *Los jefes* (Barcelona: Bruguera, 1983), pp. 101–13.

[17] Mario Vargas Llosa, *La Chunga* (Barcelona: Seix Barral, 1986); Mario Vargas Llosa, *La Chunga*, in *Three plays. The Young Lady from Tacna. Kathie and the Hippopotamus. La Chunga*, trans. David Graham-Young (London: Faber and Faber, 1990), pp. 155–217.

[18] The evocation of music plays an important role in this novel. Music has the power to bridge the social gap between the two lovers. Other sounds, especially those of animals, accompany the action almost like the soundtrack to a film, either in a complementary manner or in the form of an ironic counterpoint. See also Keith M. Taggart, 'La técnica del contrapunto en *¿Quién mató a Palomino Molero?*', in *Mario Vargas Llosa. Opera Omnia*, ed. Ana María Hernández de López (Madrid: Pliegos, 1994), pp. 151–8.

[19] Mario Vargas Llosa, *La ciudad y los perros* (Barcelona: Seix Barral, 1983); Mario Vargas Llosa, *The Time of the Hero* (London: Picador, 1986).

this novel, and a motive is established. However, the investigation into the background of the case throws up unexpected facts, and several twists in the narrative maintain the level of suspense. But there is no release of tension at the end and other questions remain open, so that ultimately the novel responds only superficially to what is expected of a thriller.

Vargas Llosa explores the detective genre, sticks to it up to a certain point, but then turns its conventions on its head: the constellation of the cunning Lieutenant Silva and his assistant Lituma, who observes the investigative skills and combinatory gifts of his boss with admiration, follows the famous model of Sherlock Holmes and Dr Watson. The murdered Palomino Molero is the innocent victim of a hate crime who, with his romantic love and musical gifts, has all the sympathies of the reader. But when it comes to Alicia and her father the distinction between good and bad becomes unclear. Alicia, the victim of a horrible crime against her lover, is also an arrogant, racist and strangely cold-hearted young woman. In the complicated relationship with her father it remains ambiguous who is the victim and who is the perpetrator, and the abuse she accuses him of might or might not be a product of the delusions he says she suffers from. This is where Vargas Llosa's novel deviates from a simple thriller. The ambiguities are not resolved, the culprits of the murder are not punished, justice is not being done. Meanwhile the truth that the two policemen managed to establish is ignored by the public who would rather believe in the fictions that their imagination and their prejudices dictate, and the story finishes with two more unresolved deaths. Colonel Mindreau kills his daughter and then himself, either to cover up his abuse of her, or to protect their reputation from the false accusations of his mentally ill daughter. The novel ends the way it started: with a case of violent death.

This circular structure is marked by the first and last sentence of the narrative, Lituma's expletive 'Jijunagrandísimas' [Sons of bitches]: at the beginning it is provoked by the sight of the sadistically murdered young man, which sets the detective story in motion; in the end, the swearing is how Lituma greets the news of his transferral to a station in the mountain region of Junín, as a consequence of the report he and Lieutenant Silva wrote on who killed Palomino Molero (this is where readers of Vargas Llosa will find the protagonist again, in the 1993 novel *Lituma en los Andes* [*Death in the Andes*]).[20] A murder case has been investigated and solved, but the result leaves no trace and nobody is punished. Instead, the successful detectives are sent far away so that the order of society can be upheld.

With its mere 188 pages ¿*Quién mató a Palomino Molero?* is an exercise in condensed writing, a new technical challenge of restraint after the sometimes excessive proliferation of adjectives in the previous novel, and the sheer

---

[20] Mario Vargas Llosa, *Lituma en los Andes* (Barcelona: Planeta, 1993); Mario Vargas Llosa, *Death in the Andes*, trans. Edith Grossman (London: Faber and Faber, 1997).

scope of the 'total novel' *La guerra del fin del mundo*. But despite its brevity, some of Vargas Llosa's typical narrative devices are present: two contrasting plot levels juxtapose the tragedy of the murder case with the comedy of Lieutenant Silva's sexual infatuation with a married woman, Doña Adriana, whose physical abundance seems to him the height of beauty. He sings her praises to Lituma, who is unable to see her in the same light. Undeterred, the lieutenant takes Lituma to a hiding place from which he regularly observes her taking a bath – an anticipation of the voyeuristic scene in the painting by Jacob Jordaens, *Candaules, King of Lydia, showing his wife to Prime Minister Gyges*, which will inspire one of the chapters in Vargas Llosa's erotic work of 1988, *Elogio de la madrastra* [*In Praise of the Stepmother*].[21] Lieutenant Silva's sharp analytical mind during the murder investigation contrasts with his illusions regarding his chances of ever fulfilling his desire for Doña Adriana. Despite her constant rebuffs, he tries to impress her with his masculinity – until she teaches him a lesson which undermines his masculine pride once and for all, a blow to his machismo which leaves him more devastated than the failure to bring the murderers to justice.

In the final chapter 8, we find the cinematic technique of quick crosscutting between Doña Adriana's report to Lituma of how she humiliated Lieutenant Silva by coarsely challenging him to prove his masculinity, and the townspeople's speculations about the 'truth' behind the murder case. Lituma's disbelief at the fantastic story of how Doña Adriana's outrageous behaviour cured Silva of his sexual obsession is juxtaposed with the fantastic stories that the public make up about the 'true' culprits of the violent deaths – 'the big guys', a smugglers' ring, a spy ring headed by Colonel Mindreau himself, the Ecuadoreans, 'the queers'. Their imagination has no bounds: fiction is much more appealing than the truth that Silva and Lituma have established. As one observer says: 'Una historia de película' (*¿Quién mató a Palomino Molero?*, p. 181) [It's like a movie] (*Who killed Palomino Molero?*, p. 144). The topic of a truth-finding mission whose results become totally distorted in the public's eye must have been influenced by Vargas Llosa's experience as the head of the commission investigating the Uchuraccay murders in 1983, when he was heavily criticized for not finding any evidence for the involvement of the military. In the novel, the public has equally preconceived ideas about the culprits. The prejudiced opinion that the truth will never come out is informed by what people have come to expect in a corrupt society: 'los verdaderos culpables no les hagan nada' (p. 179) [the real guilty parties always get away] (p. 143). Lituma feels bitter and disappointed when he learns about the public's opinion that their report is nothing but 'a made-up story', invented to protect the 'big fish' who are never caught. The townspeople are

---

[21] Mario Vargas Llosa, *Elogio de la madrastra* (Barcelona: Tusquets, 1988); Mario Vargas Llosa, *In Praise of the Stepmother*, trans. Helen Lane (New York: Penguin, 1990).

convinced that the policemen have played their part in a conspiracy of rich and powerful players in the background: 'Con esa cortina de humo consiguieron lo que querían. Que nadie hable de lo principal. Los milloncitos' (pp. 177–8) [The smoke screen was a success. Nobody's talking about the important thing: the money] (p. 142). The fictional conspiracy theories seem much more credible than the truth – a conclusion that Vargas Llosa must have come to when confronted with the critical reactions to his report.

And yet, Lituma himself is prone to flights of fancy: at every step during the investigation his vivid imagination puts before his eyes what he thinks he has established as the truth. The story of Palomino Molero – a 'cholo' like him – and his love across racial and social divides greatly appeals to Lituma. He is able to identify with the couple, to the point where he sheds tears during the interview with the owner of the house they sought shelter in:

> Y en ese momento, sin distraerse un ápice de las revelaciones de Doña Lupe, Lituma los vio. Ahí estaban, protegiéndose del sol bajo la techumbre de esteras, sentados muy juntos y con los dedos entrelazados, un instante antes de que les cayera encima la desgracia. Él había inclinado su cabeza de rizos negros y cortitos sobre el hombro de la muchacha y, rozándole el oído con los labios, le cantaba, Dos almas que en el mundo, había unido Dios, dos almas que se amaban, eso éramos tú y yo. ... Lituma sintió que lo embargaba una desoladora tristeza. (pp. 95–6)

> [At that moment, even though he missed not a one [*sic*] of Doña Lupe's revelations, Lituma saw them. They were sitting right there, in the shade, holding hands, an instant before disaster struck. He'd bent his head covered with short, black curls over her shoulder and, caressing her ear with his lips, was singing to her: 'Two souls joined by God in this world, two souls who loved each other, that's what we were, you and I.' ... Lituma felt desolated by sadness.] (p. 76)

Readers of *Lituma en los Andes* will encounter the protagonist's literary imagination and his taste for romantic stories again, when he encourages his assistant Tomasito to tell him the story of the love of his life. In *¿Quién mató a Palomino Molero?* Lituma's ability to imagine situations and take them for the truth is constantly checked by his boss Lieutenant Silva who reminds him: 'Nada es fácil, Lituma. Las verdades que parecen más verdades, si les das muchas vueltas, si las miras de cerquita, los son sólo a medias o dejan de serlo' (p. 107) [Nothing's easy, Lituma. The truths that seem most truthful, if you look at them from all sides, if you look at them close up, turn out either to be half truths or lies] (p. 86).

The detective story is thus another exploration of the shifting borders between truth and lies. It poses questions about the distorting influence of love, desire, wishful thinking (Silva's obsession), prejudices and preconceptions of what is perceived as true. *¿Quién mató a Palomino Molero?* brings a new element to the discussion, in the form of the psychiatric concept of 'delusions' (the Spanish text uses the English word), which the enigmatic character of Alicia Mindreau is said to suffer from. Her father explains that '"Delusions" quiere decir, a la vez, ilusión, fantasía, y engaño o fraude. Una ilusión que es un engaño. Una fantasía dolosa, fraudulenta. ... ella cree y vive sus mentiras ni más ni menos que si fueran verdad' (pp. 156–7) ['delusions' means illusions, fantasies, deception, and fraud. An illusion which is also a deception. A deceptive, fraudulent fantasy. ... she believes and lives her lies just as if they were the truth] (pp. 125–6). This different, harmful sort of fiction represents a new aspect in the discussion of the relationship between reality and fiction which continues to dominate Vargas Llosa's work.

***

Only a year later, in 1987, Vargas Llosa published *El hablador* [*The Storyteller*],[22] a novel told by a writer and first-person narrator clearly identifiable by his biography as 'Mario Vargas Llosa'. Comparable to *Historia de Mayta*, this writer-protagonist and implied author tells the story of how he became interested in his subject matter and wanted to write a novel about the role of the 'hablador', an oral storyteller, bringer of news and communicator of myths and traditions in the indigenous community of the Machiguengas who live in small dispersed groups spread over a large area in the Amazonian jungle. The novel has eight chapters and is built on a dual structure. In parallel with the writer-protagonist's narration, chapters 3, 5 and 7 consist of a monologue by one of these storytellers – a structure similar to *La tía Julia* where the chapters alternated between Marito's story of how he met Julia and Pedro Camacho, and the scriptwriter's radio serials. Whereas that novel dealt with two types of literature, highbrow and popular, *El hablador* juxtaposes two types of storyteller: the modern writer of fiction and the oral storyteller in an archaic, magico-religious society. Vargas Llosa's fascination with oral literature was already visible in the storytelling protagonist 'the Dwarf' in *La guerra*. In *El hablador* Vargas Llosa's alter ego explicitly draws the connection between the role of the archaic and the modern teller of tales and their importance for their respective societies:

> Son una prueba palpable de que contar historias puede ser algo más que una mera diversión ... Algo primordial, algo de lo que depende la existencia misma de un pueblo. (*El hablador*, p. 92)
>
> ... aquellos ambulantes contadores de cuentos que a mí me parecían el rasgo más delicado y precioso de aquel pequeño pueblo y el que, en todo

---

[22] Mario Vargas Llosa, *El hablador* (Barcelona: Seix Barral, 1987); Mario Vargas Llosa, *The Storyteller*, trans. Helen Lane (London: Faber and Faber, 1991).

caso, había forjado ese curioso vínculo sentimental entre los machiguengas y mi propia vocación (para no decir simplemente mi vida). (p. 152)

[They're a tangible proof that storytelling can be something more than mere entertainment ... Something primordial, something that the very existence of a people may depend on.] (*The Storyteller*, p. 94).

[... those wandering tellers of tales, who seemed to me to be the most exquisite and precious exemplars of that people, numbering a mere handful, and who, in any event, had forged that curious emotional link between the Machiguengas and my own vocation (not to say, quite simply, my own life).] (p. 157)

The novel is thus another exercise in metafiction, an integral part of Vargas Llosa's project to understand the way literature works and to explore the vital function of storytelling for humankind. But it has another dimension, as we will see. A novel partly set in the Amazon region necessarily touches on the indigenous question, which connects it to works from *La casa verde* to *El sueño del celta* [*The Dream of the Celt*].[23]

The events that frame the dual narrative of the writer-protagonist's memories and the 'hablador' discourse take place in the mid-1980s in Florence (chapters 1 and 8), where the narrator and implied author has gone for the summer to study Renaissance culture and forget about his 'unfortunate country' Peru. But by chance, in the unlikely surroundings of the Italian city, he comes across a photo exhibition about the indigenous population in the Amazon region which takes his thoughts back to Peru and to the plans for a novel that had been in the back of his mind for a long time. The indigenous people depicted in the exhibition turn out to belong to the Machiguengas, a tribe the narrator had become obsessed with through his friend from university, Saúl Zuratas, a passionate defender of their right to preserve their traditional way of life. Since then, he himself had visited the region twice, once in 1958, and the second time in 1981, in preparation for a TV programme about the Machiguengas in a series called *La Torre de Babel* [*The Tower of Babel*] (which the real-life author Vargas Llosa fronted in the early 1980s). To his amazement, the writer-protagonist recognizes in the photographs exhibited in Florence a number of people he had encountered on this last trip to the Amazon. The scenario is similar to the one in *Historia de Mayta*, where the writer-protagonist's imagination is roused by a notice about a rebellion in the Peruvian Andes involving an old school friend of his, which he reads while in Paris. It reflects the situation of Vargas Llosa and other Latin American

---

[23] Mario Vargas Llosa, *El sueño del celta* (Doral, FL: Alfaguara, 2010); Mario Vargas Llosa, *The Dream of the Celt*, trans. Edith Grossman (London: Faber and Faber, 2012).

EXPERIMENTING WITH GENRES 187

writers who find inspiration to write about their home country while living on a different continent.

The writer-protagonist's particular fascination for the Machiguengas is linked to the existence of storytellers in their community who seem to play a vital role as communicators of stories, mythology and history, as well as news and gossip. In exercising this function the 'habladores' appear to contribute to holding the dispersed communities together and maintaining their sense of identity:

> El nombre los definía. Hablaban. Sus bocas eran los vínculos aglutinantes de esa sociedad a la que la lucha por la supervivencia había obligado a resquebrajarse y desperdigarse a los cuatro vientos ... la memoria de la comunidad. ... la savia circulante que hacía de los machiguengas una sociedad, un pueblo de seres solidarios y comunicados. (pp. 90–2)

> [Their name defined them. They spoke. Their mouths were the connecting links of this society that the fight for survival had forced to split up and scatter to the four winds ... the memory of the community, ... the living sap that circulated and made the Machiguengas into a society, a people of interconnected and interdependent beings.] (pp. 92–3)

The exhibition in Florence includes a photo of what could be a 'hablador' surrounded by his listeners, a sight which stimulates the writer's senses and his imagination: 'Estuve viéndola, oliéndola, perforándola con los ojos y la imaginación' (p. 10) [I kept looking at it, smelling it, piercing it with my eyes and imagination] (p. 6). This unexpected encounter with his native Peru in the cultural heart of Europe forms the narrative framework for the retrospective narration of the writer's friendship with Saúl Zuratas, their discussions about the indigenous question, the story of his own encounter with the Machiguengas on the two trips to the Amazon region, and his invention of a 'hablador' discourse. The reader understands the three intercalated 'hablador' chapters to be the result of the writer-protagonist's long-held intention to write a novel about the Machiguenga storyteller and to give a voice to this archaic speaker. But in the course of the novel an even stronger link emerges between the two narrative levels, in the person of the writer's long-lost friend from his years at San Marcos University. Saúl Zuratas's fanatical identification with the Machiguenga tribe might – or might not – have made him join the jungle community and become their 'hablador', when he disappeared from Lima without a trace after their final year at university in 1958. This element of mystery and doubt spurs on the writer's imagination and enables him to fantasize about the extraordinary things that might have happened to his old friend. The fact that Saúl Zuratas, a person from a modern, urban background might have adopted the role of oral storyteller in the archaic world of the Machiguengas finally enables the writer-protagonist to imagine the discourse of such a speaker, something that he had struggled with ever since he had first decided to write about the storytellers in the 1960s: 'era la dificultad que significaba inventar, en español y dentro de esquemas intelectuales lógicos, una forma literaria que verosímilmente sugierese la manera de contar de un hombre primitivo, de mentalidad mágico-religiosa' (p. 152) [it was the difficulty of inventing in Spanish and within a logically consistent intellectual framework, a literary form that would suggest, with any reasonable degree of credibility, how a primitive man with a magico-religious mentality would go about telling a story] (pp. 157–8). The double reflection of an archaic way of talking imitated by a speaker from a modern background imagined by a modern novelist gives the attempt verisimilitude.

The link between Saúl Zuratas and the 'hablador' in the photo is made explicit in the last chapter that goes back to the narrative frame of the writer's stay in Florence and closes the novel in a circular movement: 'He decidido que el hablador de la fotografía de Malfatti sea él' (p. 230) [I have decided that it is he who is the storyteller in Malfatti's photograph] (p. 240). But this link is already suggested at the very beginning, in the transition from the framework to the retrospective narrative, by means of association: the first chapter ends with the writer-protagonist's words, referring to the intriguing photograph, 'Sin la menor duda. Un hablador' (p. 10) [No doubt whatsoever about it. A storyteller] (p. 7), and the next chapter starts with 'Saúl Zuratas'. Before the reader becomes aware of the possible conversion of Saúl Zuratas into a Machiguenga storyteller, this juxtaposition plants a first subliminal hint. Other indications are the name Saúl which evokes the biblical figure of Saul and his conversion to Paul, and Saúl's favourite piece of literature, *The Metamorphosis* by Franz Kafka. He owns a parrot whom he has named Gregor Samsa after Kafka's protagonist who, one morning, finds himself turned into a beetle, an outcast within his own social group. This game with intertextual references to other works of literature will continue within the 'hablador' chapters, as we will see.

In reconstructing the past, the writer-protagonist frequently admits that he is not sure what he actually remembers about his friend Saúl's development, and what he imagines: 'no me fío mucho de mi memoria en esto' (p. 37) [I don't quite trust my memory] (p. 35); 'La memoria es una pura trampa: corrige, sutilmente acomoda el pasado en función del presente' (p. 93) [Memory is a snare, pure and simple: it alters, it subtly rearranges the past to fit the present] (p. 95). These are metaliterary comments on the shifting borders between reality and fiction, which warn the reader that the story of Saúl Zuratas might be a deception born out of the writer-protagonist's imagination. But the next moment he reassures us that his memory does not deceive him when it comes to certain aspects of Saúl's character, thus involving the reader in a metafictional game that constantly veers between drawing attention to the fictional nature of the reconstruction and establishing its verisimilitude.

The Saúl Zuratas that the narrator remembers stands out from the society he lives in: of Jewish faith, with 'unruly red hair' and a huge birthmark covering one half of his face which accounts for his nickname 'Mascarita' [Mask Face], he is also of an extremely kind, 'angelic' disposition. His experience of being an outsider who does not blend in predisposes him, like so many other protagonists in Vargas Llosa's fictional universe, to a rebelliousness that can lead either to literature or to fanaticism. In Saúl Zuratas, both tendencies come together: his interest for the Machiguengas turns him into a fanatic who ends up with one single topic of conversation, and he becomes – perhaps – one of their storytellers. The narrator suggests, in the form of a question, what he wants the reader to believe – that it was Mascarita's deformed face that contributed to his extreme identification with the Amazon tribe at the margin of Peruvian society: '¿Era ésa la raíz del amor a primera vista de Mascarita por los chunchos? ¿Se había inconscientemente identificado con esos seres marginales debido a su lunar que lo convertía también en un marginal cada vez que ponía los pies en la calle?' (p. 30) [Was this the origin of Mascarita's love at first sight for the tribal Indians, the 'chunchos'? Had he unconsciously identified with those marginal beings because of the birthmark that made him, too, a marginal being, every time he went out on the streets?] (p. 28). He also ascribes Saúl's passion in defending the threatened culture of an itinerant minority people to his experience as a member of the Jewish community:

> —Bueno, un judío está mejor preparado que otros para defender el derecho de las culturas minoritarias a existir —me repuso—. Después de todo, como dice mi viejo, el problema de los boras, de los shapras, de los piros, es nuestro problema hace tres mil años.
>
> ¿Lo dijo así? ¿Se podía cuando menos, de lo que me iba diciendo, inferir una idea de esta índole? No estoy seguro. Tal vez sea una pura elucubración mía a posteriori. (p. 97)

> ['Well, a Jew is better prepared than most people to defend the rights of minority cultures', he retorted. 'And, after all, as my old man says, the problem of the Boras, of the Shapras, of the Piros, has been our problem for three thousand years.'
>
> Is that what he said? Could one at least infer something of the sort from what he was saying? I'm not sure. Perhaps this is pure invention on my part after the event.] (p. 99)

Here again Vargas Llosa's Chinese-box technique plays a vital role: the real-life novelist, who has often written about the marginalization that the profession of writer brings with it, identifies with the writer-protagonist in his work who gets into the mind of Saúl, the marginalized protagonist of the story he tells, who identifies with a community at the margins of Peruvian society. The topic of role-play that is so important in many of Vargas Llosa's works is a crucial element in the story of Mascarita, the Mask Face, who impersonates an 'hablador', thus enabling the author to speak through the mask (as in the Latin 'persona') of an oral storyteller.

The technical experiment of inventing a 'hablador' discourse seems, on the surface, to rely on what the writer-protagonist has learned about Machiguenga language and customs from his conversations with the Schneils, a couple working for the Summer Institute of Linguistics (a highly controversial institute accused of spreading US influence and Protestant faith under the mantle of ethnological work). The linguist Edwin Schneil had two personal encounters with the elusive figure of a 'hablador', one of whom he describes as an 'albino' with a birthmark on his face, who seemed very averse to his presence – which convinces the writer that it was indeed his old friend Saúl, who had been fiercely critical of the Summer Institute of Linguistics. The novelist learns that Machiguenga grammar does not clearly distinguish between past and present, a feature that is reflected in the 'hablador' chapters in frequently interspersed phrases such as 'Eso era antes' [That was before] or 'Eso fue después' [That was after]. The telling of the Machiguenga creation myth ends with the ambiguous sentence: 'Así comenzó después, parece' (p. 206) [That's how after began, it seems] (p. 214). Ambiguity and uncertainty are characteristics of the episodic 'hablador' discourse. Individual episodes, announced with a title ('Esta es la historia de' [This is the story of]), always end with the storyteller's phrase 'Eso es, al menos, lo que yo he sabido' [That, anyway, is what I have learned], a warning about the absence of absolute truths in his tales. Sometimes there are other stories within these episodes, in the form of Chinese boxes: 'Y me contó esta historia que ahora les voy a contar' (p. 52) [And he told me this story that I'm going to tell you] (p. 53). Different levels of time and reality are intermingled. The concrete realm of the danger of the common cold, for instance, which was introduced into the indigenous community through the contact with Westerners, is mixed with magical elements such as the death of spiders, ants and all other forms of life in the place where sneezing had occurred. The storyteller integrates multiple voices in direct speech into his narration which is frequently punctuated by onomatopoeic exclamations, so that it takes on the character of a lifelike representation. This impression is supported by the vivid visual description of scenes that seem to come alive in front of the listeners' eyes, a feature (so we are led to believe) that adds to the storyteller's hypnotic effect on his audience, who come to listen to him hours on end.

All these features of the 'hablador' discourse are familiar to Vargas Llosa's readers. What appears to be an imitation of an oral storyteller turns out to reflect the modern novelist's narrative strategies: the disruption of time, the mingling of different levels of reality by 'qualitative jumps', multiple juxtaposed voices, onomatopoeia (see *Los cachorros* [The Cubs][24] or Boa's monologue in *La ciudad*), episodic narration, Chinese boxes, the creation of ambiguity, the inclusion of strong visual elements – the 'hablador' discourse actually confirms the parallel that the writer-protagonist draws between himself and the archaic storyteller. This happens not only on the level of form but also of contents: the 'hablador' tells the story of how he came to be part of the community and how, by listening to others, he became a storyteller himself. This is a reflection of the autobiographical, self-referential writing that we find in most of Vargas Llosa's work. It also echoes his conviction that, in order to become a writer, one needs to read and absorb what other writers have written previously: 'Me dejaban escuchar lo que hablaban, aprender lo que eran', says the 'hablador'. 'Nada de lo que iba oyendo se me olvidaba' (p. 202) [They let me listen to what they said, to learn what they were. ... Of all the things I heard I didn't forget a one] (pp. 209–10). The 'cultural demons' of Vargas Llosa's literary theory are exemplified in the storyteller's Machiguenga version of Kafka's *Metamorphosis* (chapter 7). The 'hablador' also adapts the story of the Jewish people to the mythological world of the indigenous community and establishes parallels between Machiguengas and Jews, both 'people who walk'. The 'social demons' come into view when the storyteller talks about the epoch of the 'tree-bleeding', the traumatic time of rubber exploitation – which also crops up in the writer-protagonist's chapters, where the Japanese adventurer Tushía and the abuse of the *cacique* Jum, familiar to readers of *La casa verde*, are mentioned. The intertextuality of Vargas Llosa's fiction is mirrored on both narrative levels of *El hablador*. The storyteller gives a reason for reminding his listeners of the catastrophic consequences of the rubber boom for their community: in order to learn from history, 'Mejor ser prudentes y tener la memoria despierta' (p. 136) [Best to be prudent and to keep memory alive] (p. 141) – a clear intertextual parallel with the short-sighted journalist's resolution at the end of *La guerra del fin del mundo* to tell the story of Canudos.

The fusion of archaic and modern storyteller that is exemplified here is the only clear outcome of a novel that touches on the situation of indigenous people in Peruvian society. The narrator remembers how he discussed the controversial issue with his friend Saúl, back at university. Saúl was an ardent defender of preserving the indigenous way of living in harmony with nature, which had enabled the Amazonian tribes to survive for hundreds of years. He thought that any change would make them exploitable like the 'zombies and caricatures of men' that the semi-acculturated Andean Indians had become. By contrast, the Amazonian tribes were still living a life adapted to their environment, with a wealth of knowledge about nature that modern

---

[24] Mario Vargas Llosa, *Los cachorros* (Madrid: Cátedra, 1990); Mario Vargas Llosa, 'The Cubs', in *The Cubs and Other Stories*, trans. Gregory Kolovakos and Ronald Christ (London: Faber and Faber, 1991), pp. 1–43.

life outside their communities had destroyed. The fact that Saúl is a Jew gives his arguments against acculturation special weight since Jewish assimilation did not prevent the holocaust. But this is not made explicit. The narrator recalls how he himself, still a Marxist in those days, had argued in favour of progress for any price and provoked his friend by asking whether sixteen million Peruvians should forgo the agricultural, cattle-raising and commercial potential of the region and renounce the area's natural resources for the supposed benefit of a small number of indigenous communities. However, in retrospect he concedes that in these discussions he never came to a definite conclusion: 'Yo no lo sabía, yo dudo aún. Pero Mascarita sí lo sabía' (p. 29) [I didn't know, and I still don't. But Mascarita knew] (p. 27). At the time of their last debate, in 1958, Saúl argued with the absolute certainty of a fanatic: 'la única manera de respetar [a esas culturas] es no acercarse a ellas. No tocarlas. Nuestra cultura es demasiado fuerte, demasiado agresiva. Lo que toca, lo devora. Hay que dejarlos en paz' (p. 97) [the only way to respect [these cultures] is not to go near them. Not touch them. Our culture is too strong, too aggressive. It devours everything it touches. They must be left alone] (pp. 98–9). The narrator, however, found out during his trip to the Amazon region that Saúl's idea was no longer viable, since the tribes had already come into contact with modern life, and their traditional way of living had actually made them 'víctimas de los peores despojos y crueldades' (p. 72) [victims of the worst exploitation and cruelty] (p. 74). This is illustrated by the story of Jum, the tribal leader who had received some basic education through the Institute of Linguistics, understood how his community was being exploited by the rubber traders and tried to set up a cooperative. The story of how he was brutally tortured, part of the fictional narrative in *La casa verde*, is retold here as part of the recollections of the implied author about his voyage to the Amazonian jungle. The narrator's own conclusion, '¿Por qué, entonces, no cambiar más bien a los viracochas, para que su manera de tratar a los indígenas fuera otra?' (p. 76) [why not change the Viracochas [the non-indigenous people] so that they'd treat the Indians differently?] (p. 77) points ahead to the protagonist of *El sueño del celta*, Roger Casement, and his fight for treating the indigenous peoples of the Congo and Amazonian Peru with dignity and respect.

It is difficult to find a definitive political message behind the complex fictional game of mirrors in *El hablador*. What is remarkable is that, unlike other fanatics in Vargas Llosa's work, Saúl Zuratas is not shown to fail. The narrator and implied author points out that Saúl is well aware of the contradictions of his defence for a community in which he would not have had a place had he been born into it with the birthmark that covered his face. Like other babies with physical defects, he would have been killed by his mother: 'Yo no hubiera pasado el examen, compadre', he says. 'A mí me hubieran liquidado' (p. 27) [I wouldn't have passed the test, pal. They'd have liquidated me] (p. 25). He is also far from idealizing the Amazonian tribes in other respects, such as their brutal treatment of women, or the existence of slavery in some communities. But the writer-protagonist suggests that Saúl's own vulnerability makes him identify with the Machiguengas to a point where he becomes part of their community. Learning their ways he even becomes one of their authorities, a prestigious storyteller. In that function, so the 'hablador' chapters suggest, he subtly educates his listeners through his stories that wives should not be beaten, that having stillborn babies does not make a woman a witch, that outsiders (such as Tasurinchi-Gregorio/Gregor Samsa) should not be shunned, and that birth defects do not make a person worthless. He illustrates this last point with the parable of the parrot he has as a companion, who keeps repeating the name 'Mascarita'. The storyteller relates how he saved the bird from his mother's attempts to kill him because of his deformed feet. It seems that some of the stories the 'hablador' tells represent a subtle way to introduce Western values into indigenous communities, but from the inside, with knowledge and respect for their customs – if anything this is a Utopian model for a benevolent, slow kind of progress, brought about by none other than the storyteller. (That is, at least, what I have understood, as Vargas Llosa's 'hablador' would say.)

***

Thematically related to these three works of the 1980s is *Lituma en los Andes*, a novel which appeared in 1993 after Vargas Llosa's unsuccessful bid for the presidency of Peru. (In 1988 he had published the short erotic novel *Elogio de la madrastra* which will be discussed later, in conjunction with its sequel, *Los cuadernos de Don Rigoberto* [*The Notebooks of Don Rigoberto*].)[25] Vargas Llosa's political campaign took him to parts of the country he was less familiar with, including the Andes, and he has written about some of his encounters with local politicians and the electorate in his memoirs. Together with his participation in the investigation of the deaths in Uchuraccay, these experiences will have played a role in the sense of strangeness that his protagonist Corporal Lituma feels in the mountain post of the Guardia Civil to which he has been transferred. Lituma, the character we encountered before in his home town of Piura, perceives the natural environment as hostile and the local people as inscrutable. *Lituma en los Andes* is a detective novel set in the present of the 1990s, in a climate of violence and fear caused by the Sendero Luminoso terrorism. The corporal and his aide, Tomás Carreño, investigate the disappearance of three local men, but their attempts to solve the case are hampered by the stubborn silence of the locals. In the vicinity

---

[25] Mario Vargas Llosa, *Los cuadernos de Don Rigoberto* (Madrid: Alfaguara, 1997); Mario Vargas Llosa, *The Notebooks of Don Rigoberto*, trans. Edith Grossman (London: Faber and Faber, 1999).

of their station in Naccos, surrounded by barren mountains, is a camp for workers on a highway construction site whose only distraction consists of a cantina run by a couple, Dionisio and Adriana, who encourage the workers to forget their hardship through drink, music and dance, and through Adriana's stories of how she helped her previous husband kill a 'pishtaco', a flesh-eating monster. Names and circumstances evoke the Greek god of wine and dance Dionysios who married Ariadne, abandoned on the island of Naxos after she had helped Theseus kill the Minotaur. These references to ancient Greek myths merge with Andean superstitious beliefs and contribute to the disturbing climate of irrational violence and excess that dominates the novel. Apart from being a detective story which also draws on myths, *Lituma en los Andes* has a third, metafictional dimension: each night, Tomás Carreño tells Lituma an episode in the story of how he found and lost the love of his life, a narrative in instalments which helps storyteller and listener to forget their constant fear of an imminent attack by Sendero Luminoso terrorists and to endure the harsh conditions of their life.

The novel is divided into two parts and an epilogue. Part 1 consists of five chapters and part 2 of four, each subdivided into three sections which follow a regular sequence: the detective story unfolds in the first section, and the romantic tale that Tomás tells Lituma occupies the third segment. Each middle section of part 1 narrates an act of violence committed by Sendero Luminoso, in which the cold irrationality of the terrorists' actions is emphasized. The middle segment in part 2 is devoted to stories of equally irrational violence, of superstition and myth surrounding the 'witch' Adriana and her husband Dionisio. This suggests a continuity between the two faces of violence in the Andes, old and new. The epilogue, also subdivided into three segments, inverts the sequence: the first section contains a surprising happy ending to the love story between Tomás and Mercedes, with the reunion of the two lovers. The 'serialized' romance that had fuelled Lituma's imagination becomes reality with the appearance of Mercedes in the guard post and, as a consequence, in the second section Lituma goes to see Adriana and Dionisio for the last time before leaving Naccos, and witnesses the drunken excesses in the cantina that he had so far avoided. In the last section the gruesome truth about the deaths of the three missing people comes to light. Lituma finds out that they were not only killed as human sacrifices to appease the Andean gods, but that the ritual also involved anthropophagy. What, on all three levels, had seemed fiction to him, turns out to be reality: the beautiful Piuran woman evoked by Tomás's narration becomes a concrete reality and, in addition, turns out to be Meche, the former girlfriend of one of Lituma's drinking mates, the Inconquistables (and protagonist of the play *La Chunga*); the drink-fuelled orgies in the cantina that Lituma had so far only imagined really happen; and the mythical beliefs and archaic rituals of the Andean world turn out to be part of contemporary reality.

The model of the detective story is once again inverted, but in a way that is different from *Palomino Molero*. The truth about the disappearances is revealed to Lituma early on in the novel (chapter 2), but at that point neither he nor the reader believe in Doña Adriana's talk about human sacrifices, and Lituma's search for a rational explanation leads him to suspect that the men were victims of Sendero Luminoso. But the terrorists' method of exhibiting the bodies of those they kill does not correlate with the three men's disappearance. Neither does Lituma believe Dionisio when he tells him about 'pishtacos', the devilish monsters of popular belief, and reveals that the bodies of the three victims are deep inside a disused mine shaft, guarded by the 'muki', the devil of the mines who takes revenge for the mountains being exploited by human greed: '—Ustedes son muy crédulos, muy ingenuos — repuso Lituma—. Se tragan cualquier embuste, como eso del pishtaco o del muki, cosas que no se creen ya nadie en ningún lugar civilizado' (*Lituma en los Andes*, p. 104) ['You're very gullible, very naïve,' replied Lituma. 'You believe anything, like stories about pishtacos and mukis. In civilized places, nobody believes things like that anymore'] (*Death in the Andes*, p. 86). When he finally discovers the whole extent of the shocking truth he wishes he hadn't. One of the few remaining workmen in Naccos describes the cannibalistic ritual in Catholic terms: 'Todos comulgaron' (p. 311) [Everybody took communion] (p. 275), and Lituma says: 'Me arrepiento de haberme entercado tanto en saber lo que les pasó a ésos. Mejor me quedaba sospechando' (p. 312) [I'm sorry I tried so hard to find out what happened to them. I'd be better off just suspecting] (p. 275). The truth is much more fantastic than what Lituma had imagined.

Lituma's belief in civilization and rationality does not withstand the confrontation with Andean reality, in all its forms: it is shattered by the irrational violence of the Sendero Luminoso guerrillas, by the superstitions of the locals and by nature itself, the 'oppressive, crushing presence' of the immense mountains. He feels nostalgia for distant Piura, its hot climate and its outgoing people, 'a lost paradise' looked at from the 'hell' of the sierra. The two geographical zones seem like two different worlds to Corporal Lituma. This is an issue that Vargas Llosa had raised in his report on Uchuraccay where he drew attention to a basic national problem: the enormous gulf that divides Peruvians from different regions and cultures.[26] He spoke of the 'atavistic attitude' of the indigenous population: what had shocked Vargas Llosa in the killing of the eight journalists in Uchuraccay was the superstitious ritual carried out on their bodies: their eyes had been gauged out, they were buried face down and showed other signs of a 'típica

---

[26] Mario Vargas Llosa, 'El terrorismo en Ayacucho. Entrevista a Mario Vargas Llosa por Uri Ben Schmuel', in *Contra viento y marea, III (1964–1988)* (Barcelona: Seix Barral, 1990), pp. 129–40 (p. 133).

ceremonia de exorcismo y purificación practicada en toda el área andina' [a typical ceremony of exorcism and purification practised in the whole Andean region].[27] In the novel, it falls to a non-Peruvian outsider to draw Lituma's attention to the survival of archaic traditions in the Andes and to the fact that the most incredible explanation for the disappearance of the three men might actually be true. The Danish professor Stirmsson, a scholar of Andean culture, who has spent many years studying Peru and is acquainted with Dionisio and Adriana, points out that the ancient Chancas and Huancas sacrificed 'children, men, women' to keep the *apus*, the ancestral gods of the mountains, happy when building work was needed. This finally brings Lituma closer to the truth. But it is not until he physically experiences the terrifying forces of nature that he begins to realize that reason alone is not enough to understand reality in the Andes. Having survived a *huayco*, an avalanche of mud, rocks and ice, 'aplastó su boca contra la roca que lo había cobijado y como hubiera hecho un serrucho, susurró: "Gracias por salvarme la vida, mamay, apu, pachamama o quien chucha seas"' (p. 209) [he pressed his mouth against the rock that has sheltered him, and whispered, like a serrucho: 'Thank you for saving my life, mamay, apu, pachamama, or whoever the fuck you are'] (p. 180). Lituma experiences for himself that living at the mercy of such elemental forces challenges concepts of rationality and civilization, and renders understandable the belief that mythical deities rule nature.

Dionisio and Adriana, the two people who represent a hybrid form of European-Andean myth, actively encourage visitors to their cantina to leave behind reason and give free rein to their instincts by drinking, singing and dancing in a ritual of liberation which Dionisio describes as 'paying a visit to your animal'. Adriana, another of the novel's storytellers who bewitches listeners with her tales, explains Dionisio's philosophy:

> Bailando y bebiendo, no hay indios, mestizos ni caballeros, ricos ni pobres, hombres ni mujeres. Se borran las diferencias y nos volvemos como espíritus ... El que no pone a dormir su pensamiento, el que no se olvida de sí mismo, ni se saca las vanidades y soberbias ni se vuelve música cuando canta, ni baile cuando baila, ni borrachera cuando se emborracha. Ése no sale de su prisión, no viaja, no visita a su animal ni sube hasta espíritu. (p. 274)

> [When we're dancing and drinking, there are no Indians, no mestizos, no white señores, no rich or poor, no men or women. The differences are wiped away and we become like spirits ... The man who doesn't put his thoughts to sleep, who doesn't forget himself, or throw off his vanity and pride, or become the music when he sings and the dance when he dances

---

[27] Mario Vargas Llosa, 'Informe sobre Uchuraccay' in *Contra viento III*, pp. 87–128 (p. 126).

and drunkenness when he drinks – that man does not leave his prison, does not travel, does not pay a visit to his animal or rise up to become spirit.] (p. 239)

That is how she entices the workers of Naccos to get inebriated and drop their inhibitions, so that they will take part in the sacrifice to appease the spirits. Like a good rhetorician, Adriana structures her stories with repetitions: her warnings about the death of Naccos that has been decided by the mountain spirits end with the suggestive 'A menos que ...' [Unless ...]. She repeats this three times, suggesting that a human sacrifice is needed since 'a grandes males, grandes remedios' (p. 270) [Great troubles need great remedies] (p. 235).

Adriana and Dionisio represent an attitude that Vargas Llosa has discussed in an essay on Bataille in which he quotes the French author with the words: 'Hay en cada hombre un animal encerrado en una prisión, como un esclavo ...; hay una puerta: si la abrimos, el animal se escapa como el esclavo que encuentra una salida; entonces el hombre muere provisoriamente y la bestia se conduce como una bestia' [In every human being there is an animal locked up in a prison, like a slave ...; there's a door: if we open it, the animal escapes like the slave who finds an opening; the human being then dies for the time being, and the beast behaves like a beast].[28] Dionisio and Adriana are thus manifestations of Vargas Llosa's fascination with Bataille's idea of human sovereignty which can be achieved through violating prohibitions and taboos.

The Sendero Luminoso guerrillas are shown to set up a similarly barbaric ritual of 'liberation': they incite the inhabitants of Andamarca to mount a people's tribunal in which, in a climate of feverish excitation, they accuse other members of the community of vices and collectively stone them to death – in a 'gran explosión de aturdimiento e irrealidad' (p. 81) [great dazzling explosion of unreality] (p. 66). By exercising this cruel ritual, as the terrorists assure them, 'los andamarquinos irían tomando conciencia de su poderío. ... Ya no eran víctimas, comenzaban a ser libertadores' (p. 78) [the Andamarcans would become conscious of their own power. ... They were no longer victims, they were beginning to be liberators] (p. 64). This is a chilling sequence which exposes the absurd logic of the terrorists' strategy and the atavistic violence which they unleash amongst neighbours and family members: 'La milicia no participó en las ejecuciones. No se disparó un tiro. No se clavó un cuchillo. No se dio un machetazo. Sólo se usaron manos, piedras, garrotes' (p. 78) [the militia did not take part in the executions. No gun fired. No knife stabbed. No machete hacked. Only hands, stones,

---

[28] Mario Vargas Llosa, 'Bataille o el rescate del mal', in *Contra viento y marea, II (1972–1983)* (Barcelona: Seix Barral, 1986), pp. 9–29 (p. 11).

and sticks were used] (p. 64). This crucial scene in the novel establishes a continuity between the atavistic rituals and beliefs that have survived from pre-modern times and the violence unleashed by a twentieth-century terrorist group. As one of the engineers who have survived a terrorist attack says: '—Yo me pregunto … si lo que pasa en el Perú no es una resurrección de toda esa violencia empozada. Como si hubiera estado escondida en alguna parte y, de repente, por alguna razón, saliera de nuevo a la superficie' (p. 178) [I wonder … if what's going on in Peru isn't a resurrection of all that buried violence. As if it had been hidden somewhere, and suddenly, for some reason, it all surfaced again] (p. 153).

As early as 1966, in an article on Bataille's *Gilles de Rais*,[29] Vargas Llosa had raised the issue of violence and its origin. In that article he suggested that violence grows out of the experience of violence as something normal. Twenty-seven years later, in his novel of 1993, the road worker in Naccos who confesses to having played his part in the sacrifices of the three men says: '¿No hay muertos por todas partes? Matar es lo de menos. ¿No se ha vuelto una cojudez, como mear o hacer la caca? (p. 310) [Aren't there killings everywhere? Killing is the least of it. Isn't killing just routine, like pissing or taking a shit?] (p. 274). And Tomás Carreño, who has grown up in the sierra, tells Lituma 'Nos hemos acostumbrado a la brutalidad' (p. 68) [We've gotten used to cruelty] (p. 55). This structural violence is a factor that, in his texts on Uchuraccay, Vargas Llosa blamed for the vicious circle of violence and counter-violence ravaging the Andean region. In his journalistic report 'The Story of a Massacre' he pointed out: 'The violence astonishes us because it is an anomaly in our daily lives. For the Iquichanos, this violence is the atmosphere they live in from the moment they are born until their death'.[30] The Peruvian state has a responsibility to fight the structural basis of violence by 'sacar al campesinado de ese subdesarrollo profundo en que se encuentra' [pulling the rural population out of this state of deep underdevelopment in which it finds itself] (see chapter 3 above) in order to end ignorance and mutual misunderstanding, which he sees as the root of the problem.

In *Lituma en los Andes*, the total lack of understanding is shown in a chilling manner in the narratives of the two young French tourists and the ecologist Señora d'Harcourt who are killed by Sendero Luminoso guerrillas. Their attempts to explain to the terrorists that they have nothing to do with Peruvian politics fall on deaf ears, as the idealistic Señora d'Harcourt realizes: 'por las expresiones y las miradas de sus interrogadores, la dominaba la certidumbre de un insuperable malentendido, de una incomunicación más profunda que si

---

[29] Mario Vargas Llosa, 'Un personaje para Sade: Gilles Rais', in *Contra viento III*, pp. 33–6 (p. 36).
[30] Mario Vargas Llosa, 'The Story of a Massacre', in *Making Waves*, ed. and trans. John King (London: Faber and Faber, 1996), pp. 171–99 (p. 196).

ella hablase chino y ellos españoles' (p. 121) [the expressions and glances of her interrogators filled her with the overwhelming certainty of an insuperable incomprehension, a lack of communication more profound than if she had been speaking Chinese and they spoke only Spanish] (p. 101). Vargas Llosa's narrative device of introducing sympathetic protagonists, making the reader engage with them and share their admiration of the natural beauty of the Andes – and then, at the end of the short section, having them drop out of the narrative again since they are brutally killed – is a very effective way of bringing home to the reader the shocking reality of these senseless murders. *Lituma en los Andes* leaves the reader stunned and upset; there is no resolution at the end, just a sense of resignation that one shares with the protagonist Lituma, and an understanding for his wish to leave behind the cold, clear skies and the beautiful, but inscrutable, nature of the sierra.

With his departure from Naccos, Lituma also leaves behind the counter-world of dreams and fantasies that had played such an important part in compensating for the hostile surroundings. His adjutant's nightly storytelling had created an escape route into a better, imaginary world, a world that for Tomás was above all one of romance, whereas Lituma was particularly stimulated by the sexual encounters that he recreated in his mind: '—Yo siempre esperando cositas ricas, placitos, manoseos, polvos que me distraigan del ayuno forzoso, y tú siempre yéndote por lo romántico —se quejó Lituma' (p. 161) ['I'm always waiting for the good stuff, a little feeling up and fucking around to take my mind off having to live like a monk, and you always get romantic,' Lituma complained] (p. 137). Some of Lituma's fantasies, always containing a strong visual element, rehearse motifs that play an important role in Vargas Llosa's erotic novels. There is a clear link between Lituma's wish to fill his nights with fantasies and Don Rigoberto, protagonist of the erotic novels, and his attempt to fill the void left behind by the departure of his wife with imagined erotic scenarios involving her.

***

Don Rigoberto, Doña Lucrecia and her stepson Alfonso (or Fonchito) are the protagonists of *Elogio de la madrastra*, Vargas Llosa's erotic novel of 1988, and its sequel, *Los cuadernos de Don Rigoberto* which appeared in 1997. (A young Fonchito, son of Don Rigoberto, is also the clever little hero of Vargas Llosa's 2010 children's book *Fonchito y la luna* [Fonchito and the Moon][31] in which the boy steals a kiss from a girl by presenting the moon to her – as a reflection in a bowl of water. By playing with imagination and reality the child achieves his goal.) Erotic literature, as Vargas Llosa states in a recent

---

[31] Mario Vargas Llosa, *Fonchito y la luna*, illus. Marta Chicote Juiz (México: Alfaguara Infantil, 2010).

essay, is part of the secret world of desires and fantasies which turn sex into an intimate celebration of a culturally refined ritual. Eroticism, he writes,

> con sus rituales, fantasías, vocación de clandestinidad, amor a las formas y a la teatralidad, nace como un producto de la alta civilización, un fenómeno inconcebible en las sociedades o en las gentes primitivas y bastas, pues se trata de un quehacer que exige sensibilidad refinada, cultura literaria y artística y cierta vocación transgresora. ... Sin el cuidado de las formas, de ese ritual que, a la vez que enriquece, prolonga y sublima el placer, el acto sexual retorna a ser un ejercicio puramente físico —una pulsión de la naturaleza en el organismo humano de la que el hombre y la mujer son meros instrumentos pasivos—, desprovisto de sensibilidad y emoción.[32]
>
> [with its rituals, fantasies, its taste for the clandestine, its love of forms and theatricality, is born out of high civilization, a phenomenon that is inconceivable in primitive societies and coarse individuals, since it requires a refined sensitivity, literary and artistic culture, and a certain taste for transgression. ... Without attention to form, to this ritual which not only enriches but also prolongs pleasure and turns it into something sublime, the sexual act is reduced to a purely physical exercise – an urge inherent in the human organism that men and women are passively submitted to – devoid of sensitivity and emotion.]

This (questionable) idea that sex can only transcend its animalistic, instinctive nature by being turned into a sublime manifestation of culture, a staging of refined fantasies – which reduces sexuality in anybody who lacks cultural sophistication to some crude form of copulation – is the guiding principle of Vargas Llosa's erotic fiction. Don Rigoberto's pictorial fantasies in *Elogio*, and later Fonchito's desire to re-enact scenes from the art of Egon Schiele, are manifestations of an eroticism that links physical and emotional pleasure with the fictions of art and the imagination.

In *Elogio de la madrastra*, fifty-year-old Rigoberto (who leads an outwardly unspectacular day-to-day existence running an insurance firm) cultivates, in the intimacy of his home, a life dedicated to the pleasures of the body and the mind. He indulges in elaborate rituals of cleansing and grooming his body, in preparation for the erotic encounters with his second wife Lucrecia whom he adores. In the secrecy of their bedroom the couple act out Rigoberto's fantasies which are inspired by his extensive collection of erotic prints and art books that he keeps under lock and key. Other members of the household include the maid Justiniana and Rigoberto's son Alfonso. The narrative plot involving these four protagonists develops in the odd-numbered chapters, while the even-numbered ones contain erotic fantasies inspired by paintings

---

[32] Mario Vargas Llosa, 'La desaparición del erotismo', in *La civilización del espectáculo* (Madrid: Alfaguara, 2012), pp. 105–16 (p. 115).

that are reproduced at the beginning of each chapter. The literary genre of ekphrasis, the visual description of a painting in literature intended to make the readers visualize what they cannot see, is given a new twist here: the point of view from which a particular picture is described is not outside, but inside the painting. The ekphrastic voice identifies with someone depicted in the painting, and fantasizes about the situation they find themselves in. These situations are loosely linked to the story that develops in the narrative chapters. The paintings range from the obviously erotic depiction of a voyeuristic scene in Jordaens's *Candaules, King of Lydia, showing his wife to Prime Minister Gyges* to the modern *Head 1* by Francis Bacon and the abstract *Road to Mendieta 10* by the Peruvian artist Fernando de Szyszlo. Even this abstract painting receives a very personal interpretation as representing a woman's body from the inside. In this and one other case, the voice describing these paintings is that of Lucrecia, who adds her own fantasies to the mental role-play that is usually orchestrated by Rigoberto. Lucrecia willingly plays along to her husband's 'flights of fancy' despite the fact that they regularly carry him 'far away' from her to some 'unreachable' place of his own imagination.

Lucrecia, meanwhile, lives out a very concrete fantasy by allowing herself to be drawn into an affair with her stepson Fonchito, an angelic-looking young boy on the verge of manhood. Out of an anguished desire to be accepted and liked in the role of stepmother Lucrecia falls for the boy's manipulations. Looking like the personification of innocence, his face of a cherub hides a demonic deviousness. Discovering that he spies on her in the bath Lucrecia deliberately exposes herself to him. She is drawn into the voyeur–exhibitionist pact with her stepson, while Rigoberto only imagines himself to be King Candaules who shows off his wife's opulent body to his Prime Minister. The secret fantasies of transgression of the husband and father become, behind his back, a reality, and Lucrecia wonders whether her taboo-breaking, quasi-incestuous desires are ultimately 'un efecto de esas fantasías y extravagancias nocturnas de su marido' (*Madrastra*, p. 64) [a consequence of those nocturnal fantasies and bizarre caprices of her husband] (*Stepmother*, p. 44).

Rather than implying any judgement on Lucrecia's behaviour, the novel reverses the categories of innocence and corruption. Whereas, at first, she feels guilty about her corrupting influence on the child, it soon becomes clear that Fonchito is an accomplished manipulator who uses his beatific looks and childish charm to achieve his goal: driving father and stepmother apart. With feigned innocence he exposes his and Lucrecia's intimate relationship with his father who suffers the sudden collapse of his 'rico y original mundo nocturno de sueño y deseos en libertad que con tanto empeño había erigido' (p. 176) [splendid, original nocturnal world of dreams and desires given free rein that he had so carefully erected] (p. 134). Rigoberto had tried to keep the two worlds of his unspectacular daily existence and his exciting nocturnal passions and rituals strictly apart. But the two extremes merge: his son who had seemed innocent reveals a carnal knowledge and deviousness beyond his age; his beatific face now seems to Rigoberto 'what Lucifer must have looked like'. The beautiful, devoted wife has committed an ugly betrayal. Reality turns out to surpass Rigoberto's imagination. His neatly organized dual existence has become a mess, the 'beautiful house of cards' has collapsed, his wife will have to leave the home. Rigoberto seeks refuge in art and reacts with a flight into his own imaginary world:

> Y, súbitamente, su maltratada fantasía deseó, con desesperación, transmutarse: era un ser solitario, casto, desasido de apetitos, a salvo de todos los demonios de la carne y el sexo. Sí, sí, ése era él. El anacoreta, el santón, el monje, el ángel, el arcángel que sopla la celesta trompeta y baja al huerto a traer la buena noticia a las santas muchachas. (pp. 176–7)

> [And, all of a sudden, his ruined fantasy desired, desperately, to be transmuted: he was a solitary being, chaste, freed of appetites, safe from all the demons of the flesh and sex. Yes, yes, that was how he was. The anachorite, the hermit, the monk, the angel, the archangel who blows the celestial trumpet and descends to the garden to bring the glad tidings to pure and pious maidens.] (p. 134)

This leads to a fantasy about Fra Angelico's painting of *The Annunciation* in the last of the ekphrasis chapters. While Rigoberto finds solace in art and imagination, Fonchito finds a new victim for his corrupting charm: in the epilogue he makes a pass at the maid Justiniana.

In contrast to Rigoberto, Lucrecia had come to realize even before she had to leave the house that things were not as clear-cut as her husband liked to think. She had asked herself, wondering about Fonchito: '¿Era la niñez esa amalgama de vicio y virtud, de santidad y pecado?' (p. 148) [Was childhood, then, that amalgam of vice and virtue, of sanctity and sin?] (p. 112).[33] She had been feeling that Rigoberto's 'utopia' of matrimonial bliss and her own happiness making love to both father and son could not last, and come to the conclusion that 'las cosas sólo ocurrían así en las películas y en las novelas, mujer. Sé realista: tarde o temprano, acabará mal. La realidad nunca era tan perfecta como las ficciones, Lucrecia' (p. 150) [things turn out this way only in novels and in the movies, woman. Be realistic: sooner or later, the

---

[33] Roy C. Boland sees Fonchito as the personification of 'Bataille's unity of contraries. He represents good and evil, innocence and perversion, virtue and vice, purity and filth, candour and cunning, light and shadow, the corrupter and the corrupted', in 'The erotic novels. *In Praise of the Stepmother* and *The Notebooks of Don Rigoberto*', in *The Cambridge Companion to Mario Vargas Llosa*, ed. Efraín Kristal and John King (Cambridge: Cambridge University Press, 2012), pp. 102–15 (p. 107).

whole thing will end badly. Reality is never as perfect as fiction, Lucrecia] (pp. 113–14). This adds an interesting new aspect to the overarching theme of Vargas Llosa's writing, the relationship between reality and fiction. To judge from *Elogio de la madrastra* and also from its sequel, men like Don Rigoberto are prone to inhabit their own fictions while women like Lucrecia and Justiniana might be seducible by fictions, but they never lose the sense of reality – a mildly ironic gender typecasting which, nevertheless, fits into some of the ironic comments Vargas Llosa has made about his own marriage, for example in his memoirs *El pez en le agua* (see chapter 8 below).

Elogio de la madrastra appeared at a point when Vargas Llosa was already deeply involved in Peruvian politics. It caused a scandal when it was used by his political adversaries to prove that the presidential candidate was a pornographer with a sick imagination. Vargas Llosa describes in his memoir of the political campaign how the entire book was read a chapter at a time on prime-time television, followed by a discussion with a panel of experts analysing his personality. This bizarre intermingling of reality and fiction continued one of the subject matters of the novel, the way in which life has a tendency to imitate art – up to a point where life turns out to be far stranger than fiction.

***

Los cuadernos de Don Rigoberto picks up the story of Rigoberto, Lucrecia, Alfonso (Fonchito) and Justiniana some time later. Alfonso is now an art student who unexpectedly turns up at the modest house where Lucrecia lives with her maid Justiniana. This visit sets the whole cycle of seduction, manipulation and lies in motion again. The son has obviously inherited the father's fixation with erotic art, and Alfonso is completely obsessed with the Austrian painter Egon Schiele. The book does not contain reproductions of Schiele's work but small drawings inspired by him at the end of each of the nine chapters plus epilogue. Fonchito comes to talk to Lucrecia and Justiniana about Schiele's work and his life, and he persuades them to adopt poses from his paintings. These *tableaux vivants* go a step further than his father's imagined re-enactment of pictorial scenes which only happens in his mind. Fonchito, by contrast, involves the two women in an elaborate erotic game, even though they realize that he is a diabolical manipulator, 'so shameless, so cynical, so perverse' despite being so young. But Lucrecia can't resist his charm, the 'canto de esas sirenas que llaman desde los abismos' (*Cuadernos*, p. 33) [siren song calling her down to the abyss] (*Notebooks*, p. 23). Her natural taste for danger and excitement was enhanced by her husband introducing her to the notion of life as play, according to the book *Homo ludens* by Johan Huizinga (another cultural allusion to prevent their sex life from becoming trivial). This game of spicing up their nocturnal encounters with 'endlessly renewed fictions' had intrigued her so much that she now falls for Fonchito's playful erotic scenarios, and even invents one herself when she goes on an adventure dressed as a hooker. The plot involving Fonchito and the two women is narrated from Lucrecia's perspective, in each first section of the novel's nine chapters.

The second section contains Rigoberto's voice, in letters expressing his extremist views about followers of 'collectivist conspiracies' such as ecologists, feminists, Rotarians, sportsmen, patriots, readers of *Playboy* magazine and bureaucrats – a self-parody of Vargas Llosa's well-known dislike for any sort of collective identity. This he projects onto the slightly deranged manner in which his embittered protagonist takes refuge in his own mental world, his 'enclave de libertad y fantasía' (p. 330) [enclave of freedom and fantasy] (p. 264), following the loss of the private empire of happiness that he had built himself with his wife. Having completely withdrawn into his world of thoughts and fantasies, Rigoberto does not send off these letters but records his anti-collectivist feelings in his notebooks, one of the occupations with which he fills the loneliness that remains after Lucrecia's departure. The tone of Rigoberto's letters is extremely polemical, reflecting Vargas Llosa's own extreme individualism, but hilariously exaggerated: modern sportsmen, for instance, are denounced for providing meaningless mass entertainment so that 'muchedumbres insanas se desexualicen con eyaculaciones de egolatría colectivista' (p. 127) [maddened crowds can be desexed by ejaculations of collective egotism] (p. 101). The sexual undertone of many of Rigoberto's diatribes speaks of his sexual frustration, for example when he writes about vegetarians:

> Yo confieso paladinamente que para mí los animales tienen un interés comestible, decorativo y acaso deportivo (aunque le precisaré que el amor a los caballos me produce tanta desagrado como el vegetarianismo y que tengo a los caballistas de testículos enanizados por la fricción de la montura por un tipo particularmente lúgubre del castrado humano). (p. 41)

> [I openly admit that for me, animals are of edible, decorative, and perhaps sporting interest (though I state specifically that I find love of horses as unpleasant as vegetarianism, and consider horsemen, their testicles shrunken by the friction of the saddle, to be a particularly lugubrious type of human castrato).] (p. 29)

In another letter Rigoberto declares feminism to be a collectivist illusion for wanting to divide into dual categories what, from his 'solitaria esquina de libertario hedonista' [solitary corner [of a] libertarian hedonist], is a humanity made up of individuals: 'falos aquí, clítoris del otro lado, vaginas a la derecha, escrotos a la izquierda. Ese esquematismo gregario no corresponde a la verdad' (p. 86) [penises here, clitorises there, vaginas to the right, scrotums to the left. This slavish schematic does not correspond to the truth] (p. 66). This particularly outrageous letter to a feminist ends with the greeting

'Abur y polvos, amiga' (p. 88) [Farewell and fine fucking, my friend] (p. 67). It is not difficult to imagine Vargas Llosa chuckling in the background. There is one particular letter in which the extraliterary author appears only thinly disguised behind his protagonist Rigoberto, a letter that deals with patriotism, one of Vargas Llosa's most ardent concerns of the 1990s. Rigoberto addresses a typical flag-waving patriot with words that are lifted almost literally from an essay Vargas Llosa published on the dangers of nationalism:[34]

> El cordón umbilical que los enlaza a través de las centurias se llama pavor a lo desconocido, odio a lo distinto, rechazo a la aventura, pánico a la libertad y a la responsabilidad de inventarse cada día, vocación de servidumbre a la rutina, a lo gregario, rechazo a descolectivizarse para no tener que afrontar el desafío cotidiano que es la soberanía individual. (p. 247)
>
> [The umbilical cord that connects you across the centuries is called terror of the unknown, hatred for what is different, rejection of adventure, panic at the thought of freedom and the responsibility it brings to invent yourself each day, a vocation for servitude to the routine and the gregarious, a refusal to decollectivize so that you will not be obliged to face the daily challenge of individual sovereignty.] (p. 199)

It seems fair to say that Rigoberto, the individualistic erotomane, is one more fictional alter ego of Vargas Llosa – even though a parodistically exaggerated one – and a number of the erotic fantasies which make up each third section of the novel's nine chapters confirm this. They are based on some of Vargas Llosa's favourite literary texts: Juan Carlos Onetti's *La vida breve* [*A Brief Life*] and Calderón de la Barca's *La vida es sueño* [*Life is a Dream*]. Rigoberto fills his sleepless nights by imagining elaborate erotic encounters between his wife and other men (or women) inspired by the literary quotations, personal observations, newspaper cuttings, or cross-references to works of art, which fill his notebooks. The motifs are familiar from *Elogio de la madrastra*: voyeurism, homoeroticism and intimate role-play starting with the question 'Who am I?'; Rigoberto's overlarge ears and nose as erotic objects; his obsession with cleanliness and bodily functions; sex across the boundaries of race, age and social status; bodily odours and synaesthesia, etc. At some point, leafing through his notebooks, Rigoberto comes across a quotation from a poem by Kipling, 'If you can dream – and not make dreams your master', which he sees as a warning: 'Seguía siendo dueño de sus sueños, o éstos lo gobernaban ya, por abusar tanto de ellos desde su separación de Lucrecia?' (p. 261) [Was he still master of his dreams, or did they now rule him because he had abused them so much since his separation

---

[34] Mario Vargas Llosa, 'Cuestión de fondo', in *Desafíos a la libertad* (Madrid: El País/Aguilar, 1994), pp. 247–51 (pp. 248–9).

from Lucrecia?] (p. 209). That is a question that hovers over *Los cuadernos de Don Rigoberto* as a whole: does there have to be a necessary balance between reality and fiction? At which point does the imaginary counter-world take over and turn from an enriching to a destructive factor of life? Lucrecia feels the corrupting influence of her husband's taboo-breaking imagination on her own, very real desires. In Fonchito's case his identification with Schiele has become an unhealthy obsession. He imagines himself suffering from the same kind of schizophrenia, and he is obsessed with the same kind of paedophilic scenarios as his hero. Both father and son are prone to get lost in their imaginary worlds of cultural references which they mistake for the real world.

But Fonchito is also a very real manipulator who sets out to bring his father back together with Lucrecia. His motives remain ambiguous, although Lucrecia's suspicions are supported by her stepson's ruthless betrayals of trust: '¿Que quería? ¿Qué intriga tramaba? ¿Por qué esa farsa? ¿Divertirse, divertirse disponiendo de sus emociones, de su vida? Era perverso, sádico. Gozaba ilusionándola y viéndola luego desmoronarse, desengañada' (p. 280) [What was he after? What scheme was he devising? Why the farce? For the fun, the sheer fun of manipulating her emotions, her life? He was perverse, sadistic. He enjoyed leading her on and then watching her crumbling hopes, her disillusionment] (p. 224). Fonchito manipulates both his father and stepmother into thinking that they want to get back together, by writing anonymous letters making each believe they come from the other. These letters make up the fourth section of each chapter, and the reader is left wondering until the end as to who is their author. Half of them are full of cultural allusions as if they were written by Rigoberto, the other half elaborate on erotic scenarios as if Lucrecia were teasing her husband's imagination. All of them seem to suggest a longing for the other person and a wish to reunite, making Lucrecia feel 'extraviada en un bosque de conjeturas, divagaciones, sospechas, fantasías' (p. 281) [lost in a forest of conjectures, speculations, suspicions, fantasies] (p. 225).

In the epilogue, the family is indeed reunited, the letters have fulfilled their function. But Fonchito's corrosive influence destroys the happiness again by revealing his frequent visits to Lucrecia. She then feels the need to tell Rigoberto that her attraction to Fonchito is irresistible as long as he is present. The couple finally discover the deceit of the anonymous correspondence. They read the letters addressed to the other person and find out that Fonchito had not only forged Rigoberto's handwriting, but also quoted directly from his father's secret notebooks. For the letters supposedly from Lucrecia, Fonchito had lifted passages from the trivial romances of Corín Tellado (one of Vargas Llosa's often mentioned 'cultural demons'). The fact that the couple had believed in the authenticity of these steamy, kitsch[35] pieces

---

[35] For the interesting thesis that these letters constitute the novel about the specifically Peruvian form of kitsch, 'lo huachafo', that Vargas Llosa had always intended to write, see

of writing ridicules their whole edifice of refined erotic fantasies. It confirms that such fantasies constitute a private pact between two (or more) people, 'un dominio privado y secreto' [a private and secret domain], as Vargas Llosa puts it ('La desaparición del erotismo', p. 110). Fonchito's violation of this pact by reading Rigoberto's notebooks and imitating the couple's private fantasies destroys their secret world of happiness.

Whether the erotic pact between the reader and the novel works is another question. The nature of the fantasies in Vargas Llosa's two erotic novels is a matter of personal taste. The 'refinement' that turns the sexual act into 'a work of art' ('La desaparición del erotismo', p. 111) is a very private concept, and Vargas Llosa's game with a multitude of cultural references cannot hide that. But there is also an issue with repetitive metaphors. This reader, at least, got a bit tired after the third mention of a 'serpentine tongue' slithering into some crevice. Behind all the cultural and intertextual references meant to detrivialize the erotic encounters, there is still an awful lot about 'croups', 'rods', 'wetness', 'depilated hollows', etc. The problem is one that Vargas Llosa himself describes in his essay on eroticism: 'los libros *sólo* eróticos pronto sucumben a la repetición y a la monomanía, porque la actividad sexual, aunque intensa y fuente maravillosa de goces, es limitada' [books which are *solely* erotic soon succumb to repetition and monomania, since sexual activity, although intense and a wonderful fount of pleasure, is limited] ('La desaparición del erotismo', p. 114). The novel's intriguing story, its ambiguous play with innocence and corruption, the interesting question of the fragile balance between reality and fiction seem to me, in the end, not enough to outweigh the repetitiveness of the erotic fantasies in Los cuadernos de Don Rigoberto. Elogio de la madrastra, by contrast, is a much more interesting work due to its brevity and the originality of its experimentation with ekphrasis. Form, contents, language and pictorial representation, not least the intriguing choice of paintings, work together to produce an erotic fiction that can be enjoyed on many different levels.

***

Travesuras de la niña mala [*The Bad Girl*],[36] a novel which appeared in 2006, continues some motifs of these two erotic works. Although not an expressly erotic novel, there is a strong sexual element in the story of protagonist Ricardo Somocurcio's lifelong infatuation with the elusive 'bad

Brigitte König, 'Ama et impera! Linguistische (und andere) Betrachtungen zum erotischen Imperativ bei Mario Vargas Llosa', in *Das literarische Werk von Mario Vargas Llosa. Akten des Colloquiums im Ibero-Amerikanischen Institut, Berlin 5.–7. November 1998*, ed. José Morales Saravia (Frankfurt am Main: Vervuert, 2000), pp. 305–33, in particular pp. 327–9.

[36] Mario Vargas Llosa, *Travesuras de la niña mala* (Madrid: Alfaguara, 2006); Mario Vargas Llosa, *The Bad Girl*, trans. Edith Grossman (London: Faber and Faber, 2008).

girl' whom he meets as a teenager in Lima and re-encounters in various incarnations in different cities throughout his life. Explicit descriptions of their sexual encounters, certain motifs such as voyeurism, the different masks that the 'bad girl' appears under, and Ricardo's use of the 'cheap, sentimental' language of the 'huachaferías' to woo her are the most obvious links between this later work and Vargas Llosa's two erotic novels. But *Travesuras de la niña mala* is also Vargas Llosa's contribution to another genre, the 'novela de amor', even though it is a rather one-sided love story. Ricardo's fascination for the 'bad girl', whose real name and identity remain a mystery until the later stages of the novel, is based on an erotic attraction awakened in the proper young man from middle-class Miraflores by the girl's provocative manner of dressing and dancing. Her bold and mischievous behaviour and the sense of mystery, danger and transgression that the presumed Chilean girl exudes have a lasting effect on the 'good boy', as she calls Ricardo. But whenever Ricardo wants to commit himself to the 'bad girl' she disappears – until she enters his life again in a different incarnation: as a guerrilla fighter on her way to Cuba; as Madame Arnoux (a reference to Flaubert's *Education Sentimentale*), married to a French diplomat; as the wife of a horse-breeding country gent in Newmarket; the mistress of a Japanese gangster in Tokyo. Sometimes they run into each other by pure chance – demands on the reader's credulity become ever greater in the course of the novel – while at other times the 'bad girl' seeks him out because she needs this reliable, steady friend whose love for her is never destroyed by her deceitful, cruel and selfish behaviour. After her many role-plays it turns out that she is actually a Peruvian trying to run away from her background of poverty and chasing her dream of living an exciting life in great wealth. There are traits of Emma Bovary about the 'bad girl': when Ricardo nurses her back to health after a crisis and, for a while, they live a settled, bourgeois life together in his small Parisian apartment, the 'bad girl' flees the mediocrity she cannot accept in search of new adventures, this time with the husband of her boss. She returns to Ricardo when she develops terminal cancer and makes him happy by letting him nurse her to the end – a sentimental and somewhat infuriating story of a ruthlessly ambitious and thrill-seeking woman exploiting a decent, but weak and unambitious man. Some critics have detected humour and irony in this inversion of machismo.[37] But the 'bad girl's' belief that life is a jungle 'where only the worst triumph' – which relates her to the alpha-male Jaguar from *La ciudad y los perros* – make her act in a stereotypically female way: by becoming the trophy wife of rich and powerful men she uses her beauty to achieve wealth.

---

[37] For example, see José Miguel Oviedo's review, 'Travesuras de la niña mala, de Mario Vargas Llosa', *Letra Libres*, July 2006, <http://www.letraslibres.com/revista/libros/travesuras-de-la-nina-mala-de-mario-vargas-llosa> [accessed 29 October 2012].

The sentimental love story is told by the first-person narrator Ricardo and progresses in a linear manner, beginning with the lovers' encounter in 1950s Lima and ending with the 'bad girl' near to death in the late 1980s in France. The themes of ageing, illness and death link *Travesuras de la niña mala* to the other three novels from the first decade of the new millennium which will be discussed in chapter 9 below, the final part of this study of Vargas Llosa's narrative work. But *Travesuras* is not in the same category as these renewed attempts at a 'total novel'. Technical innovation is absent from this simple, straightforward narration, but on the level of content it fulfils Vargas Llosa's recipe for interesting fiction: sex, violence, melodrama and rebellion are the prevalent ingredients of this love story. The book's seven chapters have descriptive titles such as 'Retratista de caballos en el *swinging London*' [Painter of Horses in Swinging London] (chapter 3) or 'Marcella en Lavapiés' [Marcella in Lavapiés] (chapter 7), which indicate the episodic nature of the individual chapters unfolding in different periods and places. Each of these titles refers to a secondary character who only appears in one chapter and acts as a catalyst to the development of the love story between Ricardo and the 'bad girl'. The majority of them are Latin American friends whom Ricardo is attached to during a particular period of his nomadic life. They represent the link to his home country and give Vargas Llosa the opportunity to fill in the background of Peru's historical and social development from the 1950s to the 1980s, complementing the depiction of the *zeitgeist* of these decades in European and Asian cities.

The novel once again plays with autobiographical material. Some stages of Ricardo's life run in parallel with Vargas Llosa's own development: from his youth in Miraflores to the fulfilment of his dream of living in Paris, the move to London during the 1960s, the frequent changes of place in the 1970s and the stay in Madrid in the 1980s – these are reflections of Vargas Llosa's own experiences. The changes of scenery give him the chance to depict the atmosphere of different decades and the local colour of the various cities, and to highlight the cultural changes that happened during his lifetime. He describes, for example, the shift from the bookish, intellectual culture of Paris in the early 1960s to the music-dominated scene in 'swinging' London which he perceives as uninterested in ideas. This kaleidoscope of various youth cultures, ending with the vibrant multicultural scene in 1980s Madrid that the protagonist is introduced to through a much younger woman, is written with a nostalgic tone, as Vargas Llosa has said in a number of interviews. The changes of scene and the episodic character of the narration provide easy, entertaining reading, but they necessarily remain superficial. The light-hearted romp through epochs and places takes in the 1960s enthusiasm for Cuba in the same tone as more sinister aspects such as the emergence of Aids.

The episodic narration is also full of – at times rather uncomfortably so – clichés. Particularly hard to digest is the plot involving the cruel, inscrutable and cold Asian male Fukuda, the only man who provokes real feeling in the 'bad girl', despite his brutal sexual abuse of her. The 'bad girl's' masochistic attachment to Fukuda is not explored further despite the potentially intriguing fact that her usual lack of passion in the sexual encounters with Ricardo gives way to a great ardour in the scene where she makes loves to him while Fukuda is watching in the background. Before encountering him in person, Ricardo is afraid that the Yakuza boss 'no la cortara en canal y echara su cadáver a los perros, como hacía el malvado en una película japonesa que acababa de ver' (*Travesuras*, p. 167) [wouldn't slit her open from head to toe and throw her body to the dogs, as the villain had done in a Japanese film I had just seen] (*Bad Girl*, p. 175). This might pass as irony, but when Ricardo actually meets him, Fukuda lives up to the stereotype: 'una cara inexpresiva y neutral, apergaminada, ... una cara que parecía una máscara' (p. 187) [the same inexpressive, neutral, parchment-like face, ... a face that looked like a mask] (p. 197); 'podía permanecer inmóvil y mudo mucho rato ... como petrificado' (p. 188) [he could remain motionless and silent for a long time ... as if he were petrified] (p. 197). During their encounter the Japanese appears 'rígido e inescrutable ... como un muñeco articulado' (p. 192) [rigid and inscrutable ... like an articulated puppet] (p. 201). What Ricardo later finds out about Fukuda's preferred sexual practices and the injuries that he has inflicted on the 'bad girl's' body and mind answers to the cliché, well-known from movies, that the inscrutable mask and cold politeness of the Asian man hide cruelty and ruthlessness. Ricardo's Latin American friends, by contrast, are all warm-hearted, good-natured people, friends 'a la Peruana' [in the Peruvian style], as he puts it several times. This 'amistad visceral a la sudamericana' (p. 275) [South American kind of visceral friendship] (p. 293) makes up for his lack of friends amongst the Parisians. The novel also touches on questions of identity when Ricardo asks himself: 'Había dejado de ser un peruano en muchos sentidos, sin duda. ¿Qué era entonces? Tampoco había llegado a ser un europeo, ni en Francia, ni mucho menos en Inglaterra. ¿Qué eras, pues, Ricardito?' (p. 141) [I undoubtedly had stopped being a Peruvian in many senses. What was I, then? I hadn't become a European either, not in France and certainly not in England. So what were you, Ricardito?] (p. 147) – a question that must have haunted Vargas Llosa many times during his lifetime of travelling from place to place, meticulously recorded in the way he signs off his many articles, and carefully documented on his website.

Another – unintentionally funny – stereotype concerns the wholesome beauty of a Danish woman whom Ricardo meets at a conference. She takes him to a hotel room where they make love in a 'healthful way' that has 'more to do with gymnastics' than with passion: 'Hacía el amor sin que la sonrisa se retirara de su cara, incluso en el momento del orgasmo' (p. 206) [She made love and the smile didn't leave her face, not even when she had an orgasm] (p. 219). To Ricardo this is not attractive compared to the contorted infatuation that binds him to the 'bad girl', even though she does not show any passion during their lovemaking and instead retreats into her own world – a motif already known from Don Rigoberto of the erotic novels. The bad girl also resembles Rigoberto in her desire to compensate for the mediocrity of life with the fictions of role-play, forever reinventing herself as someone else. Only, in her case, these fictions take over her whole life. She goes a step further than Don Rigoberto, who wondered whether he could keep his fantasies at bay, and immerses herself in the different fictional lives she creates for herself. The border between reality and fiction is abolished, as one psychiatrist explains to Ricardo: 'ella, y todos quienes viven buena parte de su vida encerrados en fantasías que se construyen para abolir la verdadera vida, saben y no saben lo que están haciendo. La frontera se les eclipsa por períodos y, luego, reaparece. Quiero decir: a veces saben y otras no saben lo que hacen' (p. 268) [she, and all those who live a good part of their lives enclosed in fantasies they erect in order to abolish their real life, both know and don't know what they're doing. The border disappears for a while and then it reappears. I mean, sometimes they know and other times they don't know what they're doing] (p. 285). The bad girl is also a reincarnation of Alicia Mindreau, the delusional protagonist of *Palomino Molero*.

It seems to me that the story of a compulsive liar with an untameable desire for adventure, excitement and danger is as self-referential as many of Vargas Llosa's more obviously metafictional novels. In his book review, José Miguel Oviedo states that *Travesuras de la niña mala* deviates from the dual patterns which structure Vargas Llosa's novels. But Ricardo and the 'bad girl' are two sides of the same coin, for they are the coexisting opposites that simultaneously repel and attract each other: the civilized, polite and amiable 'niño bueno' who used to be a shy young man from Miraflores, and the 'niña mala' avid for adventure, transgression and the thrills that a life full of lies can provide. Ricardo is the incurable romantic who struggles with his desire for the mysterious and elusive woman. The 'bad girl' longs for an alternative existence that allows her to overcome the shortcomings of her childhood and adolescence, 'de huir para siempre de esa trampa, cárcel y maldición que era para ella el Perú' (p. 323) [to flee forever the trap, the prison, the curse that Peru meant for her] (p. 347). Both protagonists carry traits of Vargas Llosa himself. The 'bad girl' embodies the exciting life that he lives out in his fictions, adopting roles and imagining himself in different incarnations. His other double Ricardo settles in Paris, the city of his – and Vargas Llosa's – dreams where he is happy with the uneventful life that Vargas Llosa could have had, had he not, in his literary fantasies, followed the path of the 'bad girl', obsessively looking for the next adventure. Pursuing her never satisfied dreams she represents the uncompromising, exploitative and devouring existence that a life dedicated to fiction demands. Vargas Llosa's autobiographical persona that he uses so often in his writing is split into two: the timid Ricardo, translator of other people's words, whose love does not make any demands and expresses itself in terms of 'kitsch' (doesn't his name Somocurcio evoke 'somos cursi'?) lives a real, bourgeois existence, while, on the other side, there is the 'bad girl' who is at home in fictions, rejecting real life and not allowing herself to be reigned in by obligations. Like literature's demands on Vargas Llosa, she requires Ricardo's total dedication as someone who puts up with all her whims. She terrorizes and tortures her loyal lover by needing him one moment and rejecting him the next, 'demostrando al pichiruchi insolente que no estaba enamorada en absoluto, que podía prescindir de él como de una baratija inservible' (p. 140) [showing the insolent little pissant that she absolutely was not in love and could dispose of him like a useless trinket] (p. 145). Ricardo is that person willing to submit himself totally to her demands, even though this attachment almost drives him to suicide. But despite all her whims she makes Ricardo feel alive, she is his inspiration and the motor of his existence. Once, when she has left him again, he muses: 'las ilusiones que hacen de la existencia algo más que una suma de rutinas, se ma habían apagado. A ratos, me sentía un viejo' (p. 207) [the illusions that make existence something more than the sum of its routines had been extinguished for me. At times I felt like an old man] (p. 220). (*Travesuras* is also a novel about growing older, with at times clinical descriptions of bodies ravaged by old age and illness.)

When the 'bad girl' has lived out her life driven by the destructive desire to explore ever more exciting and dangerous paths, she comes back to rely on Ricardo, her last and only friend. In the end she tells him that she can give him one thing: her life story to write about, 'Porque siempre has querido ser un escritor y no te atrevías. ... Por lo menos, confiesa que te he dado tema para una novela' (p. 375) [Because you always wanted to be a writer and didn't have the courage. ... At least admit I've given you the subject for a novel] (p. 403). Thus we are, once more, reading the very novel that its protagonist sets out to write. In the end, *Travesuras de la niña mala* is not only a sentimental love story which has traits of a travelogue, an erotic and a *zeitgeist* novel, but also a self-referential work of metafiction. Like Ricardo's obsession with the 'bad girl' and her imagined lives, Vargas Llosa's fictional and (as we will see in chapter 8) non-fictional writing always revolves around turning his life's experiences into literature.

8

Interlude: the Demons of Literature and Politics (*El pez en el agua*, 1993)

When I met Mario Vargas Llosa in November 1991 at the Wissenschaftskolleg [Institute for Advanced Study] in Berlin and had the chance to put some questions to him about literature and politics,[1] he had already published an account of his unsuccessful bid for the Peruvian presidency in the English journal *Granta*[2] and was working on an extended version of that essay, planned as a book-length memoir of the political campaign leading up to his defeat in the second round election in June 1990. His *Granta* essay was appropriately named 'A Fish out of Water', tracing the phase of his life from 1987 to 1990 when politics took precedence over literature: from the moment he became the figurehead of the protest movement against President Alan García's plans to bring banks, insurance companies and financial institutions under government control, a move which consequently turned the writer into a full-time politician, up to Vargas Llosa's electoral defeat allowing him to return to his true vocation, literature. In a condensed form, and from a perspective still very close to the events, he presented a testimony of his motivations for entering politics, the intentions and methods he followed in his campaign, the obstacles he encountered and misjudgements he made. The essay ends with the disillusioned résumé of his period as an intellectual in politics, a 'fish out of water': 'No, finally, I don't believe that I succeeded in putting across what I wanted to. Peruvians did not vote for *ideas* in the elections' (p. 74). *Granta* complemented Vargas Llosa's account of his campaign with two shorter articles in which his son Álvaro (who acted as his press officer) and Mark Malloch Brown (who was the adviser for the political consultancy Sawyer Miller overseeing his campaign) gave their perspective on the failed candidacy.[3]

---

[1]   At the time I was working on my doctoral dissertation *Literatur und Politik – Mario Vargas Llosa*, submitted to the University of Zurich in 1995 and subsequently published by Peter Lang (Bern, 1996).
[2]   Mario Vargas Llosa, 'A Fish out of Water', trans. Helen Lane, *Vargas Llosa for President* (*Granta*, 36 (1991)), 15–76.
[3]   Alvaro Vargas Llosa, 'The Press Officer', trans. Shaun Whiteside, and Mark Malloch Brown, 'The Consultant', *Vargas Llosa for President* (*Granta*, 36 (1991)), 77–85 and 87–95 respectively.

The book about Vargas Llosa's political adventure appeared in 1993 under the surprising title *El pez en el agua. Memorias* [*A Fish in the Water. A Memoir*][4] and turned out to be much more than what the English subtitle suggests: the memoir of his political campaign to become president of Peru alternates with chapters recounting the formative years in which the young Mario developed into a professional novelist. The chronicle of a specific episode in Vargas Llosa's life dominated by his political commitment is juxtaposed with the autobiographical narration of his childhood, adolescence and youth, recollecting the many factors and people that played a role in turning him into what, from early on, he wanted to be: a writer. Two different genres, autobiography and political memoir, set within two different time frames, the distant past of the 1940s and 1950s and the immediate past of the late 1980s, complement each other in alternate chapters. The book begins on the autobiographical level, with the traumatic event in the author-protagonist's childhood when he realized that his father, whom he had thought dead, was alive and would rip him out of the security of his pampered early life with his mother, grandparents and the extended Llosa family, all of whom had encouraged him in his precocious attempts to write fiction. In a symmetrical way chapter 2 relates how, in July 1987, a piece of news that reached Vargas Llosa during a peaceful family holiday on a remote Peruvian beach would bring turmoil into the steady life of writing that he had mapped out for himself, with a set of literary projects. The fact that the parallel treatment of these two unexpected, life-changing events starts with the autobiographical narration, rather than the political memoir, shows that the emphasis of the book is on the author-protagonist's formative experiences which made him turn to literature, an area where he would swim like a fish in water, rather than on the interlude in politics where he felt like a fish out of water, unable to influence things the way he wanted to.[5] Both narrative strands end with his

---

[4]   Mario Vargas Llosa, *El pez en el agua. Memorias* (Barcelona: Seix Barral, 1993); Mario Vargas Llosa, *A Fish in the Water. A Memoir*, trans. Helen Lane (London: Faber and Faber, 1995).

[5]   This is a thought underlined in the epigraph that precedes *El pez en el agua*, a quotation from Max Weber's 1919 lecture on *Politik als Beruf* [Politics as a Vocation], published in 1919 and reprinted in the same form as a separate booklet (Berlin: Dunker & Humblot, 1987), which states (in what seems to be Helen Lane's translation) that 'the world is ruled by demons ... anyone who becomes involved in politics ... has sealed a pact with the devil, so that it is no longer true that in his activity the good produces only good and the bad bad'. This epigraph has been widely commented on by critics (for example, see Sergio R. Franco, 'The Recovered Childhood', in *Vargas Llosa and Latin American Politics*, ed. Juan E. De Castro and Nicholas Birns [New York: Palgrave Macmillan, 2010], pp. 125–36). I was surprised and amused to find it on opening Vargas Llosa's book, remembering that in 1991 on a visit to the Vargas Llosas (who were so very open and generous to invite me together with my husband and baby daughter into their home in Berlin), my husband presented them with a book of his on Shakespeare which included an essay on *Coriolanus*, preceded by that exact same epigraph from Weber which we thought very fitting – an indication of how writers, consciously or unconsciously, absorb and rework everything that catches their imagination.

departure from Peru to Europe where, in 1958, he would begin, and thirty-two years later resume pursuing his true vocation: writing fiction. In both cases, he experienced this departure as a liberation from the constraints of his native country and its overwhelming problems which made it impossible to be a writer and nothing but a writer. The last of the book's twenty titled chapters ends with the metaphorical image of the plane, on the morning of 13 June 1990, carrying him into the blue skies, leaving the oppressive grey clouds of Lima behind:

> Cuando el aparato emprendió vuelo y las infalibles nubes de Lima borraron de nuestra vista la ciudad y nos quedamos rodeados sólo de cielo azúl, pensé que esta partida se parecía a la de 1958, que había marcado de manera tan nítida el fin de una etapa de mi vida y el inicio de otra, en la que la literatura pasó a ocupar el lugar central. (*El pez*, p. 529)

> [When the plane took off and the infallible clouds of Lima blotted the city from sight and we were surrounded only by blue sky, the thought crossed my mind that this departure resembled the one in 1958, which had so clearly marked the end of one stage of my life and the beginning of another, in which literature came to occupy the central place.] (*Fish*, pp. 522–3)

However, in the short 'Colophon' Vargas Llosa narrates how, in the years immediately following his departure after the defeat in the elections, he found himself unable to shake off Peruvian politics and was drawn back into publicly taking a stand when Alberto Fujimori, who beat him in the elections, pronounced his 'autogolpe' [self-coup]. This underlines a number of points that Vargas Llosa makes throughout the book: that for him literature and politics are intertwined since the interest in them developed in parallel, and that, despite his self-definition as a citizen of the world, Peru remains closest to his heart and events there will always hold him in his grip. Earlier on in the book he says:

> Quizá decir que quiero a mi país no sea exacto. Abomino de él con frecuencia y, cientos de veces, desde joven, me he hecho la promesa de vivir para siempre lejos del Perú y no escribir más sobre él y olvidarme de sus extravíos. Pero la verdad es que lo he tenido siempre presente y que ha sido para mí, afincado en él o expatriado, un motivo constante de mortificación. No puedo librarme de él. (p. 48)

> [Perhaps saying that I love my country is not true. I often loathe it, and hundreds of times since I was young I have promised myself to live a long way from Peru forever and not write anything more about it and forget its aberrations. But the fact is that it is continually on my mind, and whether I am living in it or residing abroad as an expatriate, to me it is a constant torment. I cannot free myself from it.] (p. 43)

Despite the factual character of *El pez en el agua*, its dual structure alternating between two narrative strands, its framework of an epigraph and an epilogue (or in this case 'colophon'), the wealth of colourful anecdotes contained in both strands, and the carefully constructed parallels between the two levels of narration continue characteristics of Vargas Llosa's fictional work. Some bibliographies categorize the memoirs under essays, others under narrative. On his official website[6] the 'memorias' appear as a separate category. The special, hybrid character of *El pez en el agua* is not least due to the fact that the book recounts many events in Vargas Llosa's life which are familiar to readers of his fiction. His way of writing literature on the basis of his own experiences, and the reality surrounding him and the people he knows (the 'demonios personales') means that we recognize episodes and characters from his novels in the account of real-life occurrences. In some cases, the realization of how closely the fictitious world mirrors reality can have a disillusioning effect. Chapter 7, 'Periodismo y bohemia' [Journalism and Bohemia], for example, narrates Vargas Llosa's experiences as a journalist at *La Crónica* and contains near word-for-word repetitions of dialogue that we have taken to be part of the fictional world of the 1969 novel *Conversación en la catedral*. That leaves a stale taste, retrospectively destroying part of the magic of fiction that Vargas Llosa often invokes. Since his novelistic output has always closely followed his autobiographical experiences, there are many such disillusioning 'déjà lu' moments in the sequence of the chapters: 'El cadete de la suerte' [The Cadet] and its retelling of Vargas Llosa's time at the Leoncio Prado Academy; 'Camarada Alberto' [Comrade Alberto] and the Communist cell Cahuide at San Marcos University; 'La tía Julia' [Aunt Julia] and the search for a mayor who would marry the underage Mario, to name just a few.

The blurring of the border between reality and fiction works both ways: not only does the real background for Vargas Llosa's fictional creations come into view and tarnish his fiction with too much reality; in some instances Vargas Llosa's memories have become distorted by fiction – his own and that of other authors – as he expressly warns his readers. On the autobiographical level, for instance, he admits that he is no longer sure about the extent of reality and fantasy in his recollections of the trip he made in 1958 to the Alto Marañon, an excursion that provided him with material for several novels. He concedes the possibility that his unconscious and his imagination might 'have continually incorporated changes' into the memory of that expedition. Something similar happens on the level of political memoir, for example in the episode of the archbishop of Lima's secret visit to Vargas Llosa's house before the second round of the elections: 'La media hora o tres cuartos de hora que conversamos ha quedado en mi memoria confundida con algunos de los episodios

---

[6] <http://www.mvargasllosa.com>.

más inusuales de las buenas novelas que he leído' (p. 484) [The half- or three-quarters of an hour that we talked together has become confused in my memory with certain of the most unusual episodes of the good novels that I have read] (p. 477). This sums up a paradox in Vargas Llosa's life and work: he writes fiction starting from real life, but is most stimulated by real life when it seems like fiction. As he puts it in one of the early autobiographical chapters of *El pez*: 'Desde chico, las cosas y los seres de la realidad que me han conmovido más han sido los que más se acercaban a la literatura' (p. 191) [Ever since I was a small boy, the real-life things and people that have moved me most have been the ones that most closely resembled literature] (p. 188). Here also lies part of the motivation for his step into politics: the hunger for adventure and the desire to live through extraordinary and possibly dangerous experiences that drive him to read and write has played a role in his decision to accept the 'almost impossible challenge' of wanting to govern a country like Peru with its 'decadence, impoverishment, terrorism, and multiple crises'. Quoting his wife Patricia's retrospective judgement – 'Fue la aventura, la ilusión de vivir una experiencia llena de excitación y de riesgo. De escribir, en la vida real, la gran novela' (p. 46) [It was the adventure, the illusion of living an experience full of excitement and risk. Of writing the great novel in real life] (p. 41) – he admits:

> Tal vez tiene razón. Es verdad que si la presidencia del Perú no hubiera sido, como le dije bromeando a un periodista, el oficio más peligroso del mundo, jamás hubiera sido candidato. ... no descarto que, en ese fondo oscuro donde se traman nuestros actos, fuera la tentación de la aventura, antes que ningún altruismo, lo que me empujara a la política profesional. (p. 46)

> [This may well hit the nail on the head. It is true that if the presidency of Peru had not been, as I said jokingly to a journalist, 'the most dangerous job in the world', I might never have been a candidate. ... I can't discard the possibility that, in those dark depths where the most secret motivations of our acts are plotted, it was the temptation of adventure, rather than some sort of altruism, that induced me to enter professional politics.] (pp. 41–2)

On the other hand, the sum of the autobiographical chapters renders a coherent account of Vargas Llosa's personal and intellectual formation and maps out the sense of moral responsibility with which he would later enter politics, as well as his contrariness and stubbornness in pursuing his political goals, often against the advice of his team. The two narrative strands of *El pez* complement each other in explaining how Vargas Llosa's experience of unhappiness, injustice and violence on the personal level have shaped the sense of justice and morality with which he approached the problems of his country. When his father entered his life, nine-year-old Mario began to feel the basic evils of Peruvian society in his own existence: he came to hate the authoritarian attitude of his father, and fear his outbreaks of physical and verbal violence, often directed against his son's love of literature, an 'effeminate' occupation unacceptable in the father's value system which reflected society's machismo. The father seemed to him 'la encarnación de la crueldad, el mal hecho hombre' (p. 75) [the very embodiment of cruelty, the evildoer personified] (p. 71). But in retrospect Vargas Llosa understands the social dimension to his parents' problems, the fact that his father, from an impoverished family, felt socially inferior to his mother's family background. This crucial analysis is given already on the third page of *El pez*, establishing the link between early biography and later political career, between his personal experience of the effects of social inequalities and his later political attempt to bring about social change:

> Pero la verdadera razón del fracaso matrimonial no fueron los celos, ni el mal carácter de mi padre, sino la enfermedad nacional por antonomasia, aquella que infesta todos los estratos y familias del país y en todos deja un relente que envenena la vida de los peruanos: el resentimiento y los complejos sociales. (p. 11)

> [But the real reason for the failure of their marriage was not my father's jealousy or his bad disposition, but the national disease that gets called by other names, the one that infests every stratum and every family in the country and leaves them all with a bad aftertaste of hatred, poisoning the lives of Peruvians in the form of resentment and social complexes.] (p. 5)

In the political chapters Vargas Llosa shows how the same kind of social rancour, resentment and violence also poisoned his electoral campaign. His defeat was not least due to the fact that the electorate perceived him as representing a rich and powerful white minority. The same racial and social divisions that he had set out to fight ended up defeating him.

The violence and fear that overshadowed his childhood and youth is symbolized by the revolver that his father wields on occasions: 'Ese revólver ... fue un objeto emblemático de mi infancia y juventud, el símbolo de la relación que tuve con mi padre mientras viví con él. ... lo veía sin tregua, en mis pesadillas y en mis miedos' (p. 63) [That revolver ... was an emblematic object of my childhood and adolescences, the symbol of the relationship I had with my father as long as I lived with him. ... I saw it constantly, in my nightmares and in my moments of terror] (p. 60). Literature becomes a refuge from this threat, a secret world apart, but also a rebellion against the father's values. In the military academy that his father sends him to Vargas Llosa experiences institutionalized authoritarianism, with its 'mechanical hierarchies', 'authorized violence' and rituals to prove one's 'hombría' [manhood]. This microcosm assembles all the social and racial prejudices, complexes and animosities that exist in Peruvian society. Again it is literature that provides him with a counter-world. He reads voraciously and begins to write regularly. 1952, the year he returns to Piura to finish his studies, living with his uncle Lucho and his family, turns out to be a crucial period in his life when he becomes aware of politics, loses the disgust of sex that had plagued him as a boy, stages his play *La huida del inca* [The Inca's Escape] in the local theatre, and lives in a general state, hitherto unknown to him, of 'entusiasmo intelectual y vital' (p. 183) [intellectual enthusiasm and joie de vivre] (p. 180). Uncle Lucho encourages his literary inclinations and explains political concepts to him, so that his literary vocation and his interest in politics develop in parallel. Both areas of his later activities, literature and politics, will be marked by his strong opposition to authoritarianism, violence, machismo and social injustice. In that year Vargas Llosa becomes aware that 'el Perú era un país de feroces contrastes, de millones de gentes pobres y de apenas un puñado de peruanos que vivían de manera confortable y decente, y de que los pobres —indios, cholos y negros— eran, además de explotados, despreciados por los ricos, gran parte de los cuales eran "blancos"' (p. 203) [Peru was a country of contrasts, of millions of poor people and barely a handful of Peruvians who had a comfortable, decent standard of living, and that the poor – Indians, mestizos, and blacks – were, in addition to being exploited, looked down on by the rich, a large part of whom were whites] (pp. 200–1). His ardent desire to change this injustice which, at the time, makes him turn to revolutionary socialist politics, is still the same that, thirty-six years later, urges him to enter the presidential race with a programme of economic liberalization and democratic consolidation, 'un proyecto integral de desmantelamiento de la estructura discriminatoria de la sociedad, removiendo sus sistemas de privilegio, de manera que los millones de pobres y marginados pudieran por fin acceder a aquello que Hayek llama la trinidad inseparable de la civilización: la legalidad, la libertad y la propiedad' (p. 533) [an integral plan to dismantle the discriminatory structure of society, removing its systems of privilege, so that the millions of impoverished and marginalized Peruvians could finally accede to what Hayek calls the inseparable trinity of civilization: legality, freedom, and property] (pp. 526–7). Vargas Llosa's indignation about the effects of social injustice is exacerbated during the campaign by witnessing the 'savagery' amid which so many Peruvians live their lives, 'los casi inconcebibles niveles de deterioro a que había descendido la vida para millones de Peruanos' (p. 521) [the almost inconceivable levels of deterioration to which life for millions of Peruvians had sunk] (p. 514).

His early commitment to socialism and his later campaign to implement a neoliberal programme for social change both end in disappointment and failure. The youthful enthusiasm with which Vargas Llosa throws himself into clandestine socialist activism at San Marcos University soon leads to disillusionment and dissidence. His boredom with the 'inanity' of the Marxist student cell's actions, his revulsion at the 'catechism of stereotypes and abstractions' used to interpret reality make him realize his 'incapacidad visceral para ser ese militante revolucionario paciente, incansable, dócil, esclavo de la organización, que acepta y practica el centralismo democrático' (p. 250) [visceral inability to embody that patient, tireless, docile revolutionary, a slave to the organization, who accepts and practices democratic centralism] (pp. 248).[7] In the late 1980s, the presidential candidate experiences the same kind of inability to adapt to political rituals or put up with opportunist *caciques* [local political bosses], and he admits feeling 'asphyxiated' by the 'byzantine maneuvers' of his own allies. His disillusionment with the 'petty, pedestrian practice of day-to-day politics' is as great in the 1980s as it was in the 1950s Communist cell. Vargas Llosa comes to the conclusion that, as an individualist concerned with ideas but uninterested in power, he is ill-suited to the profession of politics:

> Está hecha casi exclusivamente de maniobras, intrigas, conspiraciones, pactos, paranoias, traiciones, mucho cálculo, no poco cinismo y toda clase de malabares. Porque al político profesional, sea de centro, de izquierda o de derecha, lo que en verdad lo moviliza, excita y mantiene en actividad es *el poder*: llegar a él, quedarse en él o volver a ocuparlo cuanto antes. ... Quien no es capaz de sentir esa atracción obsesiva, casi física, por el poder, difícilmente llega a ser un político exitoso. (p. 90)
>
> [It consists almost exclusively of maneuvers, intrigues, plots, paranoias, betrayals, a great deal of calculation, no little cynicism, and every variety of con game. Because what really gets the professional politician, whether of the center, the left, or the right, moving, what excites him and keeps him going is *power*, attaining it, remaining in it, or returning to it as soon as possible. ... Anyone who is not capable of feeling this obsessive, almost physical attraction to power finds it nearly impossible to be a successful politician.] (pp. 87–8)

The political chapters of *El pez en el agua* deliver a frank assessment of his own misjudgement in believing that honesty and integrity, ideas and principles would help him gain the elections. With tangible repulsion he describes how he had to adapt his speeches to the expectations of his public, something which he ascribes to the backwardness of Peru – even though what he denounces here concurs exactly with what ancient rhetoricians already knew and taught:

---

[7] An iconic photo illustrating this unease shows the young Vargas Llosa, grinning awkwardly and raising his fist in a half-hearted Communist salute. It is widely reproduced on the Internet, for example at <http://www.listal.com/viewimage/1298008> [accessed 18 February 2013].

En el Perú la oratoria se ha quedado en la etapa romántica. El político sube al estrado a seducir, adormecer, arrullar. Su música importa más que sus ideas, sus gestos más que los conceptos. La forma hace y deshace el contenido de sus palabras. El buen orador puede no decir absolutamente nada, pero debe decirlo bien. Que suene y luzca es lo que importa. La lógica, el orden racional, la coherencia, la conciencia crítica de lo que está diciendo son un estorbo para lograr aquel efecto, que se consigue sobre todo con imágenes y metáforas impresionistas, latiguillos, figuras y desplantes. (pp. 172–3)

[For in Peru political oratory has remained at the romantic stage. The politician goes up onto the platform to charm, to seduce, to lull, to bill and coo. His musical phrasing is more important than his ideas, his gestures more important than his concepts. Form is everything: it can either make or destroy the content of what he says. The good orator may say absolutely nothing, but he says it with style. What matters to his audience is for him to sound good and look good. The logic, the rational order, the consistency, the critical acumen of what he is saying generally get in the way of his achieving that effect, which is attained above all through impressionistic images and metaphors, ham acting, fancy turns of phrase, and defiant remarks.] (p. 169)

With this purist attitude it is not surprising that his consultant Mark Malloch Brown told Vargas Llosa that he was the 'worst candidate he ever worked with' ('The Consultant', p. 95).

The political memoir clearly reveals that Vargas Llosa was unable to deal with the demons of politics, in the sense of the Max Weber epigraph. He was appalled to find his good intentions distorted, his programme and his person misrepresented, and his principles betrayed by his own supporters (some of whom used racist slanders against Fujimori in the final round of the campaign). He sets the record straight on the political mechanisms that he could not control, making him feel 'trapped in a spider web of misunderstandings', and he exposes details of the 'dirty war' waged against his candidacy. But he also admits that he was naive to enter into that 'pact with the devil' in the shape of professional politicians. He concedes being personally responsible for making wrong choices and for 'giving signs of intransigence'. What he does not do at any point in the book is question his political programme.[8] The bitter résumé of his failure in politics turns extremely acerbic in the chapter on what he calls 'cut-price intellectuals' ('El intelectual barato', chapter 14),[9]

---

[8] As Sergio R. Franco puts it: 'What never crosses Vargas Llosa's mind is that someone could reject his proposals *rationally* due to their different way of looking at things' (p. 131).

[9] This chapter develops a subject matter that Vargas Llosa had already written about in an article of 1979 under the same title: see *Contra viento y marea, II (1972–1983)* (Barcelona: Seix Barral, 1986), pp. 143–55.

culpable of inauthentic, opportunistic behaviour, some of whom he names as having been involved in the mud-slinging hate campaign against his candidacy, his person and his family. The unsavoury role of intellectuals in an authoritarian regime is a topic that Vargas Llosa will go on to explore in depth in *La Fiesta del Chivo* [*The Feast of the Goat*].[10] Here, he reveals the names of the 'resentful and scheming' writers and journalists in the service of Alan García's 'hate-office', describing their publications with metaphors of filth and excrement: 'el periodismo de estercolero' (p. 314) [that dung-collecting journalism] (p. 310); 'la cloaca hecha prensa' (p. 315) [a sewer metamorphosed into a paper] (p. 311); 'las sentinas literarias locales' (p. 315) [the local literary pigsties] (p. 310). In one of the earlier chapters he had already expressed his extreme disappointment with the economist Hernando de Soto, to whose book *El otro sendero* he had written a long preface.[11] De Soto turned out to be 'un hombre con más ambiciones que principios y de dudosa lealtad' (p. 176) [a man with more ambitions than principles and one whose loyalty was dubious] (p. 173), who would show his true colours as a ruthless opportunist when he worked for Fujimori after the elections.

All in all, Vargas Llosa's political memoir conveys a feeling of having been soiled by dirty politics, and he speaks of 'el disgusto visceral que la acción política me había dejado en la memoria' (p. 535) [the visceral disgust that political action had left in my memory] (p. 529). When, during the years of the campaign, he tried to continue writing fiction, he found that 'impure' preoccupations of the moment interfered: 'interferían preocupaciones impuras, inmediatas' (p. 211). As the elections approached and he could no longer find the time to read novels, he turned to the 'purity' of Góngora's poetry: 'Pero ni siquiera el día de la elección dejé de leer un soneto de Góngora, o una estrofa del *Polifemo* o *Las soledades* o alguno de sus romances o letrillas y de sentir con esos versos que, por unos minutos, mi vida se limpiaba' (p. 212) [But not a single day, not even the day of the election, went by without my reading a sonnet of Góngora's, or a strophe of his *Polifemo* or his *Soledades* or one or another of his ballads or rondelets, and through these verses to feel that, if only for a few minutes, my life became purer] (pp. 210–11). Compared to 'la mugre', the filth he found in politics, literature provided him with a pure counter-world and reading had a purifying effect.

---

[10] Mario Vargas Llosa, *La Fiesta del Chivo* (Madrid: Alfaguara, 2000); Mario Vargas Llosa, *The Feast of the Goat*, trans. Edith Grossman (New York: Farrar, Straus and Giroux, 2001).

[11] Mario Vargas Llosa, 'Prólogo', in Hernando de Soto, *El otro sendero. La revolución informal* [The Other Path. The Informal Revolution] (Lima: El Barranco, 1986), pp. XVII–XXIX.

9

The Return of the Grand Design: *La Fiesta del Chivo* (2000), *El Paraíso en la otra esquina* (2003) and *El sueño del celta* (2010)

Despite the interesting and varied nature of Vargas Llosa's experimentation with different novelistic genres, none of the works discussed in chapter 7 can compare with *La guerra del fin del mundo* [*The War of the End of the World*],[1] his central novel of 1981 which best embodies what he calls his 'totalizing ambition', the will to confront a complex reality with its fictional recreation on an equally grand scale. The publication of *La Fiesta del Chivo* [*The Feast of the Goat*][2] twenty years later marked a return to the project of the total novel, followed in 2003 by *El Paraíso en la otra esquina* [*The Way to Paradise*][3] and *El sueño del celta* [*The Dream of the Celt*][4] in 2010, all ambitious novels which turn the reality of historical events and personalities into a fictional creation that goes far beyond the portrayal of an epoch or an individual, exploring human nature, ambitions and contradictions in a social context. Comparable to *La guerra*, these three novels required extensive research, as they are not, or only partly, set in Peru and not directly rooted in Vargas Llosa's personal experience. In order to base his inventions on facts ('para mentir con conocimiento de causa', as the writer-protagonist in *Historia de Mayta* [*The Real Life of Alejandro Mayta*][5] puts it) Vargas Llosa worked through a wide range of historical and literary sources. He travelled to the regions where the novels are set and conducted interviews

---

[1] Mario Vargas Llosa, *La guerra del fin del mundo* (Barcelona: Plaza y Janés, 1982); Mario Vargas Llosa, *The War of the End of the World* (London: Faber and Faber, 1986).
[2] Mario Vargas Llosa, *La Fiesta del Chivo* (Madrid: Alfaguara, 2000); Mario Vargas Llosa, *The Feast of the Goat*, trans. Edith Grossman (New York: Farrar, Straus and Giroux, 2001).
[3] Mario Vargas Llosa, *El Paraíso en la otra esquina* (Madrid: Alfaguara, 2003); Mario Vargas Llosa, *The Way to Paradise* trans. Natasha Wimmer (London: Faber and Faber, 2004).
[4] Mario Vargas Llosa, *El sueño del celta* (Doral, FL: Alfaguara, 2010); Mario Vargas Llosa, *The Dream of the Celt*, trans. Edith Grossman (London: Faber and Faber, 2012).
[5] Mario Vargas Llosa, *Historia de Mayta* (Barcelona:Seix Barral, 1984); Mario Vargas Llosa, *The Real Life of Alejandro Mayta*, trans. Alfred MacAdam (London: Faber and Faber, 1986).

with witnesses, survivors, relatives, amongst others. Starting from this factual base, he invented the inner voices of historical personalities such as Rafael Leónidas Trujillo, Flora Tristán, Paul Gauguin and Roger Casement, thus adding an element to his fictional recreation which historiography is unable to provide. This imagined perspective of real-life personalities goes a step further than Vargas Llosa's previous fictional treatment of historical figures such as Antonio Consejero or, back in 1969, General Odría, both of whom do not have a voice of their own in his novels. Ascribing thoughts, motivations and emotions to historical characters is a bold move which has provoked criticism, especially in the case of *La Fiesta del Chivo*, as we will see. But this new level of invented reality is in line with Vargas Llosa's previous thoughts on the relationship between history and fiction: 'Una ficción lograda encarna la subjetividad de una época y por eso las novelas, aunque, cotejadas con la historia, mientan, nos comunican unas verdades huidizas y evanescentes que escapan siempre a los descriptores científicos de la realidad'[6] [Successful fiction embodies the subjectivity of an epoch and for that reason, although compared to history novels lie, they communicate to us fleeting and evanescent truths which always escape scientific descriptions of reality].[7]

The 'totalizing' design that unites these three big novels of the period 2000 to 2010 strives to encompass all the major themes of Vargas Llosa's fictional and essayistic writing: authoritarianism and the search for freedom, paternalistic power and machismo, the fight against social injustices and violence, the aberrations of nationalism and the role of traitors, the search for a counter-world, be it in ideology, religion, sexuality or art, or in adventures in far-away countries. The themes of ageing, illness and dying which become prominent in this period are also present in *Travesuras de la niña mala* [*The Bad Girl*][8] of 2006. But, as we have seen, that particular novel does not belong in the same category as the works discussed here. *La Fiesta*, *El Paraíso* and *El sueño del celta* resemble each other in the way they deal with multiple narrative strands on various levels of time and space, and combine differing perspectives in a grand design that tells a story using all the narrative strategies that Vargas Llosa has developed in his early writings, but employed in a more discreet, less disorienting manner than, for example, in *Conversación en la catedral* [*Conversation in the Cathedral*].[9] Also integrated into the

---

[6] Mario Vargas Llosa, 'La verdad de las mentiras', in *La verdad de las mentiras. Ensayos sobre literatura* (Barcelona: Seix Barral, 1990), pp. 5–20 (p. 15).

[7] Mario Vargas Llosa, 'The Truth of Lies', in *Making Waves*, ed. and trans. John King (London: Faber and Faber, 1996), pp. 320–30 (p. 327).

[8] Mario Vargas Llosa, *Travesuras de la niña mala* (Madrid: Alfaguara, 2006); Mario Vargas Llosa, *The Bad Girl*, trans. Edith Grossman (London: Faber and Faber, 2008).

[9] Mario Vargas Llosa, *Conversación en la catedral* (Barcelona: Seix Barral, 1985); Mario Vargas Llosa, *Conversation in the Cathedral*, trans. Gregory Rabassa (New York: HarperCollins, 2005).

grand design of Vargas Llosa's fiction of the new millennium is his use of various genres: elements of the adventure and mystery story are combined with characteristic traits of the historical novel and, in *La Fiesta del Chivo*, its Latin American subgenre of the dictator novel. Biographical writing is a point of reference for all three novels, and in *El Paraíso* we re-encounter Vargas Llosa's exploration of the creative process, as well as his ekphrastic description of paintings. *La Fiesta*, *El Paraíso* and *El sueño del celta* mark a confluence of the various strains of Vargas Llosa's writing, a synthesis which, in my opinion, is most successful in the first of these 'total novels'. *La Fiesta del Chivo* combines all the elements that make Vargas Llosa's work special: a strong social commitment, the dissection of the mechanisms of power, the vivid portrayal of the effects of authoritarianism on the individual, the exposure of the contradictory sides of human nature, and the questioning of what truth is, all brought together in a perfect equilibrium of narrative structure, technical mastery and an exciting, extraordinary story.

Set in the Dominican Republic, *La Fiesta del Chivo* deals with the events surrounding the killing of the country's dictator Rafael Leonidas Trujillo in 1961. His thirty-one years in power, a period known as the 'Era Trujillo', was brought to a violent end by conspirators from inside his own regime. The nickname 'el Chivo' [the Goat] refers to the tyrant's abuse of his absolute power to fulfil his sexual desires with whatever woman he wanted, including the wives and daughters of his ministers. In a society dominated by machismo the Goat's voracious sexual appetite played an important role in his popular reputation as an extraordinary leader. But the goat, as well as a symbol of lust, is also associated with the devil. (The cover illustration of the Spanish paperback version of the novel appropriately shows the horned figure resting its foot on a goat from Lorenzetti's painting *Allegory of Bad Government*.) Trujillo was equally admired for his uncommon physical and mental energy and his iron discipline, derived from his training in the US Marines, and feared for his ability to control people's minds and manipulate them into submission. These attributes made him particularly interesting for Vargas Llosa, since the 'Padre de la Patria Nueva' [Father of the New Fatherland],[10] as Trujillo liked to be called, embodied a number of Vargas Llosa's lifelong demons: dictatorship, the military, machismo and the father. Despite some critical comments about the fact that *La Fiesta* came out some twenty-five years after the dictator novel in Latin American literature had peaked,[11] the

---

[10] Unfortunately, the English translation by Edith Grossman leaves out a whole dimension of the novel by translating 'Padre de la Patria Nueva' as 'Father of the New Nation'. The patriarcal role of Latin American dictators has also been explored by other dictator novels, most prominently in Gabriel García Márquez's *El otoño del patriarca* [*The Autumn of the Patriarch*] (1975).

[11] The consensus is that the high point of the subgenre is marked by three novels: *Yo el Supremo* [*I, the Supreme*] by Roa Bastos and *El recurso del método* [*Reasons of State*]

period of authoritarian leaders was not over when Vargas Llosa published his novel: in 2000 the charismatic figure of Fidel Castro still loomed large; Alberto Fujimori and his head of intelligence Vladimiro Montesinos – an astonishing parallel with Trujillo's man for the dirty jobs, Abbes García – still held Peru in their grip, and Hugo Chávez exerted his personalized power over Venezuela.

Vargas Llosa's fascination with Trujillo's paternalistic regime of corruption, manipulation and repression, combined with an excessive taste for titles, ceremony and extravagant display, goes back to the eight months he spent in the Dominican Republic in 1975 during the filming of his novel *Pantaleón y las visitadoras* [*Captain Pantoja and the Special Service*].[12] Trujillo's shadow was still hanging over the country, and Vargas Llosa began to take notes on what he heard about him, and to read books about the Era.[13] More than twenty years later his interest became a definite novelistic project and he undertook research into the historical facts surrounding Trujillo's death. He read literary, journalistic and historical accounts, worked through newspaper archives and interviewed witnesses, amongst them Joaquín Balaguer, a key figure of the Era and the post-Trujillo years, ninety-four years of age and still in politics when the novel appeared in 2000. The work which finally resulted from this meticulous documentation is true to the historical facts concerning the end of the Trujillo regime, but it treats historical personalities such as the conspirators with great liberty. They appear with their real names, but Vargas Llosa gives them a fictitious inner perspective, attributing to them specific motivations for murdering Trujillo, a procedure which provoked controversial reactions in the Dominican Republic.[14] Other protagonists are invented but show characteristics of a number of different historical personalities.[15] The heated discussions caused by *La Fiesta del Chivo* revealed that the Era Trujillo was still an open wound in the Dominican Republic: while some Dominicans accused Vargas Llosa of falsifying and distorting history with his

---

by Carpentier, both from 1974, and García Márquez's *El otoño del patriarca* published the following year.

[12] Mario Vargas Llosa, *Pantaleón y las visitadoras* (Barcelona: Seix Barral, 1986); Mario Vargas Llosa, *Captain Pantoja and the Special Service* (London: Faber and Faber, 1987).

[13] See Enrique Krauze, 'La seducción del poder. Conversación entre Mario Vargas Llosa y Enrique Krauze', *Letras Libres*, 2 (2000), 22–6 (p. 22).

[14] For a well-documented account of the novel's reception in the Dominican Republic, see Frauke Gewecke, '*La fiesta del Chivo* de Mario Vargas Llosa: perspectivas de recepción de una novela de éxito', *Iberoamericana*, 1.3 (2001), 151–65.

[15] Especially interesting is the protagonist Henry Chirinos, a despicable opportunist based on a number of different Dominican models, but with a name that is reminiscent of the Peruvian politician Enrique Chirinos who, during Vargas Llosa's election campaign, was involved in his 'Movimiento Libertad' [Freedom Movement], a 'clear and ferocious caricature', as Ismael Pinto writes in 'La oscura fascinación por el poder', *Expreso* (Lima), 12 March 2000, <http://www.expreso.com.pe/ediciones/2000/mar/12/cultural/%5F01.htm> [accessed 17 May 2000].

inventions, other critics questioned the novel's fictional value, accusing him of lifting too much detail from his sources[16] or following historical reality so closely that in places it resembled a mere chronicle.[17]

A look at the structure of *La Fiesta del Chivo* reveals the novelistic craft that has gone into turning the historical events into an original fiction with its very own literary power of persuasion and, therefore, truth. Three alternating narrative strands complement each other in forming an image of the Era Trujillo from differing points of view, which are nonetheless all dominated by the personality of the tyrant, even after his death. That reflects a totalitarian regime based on the charismatic power of one person. The first of these narrative strings, the one which provides the framework for the whole book, renders the voice of a fictitious character, Urania Cabral, daughter of a former member of the regime, in the present of the 1990s. She returns to the Dominican Republic for the first time after thirty-five years and confronts her invalid father (who, after a stroke, is unable to talk) and her remaining family with the traumatic events that still overshadow her life: the dictator's attempt to rape her as a fourteen-year-old girl, and her father's complicity in the events. The whole extent of what she had gone through is only made explicit in the last chapter of the book, a literary device that maintains the suspense until the end.

In contrast to this retrospective look at the Era Trujillo and its horrors which still have consequences to the present day, the narrative strand narrating the last day of the dictator through his own perspective possesses great immediacy. From his own point of view we witness the last hours of an ageing tyrant who feels his legendary physical power diminish at a time when his political and economic position is under severe threat from various sides. Nevertheless he indulges in his usual cruel game of manipulating his courtiers by granting or withdrawing his benevolence. Later that day, on the way to his retreat in the country where he expects to find a young girl waiting on his orders to reassure him of his virility, he is intercepted and mortally wounded.

The third string of narrative shows the conspirators, all involved in the regime, during their tense wait to ambush and kill the tyrant. The reader learns through the perspective of each of the four main conspirators why they have turned against Trujillo. The tyrannicide, experienced from their point of view, takes place exactly in the middle of the book. After this central chapter 12, the focus of the three narrative strings changes, from Urania at

---

[16] This refers particularly to the journalistic account by Bernard Diederich, *Trujillo. The Death of the Goat* (Boston and Toronto: Little, Brown and Company, 1978), one of Vargas Llosa's main sources. In the novel, Vargas Llosa actually mentions another standard work on the Era Trujillo, Robert D. Crassweller's *Trujillo: The Life and Times of a Caribbean Dictator* (New York: Macmillan, 1966).

[17] See Gewecke, pp. 158–9.

her father's to Urania visiting her aunt and her cousins, from the assassins waiting in their car to the confusion amongst the conspirators after Trujillo's death, and the repression of the regime against them and their families. The second narrative line reporting the dictator's inner view shifts more and more to other members of the regime, focusing in the last chapters of the book on the inscrutable Joaquín Balaguer, who steps into the vacant role as the country's leader.

The attack on Trujillo's life as seen from the tyrant's own perspective is not related until chapter 18, that is six chapters after it was rendered from the assassins' point of view. The intermediate chapters, which narrate events *after* Trujillo's death in parallel with his own experiencing of the last hours *before* the assault, reproduce by narrative means the strong presence of the dictator even after his physical elimination. Furthermore, the technique of narrating a main event twice, from differing points of view, already used in *La guerra*'s depiction of Moreira César's defeat, has the purpose of revealing the whole range of causes and effects to the reader, while they remain hidden to the acting protagonists. In *La guerra* this technique revealed the incredible misjudgement on the part of the military hero Moreira César, who totally underestimated his adversary. A similar effect is produced in *La Fiesta* when we first see the decisive events following Trujillo's death through the eyes of the leader of the armed forces, General José René Román. Acutely aware of his crucial role in the conspiracy, he is unable to act according to plan (chapter 20) because the dictator's shadow still paralyses him. Two chapters later, we see the general's confused state through the eyes of the totally underestimated president, Joaquín Balaguer, who takes advantage of the failing coup d'état and seizes power.

The fact that Vargas Llosa succeeds in maintaining the narrative tension and suspense right through to the end of the book speaks for his careful construction of the novel. His conception, ending the narrative with Urania's final revelation of the dictator's use of sex as an instrument of power and the traumatic effect this had on her, allows him to show the devastating consequences of totalitarianism on the individual and its long-lasting impact on society. By inventing a network of relations between the different protagonists, historical and fictional, and linking their individual life stories, Vargas Llosa makes his literary representation of history coherent and truthful in its own right, rounding it off to present a 'total' fiction.

The dominant narrative mode in all three plot lines is the free indirect style which enables the impersonal narrator to approach each chapter's main character, temporarily entering his or her mind, conveying their stream of consciousness, their inner monologue or, in Urania's case, pseudo-dialogue (Urania addresses herself in the second person singular, as in the following case where she refers to her invalid father): 'No te hagas ilusiones, Urania. Entiende por segundos y lo olvida. No te comunicas con él. Sigues hablando sola, como todos los días desde hace más de treinta años. ... No está triste ni deprimida' (*La Fiesta*, p. 140) [Don't kid yourself, Urania. He understands for a couple of seconds and then he forgets. You're not communicating with him. You're still talking to yourself, as you've done every day for more than thirty years. ... She isn't sad or depressed] (*Feast*, p. 104). This narrative mode, which approaches a protagonist's perspective and then becomes distant again, is frequently interspersed with direct speech, a technique that can highlight the contrast between a character's thoughts and his or, in this case, her words: 'Yo fui siempre un poco loca, Lucindita', Urania says to her cousin. 'Eso sí, aunque no les escribiera, los recordaba mucho. En especial, a ti. ... Mentira. No echaste de menos a nadie' (p. 195) ['I was always a little crazy, Lucindita. And really, even though I didn't write, I thought about all of you a lot. Especially you.' A lie. You didn't miss anyone, not even Lucinda] (p. 148). The clash between inner voice and direct speech is particularly revealing in the case of Trujillo himself and his puppet president Balaguer, both impenetrable personalities to the outside world. In the following quotation the narrator adopts Balaguer's perspective to show how the president manipulates Trujillo's son Ramfis after the dictator's death:

> El doctor Joaquín Balaguer siempre supo que de esta conversación dependía su futuro y el de la República Dominicana. Por eso, decidió algo que sólo hacía en casos extremos, pues iba contra su natural cauteloso: jugarse el todo por el todo, en una suerte de exabrupto. ... siempre con su manera calmada, sin denotar la más mínima inquietud, le dijo lo que había cuidadosamente preparado: —De usted, y sólo de usted, depende que perdure algo, mucho, o nada, de la obra realizada por Trujillo. Si su herencia desaparece, la República Dominicana se hundirá de nuevo en la barbarie ... Durante el largo rato que habló, Ramfis no lo interrumpió una sola vez. ¿Lo escuchaba? (p. 458)

> [Dr Joaquín Balaguer always knew that his future, and the future of the Dominican Republic, depended on this conversation. As a consequence, he decided on something that he did only in extreme cases, since it went against his cautious nature: he would gamble everything on a single play. ... and not wavering from his tranquil manner, not betraying the slightest uneasiness, he said the words he had carefully prepared: 'It depends on you, and only on you, whether some, a good deal, or nothing at all of Trujillo's work endures. If his legacy disappears, the Dominican Republic will sink back into barbarism ...' He spoke at length, but Ramfis did not interrupt once. Was he listening?] (p. 356)

Balaguer coaxes Trujillo's oldest son into trusting him, whereas he really thinks of him as an intelligent but brutal good-for-nothing, who might endanger his plan for a new regime under his own leadership. In his Machiavellian way, Balaguer makes a concession to Ramfis's need for bloody revenge – 'Nadie, y yo menos que nadie, obstaculizará su empeño en hacer justicia. Ése es, también, mi más ferviente deseo' (p. 459) [No one, least of all me, will stand in the way of your determination to see justice done. That, too, is my most fervent desire] (p. 357) – and thus persuades him to give up power. This is a crucial scene which fictionalizes something that historiography is not certain about, the extent of knowledge and control that Balaguer had over the situation before and after Trujillo's death. But Vargas Llosa's concern is not the 'historical truth' – a problematic concept in any case – but a story brought alive through a personalized narration full of suspense, which has the potential to express 'profound truths' about the human condition: 'Ése es el poder de la literatura, y su anécdota es un pretexto para hablar de la condición humana' [This is the power of literature, and its anecdote is just a pretext for talking about the human condition].[18] The protagonist Balaguer, quiet, modest and a lover of poetry, represents the opposite pole to the regime's virile brutes such as the powerful General Román, the big, loud and fierce brothers of the dictator and the bloodthirsty, mentally unstable Ramfis. This gives Vargas Llosa the opportunity to create a series of dramatic confrontations between the small, unmanly but secretly ambitious intellectual and the bullying strong men who have no chance against Balaguer's own weapons: an analytical mind, a capacity to adapt quickly to a new situation, and persuasive eloquence. The insight into the controlling mind of this character through Vargas Llosa's use of the free indirect style gives his fictional portrait credibility.

Vargas Llosa employs another of his favourite literary techniques in order to evoke, in a present situation, events of the past by zooming in and out of past situations. One of the advantages of this direct link between different levels of time is that additional background information to what is happening in the present is provided without the need for long explanations by the narrator. Readers are invited to judge for themselves and to feel, by means of telescopic dialogue or narration, what it is like to live under a dictatorship which invades the most personal realms of one's life. This aspect comes out strongest in the narrative line dealing with the conspirators. In chapter 3, for instance, the focus is on Amado García Guerrero, a member of Trujillo's special guard. He had to prove his loyalty to the dictator by abandoning his fiancée, because her brother turned out to be a dissident. In addition to this painful 'sacrifice for the Fatherland' he had to give another proof of his unconditional obedience by killing an opponent of Trujillo with his own hands. This so-called 'óbolo de sangre al Jefe' [blood offering to the Chief] was used as a routine measure to compromise the young adjutants in Trujillo's guard, binding them to the regime and its practices. In these

---

[18] Sol Alameda, interview with Mario Vargas Llosa, *El País*, 8 March 2000; also in <http://www.sololiteratura.com/var/entrevistapais1.html> [accessed 31 October 2012].

details, *La Fiesta del Chivo* follows historical sources such as Diederich's account of García Guerrero's motives for murdering Trujillo (see Diederich, pp. 76–8). But in the novel Vargas Llosa adds a fictitious link between the two episodes, highlighting the perfidious nature of the scheme that Trujillo and his helper Johnny Abbes devise to test the adjutant's loyalty. Having executed the helpless prisoner, they tell Amado that he has killed the brother of his former bride, leaving him full of disgust and self-hatred, prone to be manipulated further. These facts are reflected in the protagonist's thoughts while he is waiting in the ambush to kill his boss. In the form of a flashback, the narration switches directly to the past, the night after the killing when he went to see his friend Salvador Estrella Sadhalá to tell him what had happened and that, as a result, he intended to kill Trujillo. From that point in the middle distance, the narration switches further back to the direct situation of Amado's test of loyalty, and back even further to his first face-to-face encounter with the dictator. Vargas Llosa's use of this telescopic technique enables the reader to live through the experience, share Amado's disgust at finding himself a part of Trujillo's murderous system, understand how he came to be part of the conspiracy that his friend Estrella Sadhalá was involved in, and empathize with his vital need to end once and for all the destructive power emanating from Trujillo's personality. Back in the present, one feels with him his grim determination to empty his pistol right into Trujillo's 'ojos fríos de iguana' (p. 49), the 'cold iguana eyes' (p. 33) whose power had turned him into a 'slave'.

Similar narrative techniques of creating immediacy reveal the motivations of the other three main conspirators lying in wait for Trujillo's car. The novel ascribes to each of them one particular aspect of the many reasons why members of the regime wanted Trujillo dead. The hot-headed Antonio de la Maza wants revenge for his brother's assassination and retrospective denunciation (Trujillo involved him in the notorious abduction of the Basque professor Galíndez in the middle of New York)[19] and wants to end the 'parálisis, el adormecimiento de la voluntad, del raciocinio y del libre albedrío que aquel personajillo acicalado hasta el ridículo, de vocecilla aflautada y ojos de hipnotizador, ejercía sobre los dominicanos pobres o ricos, cultos o incultos, amigos o enemigos' (p. 119) [paralysis, the numbing of determination, reason, and free will, which this man, groomed and adorned to the point of absurdity, with his thin high-pitched voice and hypnotist's eyes, imposed on Dominicans, poor or rich, educated or ignorant, friends or enemies] (p. 88).

Whereas these two conspirators are driven by a personal motivation to end the perfidious system of lies and manipulation, and to reestablish the

---

[19] See Crassweller, *Trujillo*; Diederich, *Trujillo*; as well as the fictionalization of this event in a novel by Manuel Vázquez Montalbán, *Galíndez* (1991).

individual's free will, Salvador Estrella Sadhalá, 'el Turco' [the Turk], has moral reasons for wanting to see Trujillo dead. A devout Catholic, he is respected and admired by the other conspirators for his firm moral beliefs, his strong sense of justice and his attempts to live according to his faith. Estrella Sadhalá belongs to the category of 'puros', of 'pure' idealists in Vargas Llosa's fiction, who are totally convinced by their beliefs and, therefore, often prone to turn into fanatics. But Estrella Sadhalá is not a zealot. He is well aware of his human weaknesses and imperfections: 'No soy beato, ni fanático. Un practicante de mi fe, nada más. Y, desde la Carta Pastoral de los obispos del 31 de enero del año pasado, orgulloso de ser católico' (p. 42) [I'm not a saint or a fanatic ... I practice my faith, that's all, And ever since the bishops sent their Pastoral Letter on January 24 last year, I'm proud to be a Catholic] (p. 27). The Catholic Church's support for Trujillo over many years, which finally stopped with the bishops' message of 1960 mentioned here, had thrown him into a deep moral dilemma: '¿Cómo podía equivocarse la Iglesia inspirada por Dios apoyando a un desalmado?' (p. 239) [how could the Church inspired by God make the mistake of supporting a cruel, merciless man?] (p. 182). The criticism of totalitarianism, with its arbitrariness and lack of freedom, read out from the pulpits all over the country, dissolves his doubts. But the subsequent brutal repression of priests presents him with a new dilemma. He is convinced he has to put an end to these outrageous injustices against men of the Church by killing 'the Beast', as he calls Trujillo. His worries about committing such a mortal sin are relieved by the Papal Nuntius who shows him the decisive passage about tyrannicide in Thomas Aquinas: 'La eliminación física de la Bestia es bien vista por Dios si con ella se libera a un pueblo' (p. 243) [God looks with favor upon the physical elimination of the Beast if a people is freed thereby] (p. 185). This revelation puts his mind at ease: 'Mataría a la Bestia y Dios y su Iglesia lo perdonarían, manchándose de sangre lavaría la sangre que la Bestia hacía correr en su patria' (p. 243) [He would kill the Beast, and God and his Church would forgive him; staining his hands with blood would wash away the blood the Beast was spilling in his homeland] (p. 185). Salvador Estrella Sadhalá's moral justification for tyrannicide has particular weight since it immediately precedes the actual assault on Trujillo. The last words in his inner monologue before the dictator's car appears in sight establish the link between Trujillo and the devil: 'Trujillo había sido uno de los más efectivos aliados del demonio' (p. 246) [Trujillo had been one of Satan's most effective allies] (p. 187). When action takes over from reflection, this judgement remains standing as a moral justification for the deed, confirmed by the regime's violent, unrestrained repression following the assassination. But in the moment of triumph over Evil the 'Turk' burdens himself with guilt, shooting by mistake one of the other conspirators, who then falls into the hands of Johnny Abbes and his torturers: 'Fue como si se abriera la tierra, como si, desde ese abismo, se levantara riéndose de él la carcajada del Maligno' (p. 251) [It was as if the earth had opened up, as if, from the bottom of the abyss, he could hear the sound of the Evil One laughing at him] (p. 191). This is a very effective and dramatic way to end the central chapter about the actual tyrannicide. It highlights the impossibility of remaining 'pure', a recurrent theme in Vargas Llosa's work. In terms of the novel's structure it points towards the horrors yet to come, even though the dictator is dead.

The motivations ascribed to the fourth conspirator, Antonio Imbert, are clearly shaped to represent Vargas Llosa's own abhorrence of dictatorships: an individualist, Tony Imbert intends to restore the freedom and integrity which have been suppressed by a system of official lies. He had himself fallen under the dictator's spell when he was a young governor of Puerto Plata, publicly announcing his absolute obedience to Trujillo: '"Usted ordene y yo quemo Puerto Plata, Jefe." La frase que más lamentaba en su vida. La vio reproducida en todos los periódicos' (p. 172) ['Give the order and I'll burn Puerto Plata, Chief.' The words he regretted most in his life. He saw them reprinted in every newspaper] (p. 130). This is not a historical detail; instead it establishes an intertextual relation to a work of literature that is mentioned several times in *La Fiesta del Chivo* as Trujillo's favourite, Sienkiewicz's popular novel of 1896, *Quo Vadis*.[20] The dictator makes frequent references to its protagonist Petronius, arbiter of good taste in the service of the Roman emperor Nero. In *Quo Vadis* the character Tigellinus, rival of Petronius for Nero's favour, says: 'Speak a word, o Divinity, I will take a torch, and before the night passes thou shalt see blazing Antium'. Vargas Llosa ascribes a variant of this declaration of extreme submission to Tony Imbert to show the complete reversal of a devoted follower of Trujillo. Imbert's decision to assassinate the dictator derives from his disgust with the systematic distortion of truth and the total corruption of values in Trujillo's state, resulting in a split between thinking and acting,

> la entronización por la propaganda y la violencia de una descomunal mentira. ... Había sido ese malestar de tantos años, pensar una cosa y hacer a diario algo que la contradecía, lo que lo llevó, siempre en el secreto de su mente, a sentenciar a muerte a Trujillo, a convencerse de que, mientras viviera, él y muchísimos dominicanos estarían condenados a esa horrible desazón y desagrado de sí mismos, a mentirse a cada instante y engañar a todos, a ser dos en uno, una mentira pública y una verdad privada prohibida de expresarse. (pp. 186–7)

---

[20] Henryk Sienkiewicz, *Quo Vadis* (Uhrichsville, OH: Barbour, 2000). For an analysis of the multiple intertextual relations to this novel see the chapter on *La Fiesta del Chivo* in my study *Vargas Llosa's Fiction & the Demons of Politics* (Oxford: Peter Lang, 2002), pp. 239–301.

[the enthronement, through propaganda and violence, of a monstrous lie. ... It had been this malaise of so many years' duration – thinking one thing and doing something that contradicted it every day – that led him, in the secret recesses of his mind, to condemn Trujillo to death, to convince himself that as long as Trujillo lived, he and many other Dominicans would be condemned to this awful queasy sickness of constantly having to lie to themselves and deceive everyone else, of having to be two people in one, a public lie and a private truth that could not be expressed.] (p. 141)

In an interview after the novel was published, Vargas Llosa commented on the 'generalized corruption' in a despotic system, 'donde es imposible mantener una dignidad, una honra personal, porque uno está obligado a entrar en los mecanismos de impostura' [where it is impossible to preserve one's personal dignity and honour, because one is forced to go along with the mechanisms of imposture].[21] His choice of words, especially the 'imposture' which plays such a big role in Vargas Llosa's novels ever since *La ciudad y los perros* [*The Time of the Hero*][22] (originally entitled 'Los impostores' [The Impostors]), shows how much the protagonist Antonio Imbert represents some of the extraliterary author's most ardent concerns,[23] and is shaped with several intertextual references in mind. The general corruption of an authoritarian state had already been the subject of *Conversación en la catedral* more than thirty years earlier. In *La Fiesta del Chivo* corruption and lies are centred around one person, the megalomaniac dictator, and Tony Imbert has come to realize that change is only possible by liberating his country from the despot: 'Había que liquidar a la persona en la que convergían todos los hilos de esa tenebrosa telaraña' (p. 173) [You had to eradicate the person in whom all the strands of the dread spiderweb converged] (p. 131). The decisive event for his joining the conspiracy was Trujillo's murder of the Mirabal sisters, three much-respected leading figures of the clandestine opposition. In a move that is typical for *La Fiesta*, Vargas Llosa personalizes this historical event which, indeed, caused an outrage against the regime in the Dominican population, by turning Imbert into a secret admirer of Minerva Mirabal. It is this ingenious interlinking of historical and fictional elements that makes the story of Trujillo's death such a compelling historical novel.

The counterpoint to the conspirators' perspective of the totalitarian system, which has granted them favours in return for abandoning their free will and submitting totally to the dictator, is Trujillo's own point of view. His inner

---

[21] See Alameda, interview with Mario Vargas Llosa.
[22] Mario Vargas Llosa, *La ciudad y los perros* (Barcelona: Seix Barral, 1983); Mario Vargas Llosa, *The Time of the Hero* (London: Picador, 1986).
[23] By contrast, Imbert's characterization in Diederich, pp. 74–5, is not all that positive. His political dealings after the end of the Era seem to have been rather dubious, and not in support of freedom (see Diederich, p. 255).

voice confirms what a cold and ruthless tyrant he is, but it also shows him as a human being with obsessions and fears, prone to vanity and flattery as much as to self-deception and hubris. In entering the tyrant's mind Vargas Llosa uses a narrative device known from some of the most famous dictator novels of the 1970s, such as *El recurso del método* by Carpentier and *El otoño del patriarca* by García Márquez. This technique is sometimes criticized for humanizing the dictator in question, but the effect Vargas Llosa produces here is in line with his fictional exploration of the dark side of human nature. In an essay which appeared in the same year as the novel, he ascribes literature the function of 'bucear las simas del fenómeno humano y descubrir el escalofriante potencial destructivo y autodestructor que también lo conforma' [exploring the depths of human nature and discovering the chilling destructive and self-destructive potential which it also consists of] ('Un mundo sin novelas', p. 44). 'Lo peor', he continues, 'es descubrir que esa violencia y desmesura no nos son ajenas, que están lastradas de humanidad' [The worst is to discover that violence and excess are not outside our nature, but that they are part of what is human] (p. 43). Thus Vargas Llosa's intention in giving his dictator protagonist a human dimension and an inner perspective is not to play down the evil in his conduct but to provoke the reader's horror in discovering that evil is part of human nature and cannot simply be ascribed to a particularly monstrous person. In all his monstrosity and ruthlessness Trujillo is not a special case, he is the dictator *par excellence*, 'el dictador emblemático',[24] as Vargas Llosa says, with his absolute, personalized power based on charisma, his megalomania and his vain delight in spectacle and pomp: 'Una de mis preocupaciones cuando escribí la novela era mostrar cómo lo que ocurre en la República Dominicana de ninguna manera es privativo ni de ese país ni, en consecuencia, de ese personaje' [One of my concerns in writing this novel was to show how the things that happened in the Dominican Republic were by no means special to that country nor, as a consequence, to that personality], said Vargas Llosa in his dialogue with Enrique Krauze.[25] *La Fiesta del Chivo* highlights the need to rein in the human potential for evil. In the novel, the puppet president Balaguer, who turns out to be the shrewdest and most cold-blooded player in the fight for power after the dictator's death, assigns this function to Catholicism, an irreplaceable 'instrument for the social restraint of the human animal's irrational passions and appetites' (p. 231). But in a state like Trujillo's where not even clerics are safe from persecution and murder the existence of these 'appetites', which turn people like Balaguer into willing accomplices of a murderous system, calls for political mechanisms to prevent

---

[24] Mario Vargas Llosa, 'El suicidio de una nación', in *El lenguaje de la pasión* (Madrid: Ediciones El País, 2000), pp. 299–304 (p. 301).
[25] Krauze, p. 22. For parallels with the Roman emperor Nero, which are suggested by the frequent mentions of *Quo Vadis* in *La Fiesta*, see my book *Vargas Llosa's Fiction*, pp. 258–60.

the assembling of excessive personal power. As such, *La Fiesta del Chivo* is part of Vargas Llosa's political discourse calling for democratic institutions to restrict power and block the temptations for its abuse: 'Una dictadura como la de Trujillo muestra hasta qué punto es importante limitar el poder, cómo cuando éste carece de frenos saca lo peor que hay en el ser humano [y] puede convertir a los hombres en una especie de monstruos de crueldad y exceso' [A dictatorship like Trujillo's shows how important it is to limit power, how unrestricted power brings out the worst in human beings [and] turns them into monsters of cruelty and excess].[26]

Like so many of these charismatic autocrats Trujillo is simultaneously revered and feared. He provokes 'respeto y hechizo' (p. 109) [respect and fascination] (p. 80), thus affecting people on the intellectual as well as the emotional level. The novel describes the dictator's reputation as based on his great determination and his capacity for work with little rest: 'Su capacidad de recuperación física, con un mínimo de reposo, contribuyó a su aureola de ser superior' (p. 26) [His ability to recover physically with a minimum of sleep contributed to his aura of superiority] (p. 16). On the one hand, this connects him to other protagonists in Vargas Llosa's work: 'Esa disciplina despiadada, de héroes y místicos' (p. 24) [the merciless discipline of heroes and mystics] (p. 14) is reminiscent of *La guerra*'s two charismatic, legendary leaders, the hero Moreira César and the mystic Antonio Consejero. On the other hand, it establishes a link between Trujillo in the novel and the Cuban leader Fidel Castro, of whom Vargas Llosa wrote in an article following an encounter with him: 'quedé también enormemente impresionado con su energía y su carisma. ... Habló doce horas, hasta bien entrada la mañana, ... sin dar la menor señal de fatiga. ... Cuando se fue, tan fresco como había llegado, todos estábamos exhaustos y maravillados' [I was also enormously impressed by his energy and his charisma. ... He talked for twelve hours, well into the morning ... without the slightest sign of fatigue. ... When he left, as fresh as on his arrival, we were all exhausted and amazed].[27] The Cuban leader's bewitching charisma – Vargas Llosa describes him as a 'maestro supremo de la hechicería' [supreme master of witchcraft][28] – has found its equivalent in the bewitching effect that *La Fiesta* ascribes to Trujillo, especially through his arresting eyes and his

---

[26] Emma Rodríguez, interview with Mario Vargas Llosa, *El mundo*, 7 March 2000, <http://www.el-mundo.es/2000/03/07/cultura/07N0128.html> [accessed 16 July 2000]. This is in line with Vargas Llosa's ongoing political campaign against such regimes as that of Hugo Chávez in Venezuela. In many articles he draws attention to the fact that Chávez had assembled a dangerous amount of personal power, violating more and more democratic rules about the separation of power. See Vargas Llosa, 'El suicidio de una nación'.

[27] Mario Vargas Llosa, 'El gigante y la historia', in *Contra viento y marea, III (1964–1988)* (Barcelona: Seix Barral, 1990), pp. 423–8 (p. 424).

[28] Mario Vargas Llosa, 'Desbarajuste con samba', in *Desafíos a la libertad* (Madrid: El País/Aguilar, 1994), pp. 241–6 (p. 242).

look that nobody can resist. This feature, mentioned in passing in the sources, is given prominence in the novel and illustrates the dictator's hold on people. His penetrating gaze, which seems to intrude into the most secret thoughts of a person and strip them of their free will, symbolizes Trujillo's absolute power. It is yet another feature that links him to the charismatic, fanatical and self-possessed characters Antonio Consejero and Moreira César, whose striking eyes summed up their personalities in *La guerra*.

In a number of different ways Vargas Llosa integrates the historical dictator into his own fictional universe. In a move comparable to *Conversación* and its most negative protagonist Cayo Bermúdez, *La Fiesta* makes the protagonist Trujillo himself disclose his strategies of brutal repression, propaganda and manipulation, sometimes in conversations with his collaborators and sometimes in his inner monologue. From the tyrant's own perspective we learn how he has systematically built up an image of himself and his family as the benefactors of the country via pompous titles, dazzling ceremonious displays and generous gifts and favours, thus turning the Dominican Republic into his personal fiefdom and making every household in it an obligatory part of his web of lies and personal allegiances. An all-embracing system of propaganda and manipulation has established an indissoluble link between the welfare of the country and its 'Father' and 'Benefactor'. His systematic invasion of the private realm manifests itself in the obligatory sign in every household saying 'En esta casa Trujillo es el Jefe' (p. 18) [In this house Trujillo is the Chief] (p. 8), a historical fact. But Vargas Llosa exercises restraint in his use of the more grotesque manifestations of Trujillo's vain megalomania. There are many colourful details in his sources (especially in Crassweller's biography) that *La Fiesta* omits, as they would have simply ridiculed the dictator and taken away his credibility within the fiction.

The novel adopts a different strategy, having the reader experience the tyrant's hubris through his own perspective, making it tragically clear that he has fallen victim to his own web of lies. He has ended up believing the myths he created about himself: 'Trujillo podía hacer que el agua se volviera vino y los panes se multiplicaran, si le daba en los cojones' (p. 28) [Trujillo could turn water into wine and multiply loaves of bread if he fucking well felt like it] (p. 17), as he defiantly reassures himself when he becomes aware of the gradual loss of his political as well as his physical power. He overestimates his abilities to 'sniff out' any traitor, when the reader knows full well how wrong that is from the narrative line dealing with the conspiracy. In another revealing instance, the reader is made to understand how Balaguer's speech 'Dios y Trujillo' [God and Trujillo], which deified the dictator as an 'instrument of God', is too seductive for a megalomaniac character not to fall for: 'Aquel discurso de Balaguer lo estremeció, lo llevó a preguntarse muchas veces si no expresaba una profunda verdad, una de esas insondables decisiones divinas que marcan el destino de un pueblo' (p. 292) [Balaguer's speech had moved him deeply and often led him to wonder if it might not express a profound truth, one of those unfathomable divine decisions that mark the destiny of a people] (p. 224). Seeing it through Trujillo's conscience provokes pity for the dictator's foolishness to believe in his mission from God, and disbelief for Balaguer's concoction. Similarly, we see how the waning US support leaves Trujillo bitterly disappointed. The great manipulator feels betrayed – a different sort of irony from the easy ridicule that his operetta-like public appearances would have offered: 'El Generalísimo sintió un vacío en el estómago. No era la cólera lo que le producía acidez, sino la decepción. ... —No me cabe en la cabeza que se porten así conmigo' (p. 161) [The Generalissimo felt a hollow in his stomach. It wasn't anger that produced acid, it was disappointment. ... 'I can't get it into my head that they're treating me this way'] (p. 121).

In addition to his loss of support the unmistakable signs of ageing – his prostate cancer and the threat of impotence – make him alternately desperate and livid: 'Éste no era un enemigo que pudiera derrotar como a esos cientos, miles, que había enfrentado y vencido, a lo largo de los años, comprándolos, intimidándolos o matándolos. Vivía dentro de él, carne de su carne, sangre de su sangre' (p. 26) [This wasn't an enemy he could defeat like the hundreds, the thousands he had confronted and conquered over the years, buying them, intimidating them, killing them. This lived inside him, flesh of his flesh, blood of his blood] (p. 16). *La Fiesta* sums up Trujillo's personal tragedy in the revealing desperate thought forming in his mind: 'Podía dominar a los hombres, poner a tres millones de dominicanos de rodillas, pero no controlar su esfínter' (p. 165) [He could dominate people, bring three million Dominicans to their knees, but not control his sphincter].[29] The ageing dictator in *La Fiesta* provokes contradictory feelings of outrage, disgust, pity and *Schadenfreude* in the reader. There is an element of poetic justice in Vargas Llosa's portrayal of the end of an era of absolute power: Trujillo, so meticulous about cleanliness and immaculate attire on himself and others, is terrified of the appearance of the telltale signs of his incontinence on his uniform. His ruthless use of sex as an instrument of power and his self-projection as the potent Goat turns into the haunting memory of his impotence with the 'skinny little bitch' (which refers to Urania, as we find out at the end).[30]

---

[29] This is my own translation, since Edith Grossman avoids the blunt expression – and with it the raw sentiment – of the original.

[30] *La Fiesta del Chivo* abounds with instances where a person is punished in a way particularly appropriate to his or her previous behaviour. Such poetic justice does not only apply to the dictator himself: in the case of Agustín 'Cerebrito' [Egghead] Cabral, the abuse of his extraordinary intelligence for the wrong cause ends in an 'ataque cerebral', a stroke leading to dementia. A similarly ironic fate waits for Trujillo's wife whose avarice is punished with poverty in old age, since she forgets the numbers of her secret accounts, which she had not

Getting inside the tyrant's mind is an uncomfortable but revealing experience, producing a criticism of dictatorships that goes beyond the straightforward denunciation of their horrors. Readers discover through Trujillo's own perspective what effect an excess of power can have on a person, and what abuses of such power human beings are capable of when nothing holds them back. And the reactions the novel provokes in its readers are equally ambiguous. Through the dictator's perspective one is made to share his contempt for the courtiers who degrade themselves in the hope of remaining in his favour, a narrative strategy which simultaneously provokes revulsion at the sycophancy of Trujillo's entourage and disgust at the dictator's delight in playing with their fear of falling into disgrace. Nevertheless, behind the various levels of official lies, flatteries and self-deception, Trujillo is aware of the basis of his regime: the personal loyalties which he has carefully created and systematically sustains with a perfidious system of fear and terror. His collaborators know that the 'Father of the New Fatherland' enjoys committing symbolic filicides by arbitrarily withdrawing his sympathies, or actually killing people close to him who are in his way. In the end, this practice leaves no other solution than the murder of the patriarchal dictator. Filicide ultimately leads to parricide, a pattern which repeats itself on another level of the story, where Urania confronts the father who has destroyed her life.

Vargas Llosa's novel not only explores the evil side of human nature by showing Trujillo's tendencies to dominate, humiliate and destroy others. It also deals with the mutually dependent mechanisms of oppression and submission (a theme explored further in *Travesuras de la niña mala*), and investigates the manifold reasons for submitting to a powerful tyrant, to obey and to allow oneself to be humiliated. This is particularly striking in the case of the intellectuals who play their part in upholding the regime's power structure, such as Agustín Cabral. He is the most extreme case since he is willing to turn his virgin daughter Urania into a peace offering in order to win back the Goat's good will. In Diederich's account of Trujillo we read: 'And this man ... had reached a height where he could expect from a "loyal" subject tribute in the form of a daughter's virginity, to satisfy his extraordinary sexual appetite' (Diederich, p. 14). Vargas Llosa turns this snippet of information into the central plot of his novel, combining the themes of absolute power and extreme machismo with the father–child relationship, and with the sycophancy of intellectuals towards an autocratic leader.

---

even communicated to her children. Manuel Alfonso, the handsome former model and personal advisor to Trujillo in questions of taste, who is also responsible for preparing the selected young girls, such as Urania, for their encounter with the 'Benefactor' (afterwards being allowed to abuse them himself – another parallel with Petronius from *Quo Vadis*) has his good looks destroyed by a cancer of the tongue which leaves him mutilated.

The theme of the father, admired and trusted, who then disappoints and abuses the unconditional love he receives is explored on two interconnected levels. For Cabral, Trujillo is an adored father figure: 'para él, Trujillo no sólo había sido el Jefe, el estadista, el fundador de la República, sino un modelo humano, un padre' (p. 280) [for him, Trujillo had been not only the Chief, the statesman, the founder of the Republic, but a human model, a father] (pp. 214–15). He did not serve him out of self-interest or opportunism but out of conviction, as Urania states with disgust. This is why he recurs to desperate measures to regain the 'love' of the 'Father of the New Fatherland' – by offering him his own daughter as a living gift. This monstrous act of deception amounts to a filicide, since Urania is so traumatized that she never trusts a man again in her private life. She returns to her father for revenge and commits a symbolic parricide by torturing the helpless invalid with her reproaches: 'Luego de tantos años de servir al Jefe, habías perdido los escrúpulos, la sensibilidad, el menor asomo de rectitud ... ¿Era ese el requisito para mantenerse en el poder sin morirse de asco? Volverse un desalmado, un monstruo como tu Jefe' (p. 137) [After so many years of serving the Chief, you had lost your scruples, your sensitivity, the slightest hint of rectitude. ... Was that a requirement for staying in power and not dying of disgust? To become heartless, a monster like your Chief?] (p. 102). The submission of her father and of the other intellectuals to the dictator's whims, and their complicity in his murderous system, is something that Urania has tried to understand all those years living abroad and investigating the Era Trujillo. But she can only speculate that 'Trujillo les sacó del fondo del alma una vocación masoquista, de seres que necesitaban ser escupidos, maltratados, que sintiéndose abyectados se realizaban' (p. 76) [Trujillo pulled a vocation for masochism up from the bottom of your souls, that you were people who needed to be spat on and mistreated and debased in order to be fulfilled] (p. 54). And later on she herself draws the comparison between the relationship of a child to an abusive father and the way that so many Dominicans came to worship Trujillo: 'No sólo a temerlo, sino a quererlo, como llegan a querer los hijos a los padres autoritarios, a convencerse de que azotes y castigos son por su bien' (p. 75) [Not merely fear him but love him, as children eventually love authoritarian parents, convincing themselves that the whippings and beatings are for their own good] (p. 53). Vargas Llosa's recurring demon of the authoritarian father is projected here onto Urania and her relationship with her father, as well as onto the father's own relationship with the 'Father of the Fatherland'. (There is also the public denunciation of Salvador Estrella Sadhalá's father for his son's assassination of Trujillo which, to the son, is worse than the torture he has to endure.)

Urania returns in order to question patriarchal power, having investigated in great detail every aspect of the dictatorship. The obsessiveness with which she has pursued this issue all through her life presents a mirror image of

Vargas Llosa and his lifelong exploration of authoritarian power in his novels and essays. Urania says to her father: 'Me he convertido en una experta en Trujillo. ... mi hobby ha sido enterarme de lo que pasó en esos años' (p. 66) [I've become an expert on Trujillo. ... my hobby has been finding out what happened during those years] (p. 46). This reflects Vargas Llosa's repeated statements that his invincible repugnance for totalitarian regimes has turned him, against his will, into a specialist in dictatorships. Urania's monologue, spoken in front of her incapacitated father, echoes Vargas Llosa's lifelong fictional monologue about his own father, which replaces through literature the impossible dialogue with the real person. In this context Urania, who comes back to tell the terrible truth, is once more a narrator figure within the fiction. When, at the end of the novel, she tells her family in a cathartic act what happened to her at the hands of the dictator and of her father, in cruel language and with every brutal detail included, she wonders whether this will exorcize the demons that have overshadowed her whole life: '¿Vas a sentirte distinta, liberada de esos íncubos que te han secado el alma? Desde luego que no. Ha sido una debilidad' (p. 516) [Are you going to feel different, free of all the incubi that have sucked out your soul? Of course not. It was a weakness] (p. 403). Despite her doubts about the healing effect on herself, the story she finally tells has a big impact on her niece Marianita, for whom the Era Trujillo is part of a remote historical period, sometimes regarded with a certain nostalgia. Marianita's reaction makes Urania feel that her coming back to tell the truth has an important effect. A link between her and her family, but also between the past and the future, represented by the twenty-year-old niece, has been re-established, a link Urania will not break off again. The novel ends with her decision 'Si Marianita me escribe, le contestaré todas las cartas' (p. 518) [If Marianita writes to me; I'll answer all her letters] (p. 404). Communication and therefore mutual understanding will be re-established. While, at first, Urania's story seemed to the niece as unreal and exciting as a film, there is the hope that knowing the horrors of the past might change her perspective on reality and provide her with 'a less naive and more critical vision', 'una visión menos ingenua y más crítica' ('La muerte de la novela', p. 16). This is how Vargas Llosa has defined the social function of storytelling: listening to – or reading – the stories of the past has the potential to encourage a critical attitude to the present. Similar to the journalist in the novel *La guerra del fin del mundo* who set out to write his book about Canudos so that its horrors would not be forgotten, Urania represents within the novel the intention of *La Fiesta del Chivo* as a whole: it retells the past of one of the most horrible Latin American dictatorships, just as Urania retells her past under this regime, in the hope that it may affect the present and the future.

***

The novel which follows *La Fiesta* also features a female protagonist with a traumatic experience of abuse. But unlike the invented character Urania Cabral, the historical heroine of *El Paraíso en la otra esquina*, Flora Tristán, turns her personal experience of an abusive marriage into the motor of her social project of establishing a workers' union to attain social justice and gender equality. *El Paraíso* has a dual structure, its twenty-two chapters alternating between the story of Tristán, the French socialist activist, writer and feminist pioneer who lived from 1803 to 1844, and that of her grandson, the painter Paul Gauguin (1848–1903) and his project of revolutionizing art. On the surface, the two stories do not touch. Their protagonists' lives do not overlap, and their concerns and avant-garde ideas are totally different. Tristán works for a collectivist goal, guided by the wish to change the situation of women and of the poor in equal measure. By contrast, Gauguin's is an individualistic project; he seeks freedom from social and moral constraints in order to achieve a more authentic form of art. But, as with all of Vargas Llosa's binary structured works, there are a number of significant parallels as well as contrasts between the two narrative strands of Flora Tristán and Paul Gauguin, both personalities who break with their secure bourgeois existence to go out in pursuit of a Utopian ideal.

This is the first time that Vargas Llosa chooses European protagonists for a novel, even though there is a connection to Peru: Flora Tristán's father, Don Mariano Tristán y Moscoso, a colonel in the Spanish army, was from Peru which complicated the family's situation after his premature death. After leaving her abusive husband, Flora travels to Latin America in order to establish her legitimacy as a member of the Tristán family in Arequipa. Flora's grandson Paul Gauguin spends part of his childhood in his great-great-uncle's house in Arequipa and later boasts about his 'Inca' heritage. It must have been fascinating for Vargas Llosa, whose own dream as a young man from Peru was to become a writer in Paris, to find two personalities who left behind French culture to look for a 'paradise' which was located far away from that cultured city that Vargas Llosa had set his heart and his hopes on.

The juxtaposition of two biographies goes back to Plutarch and his famous *Parallel Lives*, in which the Roman author pairs well-known Greek and Roman personalities to compare, contrast and open up new perspectives on their characters. Each of the double biographies are followed by Plutarch's comments, evaluations and ethical reflections. In Vargas Llosa's fictionalized version of a double biography he leaves it entirely to the reader to find links between his two protagonists. The main clue for understanding his pairing is in the title of the book which refers to a children's game: a blindfolded child in the middle of a group of friends approaches one after the other of her friends asking 'Is this where Paradise is?' The answer is always the same since the players keep changing places: 'No, Paradise is in the other corner'. In the novel's first chapter, Flora Tristán discovers that the game she used to play as a child in Paris is still popular with children not only in France but also in Peru, as she witnesses on her visit to Arequipa: 'Bueno, qué tenía de raro, ¿no era una aspiración universal llegar al Paraíso?' (*El Paraíso*, p. 19) [And why not? Didn't everyone dream of reaching Paradise?] (*Paradise*, p. 8). In a circular move, the novel's closing chapter about Paul Gauguin picks up this thread when, shortly before his death on the Marquesa island of Hiva Oa, the painter comes across some native children playing, in their own language, the game of Paradise that he used to play in Spanish in his great-great-uncle Pío Tristán's house in Lima: '¡El juego del Paraíso! todavía no encontrabas ese escurridizo lugar, Koke. ¿Existía? ¿Era un fuego fatuo, un espejismo?' (p. 467) [The game of Paradise! You had yet to find that slippery place, Koké. Did it exist? Was it an illusion, a mirage?] (p. 407). Tristán and Gauguin both travel to far-away places in pursuit of their happiness or artistic fulfilment, but there, in the places of their dreams, in Arequipa and in the South Seas, they find that 'Paradise' is always 'in the other corner'. The longing for a Utopian ideal is a universal human trait, but the place of dreams can never be reached. Nevertheless, despite the chimerical nature of their pursuit, the Utopian striving is the source of hope and the driving force behind Tristán's and Gauguin's innovative action. The two protagonists of the novel share the rebellious spirit, energy and stubbornness necessary to chase their ideal against all odds. But their breaking away from the norms of society in both cases leads to suffering, illness and premature death, a powerful symbol of the impossibility of achieving a Utopian ideal.

El Paraíso en la otra esquina is rich in intertextuality. Flora Tristán herself is a writer whose books, especially the *London Journal*[31] and *Peregrinations of a Pariah*[32] caused much controversy at the time and are referred to and commented on within the narrative. Paul Gauguin was a prolific – and feisty – writer of letters and other prose texts which form the basis of Vargas Llosa's fictionalized biography of the artist.[33] As he did for other 'total novels', Vargas Llosa travelled to the settings of his narrative about Flora Tristán and Gauguin in order to capture the spirit of these places. For the chapters on Gauguin he undertook a voyage to the Marquesa Islands where the painter had spent the last years of his life. Vargas Llosa was not only accompanied by his daughter Morgana (who later published a book of photographs complementing her father's novel, *Las Fotos del Paraíso* [Photos of Paradise]),[34] but also by a film crew from the Spanish TV channel Canal+ who he allowed to

---

[31] Flora Tristán, *The London Journal 1842*, trans. Jean Hawkes (London: Virago, 1982).
[32] Flora Tristán, *Peregrinations of a Pariah: 1833–1834*, trans., ed. and intro. Jean Hawkes (London: Virago, 1986).
[33] See Belinda Thomson (ed.), *Gauguin by Himself* (London: Little, Brown and Company, 2000), a book that reproduces Gauguin's artwork side by side with his writings.
[34] Morgana Vargas Llosa, *Las Fotos del Paraíso* (Madrid: Alfaguara, 2003).

document his work on the novel while tracing the stations of his protagonists' lives. He was filmed visiting the places where Gauguin had stayed, and the graveyard on Hiva Oa where he is buried. Shown on 8 April 2003,[35] the documentary aimed to offer a unique insight into a novelist at work. It is a variation on Vargas Llosa's 1967 *Historia secreta de una novela*, the book in which he documents the genesis of *La casa verde*, only in 'real time' and through the medium of film. In another fascinating twist the programme sets out to document the creative process of writing a novel which itself is a work about the creative process of an artist.

While finishing his narrative about the two nineteenth-century French personalities, Vargas Llosa was also preparing his essay on Victor Hugo with a title that links it to the novel's Utopian theme: *La tentación de lo imposible* [*The Temptation of the Impossible*]. In the person of Victor Hugo politics and art go hand in hand whereas, in *El Paraíso*, this dual concern is split between the two protagonists: Flora Tristán's aim of radical change in society and Paul Gauguin's project of a renewal of art remain separate projects. But both the political activist and the painter strive to abolish the status quo for an ideal that, for Tristán, lies in the future – 'La Unión Obrera nace para evitar la [revolución], para que triunfe la justicia sin el menor derramamiento de sangre' (p. 20) [The Workers' Union is conceived to avoid revolution, so that justice may triumph without the least bit of bloodshed] (p. 10) – while Gauguin wants to go back to a mythical state of primitivism which he understands as authenticity: 'Para pintar de verdad hay que sacudirse el civilizado que llevamos encima y sacar al salvaje que tenemos dentro' (p. 34) [To truly paint we must shake off our civilized selves and call forth the savage inside] (p. 23). There are similarities between Gauguin's project of renewing art by releasing the untamed, uncivilized side of human nature and Victor Hugo's aim of giving literature a radically new direction by bringing out the grotesque side of life. Both are attempts to free art from the shackles of convention.[36] Flora Tristán's work, by contrast, attacks the suffocating conventions of a society 'que gime bajo el peso de las cadenas que se ha forjado, y que no perdona a ninguno de sus miembros que trata de liberarse de ellas' [that aches under the weight of the chains it has forged for itself, and that has no mercy for anyone trying to break free from them].[37]

The narrative strand about Tristán touches on one of Vargas Llosa's

---

[35] See <http://www.clubcultura.com/clubliteratura/clubescritores/vargasllosa/paraiso_001.html> [accessed 31 October 2012]. Unfortunately, I was unable to access the programme itself, due to technical problems.

[36] Gauguin was also an admirer of Victor Hugo's novel *Les Misérables*, and even painted a portrait of himself as Jean Valjean.

[37] Flora Tristán, 'Prefacio', in *Peregrinaciones de una Paria* (Selección), <http://digicoll.library.wisc.edu/cgi-bin/IbrAmerTxt/IbrAmerTxt-idx?type=HTML&rgn=div1&byte=11283680&q1=que%20gime%20bajo> [accessed 31 October 2012].

major concerns, the existence of social injustices, and possible ways to reform society. It contains moving descriptions of Tristán's discovery of the horrendous inequalities in her own country and those she visits on her travels, and gives Vargas Llosa the opportunity to portray various strands of nineteenth-century socialist Utopianism through the – unforgiving – eyes of his heroine who encounters Fourierists, Saint-Simonians, anarchists and less well-known splinter groups. The chapters on Paul Gauguin tie in with Vargas Llosa's many writings on the origin of the creative impulse and on the creative process. Accordingly, the novel's duality of artistic and political concerns leads the critic Dieter Oelker[38] to the interesting conclusion that the two seemingly contrasting protagonists 'become fused in a double character' which points back to Vargas Llosa himself. In his understanding *El Paraíso* is not only a fictionalized double biography but also an 'autobiographical fiction' representing the various facets of the 'Utopian desire' and its frustrations.

Despite the secret links between the two levels of narration there is a noticeable imbalance in the novel. While Vargas Llosa has stated that his original intention was to write a book about Flora Tristán and that, of the two protagonists of the final novel, his personal sympathies are more with the feminist activist and her relentless fight for social justice, he also admits that he finds Gauguin's life story more seductive.[39] This results in the book's unevenness which is palpable beneath the symmetrical narrative structure: the chapters relating Paul Gauguin's colourful life are much more engaging than Flora Tristán's travels through various provincial cities of France and the endless number of meetings she sets up in order to organize a Workers' Union, which all end up in frustration and physical exhaustion. The lively and sometimes hilarious depictions of representatives of various socialist Utopian movements whom Flora Tristán encounters cannot counterbalance the tedium of her countless frustrating meetings with groups of hostile male workers. In comparison with the tiring and repetitive accounts in the odd-numbered chapters, the depiction of Gauguin's larger-than-life personality in the even-numbered chapters, combined with the ekphrastic descriptions of some of his best-known paintings and the fictionalized stories of their genesis, contributes to the greater appeal of this narrative strand.

Even though both protagonists are overshadowed by illness and approaching death they generate enormous energy in the pursuit of their projects. Gauguin suffers from syphilis, only referred to as the 'unspeakable illness'; Tristán is affected by pain and frequent states of exhaustion that derive from her relentless lifestyle, but she also has a bullet lodged in her chest after her

---

[38] Dieter Oelker, 'Cuando el mundo posee el sueño de una cosa. (Para una lectura de *El Paraíso en la otra esquina* de Mario Vargas Llosa)', *Atenea*, 490 (2004), 59–85.

[39] See Collectif autour de Mario Vargas Llosa, *De Flora Tristán à Mario Vargas Llosa* (Paris: Presses Sorbonne Nouvelle, 2004), p. 230.

abusive husband shot her for leaving him. The events of the past are narrated by the protagonists looking back at their existence from the final period of their lives and the chapter headings include indications of dates and places to clarify the chronology. Again, in these past events Gauguin's abandonment of his successful career as a stockbroker, his separation from his wife and children, his association with bohemian friends in Brittany, and his stay with the painter van Gogh in Arles are much more fascinating than Flora Tristán's desperate attempts to establish her legitimate status as part of her Peruvian family, her brusque rejection of any male interest in her person, and her ruthless manipulations of men who find her attractive. In fact, neither protagonist is sympathetic enough to make the reader engage with their perspective. Nor is one drawn into the thought processes of an entirely negative character as was the case with Trujillo in *La Fiesta*. From an emotional distance the reader comes to admire the goals of Tristán and Gauguin, but the means to achieve them are often reprehensible. Both protagonists have suffered the traumatic experience of being expelled from a childhood paradise, in Flora's case through her father's death when she was five years old, in Paul's through his mother remarrying and sending him off to boarding school. But neither of them has any scruples about abandoning their own families in order to pursue their projects, thus perpetuating a cycle of traumatic life experiences. One recognizes Vargas Llosa's theme of the difficult balance between means and ends, but it is not pronounced enough to make the reader identify with this dilemma. Equally, the topic of fanaticism is there, but it is not in the foreground. The first words of the novel depict Flora Tristán as a single-minded person who is absolutely sure of her role as the 'Woman-Messiah' ('mujer-mesías'): 'Abrió los ojos a las cuatro de la madrugada y pensó: "Hoy comienzas a cambiar el mundo, Florita"' (p. 11) [She opened her eyes at four in the morning and thought, Today you begin to change the world, Florita] (p. 1). She is totally convinced of her world-view, in the manner of all the fanatics in Vargas Llosa's novels: 'Ahora te sentías segura, Andaluza, capaz de enfrentarte a todas las burguesas y burgueses del mundo, con tus excelentes ideas. Porque tenías una noción muy clara de lo bueno y lo malo, sobre victimarios y víctimas, y sabías la receta para curar los vicios de la sociedad' (p. 58) [Now you felt confident, Andalusa, capable of confronting all the bourgeois in the world with your excellent ideas. Because you had a very clear notion of good and bad, of victimizers and victims, and what the cure was for society's ills] (p. 45). But an insight into her thoughts also reveals an unpleasant sense of superiority in the way she dismisses other social reformers: '¡Pobres sansimonianos …! Los habías dejado muy atrás, Andaluza' (p. 11) [Poor Saint-Simonians …! You had left them far behind, Andalusa] (p. 1).

As in previous novels, Vargas Llosa shows his protagonists with all their contradictions, but for large sections of *El Paraíso* his narrative strategy leaves the reader at a sceptical distance to them. This lack of emotional power of persuasion derives in part from Vargas Llosa's use of an ambiguous second person singular voice. The narrative 'tú', as Vargas Llosa has explained in his *Cartas a un joven novelista* [*Letters to a Young Novelist*],

> podría ser el de un narrador-omnisciente, exterior al mundo narrado, que va dando órdenes, imperativos, imponiendo que ocurra lo que nos cuenta, algo que ocurriría en ese caso merced a su voluntad omnímoda y a sus plenos poderes ilimitados de que goza ese imitador de Dios. Pero, también puede ocurrir que ese narrador sea una conciencia que se desdobla y se habla a sí misma mediante el subterfugio del tú, un narrador-personaje algo esquizofrénico, implicado en la acción pero que disfraza su identidad al lector (y a veces a sí mismo) mediante el artilugio del desdoblamiento.[40]

> [could be spoken by an omniscient narrator from outside the fictional world who goes about giving orders and commands and imposing his word as law, causing everything to happen in obedience to his will and the fully fledged, limitless powers he enjoys as an imitator of God. But the narrator might also be a consciousness turned inward and speaking to itself through the subterfuge of the you, a somewhat schizophrenic narrator-character who is involved in the novel's action but disguises his identity from the reader (and sometimes from himself) through the device of the split personality.][41]

Whereas the 'tú' used for *La Fiesta*'s protagonist Urania represented the latter case of a character engaged in a credible pseudo-dialogue with herself, the second person narration in *El Paraíso* seems to be coming from a narrator holding a fictitious dialogue with his protagonists towards whom he feels ambivalent. The frequent shifts from third-person to second-person-singular narrative voice and back do not hide but, on the contrary, underline the strong presence of the omniscient narrator in the background. For large parts of the book, Vargas Llosa uses this particular way of approaching the protagonists to put things into question, plant doubts in the minds of characters and readers alike, express a patronizing evaluation of their actions from a retrospective point of view, or pretend to represent the protagonists' voice of conscience. The effect can be disillusioning and somewhat irritating: 'Al mal tiempo, buena cara, Florita. No le había ido muy bien, pero tampoco tan mal. Rudo oficio el de ponerse al servicio de la humanidad, Andaluza' (p. 22) [She wasn't discouraged. Chin up, Florita. Things hadn't gone well, but they hadn't gone badly either. Putting yourself at the service of humanity was hard work, Andalusa] (p. 12). This last phrase sounds just as awkward as the intended irony in the following example from the chapters on Gauguin: 'Cuando pensabas que, tal vez, la solución sería lanzarte desde uno de los

---

[40] Mario Vargas Llosa, *Cartas a un joven novelista* (Barcelona: Planeta, 1997), p. 54.
[41] Mario Vargas Llosa, *Letters to a Young Novelist*, trans. Natasha Wimmer (New York: Farrar, Strauss & Giroux, 2002), p. 44.

puentes, ... encontraste trabajo: pegador de carteles publicitarios en las estaciones de París. ¡Albricias, Koke!' (p. 429) [Just when you thought the solution might be to throw yourself from a bridge ... you found work: as a bill poster in the stations of Paris. Congratulations, Koké!] (p. 375). The way of addressing the characters with nicknames such as Florita, Andaluza or Koke establishes a familiarity between narrator and character and blurs the borders between the two. But it has little credibility that they would address themselves in their inner dialogues with the nicknames that other people have given them. In the following example of a sexual encounter between the painter and a young Polynesian, the tut-tutting voice is highly unlikely to represent the inner voice of an egomaniacal, sexually voracious and decency-defying character such as Paul Gauguin:

> La sangre de Koke hervía; tenía los testículos y el falo en ebullición, se ahogaba de deseo. Pero —¡Paul, Paul!— no era exactamente el deseo acostumbrado, saltar sobre ese cuerpo gallardo para poseerlo, sino, más bien, abandonarse a él, ser poseído por él igual que posee el hombre a la mujer. ... lo dejaba hacer, sin asco, con gratitud y —¡Paul, Paul!— también gozando. (pp. 72–3)

> [Koké's blood boiled; his testicles and phallus throbbed; he was choked with desire. But – Paul! Paul! – it wasn't exactly the familiar desire, of leaping on that fine body and possessing it, but rather of abandoning himself, of being possessed the way man possesses woman. ... he let the boy have his way, feeling not disgust but gratitude, and – Paul! Paul! – pleasure.] (pp. 57–8)

The intermission is the thinly veiled voice of the extratextual narrator. This way of telling a story is a constant reminder that what we are reading is a novel and not the real life story of Tristán and Gauguin. Comparable to the writer-protagonist in *Historia de Mayta*, the narrator of *El Paraíso* is in an ongoing imagined dialogue with his characters, questioning their motivations where he cannot decide what to think about some of their actions, or uttering his disapproval. In a description of one of Gauguin's paintings we read: 'y, detrás de él, como siempre en tus cuadros (¿por qué, Koke?), dos mujeres sumergidas en la floresta' (pp. 429–30) [and behind him as always in your paintings (why, Koké?), two women buried in a leafy glade] (p. 375). And in a sequence in which Flora Tristán remembers Captain Chabrié, an honourable man who fell desperately in love with her, the narrator cannot help but reproach her: 'Habías jugado con él sin el menor escrúpulo, alentándolo con tus ambiguas respuestas y esos estudiados abandonos en que permitías a veces al marino ... que te besara las manos ... No te arrepentías? "No"' (pp. 184–5) [You manipulated him shamelessly, tantalizing him with your ambiguous responses and those calculated moments of abandon when you permitted him to kiss your hands. ... Weren't you sorry? No] (pp. 154–6). In the Spanish original Tristán's answer is put into direct speech, a clear indication of a dialogue situation between narrator and protagonist.

The voice of the omniscient narrator also manifests itself in an irritating manner by frequent repetitions of phrases such as 'the unspeakable illness', 'the mad Dutchman' (for van Gogh), 'good old Schuff' (Gauguin's mentor Schuffenegger), 'the Viking' (for Gauguin's Danish wife) and the insistence on Tristán's 'pain in her abdomen and in her uterus'. Sometimes, behind all the shifting narrative instances, we hear an echo of Vargas Llosa's opinions about utopia – 'La realidad no estuvo a la altura de tus sueños, Koke' (p. 245) [Reality hadn't lived up to your dreams, Koké] (p. 209) – or about the lamentable nature of politics in Peru, driven by 'el desenfrenado apetito de poder, la enfermedad que compartían todos esos generales y generalitos que, desde la Independencia, se disputaban la presidencia del Perú, por medios legales, y, más a menudo, a tiros y cañonazos' (pp. 273–4) [the insatiable appetite for power that afflicted all the generals and petty tyrants who had been disputing the presidency of Peru since independence – by legal means and, more frequently, with gunfire and cannon blasts] (p. 233).

As a consequence, a number of critics have spoken of the didactic, almost essayistic quality of *El Paraíso en la otra esquina* where action is filtered through the protagonists' reflection, with a dominant narrative authority in the background. However, the uneven quality of the narration with its many shades of narrative perspective gains an immediate, lively quality when it comes to Gauguin's paintings and the creative process behind them. This is where Vargas Llosa's imagination takes over, and he is able to let his fantasy and his demons determine the narration, for instance in depicting the scene that Gauguin finds on coming home to the house he shares with a very young native companion whose fear of the spirits of the dead he portrays in his painting *Manao Tupapau* (*The Spirit of the Dead Watches*). Gauguin's actual letters contain some indications about the background to his paintings, but Vargas Llosa invents whole episodes around this basic information. In this case, the effect of the girl's terrified but sexually provoking attitude in the painting on Vargas Llosa is transformed into an erotic scene between her and the artist preceding the act of painting, where Gauguin is aroused by 'el espectáculo imborrable de esas nalgas fruncidas y levantadas por el miedo ... Un altar de carne humana sobre el cual oficiar una ceremonia bárbara, en homenaje a un diosecillo pagano y cruel' (pp. 33–4) [the indelible spectacle of those buttocks tightened and raised by fear ... an altar of human flesh on which to celebrate a barbaric ceremony, in homage to a cruel and pagan god] (pp. 22–3). As in *Elogio de la madrastra* [*In Praise of the Stepmother*],[42]

---

[42] Mario Vargas Llosa, *Elogio de la madrastra* (Barcelona: Tusquets, 1988); Mario Vargas Llosa, *In Praise of the Stepmother*, trans. Helen Lane (New York: Penguin, 1990).

Vargas Llosa's ekphrasis of the paintings is very personal, and the stories around the creative act that brought them to life are only loosely based on Gauguin's testimony. They reveal as much of the writer's as of the painter's demons: androgyny[43] and homosexual attraction (in the painting *Pape moe* or *Mysterious Water*, a topic Vargas Llosa explores further in *El sueño del celta*), death (in the famous canvas entitled *Nevermore*), and religion (*Vision after the Sermon* or *Jacob Wrestling with the Angel*).[44] But Gauguin himself delivers the justification for this procedure in his notes: 'Painting is the most beautiful of all the arts; it is the summation of all our sensations, and contemplating it we can each, according to our imagination, create the story, in a single glance our souls can be flooded with the most profound reflections'.[45]

El Paraíso's exploration of the creative process is one of the most interesting aspects of the novel, and puts a strong emphasis on the link between sex and creativity. Gauguin's sexual liberation runs in parallel with the emergence of his creative energy: 'El sexo había irrumpido en su vida, como la luz en sus cuadros, con beligerancia irresistible, llevándose de encuentro todos los remilgos y prejuicios que hasta entonces lo mantenían apagado' (p. 82) [Sex had burst into his life too, like the light in his paintings, with uncontainable belligerence, sweeping away all the scruples and prejudices that until then had kept it in check] (p. 66), is how the impersonal third-person narrator puts it. His artist friend van Gogh advises Gauguin to paint 'with the phallus, not the brush'. Once he has left behind the continent of 'freezing winters and frigid women', freeing himself from conventions and inhibitions, he lives out his dream of life as a savage: 'Nada más instalados en Mataiea, empezó a pintar, con verdadera furia creativa' (p. 27) [As soon as they were established in Mataiea, he began to paint, with true creative fury] (pp. 16–17). In Polynesia, he makes sure that he always has a young woman around to fulfil his needs. Sex becomes his 'fuente de energía y de salud, una manera de renovarte, de recargar el ánimo, el ímpetu y la voluntad, para crear mejor, para vivir mejor' (p. 79) [source of health and energy, a way of renewing yourself and restoring your enthusiasm, drive, and will, to create better and live better] (p. 64). Living and creating become one, and he produces his best paintings when his 'demons' (as Vargas Llosa would describe his own creative source) are involved:

---

[43] In the novel, Gauguin is obsessed with the 'mahu', the man-woman in Polynesian culture. Vargas Llosa has also published an article on this topic: see Mario Vargas Llosa, 'The Men-Women of the Pacific', in *Touchstones. Essays on Literature, Art and Politics*, select., trans. and ed. John King (London: Faber and Faber, 2007), pp. 195–200. Flora Tristán, on the other hand, spends months going around brothels and other places dressed in men's clothes to do her research.

[44] Some of the titles of Gauguin's paintings become chapter headings in the novel.

[45] Thomson, p. 33.

> No sólo habías pintado tu mejor cuadro con las manos, con tus ideas, con tu fantasía, con tu viejo oficio. También, con esas oscuras fuerzas venidas del fondo del alma, el crepitar de tus pasiones, la furia de tus instintos, esos impulsos que irrumpían en los cuadros excepcionales. (p. 254)

> [It was not simply with your hands, your ideas, your fantasies, and your old skill that you had painted your greatest work, but also with the dark forces deep in your soul, the seething of your passions, the fury of your instincts, the urgency that surfaces in exceptional paintings.] (p. 217)

This approach to creativity resembles Vargas Llosa's own, with its mixture of rational and irrational factors, of technique and passion, giving free rein to the demons and dark forces in order to fulfil a boundless ambition.

The primitivism that Gauguin aims for contains a whole lot of ideas that the painter projects onto the natives of the South Seas, derived in part from a European literary model, a novel by Pierre Loti: 'Traía muchas ilusiones consigo' (p. 24, a crucial phrase that should be translated as: 'He brought many illusions with him'). When he tries to act in the liberated way that he believes to be the natural manner of the natives, his Polynesian neighbours react with indifference. The same goes for the secret savage rituals of anthropophagy and magic that he imagines: 'y cada vez que Koke trataba de sonsacar algo a los nativos sobre sus viejas creencias, el tiempo en que eran libres como sólo pueden serlo los salvajes, ellos lo miraban sin comprender' (p. 33) [and every time Koké tried to get something out of the natives about their old beliefs, about the days when they were free as only savages can be free, they looked at him blankly] (p. 21). The authenticity he is looking for[46] does not exist any longer, and has perhaps never existed outside his mind.

With his wild behaviour and looks Gauguin provokes the attention of the authorities and has to realize that reality contradicts his dreams. His idea of Paradise is an extremely egoistic one, where he can indulge in his obsession with fourteen-year-old girls, experiment with boys, and live the illusion of having returned 'a sus orígenes, ese esplendoroso pasado en el que religión y arte, esta vida y la otra, eran una sola realidad' (p. 36) [to his roots, that splendid past in which religion and art and this life and the next were a single reality] (p. 25). In trying to live his dream he uses the girls he lives with to fulfil his every need – sex, cooking, cleaning, modelling for him, entertaining him, as long as they know when to be quiet and get out of his way – but he is unimpressed (apart from once) when they become pregnant, and has no qualms whatsoever about spreading his deadly illness. He has excluded love from his existence since he regards it as counterproductive to a life devoted

---

[46] Much in the same way as the protagonist Saúl Zuratas in Vargas Llosa's *El hablador* [*The Storyteller*] (1987) who, as an outsider amongst the Machiguengas, was the most anxious defender of their authenticity.

to creativity: 'aburguesaba a los hombres' (p. 43) [it made men bourgeois] (p. 31).[47]

In his ruthless egocentrism he represents the male attitude to women that his grandmother Flora Tristán was so repulsed by. In the end, Gauguin's sexual self-indulgence leads to the same result as Tristán's 'horror of sex' with men and her renunciation of the pleasure she finds with a woman in favour of her love for humanity: they both die a premature death, consumed by their projects, hardly loved by anyone, bitter and disillusioned, having failed during their lifetime to achieve their goals. Gauguin ends disconnected from reality, on the verge of madness, imagining that he 'regeneraría su organismo comiendo carne de su prójimo' (p. 209) [would regenerate himself by eating the flesh of his fellow man] (p. 178).

One of the most moving episodes of the novel concerns Gauguin's failed attempt to kill himself after he has finished a large canvas which he regards as his masterpiece. As so often in Vargas Llosa's work, this crucial episode occupies a central place in the novel: chapter 12, exactly in the middle of the book, is entitled '¿Quienes somos?' after the title of the painting Gauguin finished in 1898, *Where do we come from? What are we? Where are we going?* The narrative is at its best where it deals with the doubts of the artist who has laboured for months, in a 'state of incandescence', on a work that has taken the lifeblood out of his existence ('vampirizado' is the word used). This immense effort over, he falls into a deep depression asking himself whether this will be his last work, and whether anybody will be interested in it. Vargas Llosa's imagination reworks the indications we find in Gauguin's letters from February and March 1898[48] of his fear that he has exhausted his creative powers, and turns them into the inner view of the painter going off into the mountains to a beautiful spot that represents the pure and primitive, untouched paradise that he has been looking for. There he swallows a large amount of powdered arsenic and waits 'with distant curiosity' for the poison to take effect: 'Casi de inmediato, comenzó a bostezar. ¿Ibas a dormirte? ¿Pasarías de manera dulce, inconsciente, de la vida a la muerte? Tú creías que morir por veneno era dramático, dolores atroces, desgarramientos musculares, un cataclismo en las entrañas. En vez de eso, te hundías en un mundo gaseoso y empezabas a soñar' (pp. 245–6) [Almost at once, he began to yawn. Were you going to fall asleep? Would you slip gently, unconsciously, from life to death? You had thought that death by poison would be dramatic, with horrific pains, convulsions, a cataclysm in your guts. Instead, you sank into a hazy

---

[47] This is reminiscent of *La tía Julia*'s protagonist Pedro Camacho and his statement that in every vagina an artist is buried: Mario Vargas Llosa, *La tía Julia y el escribidor* (Barcelona: Seix Barral, 1986), p. 193; Mario Vargas Llosa, *Aunt Julia and the Scriptwriter*, trans. Helen R. Lane (London: Picador, 1984), p. 159.

[48] See Thomson, pp. 257–8.

world and began to dream] (p. 209). In this instance, the shifting position of the narrative voice – third-person distant voice, changing to second-person voice still remaining outside the protagonist, approaching the character to reveal his inner thoughts, and back to an outside perspective again – works very well in making the reader see, as well as live through, the protagonist's agonizing experience.

The idea of a horrible, cataclysmic death is an intertextual allusion to Flaubert's depiction of Emma Bovary's suicide by arsenic, a scene which has left an indelible mark on Vargas Llosa's imagination, as he has revealed in *La orgía perpetua* [*The Perpetual Orgy*].[49] But Gauguin does not die. He wakes up 'confused, dazed and ashamed' at his failure to commit suicide, but with the certainty that the finished canvas is a masterpiece for which he has finally found a title:[50]

> En aquel rincón superior presidirían la tela esas preguntas tremendas. No tenías la menor idea de las respuestas. Pero, sí, la seguridad de que en las doce figuras del cuadro, que trazaban, en un arco de sentido contrario al de las agujas del reloj, la trayectoria humana desde que la vida comienza en la infancia hasta que termina en la indigna vejez, estaban esas respuestas para quien supiera buscarlas. (p. 248)
>
> [In that upper corner, those tremendous questions would preside over the canvas. You hadn't the slightest idea what the answers might be. But you were sure that anyone who knew how to look could find them in the painting's twelve figures, which traced, in a counterclockwise arc, the human trajectory from the beginning of life in infancy to its end in ignominious old age.] (p. 212)

This is an ingenious way to combine ekphrasis with an internal view of a near-death experience.

Illness and death are growing concerns in Vargas Llosa's novels of the new millennium. In both narrative strands of *El Paraíso* there is a parallel movement towards the inexorable death of the two main protagonists. Perhaps the biggest challenge of this 'novela total', which is not altogether successful in its grand design of bringing together many different levels of narration, is its attempt to narrate the process of dying from the perspective of the person experiencing it. The tone is one of tender empathy, especially in Flora Tristán's case. The ambiguous second-person narrator sums up her life in a positive way, despite the fact that her 'Paradise' of equality and justice could not be attained:

---

[49] Mario Vargas Llosa, *La orgía perpetua. Flaubert y 'Madame Bovary'* (Barcelona: Seix Barral, 1975), pp. 25–6; Mario Vargas Llosa, *The Perpetual Orgy. Flaubert and 'Madame Bovary'*, trans. Helen Lane (London: Faber and Faber, 1987), pp. 16–17

[50] In a letter Gauguin declares that it is 'not a title but a signature'. Thomson, p. 262.

> Lo habías hecho, Florita. Pese a la bala junto al corazón, a tus malestares, fatigas, y a ese ominoso, anónimo mal que te minaba las fuerzas, lo habías hecho en estos ocho últimos meses. Si las cosas no habían salido mejor no había sido par falta de esfuerzo, de convicción, de heroísmo, de idealismo. Si no habían salido mejor era porque en esta vida las cosas nunca salían tan bien como en los sueños. Lástima, Florita. (p. 459)
>
> [You had done it, Florita. Despite the bullet next to your heart, your ill health, your exhaustion, and the ominous, anonymous malady eroding your strength, for eight months you had done it. If you hadn't had more success, it wasn't for lack of effort, conviction, heroism, or idealism. It was because things never succeed as well in this life as they do in dreams. A pity, Florita.] (p. 402)

The tone of empathy for this woman who ruined her health and risked everything to follow her Utopian dream is modified when, here as well as in Gauguin's case, the novel introduces an element of farce into the tragedy of an early death. The narrator imagines Flora Tristán remembering on her death bed, perhaps induced by the opium she receives to ease her pain, how she organized a contest for composing an anthem for the Workers' Union, an undertaking that ended in farce. '¿Te estabas riendo, Florita?' (p. 458) [Were you laughing, Florita?] (p. 400), asks the second-person narrator and approaches her inner view: 'Oías vagamente las voces, pero no tenías suficiente concentración y lucidez para saber qué decían' (p. 448) [You could hear voices faintly, but you weren't able to concentrate or think clearly enough to know what they were saying] (p. 400). The helplessness of the dying person who might still be conscious but is at the mercy of the people around her is exposed when Tristán, a lifelong enemy of the Church, is tricked into receiving the last rites, an 'obscurantist bit of pantomime', in the words of her friend Eléonore Blanc. In the end, even her dying will to donate her body to science and not have a burial is disregarded.

The impossibility of having control over the way one dies, and is treated and remembered when dead, is portrayed in an even more intense way in the last chapter of *El Paraíso*. It narrates the slow process of Paul Gauguin's passing away on Hiva Oa island. He is lonely, nearly blind, and pursued by the authorities in the shape of gendarme Claverie (his nemesis much in the same way as Javert was for Jean Valjean in Gauguin's favourite novel, *Les Misérables*). But he is still thinking about art, now convinced that he should have looked for Paradise in Japan, rather than in colourful, but 'mediocre' Polynesia: 'El arte no consistía en imitar a la Naturaleza, sino en dominar una técnica y crear mundos distintos del mundo real' (p. 474) [Making art didn't mean imitating Nature, but mastering a technique and creating worlds different from the real world] (pp. 413–14) – an idea very close to Vargas Llosa's concept of literature, put into practice in a masterly fashion in this last, extremely moving chapter. The novel evokes the slowly waning conscience of the painter on his deathbed, who can hear the people surrounding him talking about his person but is unable to communicate with them. Here, as in the last chapter on Flora Tristán, the narrative 'tú' works very well in making the reader feel what it is like to slowly slip away from life, at one point being still able to hear and see, 'aunque de una manera extraña, como si te separara de tus amigos de Atuona una cortina de agua' (p. 475) [but in a strange fashion, as if a curtain of water separated you from your Atuona friends] (p. 415). In the next stage, a growing feeling of disembodiment takes possession of the artist whose 'painter's eyes' are now failing as well: 'Ahora, eras puro espíritu. Un ser inmaterial, Koke. Intangible al sufrimiento y a la corrupción, inmaculado como un arcángel' (pp. 476–7) [Now you were pure spirit. An immaterial being, Koké. Beyond the reach of suffering and decay, immaculate as an archangel] (p. 416). But he is still thinking, remembering, and feeling the disappointments of the past. A while later, 'se había esfumado aquella frontera que, antes, separaba de manera tan estricta el sueño y la vida. Esto que estabas viviendo ahora es lo que siempre quisiste pintar, Paul' (p. 480) [the sharp dividing line between life and dreams had vanished. What you were living now was what you had always wanted to paint, Paul] (p. 419).

Until the very last moment, the things happening around his deathbed are filtered through the consciousness of the protagonist, whose slow process of slipping away is marked by the twice repeated phrase 'no debías estar muerto aún' (pp. 480, 481) [you must not have been dead yet] (p. 420). The repetition of this exact phrase is unfortunately not recognized as an intentional rhetorical figure (anaphora) in the English translation which varies the wording. But the repetition is a literary device to evoke 'ese tiempo sin tiempo' [this time outside of time], itself a phrase repeated twice (pp. 480, 481/pp. 420, 421). The surprise felt by the protagonist himself that he is not dead yet places the reader right in the consciousness of the dying person. He is still faintly aware of the farcical struggle between the Catholic bishop and the Protestant pastor, 'locked in a permanent fight' for the island's souls, and the gendarme Claverie representing the local authority, who have all come to his hut, the provocatively called House of Pleasure. He can hear the heated dispute flaring up over his not yet dead body, over the way to deal with his remains and his possessions. He fades away when he hears that his arch-enemy Claverie claims the last word in this case.

The moment of death is the last time the second-person-singular is used, in a phrase that juxtaposes third- and second-person narrative voices (again something that the official English translation ignores): 'A partir de allí, ya no vio ni oyó ni supo nada, porque te habías acabado de morir del todo, Koke' (p. 484) [And then [he] didn't see or hear or know anything, because you were finally altogether dead, Koké] (p. 423). From then on the narrative voice establishes itself at a distance again, consistently narrating in the third person. The slow process of gaining distance from the intensely emotional reading experience of living through a character's own perception of dying is marked by the repetition of the phrase 'no vio ni oyó ni supo' [he didn't see, hear or know], used four times in the novel's last two pages (pp. 484–5/pp. 423–4), a phrase that echoes the earlier motif of the dying painter still able to see and hear things around him. What he did not see or hear or know any more was the farce of the bishop getting in there early, snatching his body for a Catholic burial before the Protestant pastor could arrive, and taking away the infamous pornographic postcards from Gauguin's House of Pleasure. The novel ends with an ironic footnote of history: the bishop's laconic letter informing his superiors about the death of 'un artista reputado pero enemigo de Dios y de todo lo que es decente en esta tierra' (p. 485) [a reputed artist but an enemy of God and everything that is decent in this world] (p. 424) has been quoted many times in works on the now famous artist – as the narrator comments, wrapping up the novel's theme of utopia, a 'símbolo de lo injusta que es a veces la suerte con los artistas que sueñan con encontrar el Paraíso en este terrenal valle de lágrimas' (p. 485) [symbol of the injustice that is sometimes the lot of those [artists] who dream of reaching Paradise in this earthly vale of tears] (p. 485).

***

El sueño del celta, which appeared in November 2010, continues the theme of *El Paraíso* with a protagonist in search of a better world. The novel fictionalizes the biography of the British diplomat turned Irish nationalist Roger Casement, who follows his dream of an independent Ireland only to realize that the human condition is one of 'destierro en este valle de lágrimas' (*El sueño,* p. 375) [exile in this vale of tears] (*Dream*, p. 329). This expression derives from Casement's reading of Thomas a Kempis's religious work *The Imitation of Christ*, which brings him consolation during his imprisonment for high treason. In Casement Vargas Llosa chose a complex protagonist, a hero turned anti-hero: admired and honoured with a knighthood for his relentless work in defence of human rights in the Congo and in Peru, but later despised for his attempts to fight British rule in Ireland with the help of Germany during the First World War, Casement ended up being loathed for his promiscuous homosexuality exposed in the so-called 'Black Diaries' which were found after his arrest in Ireland. The suspicion that these diaries were forgeries produced by British intelligence in order to influence public opinion against the Irish nationalist has never been totally eliminated. Casement was hanged in London in 1916.

El sueño del celta closely follows his biography, told at times by an omniscient narrator, but related in other passages through the perspective of the protagonist himself looking back at his past experiences. Casement was born in Ireland in 1864 to a mother from a Catholic family and a Protestant father, who told him stories of his exploits with the British Army in India and Afghanistan. His mother had converted to Protestantism, but in her heart she had remained a Catholic. Casement grew up with this duplicity, knowing that his mother even had him secretly christened in the Catholic faith when he was little. An enthusiastic young idealist, Casement joins a shipping company engaged in commerce with West Africa, convinced that colonial trade will open the door for progress, civilization and European values in that continent. He sets off on his mission 'de una manera exaltada y, según le dijo su tío Edward, "como esos cruzados que en la Edad Media partían al Oriente a liberar Jerusalén"' (p. 27) [in an exalted way, and as his uncle Edward said to him, 'like those crusaders in the Middle Ages who left for the East to liberate Jerusalem'] (p. 16). Within Vargas Llosa's fictional world, Roger Casement is another example of the 'puro', the morally clean, idealistic type. As a young man, he has no apparent vices such as drinking or gambling, and money is of no interest to him, which sets him apart from his fellow workers in Africa. Together with the uneasiness he shows whenever they talk about women, this turns him into an outsider, comparable, for instance, to Mayta, the protagonist of Vargas Llosa's 1984 novel *Historia de Mayta*. But his strong convictions are slowly undermined by what he observes in Africa.

In 1903, by then a member of the British Consular Service, Casement is sent on a mission to the Congo to investigate reports of abuse by European companies against the indigenous population, a duty he fulfils with 'apostolic zeal'. His detailed report of unimaginable atrocities committed in the name of civilization sends shock waves through the Western world, and his exposure of the lies and illusions of colonial ventures in Africa turn him into a strong opponent of any form of colonial rule, including that of the British in Ireland. Nevertheless, he continues his work as a British Consul in South America where, in 1910, he becomes once again involved in investigating malpractices in the exploitation of rubber in the Amazon jungle. His report brings about the collapse of the British-owned Peruvian Amazon Company, and in 1911 Casement is knighted for his services in defence of human rights. But his loyalties have shifted to Ireland and her fight for independence from the British Empire. He becomes involved in organizing the Irish Volunteers and travels to Germany during the war to set up an Irish Brigade made up of Irish prisoners of war, but his attempts to gain German military support for an Irish uprising remain unsuccessful. Casement travels to Ireland in a German submarine to prevent the ill-conceived Easter Rising of Irish nationalists since it is bound to fail without foreign support, but he is arrested on his arrival in Ireland and incarcerated in London. The appeal against his sentence to death by hanging for high treason is quashed after details of the 'Black Diaries', containing explicit descriptions of his homosexual encounters, are made public.

Roger Casement's multifaceted character and his life full of contradictions and unexpected turns offer much scope for novelistic invention. Vargas Llosa's novel fills out some of the mysteries and ambiguities in Casement's biography by giving him an inner voice. As in other novels, his fictionalization of a historical personality is based on thorough research, and copious amounts of authentic names, dates, places and facts are given to trace Casement's activities on three continents. But the most engaging passages of the novel are those where fictional invention takes precedence over historical authentication, where the novelist attributes feelings and motivations to his protagonist, thus turning the rich and diverse material into a coherent fiction in itself. Roger Casement's story becomes an integral part of Vargas Llosa's own fictional world, reflecting some of his most ardent concerns: the human condition; the existence of evil; the shifting borders between fiction and reality (in the 'Black Diaries'); beauty and sexuality as a necessary counterweight to human suffering; narrating as a means of exorcizing personal demons (a theme that is explored in the dialogue between the protagonist and his prison guard); and nationalism, one of the foremost concerns in Vargas Llosa's thinking of the last decade.

There is an interesting intertextual relation that adds yet another dimension to Vargas Llosa's ambitious project. The part of the novel which narrates Casement's experiences in the Congo (and indeed in the Amazon, as we will see later) has a literary antecedent in Joseph Conrad's *Heart of Darkness*, a work that Vargas Llosa admires and has written about. In fact, in his 2001 essay on Conrad's masterpiece Vargas Llosa already mentions Roger Casement as a personality who 'deserve[s] the honour of a great novel'.[51] Conrad had met Casement in the Congo and was deeply impressed by his meticulous documentation of the atrocities which marred the colonial trade in rubber and ivory. In the novel, the intertextual dimension is made explicit in the form of a conversation between the main protagonist and Joseph Conrad, in which the author of *Heart of Darkness* credits Casement with having played a crucial role in his writing about the Congo: 'Usted debió figurar como coautor de ese libro. ... Nunca lo hubiera escrito sin su ayuda. Usted me quitó las legañas de los ojos. Sobre el África, sobre el Estado Independiente del Congo. Y sobre la fiera humana' (p. 74) [You should have appeared as co-author of that book ... I never would have written it without your help. You removed the scales from my eyes. About Africa, about the Congo Free State. And about the human beast] (p. 59). In his essay on *Heart of Darkness* Vargas Llosa describes the work as 'an exploration of the roots of humankind, those inner recesses of our being which harbour a desire for destructive irrationality that progress and civilization might manage to assuage but never eradicate completely'. 'Few stories', he says, 'have managed to express in such a synthetic and

---

[51] Mario Vargas Llosa, 'Heart of Darkness', in *Touchstones*, pp. 32–42 (p. 34).

captivating manner this *evil* that resides in the individual and in society' ('Heart of Darkness', p. 37). The protagonist of his novel remembers in prison, during a visit by the Irish historian Alice Stopford Green, how Joseph Conrad used the expression: 'Usted me ha desvirgado, Casement' (*El sueño*, p. 73) [You've deflowered me, Casement] (*Dream*, p. 58). The ensuing discussion about *Heart of Darkness* is a highly original piece of metaliterary writing, ascribing to Alice Stopford Green the critical view of Conrad's novel as racist which the African writer Chinua Achebe has famously made public:[52] 'Esa novela es una parábola según la cual África vuelve bárbaros a los civilizados europeos que van allá. Tu *Informe sobre el Congo* mostró lo contrario, más bien. Que fuimos los europeos los que llevamos allá las peores barbaries' (p. 76) [That novel is a parable according to which Africa turns the civilized Europeans who go there into barbarians. Your *Congo Report* showed the opposite. That we Europeans were the ones who brought the worst barbarities there] (p. 61). Vargas Llosa gives Casement the arguments that he himself developed in his essay on *Heart of Darkness*, understanding Conrad's work as 'a trenchant critique of Western civilization's inability to transcend cruel and uncivilised human nature' ('Heart of Darkness', p. 38). Echoing Vargas Llosa's assertion that the 'tragedy that Kurtz personifies has to do with both historical and economic institutions corrupted by greed, and also that deep-seated attraction to the "fall", the moral corruption of the human spirit, which Christian religion calls original sin' ('Heart of Darkness', p. 37), Casement says in the novel: 'Yo creo que [*El corazón de las tinieblas*] no describe el Congo, ni la realidad, ni la historia, sino el infierno. El Congo es un pretexto para expresar esa visión atroz que tienen ciertos católicos del mal absoluto' (*El sueño*, p. 77) [I don't think [*Heart of Darkness*] describes the Congo, or reality, or history, but hell. The Congo is a pretext for expressing the awful vision that certain Catholics have of absolute evil] (*Dream*, p. 62). Underneath the surface of the novel, there is an ongoing discussion about Catholic religion. Roger Casement's own view of why human beings are capable of the worst atrocities against each other remains ambiguous. But while this unresolved question seems to drive him to the edge of insanity, he finds refuge and strength in the Catholic belief system, in his readings of Thomas a Kempis, and his conversations with the prison chaplain Father Carey.

El sueño del celta has a complex structure. On the surface, the book is divided into three large parts, chronologically following the main stages of the protagonist's career, 'El Congo' [The Congo], 'La Amazonía' [Amazonia] and 'Irlanda' [Ireland]. Running through this partition, however, is a dual

---

[52] Chinua Achebe, 'An Image of Africa: Racism in Conrad's *Heart of Darkness*', *The Massachusetts Review*, 18 (1977), 782–94. See also Vargas Llosa, 'Heart of Darkness', especially pp. 37–8.

structure, with chapters alternating between Roger Casement's last weeks in prison and his past life: the narration in the odd-numbered chapters deals with his state of mind while he is waiting for the outcome of his appeal against the death sentence; the even-numbered chapters narrate his biography up to the events which caused his incarceration. To make things even more complicated, there are jumps forward and backward in time on either of these levels. But both strands progress inexorably towards the terminal outcome, Casement's fatal decision to depart for Ireland in a German submarine in the one case, and the result of this expedition, his execution for high treason, in the other. One of the linking elements between the two narrative strands is the blessing that Casement receives from Catholic priests: before his departure to Ireland Father Crotty places him under God's protection and reminds him that 'En nuestra religión es central el martirio. Sacrificarse, inmolarse' (p. 437) [In our religion martyrdom is central. To sacrifice oneself, immolate oneself] (p. 386). Casement accepts this message: 'mi obligación es ser consecuente e ir hasta el final' (p. 437) [my obligation is to be consistent and follow through to the end] (p. 387). Before that bitter end arrives on the gallows, he receives a final blessing from the prison chaplain Father Carey who allows him to take communion for the first and last time in his life – a strong symbol of the circularity that connects Casement in the hour of his death with his childhood and his beloved Catholic mother again.

Another instance of such a 'communicating vessel' between the two levels of narration is Casement's cousin Gertrude, or Gee. Chapter 2, which tells Roger Casement's childhood in the voice of an omniscient narrator, introduces Gee as Roger's closest confidante, and she is the first person to whom he shows his poems. (Secretly writing poems is a marker of an outsider in Vargas Llosa's work. This is one of those instances where the historical Roger Casement fits perfectly into Vargas Llosa's fictional universe.) When Gee's sister teases the two close friends that one day they will marry, Roger becomes confused and embarrassed – a first allusion to his possible homosexuality. In the following chapter, belonging to the other narrative level, Gee, now visibly aged and weary, visits Roger in prison on the same day that his homosexuality is exposed in the press. Before she leaves she asks the burning question which is present throughout the book: 'Todas esas cosas horribles que dicen los periódicos son calumnias, mentiras abyectas. ¿No es cierto, Roger?' (p. 33) [All those horrible things the papers are saying are slanders, wretched lies. Aren't they, Roger?] (p. 21). His answer is evasive, but the narrator's comment 'buscó cuidadosamente las palabras' (p. 33) [he searched carefully for his words] (p. 21) are a signal to the reader that Casement is hiding something. The ambiguity established here turns into near certainty at the end of the book when, in the final chapter 15, Roger writes a letter to Gee before his execution telling her of his hope that God will forgive his errors, a sort of answer to her question in chapter 3.

THE RETURN OF THE GRAND DESIGN 261

Such strands which run through the novel from the beginning and are resumed at the end give unity and coherence to the material. The circular structure, familiar from a number of Vargas Llosa's previous novels, also envelops the whole narrative, from the epigraph to the epilogue. *El sueño del celta* begins with a quotation by José Enrique Rodó: 'Cada uno de nosotros es, sucesivamente, no *uno*, sino *muchos*. Y estas personalidades sucesivas, que emergen las unas de las otras, suelen ofrecer entre sí los más raros y asombrosos contrastes' [Each one of us is, successively, not one but many. And these successive personalities that emerge one from the other tend to present the strangest, most astonishing contrasts among themselves]. That quotation is referenced again in the epilogue (a part of the book that will need further comment), where Vargas Llosa takes the unusual step of making an explicit judgement on his protagonist as

> uno de los grandes luchadores anticolonialistas y defensores de los derechos humanos y de las culturas indígenas de su tiempo y un sacrificado combatiente por la emancipación de Irlanda. Lentamente sus compatriotas se fueron resignando a aceptar que un héroe y un mártir no es un prototipo abstracto ni un dechado de perfecciones sino un ser humano, hecho de contradicciones y contrastes, debilidades y grandezas, ya que un hombre, como escribió José Enrique Rodó, 'es muchos hombres', lo que quiere decir que ángeles y demonios se mezclan en su personalidad de manera inextricable. (p. 449)

> [one of the great anti-colonial fighters, and defenders of human rights and indigenous cultures of his time, and a sacrificed combatant for the emancipation of Ireland. Slowly his compatriots became resigned to accepting that a hero and martyr is not an abstract prototype or a model of perfection but a human being made of contradictions and contrasts, weakness and greatness, since a man, as José Enrique Rodó wrote, 'is many men', which means that angels and demons combine inextricably in his personality.] (pp. 398–9)

Early on in the book it becomes clear what the 'Dream of the Celt' in the title refers to: Casement's friend, the sculptor Herbert Ward, had nicknamed him 'El celta' (p. 33) [the Celt] (p. 21), and in 1906 Casement himself wrote a poem called 'El sueño del celta' [The Dream of the Celt], 'un largo poema épico ... sobre el pasado mítico de Irlanda' (p. 145) [a long epic poem ... about the mythic past of Ireland] (p. 123). Later on, this title is alluded to again when the protagonist in his prison cell remembers how his friend used to warn him about his unrealistic nationalist ideas and told him to step out of this 'dream of the Celt'. Paradoxically, the Easter Rising which Casement tried to prevent because he rightly believed it would fail without foreign support, seems to him in his last days on death row as the all-too-brief realization of his dream: 'Aunque sólo por un brevísimo paréntesis de siete días, el "sueño del celta" se hizo realidad: Irlanda, emancipada del ocupante británico, fue una nación independiente' (p. 272) [Though only for an exceedingly brief parenthesis of seven days, 'the dream of the Celt' became a reality: Ireland, emancipated from the British occupier, was an independent nation] (p. 239).

Thematically, *El sueño del celta* is organized in concentric waves:[53] it focuses on a single protagonist with a multifaceted personality, whose varied activities on three continents have wide-reaching reverberations and throw up ever wider questions of ethics, politics, religion, human rights and ideology – a truly 'totalizing' design, reflected in the set-up of the novel. Its chapters expand in length and in depth until they reach their most important point: the odd-numbered, prison-based chapters grow from the initial five pages to six, twelve, fourteen, twenty-four and then – slightly less – twenty-one pages, to reach thirty-five pages in the most important chapter 13, where Casement reflects on his nationalist convictions and the events in Ireland, full of doubts over whether he chose the right path. Crucially, the protagonist also muses about his sexuality, and it becomes clear that he did indeed write the diaries, but that they contain an ambiguous mixture of reality and fantasy. He realizes that his negligence in leaving the diaries behind will, for a long time, overshadow 'la verdad de su vida, de su conducta política y hasta de su muerte' (p. 368) [the truth of his life, his political conduct, and even his death] (p. 323). This is a statement that could come from Vargas Llosa himself, explaining his motivation for writing the novel about Roger Casement. In this crucial chapter, the truth and lies about his complicated life come to the surface and help to 'set the record straight and do justice' to Roger Casement, as David Gallagher describes Vargas Llosa's intention.[54] The extensive chapter 13 ends with Casement being told that he will be hanged the next day. The remaining chapter in this narrative strand, which depicts the last day of his life, is only nine pages long. In its laconic density it is intensely moving.

The even-numbered chapters expand from ten to thirty-three, forty-four, then thirty-seven pages, and reach their widest expanse with sixty-two pages in chapter 10, right in the middle of the book. The following two chapters in this narrative strand are of similar length (fifty-five and sixty pages), signalling that the consequences of the events told in the central chapter are similarly important. But it is chapter 10 which is at the heart of the novel: it marks the turning point of Roger Casement's life when he reaches Putumayo, Peru's 'heart of darkness', where indigenous workers are branded like cattle.

---

[53] Vargas Llosa uses the metaphor of 'ondas concéntricas' (p. 52) [concentric waves] (p. 39) to describe the way the Western trade companies extended their zones of influence in the Congo.

[54] David Gallagher, 'Casement in Pentonville', *Times Literary Supplement*, 17 December 2010, 20–1 (p. 20).

This chapter is in many ways Vargas Llosa's own reworking of Joseph Conrad's novel: travelling deeper into the jungle, Casement encounters ever more cruel heads of trade stations, until he finally comes face to face with Armando Normand, the personification of evil, a mythical figure reminiscent of Kurtz in *Heart of Darkness*. The confrontation with this man, who is notorious for acting with unbelievable cruelty towards the indigenous people, brings Casement to realize that the only way for the oppressed to change their situation is by armed revolt. He notes in his diary that it is an illusion to believe that the presence of state authorities could enforce the law in this lawless region: 'En esta sociedad el Estado es parte inseparable de la máquina de explotación y de exterminio. Los indígenas no deben esperar nada de semejantes instituciones. Si quieren ser libres tienen que conquistar su libertad con sus brazos y su coraje. ... Luchando hasta el final' (p. 239) [In this society the state is an inseparable part of the machinery of exploitation and extermination. The indigenous should not hope for anything from such institutions. If they want to be free they have to conquer their freedom with their arms and their courage. ... Fighting until the end] (p. 209). The radicalization of Roger Casement, brought about by his encounter with Armando Normand, 'el paradigma de la crueldad de este mundo' (p. 232) [the paradigm of cruelty in this world] (p. 203), is crucial for the subsequent chapters in this narrative strand. The protagonist's conversion into a supporter of armed struggle explains his growing inner tensions as depicted in chapter 12, and the extremist nationalist activities in chapter 14, leading ultimately to his arrest and execution.

The narrative structure of *El sueño del celta* thus plays an important part in establishing the sort of coherence, with believable causes and effects, that Roger Casement's real life story, full of contradictions, secrets, duplicities and unresolved questions, does not seem to possess. During one of his conversations with the prison chaplain the protagonist muses about the truth and lies of historiography in trying to establish coherence where there is none, and wonders about the absurdity of his punishment for inciting an uprising which he actually wanted to stop:

> ¿Sería así toda la Historia? ¿La que se aprendía en el colegio? ¿La escrita por los historiadores? Una fabricación más o menos idílica, racional y coherente de lo que en la realidad cruda y dura había sido una caótica y arbitraria mezcla de planes, azares, intrigas, hechos fortuitos, coincidencias, intereses múltiples, que habían ido provocando cambios, trastornos, avances y retrocesos, siempre inesperados y sorprendentes respecto a lo que fue anticipado o vivido por los protagonistas. (p. 130)

> [Was all of history like that? The history learned at school? The one written by historians? A more or less idyllic fabrication, rational and coherent, about what had been in raw, harsh reality a chaotic and arbitrary jumble

of plans, accidents, intrigues, fortuitous events, coincidences, multiple interests that had provoked changes, upheavals, advances, and retreats, always unexpected and surprising with respect to what was anticipated or experienced by the protagonists.] (pp. 109–10)

Vargas Llosa has always upheld the conviction that it is the role of fiction to introduce order where there is none and establish hierarchies where real life is chaotic. Historiography attempts to deliver a coherent account of events, but Vargas Llosa goes a step further in his novel: he combines information gained from historiographical sources[55] and documentary research with his imagination and his own ideas and concerns, converting them into a 'total' narrative. His use of narrative techniques such as structure, point of view, communicating vessels, contrasts and parallelisms links his protagonist's nostalgia for Ireland to his experiences in the Congo and later in the Amazon region. Focusing his thoughts on Ireland becomes an antidote to the horrors Roger Casement encounters in his work as an envoy. The more atrocities Casement discovers in the jungle, the more he becomes convinced of the evils of colonialism in general. His growing conviction that there is a parallel between the colonial exploitation of Africa and the suppression of Ireland by an occupying force results in an ever stronger attachment to the unknown country of his childhood: '¿No era también Irlanda una colonia, como el Congo? Aunque él se hubiera empeñado tantos años en no aceptar esa verdad que su padre y tantos irlandeses del Ulster, como él, rechazaban con ciega indignación' (p. 110) [Wasn't Ireland a colony too, like the Congo? Though for so many years he had insisted on not accepting a truth that his father and so many Ulster Irishmen like him rejected with blind indignation] (p. 91). This suggests a deep underlying psychological reason for Roger Casement's development: colonialism is connected to the father. It is his authority and his convictions that Roger comes to oppose, embracing instead the idea of 'Ireland', with her nature, her culture and her Catholicism, representing the mother.

Vargas Llosa dates this conversion of his protagonist to the long, lonely voyage out of the inner Congo back into a civilization that he has learned to question. It represents a 'change of skin', as Roger Casement writes to his cousin Gee – a statement that points back to the 'successive personalities' mentioned in the novel's epigraph: 'En estas selvas ... he encontrado mi verdadero yo: el incorregible irlandés. ... Tengo la impresión de haber mudado de piel, como ciertos ofidios, de mentalidad y acaso hasta del alma' (p. 109) [In these jungles ... I've also found my true self: the incorrigible

---

[55] For example, see pp. 46–56 for echoes of Adam Hochschild, *King Leopold's Ghost. A Story of Greed, Terror and Heroism in Colonial Africa* (London: Pan Macmillan, 2006). Vargas Llosa has written a preface to the Spanish translation of this book, and it is also mentioned at the beginning of his essay 'Heart of Darkness'.

Irishman. ... I have the impression I've shed the skin, like certain ophidians, of my mind and perhaps my soul] (p. 90).

This first part of the novel, 'El Congo', successfully interweaves the protagonist's memories of his youth and his first travels with his later mission in Africa, tracing Casement's development from youthful idealism to total disillusionment with colonialism. It manages to integrate the historical background about King Leopold of Belgium, and his emissaries such as the explorer Henry Morton Stanley, in a telescopic narration which fits seamlessly into the main plot. The parallel it establishes between Casement's discovery of the lies of colonialism and the truth of his own identity is convincing. The protagonist's sense of disillusionment with the colonial project is as great as his previous unwavering commitment to the 'civilizing' activities of the British Empire in Africa. His confrontation with Stanley, the hero of his youth and another father-figure admired for his exploits, strikes a devastating blow to his illusions: 'Roger Casement llegó a la conclusión de que el héroe de su infancia y juventud era uno de los pícaros más inescrupulosos que había excretado el Occidente sobre el continente africano' (p. 40) [Roger reached the conclusion that the hero of his childhood and youth was one of the most unscrupulous villains the West had excreted onto the continent of Africa] (p. 29). Casement's previously unquestioning admiration for Britain turns into absolute hatred: 'un país que he llegado a odiar tanto como lo quise y admiré de joven. ... Dicen que los convertidos somos los peores' (pp. 133–4) [a country I've come to hate as much as I loved and admired it as a young man. ... They say converts are the worst] (pp. 112–13). This is how the novel explains the duplicity with which Casement, on the one hand, is able to pursue his work for the British government documenting human rights abuses while, on the other hand, he associates himself with the most radical elements of the Irish independence movement. Lost illusions, disappointment about his role models, and the shaming realization of his own naivety are all factors that contribute to his development.

The protagonist's radicalization happens on his subsequent mission to the Amazonian Putumayo region, where he finds even worse abuses of the indigenous population than in the Congo. The 'chicote' (a whip made out of hippopotamus skin), that brutal instrument of submission that leaves horrible marks on the bodies of those punished with it, and which came to symbolize the Congo for him, is superseded by an even more drastic form of physical abuse: the branding of workers by their 'owners'. The fact that the exploitation and brutal oppression of the indigenous population in Putumayo is even worse than in the Congo is symbolized by the fact that the Amazonian caoutchouc smells even more revolting than the African:

> ese olor rancio y penetrante, oleaginoso ... lo acompañaría mañana, tarde y noche ... un olor al que nunca se acostumbró, que lo hizo vomitar y le daba

arcadas, una pestilencia que parecía venir del aire, la tierra, los objetos y los seres humanos y que, desde entonces, se convertiría para Roger Casement en el símbolo de la maldad y el sufrimiento que ese jebe sudado por los árboles de la Amazonía había exacerbado a extremos vertiginosos. (p. 213)

[the rank, penetrating, oily stench ... would accompany him morning, noon, and night ... a smell he never became accustomed to, that made him vomit and retch, a pestilence that seemed to come from the air, the earth, objects, and human beings, and from then on would become for Roger the symbol of the evil and suffering that greed for the rubber exuded by the trees in Amazonia had exacerbated to dizzying extremes.] (p. 185)

This second part of *El sueño del celta* has an immediacy to it which makes it readable without too much background information. Geographically as well as thematically it unfolds on Vargas Llosa's home ground. He has written about the Amazon region before: the caoutchouc boom and its excesses feature in one of his early novels, *La casa verde* [*The Green House*],[56] in the story of Jum, the *cacique* who tries to organize resistance against the exploitation of indigenous workers. Vargas Llosa's familiarity with the region, and the type of low-level functionaries who are part of an all-pervading system of corruption, integrates this part of the novel into his ongoing project of exposing the mechanisms of corruption. Identifying with Roger Casement in his stubborn attempt to establish the truth, the reader finds out how the director of the Peruvian Amazon Company, Julio C. Arana (represented here with his real name) has achieved his undisputed position of power by making everybody financially dependent on him through loans and advances. Arana systematically suppresses information that he does not want to be published and makes journalists disappear. The novel builds up tension and anticipation during Casement's journey to the Amazon's heart of darkness to find out the truth about the rumours of unbelievable atrocities committed by Armando Normand at the inner station of Matanzas. However, the extensive description of abuses in the Amazonian part of the novel is at the limit of what the reader can stomach – in parallel with some members of the investigating commission for whom the descriptions of atrocities become too much. Perhaps not unlike the 'crescendo of excess' that Vargas Llosa finds in Conrad's *Heart of Darkness* which 'makes Kurtz's story, the absolute horror, quite believable' ('Heart of Darkness', p. 41), the drastic and repeated depictions of cruelties serve to make Roger Casement's sense of total demoralization understandable.

Vargas Llosa's technique of telescopic narration underlines the link between Casement's horrendous experiences in the jungle and his growing

---

[56] Mario Vargas Llosa, *La casa verde* (Barcelona: Argos Vergara, 1980); Mario Vargas Llosa, *The Green House* (London: Picador, 1986).

extremism. The narrative 'zooms in' on a visit to Ireland that the protagonist remembers while on his way into the Amazon jungle. That brings out the contrast between the negative sensations evoked in him in Iquitos and the love for the country he experienced when he went to Ireland after the publication of his Congo report. Surrounded by cacophony and pestilence in the sticky heat of Iquitos he recalls the happiness of experiencing Ireland, 'observando como un enamorado la austeridad de sus campos desérticos, su costa bravía, y charlando con sus pescadores, seres intemporales, fatalistas, indoblegables, y sus campesinos frugales y lacónicos' (*El sueño*, p. 143) [observing like a lover the austerity of her deserted fields and wild coast, chatting with her fishermen, fatalistic, unyielding men, independent of time, and her frugal, laconic farmers] (*Dream*, p. 121). The contrast between the reality that surrounds him and the idealized country he longs for could not be greater.

It is his realization of how a system of abuse and terror has turned the indigenous population into lifeless automata which brings Roger Casement to believe that a violent uprising is the only way out for a people oppressed by colonialist injustices: 'No debemos permitir que la colonización llegue a castrar el espíritu de los irlandeses como ha castrado el de los indígenas de la Amazonía. Hay que actuar ahora, de una vez, antes de que sea tarde y nos volvamos autómatas' (p. 247) [We should not permit colonization to castrate the spirit of the Irish as it has castrated the spirit of the Amazonian Indians. We must act now, once and for all, before it is too late and we turn into automata] (p. 216). Confronted with the hopeless and stagnant situation in Putumayo, where a horrendous system of exploitation is able to persist because isolated attempts at revolt are brutally crushed, he comes to the conclusion that, here as well as in Ireland, only well-organized armed resistance can bring about change.

The consequences of this conclusion are narrated in the third part of the novel, 'Irlanda', which is quite different in character from 'Amazonia', the passionately written Peruvian part of *El sueño del celta*. Narrating the protagonist's complicated interactions with Irish nationalists in various places – Ireland, Germany, the United States – this third part lacks the immediacy of the first two. An overwhelming number of facts, names, acronyms of political factions, etc. fail to engage readers who are less familiar with Irish history. Here, the novel seems to struggle with sustaining its character of a fiction, attempting instead to emulate the accuracy of historiographical writing. Only the odd-numbered chapters of this part are emotionally engaging since they show the protagonist in prison, imagining the events of the Irish Easter Rising from the bits of information that Alice Stopford Green is able to give him during her visit. Roger Casement can only envisage the short period in Ireland when, in his absence, his dream came true: '"Por unas horas, por unos días, toda una semana, Irlanda fue un país libre ...". Roger cerró los ojos. Veía la escena, nítida, vibrante' (p. 350) ['For a few hours, a few days, an entire week, Ireland was a free country ...' Roger closed his eyes. He saw the scene, clear and vibrant] (p. 308); 'Regresó a su celda con un tumulto de imágenes en la cabeza' (p. 363) [He went back to his cell with a tumult of images in his mind] (p. 319). The imaginary reconstruction of events in the protagonist's head is much more vivid than the straightforward narration of historical facts by the omniscient narrator.

Roger Casement's political extremism, so hard to understand in someone who impeccably fulfilled his duties for the British Government, is mirrored by his contradictory behaviour on a personal level. Shy, reticent, extremely polite and culturally refined, he shows a totally contrasting side in his Black Diaries. The sexual excesses described there are presented in the novel as another consequence of the horrors he had to confront in Africa and Amazonia. In the same way that *El sueño del celta* associates his conversion to fanatical nationalism with the brutal reality of exploitation that he is exposed to, it ascribes Casement's compulsive writing about real or imagined homosexual encounters to the extreme distress and enormous mental strain caused by the evil he experiences. Through the protagonist's eyes we see how physical beauty is able to make him momentarily forget his disgust at the physical abuse and mutilation he has seen. Fearing he could become 'contaminated' by the evil that reigns in the lawless caoutchouc regions, he seeks refuge in physical beauty and harmony. When in Europe, Casement is able to find pleasure in cultural beauty, especially with his friends, the sculptor Herbert Ward and his wife, 'hablando de cosas bellas y elevadas, arte, libros, teatro, música, lo mejor que había producido ese contradictoria ser humano que era también capaz de tanta maldad' (p. 263) [talking of beautiful, elevated things, art, books, theater, music, the best produced by those contradictory human beings also capable of extreme wickedness] (p. 231). During his travels, in his fleeting encounters with male lovers, he photographs his sexual partners imitating poses of antique statues.[57]

It is in Africa that the 'fever' of sexual desire starts to affect Casement as much as the fever caused by his attacks of malaria. 'Fever' symbolizes the Congo on a number of different levels: the literal fever induced by malaria; fever as a metaphor for the greed that drives the European exploiters to orgies of violence against the indigenous people; and fever as a metaphor used to depict outbreaks of otherwise suppressed homosexuality in Roger Casement who feels on one of his journeys 'que renacía en su cuerpo la antigua fiebre que se apoderaba de él' (p. 299) [in his body the rebirth of the old fever that took possession of him] (p. 262); 'En su diario resumió su estado de ánimo con tres palabras: "Ardo de nuevo"' (p. 294) [In his diary he summarized his

---

[57] Vargas Llosa's protagonist is not as openly paedophile as the real Black Diaries suggest, because this would have undermined the attempt to make the fictional Roger Casement's behaviour understandable.

state of mind with three words: 'I burn again'] (p. 258). The novel describes some of these homosexual encounters as real, while others are only played out in the protagonist's mind, in his dreams or in his diaries: 'En el pequeño diario que llevaba siempre consigo, anotó: "Muy hermoso y enorme. Lo seguí y lo convencí. Nos besamos ocultos por los helechos gigantes de un descampado. Fue mío, fui suyo. Aullé". Respiró hondo, afiebrado' (p. 113) [In the small diary he always carried with him, he wrote: 'Very beautiful and enormous. I followed him and persuaded him. We kissed hidden by the giant ferns in a clearing. He was mine, I was his. I howled.' He breathed deeply, in a fever] (p. 94). This is one of the crucial passages in the novel where it becomes clear, long before Vargas Llosa makes it explicit in his epilogue, that the diaries contain an ambiguous mixture of truth and lies. *El sueño del celta* recognizes Roger Casement as the author of the Black Diaries; but they are shown to fulfil a cathartic function in the protagonist's feverish existence. The entry quoted above is made just after he decides not to see a doctor for his declining health, since 'ver al doctor Salabert significaría hablar, recordar, contar todo aquello que por el momento sólo quería olvidar' (p. 112) [seeing Dr Salabert would mean speaking, remembering, recounting everything that for the moment he wanted only to forget] (p. 93).

The deliberately coarse, 'vulgar and telegraphic' style of his diary entries is the complete opposite to the carefully chosen, precise and neutral style of his reports. In fact, the crude and assertive language he uses to describe his sexual encounters and fantasies actually compensates for his doubts about the effectiveness of his report:

> Una tarde en que luchaba contra la sensación de impotencia que lo vencía, fantaseó así en su diario: 'Tres amantes en una noche, dos marineros entre ellos. ¡Me lo hicieron seis veces! Llegué al hotel caminando con las piernas abiertas como una parturienta'. En medio de su mal humor, la enormidad que había escrito le provocó un ataque de risa. Él, tan educado y pulido con su vocabulario ante la gente, sentía siempre, en la intimidad de su diario, una invencible necesidad de escribir obscenidades. Por razones que no comprendía, la coprolalia le hacía bien. (p. 303)

> [One afternoon, as he struggled against the feeling of impotence that overcame him, he fantasized in his diary: 'Three lovers in one night, two sailors among them. They fucked me six times! I walked back to the hotel, my legs wide like a woman in labor.' In the middle of his bad humor, the barbarity he had written made him laugh out loud. He, so well bred and polished in his vocabulary with other people, always felt, in the privacy of his diary, an irresistible need to write obscenities. For reasons he didn't understand, salacious language made him feel better.] (pp. 266–7)

In the same way that concentrating his thoughts on Ireland and his childhood help him to stabilize his mind in the middle of all the inhuman practices he has to record, the documentation of his visual impressions, fantasies and desires, first with a camera, then by writing in his private diary, functions as an antidote to the brutal reality of the rubber trade.

But with time the enormity of the horrors that confront Roger Casement have an erosive effect on his mental health. Many people he encounters on his missions explain the system of exploitation, torture and extermination that they are part of with the fact that the 'barbarity' of life in the jungle turns people into savages: 'corre mucha sangre. La gente termina por acostumbrarse. Allá la vida es matar y morir' (p. 162) [a lot of blood flows. People end up getting used to it. Life there is killing and dying] (p. 138). By contrast, Casement does not loose his humanity or his compassion, but the extreme circumstances erode the stability of his mind. The narrator imagines the nightmares that plague him, 'haciéndolo pasar del miedo al pasmo, de visiones satánicas a un estado de desolación y tristeza en que todo perdía sentido y razón de ser: su familia, sus amigos, sus ideas, su país, sus sentimientos, su trabajo' (p. 93) [moving him from fear to stunned bewilderment, from satanic visions to a state of desolation and sadness in which everything lost its meaning and reason for being: his family, his friends, ideas, country, feelings, and work] (p. 76). In his letters Roger confesses to his cousin Gee: 'Creo que estoy perdiendo el juicio ... Estoy en las orillas de la locura. ... Algo se está desintegrando en mi mente' (p. 108–9) [I believe I'm losing my mind ... I'm on the verge of madness. ... Something is disintegrating in my mind] (p. 90). The recurring metaphor for the protagonist's state of mind is that of mire – 'fango' – evoking the muddy surroundings of the Congo and the Amazon as well as representing the moral and mental morass that he is in danger of sinking into: 'Recordar el Congo o el Putumayo le hacía daño: revolvía el fango de su espíritu' (p. 132) [Recalling the Congo or Putumayo did him harm: it stirred up the mud in his spirit] (p. 111).

In these circumstances, he not only holds on to the Ireland of his childhood dreams, but also turns to the religion of his mother: 'Cuando creí que iba a perder la razón ante tanto sufrimiento. Así descubrí que un ser humano no puede vivir sin creer' (p. 127) [When I thought I would lose my mind in the face of so much suffering. That was how I discovered that a human being can't live without believing] (p. 107). The novel highlights the strong link between nationalist ideology and religion, with Irish nationalist leaders such as Robert Monteith, Patrick Pearse and Joseph Plunkett embodying the association of spirituality and fanaticism in Irish nationalism. According to Pearse, 'la fusión de esas dos tradiciones, mártires y místicos y héroes y guerreros, resultaría la fuerza espiritual y física que rompería las cadenas que sujetaban a Eire' (p. 426) [the fusion of these two traditions, martyrs and mystics and heroes and warriors, would be the spiritual and physical strength to break the chains that bound Ireland] (p. 377). Plunkett's familiarity with the Spanish mystic poets is mentioned at the same time as his exalted rhetoric and his vehement, frenetic gesticulation which fascinates his audience. He is portrayed as speaking 'con la seriedad de quien se sabe poseedor de una verdad irrefutable' (p. 420) [with the gravity of someone who knows he possesses an irrefutable truth] (p. 371) – a clear intertextual reference to other fanatics in Vargas Llosa's novels. Plunkett is depicted as the epitome of a fanatic who believes that the end justifies the means, and thus represents, within the novel, this evil that Vargas Llosa has often exposed in his extra-literary texts. Plunkett knows that the planned uprising will fail and cost many lives, yet he is absolutely convinced of the necessity to sacrifice the present for the future, comparing the self-immolation of Irish independence fighters with the martyrdom of the early Christians.

El sueño del celta highlights the appeal that both religion and nationalist ideology, with their sense of a mission and the absolute conviction of following the right path, have for Casement, thus linking Vargas Llosa's novel to his other texts about nationalism, religion and other ideologies with their devoted followers, frequently described as 'los que nunca dudan' [those who never doubt]. Casement is portrayed as an enthusiast, always ready to put his hopes and trust in people and causes – only to get bitterly disappointed. The hopes he had attached to Germany, and the ideals that he had projected onto that country during the war, result in total disillusionment. Trying to stay in contact with Irish nationalists during his feverish activities there, he feels the mental disturbance 'como en los períodos en el Congo y la Amazonía. Sintió que perdía el equilibrio mental. Su cabeza parecía a ratos un volcán en plena erupción. ¿Iba a perder la razón?' (p. 425) [as had happened during his most difficult times in the Congo and Amazonia. He felt himself losing his mental equilibrium. At times his head seemed like an erupting volcano. Would he lose his mind?] (p. 376).

Casement's fatal misjudgement in making the young, beautiful 'seducer' Eivind Adler Christensen (a shady figure who ends up denouncing him to the British) his companion, lover and confidant is also attributed to his fragile state of mind. The novel adopts the protagonist's perspective in describing Christensen as a 'Viking god' who turns out to be the incarnation of the Devil. Here again we find not only the extreme contrasts that characterize the novel, but also the pattern of love and trust bitterly disappointed and turned into hatred: 'de todos sus fracasos, el más grande había sido confiar tan ciega y estúpidamente a Eivind/Lucifer. ... era víctima de una emboscada. ¡Había caído en ella como un niño idiota!' (pp. 192–3) [But of all his failures, the greatest had been to trust so blindly and stupidly in Eivind/Lucifer. ... he was the victim of a trap! He had fallen into it like a stupid child!] (pp. 165–6). The description of Christensen's 'cara risueña y hermosa de niño travieso' (p. 194) [smiling, beautiful naughty boy's face] (p. 167) is reminiscent of the seemingly innocent seducer Fonchito in *Elogio de la madrastra*. But the deceptive innocence is, in this case, interpreted in religious terms: '¿Era ésa la cara, la mente, el retorcimiento viperino del pecado original?' (p. 196) [Was that the face, the mentality, the viperish contortion of original sin?] (p. 169). Narrative perspective plays an important role in making the reader understand Casement's misjudgement: through the use of free indirect style the omniscient narrator gets close to the protagonist until we see an inner perspective, with the effect of making Casement's motivations for trusting Eivind understandable: 'Con éste había entrado en su vida un flujo de juventud, de ilusión, y —la palabra lo hacía sonrojar— amor' (p. 407) [With him a tide of youth, of hope, and – the word made him blush – of love had entered his life] (p. 359). By rendering the protagonist's own thoughts about his flaws and the demoralization that he feels, the novel turns Casement into a tragic hero. It evokes pity for his loneliness, his longing for happiness and his marginality, and raises sympathy for his naive trust in people and causes.

On the other hand, *El sueño del celta* reflects Vargas Llosa's abhorrence for the kind of extreme nationalism that Roger Casement adopted in the course of his life. The trick the novel uses to highlight the arguments against nationalism is to have them reflected in the protagonist's mind when he remembers the words of his best friends, all very positive figures: the loyal Alice Stopford Green, Irish historian and intellectual, warns him 'No debemos dejar que el patriotismo nos arrebate la lucidez, la razón, la inteligencia' (p. 197) [We should not allow patriotism to do violence to our lucidity, our reason, our intelligence] (p. 170). The cultivated and tolerant Herbert Ward is appalled by the hatred of Britain that his friend has developed, accusing him 'de abrazar la idea nacionalista de una manera demasiado exaltada, poco racional, casi fanática' (p. 387) [of embracing the nationalist idea in a way that was too exalted, not very rational, almost fanatical] (p. 342). The discussions with his friends actually bring the protagonist to doubt his position: '"¿Me estoy volviendo un fanático?", se preguntaría desde entonces, a veces, con alarma' (p. 388) [*Am I turning into a fanatic?* he would ask himself from then on, at times with alarm] (p. 342); '¿Y si Alice tiene razón y yo me he equivocado?' (p. 410) [What if Alice is right and I've made a mistake?] (p. 362). He also remembers the cutting words of George Bernard Shaw, the dramatist who, nonetheless, defended him vociferously after his conviction: 'el patriotismo es una religión, está reñido con la lucidez. Es puro oscurantismo, un acto de fe' (p. 197) [patriotism is a religion, the enemy of lucidity. It is pure obscurantism, an act of faith] (p. 170). Tellingly, it is the Catholic cleric Father Crotty who reassures Casement: 'Debe hacer lo que crea que es lo mejor para Irlanda, Roger. Sus ideales son puros' (p. 413) [You should do what you believe is best for Ireland, Roger. Your ideals are pure] (p. 365). As we know from other works by Vargas Llosa, the word 'pure' always carries with it the connotation of fanaticism.

Perhaps even more powerful than the words of reason from his friends is the silence from his closest ally Edmund D. Morel, who breaks off contact altogether and does not sign any of the petitions in favour of Roger Casement, just like Joseph Conrad, both of whom he had met in the Congo. This is the most painful experience for Casement, who shared Morel's moral values in their joint fight against human rights violations. In their long discussions Morel had already turned against Roger Casement's attempts to explain the existence of evil in human beings in terms of the Christian idea of original sin: 'Si la razón última de la maldad es el pecado original, entonces no hay solución. Si los hombres estamos hechos para el mal y lo llevamos en el alma ¿por qué luchar entonces para poner remedio a lo que es irremediable?' (p. 196) [If the ultimate reason for evil is original sin, then there is no solution. If we humans are made for evil and carry it in our souls, why fight to find a remedy for what is irremediable?] (p. 169). The novel's gradual withdrawal of sympathies from its protagonist for his turn to extreme nationalism, of which Catholicism is an integral part, peaks in the unexplained silence of Morel, a person with strong moral credibility, during Casement's pending appeal.

El sueño del celta also addresses the question why such a conscientious person as Roger Casement could be so negligent in carrying on him, at the time of his arrest, the incriminating evidence of a German train ticket and the secret code which allowed him to communicate with the German military. This is another unsolved mystery in a life story full of contradictions. In his review of Vargas Llosa's novel, David Gallagher speculates whether, subconsciously, Roger Casement 'didn't want to put an end to so much stressful duplicity'.[58] The novel, however, leaves a certain amount of doubt and ambiguity by shifting from the omniscient narrator's explanation – 'Sin duda por los mareos y el horrible malestar durante el viaje en el U-19, olvidó ...' (p. 276) [Undoubtedly because of his nausea and horrible malaise during the trip in the U-19, he left behind ...] (p. 242) – through the use of free indirect style in approaching the protagonist's inner perspective – 'Era una pregunta que supuraba en su conciencia como una herida infectada' (p. 276) [It was a question that festered in his mind like an infected wound] (p. 243) – to the protagonist's inner doubts – '¿Eran los primeros síntomas de locura?' (p. 277) [Were these the first symptoms of madness?] (p. 243) – and back again to the omniscient narrator's evaluation: 'Quien siente una desmoralización tan profunda puede cometer distracciones tan graves como las que él cometió' (p. 277) [Someone who feels so profound a demoralization can commit oversights as serious as the ones he had committed] (p. 244). And yet the protagonist's ambiguous feelings throw this coherent explanation into doubt again: 'Estas excusas lo aliviaban unos instantes; luego, las rechazaba y el sentimiento de culpa y el remordimiento eran peores' (p. 277) [These excuses relieved him for an instant or two; then, he rejected them, and the feelings of guilt and remorse became worse] (p. 244).

[58] Gallagher, p. 21.

The portrayal of Roger Casement in *El sueño del celta* remains ambiguous. Nevertheless, the novel carefully constructs a coherent story out of the many different levels of Casement's life, establishing believable causes and effects in his erratic behaviour and resolving unresolved questions, such as the authorship of the Black Diaries – only to then add an epilogue where the author of the novel steps out of the narration to explain his personal view of things, thus compromising the fictional autonomy. Vargas Llosa explicitly states: 'Mi propia impresión —la de un novelista, claro está— es que Roger Casement escribió los famosos diarios pero no los vivió, no por lo menos integralmente, que hay en ellos mucho de exageración y ficción, que escribió ciertas cosas porque hubiera querido pero no pudo vivirlas' (p. 449) [My own impression – that of a novelist, obviously – is that Roger Casement wrote the famous diaries but did not live them, at least not integrally, that there is in them a good deal of exaggeration and fiction, that he wrote certain things because he would have liked to live them but couldn't] (p. 399). This unusual step by Vargas Llosa of giving his own opinion as the author of the book does not add anything to what the preceding narrative has not already implied. As we have seen, the novel finds a perfectly plausible way of explaining Casement's 'pestilent obscenities' in the Black Diaries, but leaves enough uncertainty and ambiguity to underline Vargas Llosa's point that 'ángeles y demonios se mezclan en su personalidad de manera inextricable' (p. 449) [angels and demons combine inextricably in his personality] (p. 399).

Adding this epilogue is a surprising move by Vargas Llosa who has always insisted on the necessary autonomy of a fictional world. There is no ambiguity or postmodern playfulness about the 'author' of this postscript or about the fact that it is no longer part of the fiction, as it is dated in the way that Vargas Llosa always signs off his non-fictional texts: 'Madrid, 19 de abril de 2010'. Does this mean that, in the end, Vargas Llosa did not trust his own historical fiction? The epilogue adds facts about the aftermath of Roger Casement's execution, such as the gruesome medical examination of the corpse which found physical 'proof' of homosexual practices, or the fact that, for a long time, he was forgotten and only much later became recognized as one of the heroes of Irish independence. It tells of Vargas Llosa's travels to places where Casement is commemorated and ends with the image of a memorial on Banna Strand in Ireland, where Casement and Robert Monteith landed, which the author finds besplattered by seagulls – a telling metaphor for the way Roger Casement's image remains besmirched by the scandal surrounding his homosexuality. But was it really necessary to make explicit the novel's intention of redressing the balance between his dubious personal life and his lasting achievements as a defender of freedom and human rights?

The last pages of the fictional narration, by contrast, make the reader experience Roger Casement's last hours and minutes through his own perspective, which is a very moving and upsetting experience. With him we hear, see and feel what is happening when he steps up onto the gallows. Vargas Llosa's use of the free indirect style is at its best when we experience with the convict that the hands of the executioner, who had shown great consideration when he had tied the protagonist's hands behind his back, worrying whether he had hurt him, are now hesitating, showing an emotion that Roger Casement himself no longer feels: 'le pareció que los dedos de Mr Ellis eran ahora menos firmes, menos dueños de sí mismos' (p. 446) [he thought Mr Ellis's fingers were less firm now, less in control] (p. 395). Vargas Llosa has narrated the death of a protagonist through his own perspective before, the most intensely moving example being Paul Gauguin's hour of death in *El Paraíso*, as we have seen. But to live through a character's execution is the most upsetting example of this challenging attempt at imagining the moment of death, not least because of the ambiguous feelings of the executioner, Mr Ellis, and his considerate, almost tender attitude towards the prisoner:

> Escuchó unos movimientos, rezos de los sacerdotes y, por fin, otra vez, un susurro de Mr Ellis pidiéndole que bajara la cabeza y se inclinara algo, *please, sir*. Lo hizo, y, entonces, sintió que le había puesto la soga alrededor del cuello. Todavía alcanzó a oír por última vez un susurro de Mr Ellis: 'Si contiene la respiración, será más rápido, sir'. Le obedeció. (p. 446)

> [He listened to some movements, the priests' prayers, and finally, again, a whisper from Mr Ellis asking him to lower his head and bend down a little, please, sir. He did, and then he felt him place the rope around his neck. He could still hear Mr Ellis's last whisper: 'If you hold your breath, it will be faster, sir.' He obeyed.] (p. 396)

The last short remark cuts off the narration in a distressing way, mirroring the cutting off of oxygen to the prisoner's brain. This upsetting piece of imaginative writing, leaving the reader choked with indignation against the injustice of the death penalty, is complemented by the information, given in the epilogue, that Mr Ellis, the executioner, later killed himself. He left a diary in which he stated that, of all the people he put to death, Roger Casement showed the most courage in dying.

PART 3:
WORKS FOR THE THEATRE

10

Life's Dreams: the Storyteller on Stage

Vargas Llosa had his first success as a writer of fiction with the play *La huida del inca* [The Inca's Escape] which he wrote in 1951, aged fifteen. Encouraged by his uncle he submitted it to a contest of children's plays organized by the Ministry of Education and won second place. In 1952, his school in Piura gave him the chance to put on a performance of this play at the Teatro Variedades under his own direction. Vargas Llosa fondly recalls the exciting process of bringing a piece of writing to life on the stage, even though he dismisses the play itself as a 'soap opera with Incas',[1] not worth remembering. He has never published the work and never revealed much about its content, but he admits carrying on him as a talisman a programme note of its performance in Piura. What he does, however, mention in his memoirs is the play's subtitle: *Drama incaico en tres actos, con prólogo y epílogo en la época actual* (*El pez*, p. 122) [*An Inca drama in three acts, with a prologue and an epilogue in the contemporary era*] (*Fish*, p. 119). It is interesting to see that this format not only anticipates the frequent use of prologue and epilogue in Vargas Llosa's later work, but also reveals the interplay between two levels of time, present and past, already in this early play, a feature that will later come to define Vargas Llosa's novels as well as his theatrical work.

'El teatro fue mi primer amor' [Theatre was my first love], he has declared on many occasions.[2] On his first visits to the theatre as a child he was fascinated to see a story come to life, acted out in front of him by people of flesh and blood. It added a new dimension to his desire to live through stories and sparked a lifelong passion for the theatre. A performance of Arthur Miller's *Death of a Salesman* which Vargas Llosa saw as a teenager in Lima moved him deeply.[3] He recalls the intensity of a production that freely juxtaposed past and present, disregarding the conventions of time and space, and this experience left an indelible mark on the future writer. Had

---

[1]   Mario Vargas Llosa, *A Fish in the Water. A Memoir*, trans. Helen Lane (London: Faber and Faber, 1995), p. 194 ('una truculencia con Incas', Mario Vargas Llosa, *El pez en el agua. Memorias* [Barcelona: Seix Barral, 1993], p. 197).

[2]   For example, see the prologue (written in 2001) to Mario Vargas Llosa, *Teatro. Obra reunida* (Madrid: Alfaguara, 2006), p. 9.

[3]   See Mario Vargas Llosa, 'El viaje de Odiseo', afterword to *Odiseo y Penélope*, photos Ros Ribas, illus. Frederic Amat (Barcelona: Galaxia Gutenberg, 2007), pp. 117–55 (p. 120).

there been a theatrical movement in 1950s Lima, he says, he might have become a playwright rather than a novelist. As that was not the case, his ambition to write for the stage lay dormant for many years until, from the late 1970s onwards, he decided that some of the material he wanted to use for his fictions was better suited to be presented in the condensed form of a stage play than in an extensive novel.[4] His strong visual memory of certain people played an important part in the decision to use them as models for his theatrical creations, such as his ancient relative Elvira, la Mamaé, protagonist of his 1981 play *La señorita de Tacna* [*The Young Lady of Tacna*],[5] the first of eight works for the theatre published to date.

Due to the metafictional element especially prominent in the early plays, some critics have regarded Vargas Llosa's dramatic works as 'a novelist's theatre'[6] and suggested that the autonomy of his plays was undermined by a surfeit of explanatory text in their prologues. It is certainly true that the introduction to *La señorita de Tacna*, 'Las mentiras verdaderas' [Lies That Tell the Truth],[7] and the prologue to *Kathie y el hipopótamo* [*Kathie and the Hippopotamus*], 'El teatro como ficción' [Theatre as Fiction],[8] are important texts in which Vargas Llosa elaborates his ideas about reality and fiction, about truths and lies, and the need for fantasies. A look at each individual theatrical work will reveal whether the actual play relies on the surrounding text to make sense. This would mean that a play needs to be read rather than experienced in the theatre. But Vargas Llosa's theatrical works have seen many successful performances, and he has made a habit of not publishing a new play until after its first staging. That puts the emphasis firmly on the text as part of a performance, not as a reading experience. Vargas Llosa adds specific stage directions to his plays, often involving music and lighting, a fact that reflects the importance of the visual, sensual element in his theatrical conception. He has always been eager to see different performances of his own works, and continues a dialogue with directors and actors.[9]

La señorita and *Kathie* put the act of storytelling itself on stage. They both

---

[4] Vargas Llosa, 'El viaje de Odiseo', pp. 128–9.

[5] Mario Vargas Llosa, *La señorita de Tacna* (Barcelona: Seix Barral, 1981); Mario Vargas Llosa, *The Young Lady from Tacna*, in *Three plays. The Young Lady from Tacna. Kathie and the Hippopotamus. La Chunga*, trans. David Graham-Young (London: Faber and Faber, 1990), pp. 1–76.

[6] For example, see Peter Standish, 'A Novelist's Theatre', *Antípodas*, 1 (1988), 133–41.

[7] Mario Vargas Llosa, 'Las mentiras verdaderas', in *La señorita de Tacna*, pp. 9–12; Mario Vargas Llosa, 'Lies That Tell the Truth', in *Three plays*, pp. 5–7.

[8] Mario Vargas Llosa, 'El teatro como ficción', in *Kathie y el hipopótamo* (Barcelona: Seix Barral, 1983), pp. 9–13; Mario Vargas Llosa, 'Theatre as Fiction', in *Three plays*, pp. 81–4.

[9] I witnessed this when *La Chunga* was staged at a small, appropriately scruffy backroom theatre behind a pub, the Phoenix Artist Club, in London in January 2012, where Vargas Llosa was present on the first night. This very good staging and performance by the Second Skin

have a writer-protagonist who is shown in the process of turning the experiences, memories and fantasies of someone's life into literature. The point of departure for both plays is Vargas Llosa's personal experience: Belisario, the writer-protagonist in *La señorita*, who pretends to study law but only wants to be a writer, reflects Vargas Llosa's teenage self living in a household with the centenarian Mamaé whose stories from her long life stimulated his imagination. In *Kathie*, we find an echo of the young author living in Paris, earning some money as a ghost-writer. Vargas Llosa's fascination with the mysterious ways in which memories are evoked and secret desires come to light in creating a story provides the subject matter for these plays, and they are as self-referential as his metafictional novels of the same period, *La tía Julia y el escribidor* [*Aunt Julia and the Scriptwriter*],[10] *Historia de Mayta* [*The Real Life of Alejandro Mayta*][11] and *El hablador* [*The Storyteller*].[12] In 'El teatro como ficción' he explains that the lies of fiction have an even greater effect in the theatre: on the one hand, the representations on stage are more obviously unreal, but on the other, they are acted out by real people which makes them more immediate, lively and bewitching. But even without the context of their explanatory prologues, these two plays illustrate Vargas Llosa's literary theory: they show on stage how turning a life into a story involves changing facts, for better or for worse, by making them more stringent, more exciting, more horrifying, beautiful or farcical, all in order to compensate for the failures, the shortcomings or the sheer tedium of a life lived.

La señorita de Tacna unfolds on two levels of time and space which Vargas Llosa's stage directions suggest to be represented side by side: Belisario's study in the year 1980, and the house of his grandparents in Lima that he and aunt Elvira, 'la Mamaé', shared with them during the 1950s. This second level of time is a recollection of Belisario who is sitting at his desk in the present, remembering the old woman in an armchair, frail, confused and surrounded by the ghosts of her past life. As a boy he used to listen to her telling him melodramatic stories of love and betrayal that turned out to be versions of her own life story, embellished by fictional elements. While Belisario is attempting to write a romantic novel inspired by Mamaé when she was 'the young lady from Tacna', events and people from various phases of her past appear on stage. Unable to keep past and present, memory and

---

Theatre company made me realize that this was definitely not 'a novelist's theatre', but an intense theatrical experience, able to bring the subject matter of truth and fiction to life.

[10] Mario Vargas Llosa, *La tía Julia y el escribidor* (Barcelona: Seix Barral, 1986); Mario Vargas Llosa, *Aunt Julia and the Scriptwriter*, trans. Helen R. Lane (London: Picador, 1984).

[11] Mario Vargas Llosa, *Historia de Mayta* (Barcelona:Seix Barral, 1984); Mario Vargas Llosa, *The Real Life of Alejandro Mayta*, trans. Alfred MacAdam (London: Faber and Faber, 1986).

[12] Mario Vargas Llosa, *El hablador* (Barcelona: Seix Barral, 1987); Mario Vargas Llosa, *The Storyteller*, trans. Helen Lane (London: Faber and Faber, 1991).

fantasy apart, Mamaé is in a dialogue with the spectres of her life, while the stories of her past invade Belisario's present. This fluidity between different layers of time and levels of reality is a challenge for any stage director, but mainly for the actress playing Mamaé. One moment she has to represent her as the young lady from Tacna, and the next as a very old woman, the transition between the two stages happening before the eyes of the audience. One stage direction reads: '*La Mamaé regresa hacia su sillón y en el trayecto va recuperando su ancianidad*' (*La señorita*, p. 31) [*As she goes back towards her armchair, she gradually takes on the characteristics of an old woman again*] (*Young Lady*, p. 18). It is hard to imagine how these transformations can be performed convincingly, but Vargas Llosa is full of praise for the first actress who played Mamaé in the 1981 Buenos Aires premiere, Norma Aleandro. Thanks to her, he says, *La señorita de Tacna* became the play that gave him most satisfaction:

> Con el simple revoloteo de un pañuelo, Norma se transformaba en una jovencita cándida e ilusionada en la ciudad de Tacna, ocupada por el Ejército chileno a comienzos del siglo veinte, o en una viejecita centenaria. ... Pasado y presente, ficción y realidad, verdad y mentira se confundían en unas imágenes de gran delicadeza y ternura, al conjuro de la expresividad de una intérprete que parecía haber abolido las barreras del tiempo y del espacio para rescatar las vivencias centrales de la oscura biografía de la Mamaé. ('El viaje de Odiseo', pp. 133–6)

> [With the simple fluttering of a scarf, Norma transformed herself into a naive young woman, full of illusions, in the town of Tacna when it was occupied by the Chilean army at the beginning of the twentieth century, or into a little old lady of a hundred years. ... Past and present, fiction and reality, truth and lies flowed together in images of great delicacy and tenderness, conjured up by the expressiveness of a performer who seemed to have abolished the borders of time and space in order to reclaim the essential experiences of Mamaé's obscure biography.]

Vargas Llosa thus found that his novelistic techniques, such as shifting levels of time and space, ambiguous narrative voices and the blurring between reality and fantasy, were indeed transferable to the stage, as was the representation of the act of writing fiction.

It is interesting to discover, in this first play, a technique that has only recently become a dominant feature of his novels: the writer-protagonist Belisario is engaged in a pseudo-dialogue with his characters, very much in the way that the narrator of *El Paraíso en la otra esquina* [*The Way to Paradise*][13] enters into an imaginary dialogue with Flora Tristán and Paul

---

[13] Mario Vargas Llosa, *El Paraíso en la otra esquina* (Madrid: Alfaguara, 2003); Mario Vargas Llosa, *The Way to Paradise* trans. Natasha Wimmer (London: Faber and Faber, 2004).

Gauguin, questioning their acts and motivations. Here we find Belisario addressing his protagonist in the second person singular: '¿Qué vienes a hacer tú en una historia de amor, Mamaé?' (p. 22) [What are you doing here, Mamaé, in the middle of a love story?] (p. 13). Like the narrator in Vargas Llosa's novel, Belisario has to come up with his own answers in order to advance the story he is writing: '¿Adónde te encargaron el vestido de novia, Mamaé? ¿Adónde era la moda encargarlo? (*Escribe, frenético.*)' (p. 35) [Where did they order your wedding dress from, Mamaé? Where was the most fashionable place? (*Writes frantically.*)] (p. 20). The spectre of Mamaé appears to Belisario as a 'personal demon' influencing the story he wants to write, without him knowing why she bothers him: '¿Qué vienes a hacer aquí? Quién te invitó? ¿No te das cuenta que me estorbas? (*Se sonríe y vuelve a su mesa de trabajo, acicateado por una nueva idea.*)' (p. 23) [What on earth are you doing here? Who invited you? Don't you realize you're stopping me from working? (*Smiles and returns to his desk, spurred on by a new idea.*)] (p. 14). The play represents the creative process with its mixture of 'demons', memories, imagination and invention that proves most fruitful for writing fiction. On the other hand, Mamaé has herself integrated fantasy, wishful thinking and role-play into a life story that abounds in elements of melodrama (the abandoned bride, the secret lover, the revealing letter, the mysterious dancer behind a mask, a deadly game of Russian roulette ...). The influence of literature on her life includes the novels of Flaubert that she likes, the radio melodramas of Pedro Camacho that she listens to (an intertextual reference to *La tía Julia*) and the poem, written on her fan by the poet from Tacna, Federico Barreto (a historical personality). Self-referentiality and intertextuality, characteristics of Vargas Llosa's narrative of the 1980s, are also prominent features of his play about Belisario and Mamaé.

They are even more evident in Vargas Llosa's second work for the theatre, the comedy *Kathie y el hipopótamo* with its frequent references to Victor Hugo. The work is dedicated to Norma Aleandro who again played the main role, of Kathie Kennety, in the first performance of the play in Caracas in 1983. Kathie Kennety is the nom de plume of a middle-aged woman in 1960s Lima who employs a ghost-writer to turn her tales of travels to exotic places into literature. Disappointed with her dull life as the wife of a philandering banker with a passion for surfing, she joins forces with the disillusioned journalist Santiago Zavala (the main character of *Conversación en la catedral* [*Conversation in the Cathedral*][14] and one of Vargas Llosa's most obvious alter egos), whose ambition to become the Peruvian Victor Hugo remains unfulfilled. Their sessions take place in the attic of Kathie's house which she

---

[14] Mario Vargas Llosa, *Conversación en la catedral* (Barcelona: Seix Barral, 1985); Mario Vargas Llosa, *Conversation in the Cathedral*, trans. Gregory Rabassa (New York: HarperCollins, 2005).

has made up to look like a 1950s Parisian artist's flat, a place where she can escape from reality and give free rein to her 'demons'. She has created herself a stage setting so that she can leave her everyday life 'full of compromises' down below when she ascends to the realm of culture, art and refinement in the mock Parisian garret. Here, the two protagonists meet to create the alternative world of a work of fiction. In the process of jointly writing the book, their individual dreams and memories begin to influence each other, and one sees how Kathie's demons become Santiago's when, touched by Kathie's anger about her husband's unfaithfulness, Santiago reviews his own betrayal of his wife. The spouses, Juan and Ana, appear on stage as reflections of Kathie's and Santiago's thoughts and fantasies during their sessions. The borders of what is real, what is memory, and what is invention become blurred. Kathie, for her part, takes over Santiago's obsession with Victor Hugo and imagines herself to be Adèle Foucher, Hugo's wife. Thus, on the stage of the theatre we find represented the theatre of life, with its fantasies and role-plays.

The process of writing Kathie's travel book seems to be strictly divided: Kathie has the ideas, while Santiago provides the language to express them. The comedy derives from the fact that neither her dreams and fantasies nor his language are as refined as they each like to think. They are melodramatic, cliché-ridden and full of coarse allusions to sex, and the hippopotamus of the title represents the unbridled sexual desire and male potency that is the subtext of the play's many dialogues on various levels, real, remembered or invented. Kathie's story of a night in Africa when she was woken by the noise of two male hippos fighting for a female is spun out in Santiago's version to represent 'una vez más la eterna historia, el triángulo amoroso, la vieja cantilena del deseo, el duelo y el estupro' (*Kathie*, p. 87) [once again the eternal story, the love triangle, the age-old tale of desire, rivalry, and violation].[15] Santiago portrays the hippopotamus as an animal with a peaceful, even delicate nature, but at the same time 'una bestia libidinosa de potencia cataclísmica' [a libidinous beast of cataclysmic potency] (p. 89).[16] In his imagination this becomes linked to his obsession with Victor Hugo's legendary sexual voracity:

> No es extraño que, a la primera experiencia, las hipopótamas queden disgustadas para siempre del cucú, como Adèle Foucher, ya que el más inapetente de los hipopótamos supera con facilidad el récord establecido

---

[15] Here, as in all the following quotations from *Kathie*, I have decided to give my own translations, since David Graham-Young's version has changed the meaning of some passages and left out important rhetorical repetitions, for instance of the word 'mediocre', a crucial term for understanding the play.

[16] Vargas Llosa has a special liking for the hippopotamus and owns a large collection of models, sculptures, toy animals and other representations of this potent beast.

para la especie humana por las nueve performances de Victor Hugo en su noche de bodas. (p. 89)

[It's no wonder that female hippos, after their first experience, remain forever disgusted by male sexual prowess, like Adèle Foucher, since even the least virile of hippopotamus can easily outdo the record set for the human species by Victor Hugo and his nine performances on his wedding night.][17]

The comedy turns into farce when the real and imagined characters on stage become mixed up in a complex role-play: Kathie and Santiago imagine themselves in a romance as Adèle and Victor Hugo while Ana persistently interferes and destroys Santiago's illusions by reminding him that he is not as virile as he would like to be. *Kathie y el hipopótamo* plays with the link between sexual and creative potency, represented here by the figure of Victor Hugo (a theme that Vargas Llosa develops further in his 2004 essay on the writer, and later continues in his novel about Paul Gauguin). But there is also a layer of irony about Santiago's socialist, anti-bourgeois rhetoric which Ana exposes as hypocritical, until Santiago has to admit: 'Qué culpa tengo si son las frivolidades burguesas de la mujeres las que le gustan al cucú. Qué culpa tengo si la sobriedad, si la seriedad de las mujeres libres y emancipadas lo anestesian y lo matan' [How am I to blame if my body tells me to like the bourgeois frivolities of women. How am I to blame if it is put off and numbed by the sober seriousness of liberated and emancipated women] (p. 71). The play about Kathie and the hippopotamus is also one about Santiago and the 'cucú', in which the discrepancy between reality and illusions, and between rational intention and irrational instinct creates comedy and farce.

In the course of the play, Santiago's detached attitude to his task as a

---

[17] The official translation does not consistently render the leitmotif-like 'cucú' with an English equivalent, which is indeed difficult to find. In the sexually charged context of the play, 'cucú' – literally translated 'cuckoo' – is a playful and child-like, but also coquettish way of referring to the male sex. It plays with the reference to adultery that resonates in the term: since Medieval times the cuckoo has been a symbol of adultery, as the female cuckoo lays its eggs in other birds' nests (hence the term 'cuckold' for the husband of an adulterous wife). The translator of *Kathie* sometimes renders the term as the much too rude 'cock', the too general 'sex', or uses paraphrases that tone down the sexual allusions. But repeated references to the 'cucú' provide much of the hilarity of the farce since it is an obsessive matter of discussion between the sexes, such as in the phrase about the surfer: 'Con tantas olas se le había congelado el cucú' (p. 63), translated as 'What with all those waves, he'd completely lost his sexual appetite' (p. 110), avoiding the more drastic but much funnier reference to the male member that is in the original. This takes away the 'huachafo' [kitsch] element of the protagonists' language, which is an ingredient of the farce, self-consciously debated between Kathie and Santiago (see pp. 78–9; *Kathie and the Hippopotamus*, in *Three plays*, pp. 77–154 [pp. 118–19]). For Vargas Llosa's definition of 'huachafería' see his *Diccionario del amante de América Latina* (Barcelona: Paidós, 2006), pp. 198–202.

ghost-writer turns into real commitment to Kathie's game of imagination and role-play. He realizes that it helps him to forget his own mediocrity and live the illusion of being a writer. Tellingly, he too adopts a nom de plume, and thus a different persona, when he enters Kathie's 'Parisian garret':

> Cuando subo a esta buhardilla, también empiezo otra vida. Abajo se queda el periodista de *La Crónica* que escribe mediocres artículos por un sueldo todavía más mediocre. Abajo se queda el profesorcito mediocre de mediocres alumnos, y aquí nace Mark Griffin, prosista, intelectual, creador, soñador, inventor, árbitro de la inteligencia, summum del buen gusto. Aquí, mientras trabajamos, tengo los amores que nunca tuve, y vivo las tragedias griegas que espero no tener. (p. 142)
>
> [When I come up to this garret, I begin a new life, too. Down there, I leave behind the journalist at *La Crónica* who writes mediocre articles for an even more mediocre salary. Down there, I leave behind the mediocre little teacher of mediocre students, and up here is born Mark Griffin, prose writer, intellectual, creator, dreamer, inventor, arbiter of intelligence, the epitome of good taste. Here, during our work together, I have the love affairs that I never had and live the Greek tragedies that I hope never to have.]

Conjuring up fictions enables them both to overcome the limitations of life. When Santiago says, 'Estas dos horitas de mentiras que se vuelven verdades, de verdades que son mentiras, también me ayudan a soportar mejor las demás horas del día' [These two hours of lies that turn into truths, and truths that are lies, also make it easier for me to bear the remaining hours of the day] (p. 141), we hear the echo of Vargas Llosa who explains in the preface to the play that to dream and invent fictions is 'una oblicua protesta contra la mediocridad de nuestra vida y una manera, transitoria pero efectiva, de burlarla' [a protest in disguise against the mediocrity of our life and a transitional but effective way to mock it] (p. 12).

The theme of truth and lies is carried on into the next play, *La Chunga*[18] of 1986, but it takes on a darker meaning than the playful mockery of mediocrity in the previous work. Once more we encounter a female protagonist who provokes the fantasies of her male counterparts, fantasies which reveal their most secret desires. La Chunga is a character known from *La casa verde* [*The Green House*],[19] the daughter born to Anselmo and Toñita in the brothel, now a tough woman who runs a bar on the outskirts of Piura. Amongst her regular guests are the 'Inconquistables' [Unconquerables] ('superstuds' in

---

[18] Mario Vargas Llosa, *La Chunga* (Barcelona: Seix Barral, 1986); Mario Vargas Llosa, *La Chunga*, in *Three plays*, pp. 155–217.

[19] Mario Vargas Llosa, *La casa verde* (Barcelona: Argos Vergara, 1980); Mario Vargas Llosa, *The Green House* (London: Picador, 1986).

Graham-Young's translation), a group of rogues known from a number of other works by Vargas Llosa, who come together to drink and gamble. The action is set in 1945, but it relates to an incident going back many years when one of the Inconquistables, Josefino, brought along his girlfriend Meche, an attractive young woman, and ruthlessly sold her to Chunga for one night when he needed money to continue with his game of dice. Meche disappeared after she spent time alone with the lesbian bar owner, who never revealed what happened during that night. The memory of that evening in the past is represented on stage on a parallel level with the present in which the four men are sitting at their table gambling, urging Chunga to tell them the truth about Meche's disappearance. As she keeps her secret, they each develop their own version of what might have happened that night. Rather than the truth about Meche's night with Chunga, their fantasies reveal their own hidden truths and desires: José imagines a voyeuristic scene in which he watches Meche and Chunga making love, a lesbian encounter which nonetheless reproduces the stereotypical male idea of sexual dominance and submission. His friend Lituma, by contrast, fears that Josefino might have killed Meche with whom he was secretly in love. In his romantic fantasy, the shy Lituma dreams that Chunga revealed to the young woman that it was him who truly loved her, urging her to escape with him from Josefino's brutality. The third 'Inconquistable', Mono, imagines himself being led by Chunga to confess in front of her and Meche how he once abused a neighbour's girl, and then indulges in the idea of being spanked by the two women for being bad. The violent gangster Josefino, finally, conjures up a scene in which he proposes a business deal to Chunga. When she rejects his idea of running a brothel with him, he brutalizes her. His fantasy is about the humiliation and submission of an independent and strong woman. Each of the men projects his own idea of women onto the enigmatic Chunga and in doing so reveals his fears, desires and secrets. Their 'demons' reflect Vargas Llosa's most prolific literary demons: voyeurism, homosexuality, romantic love hindered by shyness, sexual transgression, Catholic notions of guilt and atonement, violence and machismo.

Vargas Llosa's stage directions for representing the shift from the real to the imaginary level of the play are very specific, involving different lighting, the fading in and out of music and noises from the bar, and the change of body movements: '*Se levanta, se apresura, corre, se precipita por la escalerilla, pero allí pierde ímpetu, se demora, se apaga. Pesado, lento, apesadumbrado, vuelve a la mesa de juego*' (p. 79) [*He gets up hurriedly, rushes towards the staircase, but there he loses his impetus. He slows down – comes to a halt – and slowly returns to the gambling table*] (p. 198). These are effective instructions to visualize the changing levels of reality where each of the Inconquistables splits into his real self and his dreamlike double. On another level Chunga and Meche, as well as acting out the roles that the men ascribe to them in their fantasies, are seen spending the night together. Meche has found to her surprise that she can enjoy sex with a woman. The topic of machismo plays an important part in their conversation, and at one point Meche asks whether women are the better human beings. Chunga answers in her blunt way: 'Por lo menos, lo que tenemos entre las piernas no nos vuelve, como a los hombres, unos demonios inmundos' (p. 94) [At least what we've got between our legs doesn't turn us into foul demons] (p. 205). This marks a notable change from the hilarious, light-hearted banter about the 'cucú' and its dominance over men's minds in *Kathie y el hipopótamo* to a bitter lesson about the sinister, threatening character of machismo by the tough and independent lesbian Chunga. This layer of plot ends with Meche leaving Piura, freeing herself from the influence of Josefino. Chunga parts with her so that she herself can stay free and does not become too emotionally attached to the young woman. Whether this is Chunga's dreamt-up version of events or the truth remains ambiguous. The play ends on a note of uncertainty which refers back to the epigraph by Oscar Wilde, 'Truth is rarely pure and never simple'.

The epigraph is a part of the play that is for readers rather than theatre audiences, as are the foreword (which makes a somewhat superfluous point of explaining the play by narrating the plot), and Vargas Llosa's elaborate directions for setting the scene at the beginning. Here, he uses novelistic techniques to evoke Chunga's character by a series of questions, as well as accounts of her personality through the perspective of people in Piura. These parts of the published play are signs of Vargas Llosa's 'tendency to overstate his point', as Peter Standish puts it.[20] They are not essential for staging an otherwise convincing and gripping play that illustrates the elusiveness of truth, a subject matter that dominates Vargas Llosa's novels of the 1980s, explored here with different, theatrical means.

During the 1990s Vargas Llosa published two plays, *El loco de los balcones* [The Madman of the Balconies][21] in 1993 and *Ojos bonitos, cuadros feos* [Pretty Eyes, Ugly Paintings][22] in 1996. In both works the fantasies, passions and illusions of a person clash with a reality that shatters their dreams. A great passion for art – architecture in one case, painting in the other – ends in failure and frustration, and ultimately in suicide or attempted suicide. The protagonist of *El loco de los balcones* is an Italian-born professor of architecture with a passionate love for Lima's iconic colonial balconies, which are under threat from developers wanting to modernize the town and provide more people with better living conditions. Professor Brunelli salvages the wooden structures and stores them in his back yard in a run-down residential quarter of 1950s Lima, in order to restore them with the help of his devoted

---

[20] Standish, p. 140.
[21] Mario Vargas Llosa, *El loco de los balcones* (Barcelona: Seix Barral, 1993).
[22] Mario Vargas Llosa, *Ojos bonitos, cuadros feos* (Lima: PEISA, 1996).

daughter Ileana and a handful of idealistic volunteers. They support him in his crusade to preserve Lima's colonial heritage from the modernizers, represented by the engineer Cánepa whose son Diego becomes fascinated by Brunelli's passionate commitment, but even more so by Ileana, and joins their fight. When Diego and Ileana decide to marry and live abroad, Ileana reveals to her father that her actual motivation is to flee from his fanatical mission which she never really believed in, but was bound to by the dying wish of her mother. She releases her stored-up bitterness on her father for preventing her from living her own life and marrying the man she had truly loved, the young indigenist firebrand Teófilo Huamani, who had fiercely opposed Brunelli's campaign to save colonial buildings because it was much more urgent to solve the country's social problems. When Brunelli finds his illusions destroyed, he decides to burn down his 'graveyard of the balconies' and kill himself. This is the scene with which the play begins and ends, with Brunelli up on a balcony trying to hang himself. In this circular structure of the play, the past evolves out of his memory of dialogues which, in a telescopic manner, move back in time, or conversations that he only imagines. Stage directions ask for music and lighting to indicate transitions from one level of reality to another: '*Mientras se besan, la melodía se va extinguiendo y, lentamente, vuelve la luz de la realidad*' [*While they kiss, the melody fades away and, slowly, the light of reality returns*] (p. 75).

In the printed version, the play's seventeen individual scenes have titles. Number 3, for example, 'Magia, misterio, ratas y electricidad' [Magic, Mystery, Rats and Electricity] highlights the confrontation between the 'enemies' Brunelli and Cánepa and their ideas about the buildings of the city. Idealism stands against pragmatism, the preservation of heritage against the provision of sanitation. In scene 9 which is entitled 'Fanáticos' [Fanatics] Brunelli is haunted by an imaginary argument with Teófilo Huamani, in which the young man rebukes him for being a fanatic and for sacrificing his daughter to a dream. Brunelli, by contrast, sees in Teófilo a person who is absolutely convinced of his belief – he too a fanatic! – that the art of the colonial past is not worth looking after as long as there are urgent social problems to solve in the present. Sartre's argument that his writing was not worth anything in the face of a dying child, which had shocked Vargas Llosa in the 1960s, is reflected in Teófilo's diatribe against 'lo absurdo que es dedicar la vida a rescatar balcones viejos en un país donde la gente se muere de hambre' [the absurdity of dedicating one's life to salvage old balconies in a country where people die of hunger] (p. 90). But the play does not take sides in this argument. In scene 15, 'Padre e Hija' [Father and Daughter], the image of Ileana comes back to haunt Brunelli. She is equally convinced that 'Dedicar su vida a luchar por los balcones coloniales en un país donde la miseria y la injusticia son tan grandes, es una inmoralidad' [To dedicate your life to fight for the colonial balconies in a country with such misery and injustice is immoral] (p. 101), but underneath her rational argument there is great personal resentment. With each layer of argument that Brunelli reflects in his mind there are more factors to be taken into account, and the truth, as in the previous play, is never simple or one-dimensional. The drunkard who, in the first scene, prevents Brunelli from killing himself, becomes, in the final scene, his follower in a renewed fight for the old cause. Having watched his balconies engulfed in flames like 'Nero watched Rome burn for the love of poetry', Brunelli convinces the drunkard with a passionate speech: 'Creceremos, formaremos un ejército de soñadores' [We will rise again, we will form an army of dreamers] (p. 116). The fanatic art lover is determined to continue his Quixotic mission against wind and tide.

The problem of this play in practical terms is its long speeches: Brunelli's extensive soliloquy at the beginning of the play, addressing his beloved Lima, stops the play's action before it has really begun; an even longer speech by the engineer Cánepa takes up the whole of the fourteenth scene. The introduction, which sets the scene, is a novelist's depiction of the part of Lima called Rímac, with its history, its social make-up and its atmosphere. This is definitely for the reading public. Evelyn Fishburn, who was involved in producing a radio drama based on the play, had seen an earlier version of the manuscript that included 'two epigraphs, one on death and the other on dreams, which provided an ironic framework to the ending', but they were cut in the final published version.[23] Despite these reservations, the first performance of the play at the Gate Theatre in London in November 1993 was well received[24] whereas, according to Fishburn, the radio version was not very successful, 'as if to underscore the importance of the visual'.[25]

The visual element is less important in the staging of the 1996 *Ojos bonitos, cuadros feos*, even though it is a play about the visual arts. It has a single setting, the chic tenth-floor apartment of the renowned art critic and professor Eduardo Zanelli in contemporary Lima, and concentrates on the main dialogue between Zanelli and Rubén Zevallos, a handsome young man to whom the art critic is sexually attracted. During the main conversation, which becomes a threatening confrontation between the two men, fragments of other dialogues of the past crop up, remembered or imagined

---

[23] Evelyn Fishburn, 'The plays', in *The Cambridge Companion to Mario Vargas Llosa*, ed. Efraín Kristal and John King (Cambridge: Cambridge University Press, 2012), pp. 185–98 (p. 191).

[24] In her review Sarah Hemming calls it 'a splendid example of a successful "issue play" ... funny, rich and imaginative'. Sarah Hemming, 'THE FRINGE / Man-sized issues: Sarah Hemming reviews plays by Mario Vargas Llosa, David Epstein and Fay Weldon', *The Independent*, 3 November 1993, <http://www.independent.co.uk/arts-entertainment/the-fringe--mansized-issues-sarah-hemming-reviews-plays-by-mario-vargas-llosa-david-epstein-and-fay-weldon-1501803.html> [accessed 12 October 2012].

[25] Fishburn, p. 195.

by Rubén. They involve himself and his girlfriend Alicia, a young hopeful painter and devoted pupil of Zanelli, and between Alicia and the professor. Aware of Zanelli's homosexuality, Rubén has tricked the art critic into taking him home from a *vernissage*, in order to confront him about his devastating review of an exhibition of Alicia's paintings under the sexist, sarcastic title 'Pretty eyes, ugly paintings'. Alicia's dream of being a painter, a passion that Zanelli himself had instilled in her, was destroyed by this heartless review, a blow from which Alicia never recovered. Not only did she break off her relationship with Rubén but, as it turns out towards the end of the conversation, she killed herself because the shattering of her dreams had left her empty. Rubén confronts Zanelli with the devastating effect of his critical review which the art critic does not even remember, and threatens to kill him with a revolver. But in the end he only humiliates his terrified opponent.

The play creates an atmosphere of tension and suspense until the very end of this potentially deadly confrontation between two men, a constellation reminiscent of some of Vargas Llosa's early narrative. The conflict between the powerful and cynical critic and the vengeful young man who has lost the love of his life seems clear-cut. But in the course of the confrontation, a different truth emerges: Zanelli, the fearsome critic, turns out to be a weak, shy and unauthentic person, terrified of losing face. 'El amor de las formas' [the love of forms] and a desire for beauty play a big part in his life as a self-styled 'arbiter of elegance'. The fear of seeming ridiculous is the reason why he does not openly live out his homosexuality. Zanelli describes himself as 'un rosquete decente' [a decent faggot] (p. 20), 'Uno que lo es más en idea que en acto, más en la fantasía y el deseo que en la verdad de su vida' [One who is queer more in his mind than in his acts, more in his fantasy and desire than in the truth of his life] (p. 21).[26] Many factors play into the characterization of Zanelli through his own words: inauthentic behaviour, self-disgust, a deep sense of failure, and a paralysing self-critical attitude which he redirects into the criticism of other people's work. In Eduardo Zanelli Vargas Llosa delivers an acerbic portrayal of the professional critic who, for lack of talent, has never been able to live up to his own dream of becoming an artist: 'Nadie sueña con ser un crítico de arte. Se llega a serlo por eliminación o por impotencia' [Nobody dreams of becoming an art critic. You become one by elimination or impotence] (p. 39). Zanelli admits that he takes revenge on other mediocre painters for his own failure: 'No soy un cínico ni un malvado. Sólo un farsante, un frustrado. Artística, intelectual y sexualmente' [I am neither a cynic nor a villain. Only frustrated and a hypocrite. Artistically, intellectually,

---

[26] This ambiguous homosexuality which is set somewhere between fantasy and reality will later become an issue in the 2010 novel about Roger Casement: Mario Vargas Llosa, *El sueño del celta* (Doral, FL: Alfaguara, 2010); Mario Vargas Llosa, *The Dream of the Celt*, trans. Edith Grossman (London: Faber and Faber, 2012).

and sexually] (p. 79). He is a pathetic figure who nonetheless has the power to inspire young people to pursue their dream of becoming a painter, 'para volcar en imágenes esos demonios que llevamos dentro' [so as to turn the demons that we carry inside into images] (p. 39), but while he encourages his students to believe that they can forge their own talent by hard work, patience, discipline and conviction, he has found out for himself that this theory only raises false hopes and illusions: 'El talento es una tara de nacimiento. ... No se puede adquirir' [Talent is a weight you are born with. ... You cannot acquire it] (p. 41). Zanelli is a deeply ambiguous creation: he is a refined professor who encourages hope and illusions in his students, but also a merciless critic who releases his own bitterness and resentment on those who believe him. His attempt to hide his homosexuality while the whole of Lima's middle-class society knows about it is tragic. But his treatment of Alicia is ruthless and reflects the sexism of this society and its gender stereotypes. What upset Alicia most was the title of his review:

> No escribió lo de mis 'ojos bonitos' porque crea que los tengo bonitos. Lo hizo para que el juego de palabras, el contraste de calificativos, subrayara su desprecio. ¿Te fijaste que repite dos veces lo de 'ojos bonitos, cuadros feos'? En el título y en la última frase de la crítica. ... Está insinuando que soy una frívola, una chica de sociedad a la que le han hecho creer que podía ser pintora, un capricho más de los muchos que tiene y que los que la rodean se desviven por complacerle. (p. 51)

> [He did not write this about my 'pretty eyes' because he thinks that's what they are. He used the wordplay, the contrast of adjectives, to underline his contempt. Did you notice that he repeats 'pretty eyes, ugly paintings' twice? Once in the title and once in the last sentence of the review. ... He is insinuating that I am a frivolous society girl who was led to believe that she could be a painter, a whimsical fancy, eagerly endorsed by the people around her, like so many other caprices that she indulges.]

The power of carefully chosen words to hurt and destroy someone goes hand in hand with the sexism of a senior male, homosexual critic towards a naive young woman, a new facet in Vargas Llosa's discussion of gender issues which thus far had concentrated on exposing machismo.

Vargas Llosa's next play, *Al pie del Támesis* [On the Banks of the Thames], continues to explore the subject matter of sexuality, identity and authenticity, highlighting once more the interplay between fantasies and reality. The one-act play had its first performance in March 2008 at the Teatro Británico in Lima and was published shortly afterwards.[27] A seemingly realistic representation

---

[27] Mario Vargas Llosa, *Al pie del Támesis* (Lima: Alfaguara, 2008). The book contains photos by Vargas Llosa's daughter Morgana of the rehearsals and performance at the Teatro Británico in Lima in March 2008.

of an unexpected visit that the successful middle-aged Peruvian businessman Chispas Bellatín receives from Raquel Saavedra, who claims to be the sister of his friend Pirulo whom he has not seen for thirty-five years, develops into a multilayered game of mirrors which leaves the spectator wondering what is reality and what is fantasy. Raquel comes to talk to Chispas in his suite at the exclusive Savoy Hotel in London which overlooks the river Thames. Although Chispas does not remember that Pirulo had a sister, she seems to know many details about their past, including the violent incident that drove the friends apart: in a private moment at the gym, Pirulo had attempted to kiss Chispas who reacted by punching his friend in the face. In the course of the conversation it emerges that this incident and the following estrangement between the friends has followed Chispas 'like a shadow' all his life. It soon transpires that Raquel is actually the former Pirulo who has undergone several sex-change operations and is now a woman. She explains that Chispas's disgusted reaction to what he understood as a homosexual advance was the trigger for her decision to fully adopt her true, female identity. Raquel, it seems, has created her authentic self, accepting what she calls 'mi realidad, mi naturaleza, mi verdad' [my reality, my nature, my truth] (p. 53). Chispas, by contrast, has conformed to society's expectations, becoming a highly successful and wealthy businessman, but he has never found happiness or satisfaction inside or outside his three marriages. He admits that the reason for his frustration is the suppression of the homosexual attraction he felt himself after the attempted kiss by Pirulo, and the guilt for hitting him and driving him away: 'me provocó un verdadero trauma' [it produced a real trauma in me] (p. 33). Once they have reached that point in their conversation of admitting their secret desires and frustrations, they start engaging in a mutual game of fantasies. Raquel encourages Chispas to imagine their marriage to each other. They both enact on stage Raquel's fantasy about their wedding night, a shift in the level of reality that is signalled by different lighting and music. Back in 'reality' they reminisce about their childhood in Miraflores, talking the way they talked back then. They both feel nostalgia about the simple joys of childhood, a paradise forever lost. When Chispas's memories return to the traumatic incident of the kiss, Raquel encourages a new fantasy, imagining herself to be Chispas's mistress. But Chispas's fantasy is invaded by the memory of the punch he landed on his childhood friend's chin. Memories and fantasies mingle and turn into a violent scene of him beating Pirulo/Raquel for sexual gratification. In the end he seems to remember that he inadvertently killed Pirulo with the weights in the gym. At this point the theatre audience, likely to be confused by the different levels of role-play, experiences the biggest surprise when the violent action on stage turns back to Chispas in his incarnation as a cool and composed businessman who is called to an important meeting by a man his own age, Pirulo, who might be his assistant or business partner. Does Chispas secretly desire him?

Does he entertain himself with fantasies in between meetings? The ending remains totally ambiguous, at least on the stage.

On the page, however, Vargas Llosa has added a preface which makes the reader aware from the start that this is a play about the shifting borders between reality and fiction. He states very clearly that, in the course of the many revisions that this play has gone through, Pirulo/Raquel took on a less realistic character and became a figure settled in Chispas's fantasy and memory. Vargas Llosa relates in the preface how the play is based on a real anecdote that the Cuban writer Cabrera Infante had told him in London, about a friend, the Venezuelan poet Esdras Parra, who came to see him after many years, and who turned out to be a transsexual. But this anecdote, which Vargas Llosa had taken to be the starting point for a tragicomedy, turned into a representation of his own obsession with the ambiguous relationship between fantasy and reality. Unfortunately for the reader of the preface, Vargas Llosa delivers in advance an interpretation of the play as 'las mentiras que se cuenta el Chispas' [the lies that Chispas tells himself] (p. 20), thus giving away the imaginary nature of the action.

All of Vargas Llosa's plays explore the shifting borders between telling, showing, acting and role-play, making clever use of stagecraft – lighting, music, costumes, stage design – to bring to life the ambiguities of reality and fiction. In recent years he has himself appeared on stage in a number of experimental projects aimed at blurring the borders between theatrical performance, narrative and oral literature. The gradual shift from writing plays to acting started with a performance in the Teatro Romea in Barcelona in 2005,[28] which involved scenic readings of excerpts from Vargas Llosa's favourite works of world literature. Under the same title as his collection of literary criticism, *La verdad de las mentiras* [The Truth of Lies],[29] he appeared on stage together with the Spanish actress Aitana Sánchez-Gijón. Her part was to read aloud, but also to act out what was contained in the text fragments he had chosen, while he narrated from memory the stories in these texts, presenting them in his own words. This performance, directed by Joan Ollé, combined oral storytelling, acting and public reading, thus transcending the borders of genre in a spectacle that played with fiction and reality, showing and telling, author and interpreter, and became the first in a series of dramatizations of narrative texts that have at their heart the act of storytelling. Whereas there is no published version of the 2005 staging of *La verdad de las mentiras*, the two subsequent dramatizations of two paradigmatic narrative

---

[28] Rosa Mora, 'Vargas Llosa conquista el teatro con sus autores preferidos', *El País*, 6 October 2005, <http://elpais.com/diario/2005/10/06/espectaculos/1128549610_850215.html> [accessed 20 October 2012].

[29] Mario Vargas Llosa, *La verdad de las mentiras. Ensayos sobre literatura* (Barcelona: Seix Barral, 1990).

texts, the *Odyssey* and *The Thousand and One Nights*, were both turned into beautifully produced books, with photographs of the performances and preceding rehearsals involving Vargas Llosa, Aitana Sánchez-Gijón and the director Joan Ollé.[30] The photos render a vivid impression of the visualization techniques used to bring these hybrid performances to life.

Odiseo y Penélope was first performed in August 2006 in the Teatro Romano in Mérida during the Festival of Classical Theatre[31] and published in 2007 with the already quoted epilogue 'El viaje de Odiseo', recounting how Vargas Llosa's lifelong passion for the theatre developed into this unusual project for the stage in which he appears as a narrator who is simultaneously actor and protagonist of his own story. The retelling of the best-known episodes of the *Odyssey* is embedded into the narrative framework of the Trojan hero Odysseus (or Ulysses in the Latinized version) telling his wife Penelope the adventures of his long journey home. It is set after he has returned to Ithaca, revealed his identity, killed the queen's suitors and enjoyed his reunion with his wife. Penelope wants to hear his story, but Odysseus asks her to help him recreate the past since he is no longer sure of what really happened in those long years, and what belongs more to the realm of fantasy than memory. He wants to live through the past again with his wife, as if she had been there: 'El pasado es maleable como la arcilla, depende de nosotros tanto como el futuro, Penélope' [The past is as malleable as clay, it depends as much on us as the future, Penelope] (p. 25). The game of recreating the past that Odysseus and Penelope engage in sees them enacting the adventures that Odysseus encountered, taking on the roles of people, gods and monsters.[32] In the course of this playful recreation of the past both husband and wife shift between narrating, acting and inventing, and they mutually influence the story that comes to life on stage. Towards the end of this night of role-play Penelope begins to wonder whether her husband actually experienced any of these adventures, or whether he is such an exceptionally gifted storyteller that he has convinced himself of the truth of his inventions: 'Se me ocurre, de pronto, que, más que un aventurero, eres un fantaseador. Un contador de cuentos. Uno de esos embaucadores que divierten al público en el ágora con fantasías extravagantes' [It suddenly occurs to me that, rather than an adventurer, you are a fantasist. A storyteller. One of these conjurers who

---

[30] Vargas Llosa, *Odiseo y Penélope*; Mario Vargas Llosa, *Las mil noches y una noche*, photos Ros Ribas (Madrid: Alfaguara, 2009).

[31] See the evocative trailer of this performance posted on YouTube by the artist Frederic Amat, the play's scenographer: <http://www.youtube.com/watch?v=rDs2P6K5BsA> [accessed 10 October 2012].

[32] This game of role-play and fantasy between husband and wife is reminiscent of the games in which Rigoberto and Lucrecia, in Vargas Llosa's erotic novels (*Elogio de la madrastra* [*In Praise of the Stepmother*] and *Los cuadernos de Don Rigoberto* [*The Notebooks of Don Rigoberto*]), engage to keep their relationship alive and interesting.

entertain their public in the marketplace with the extravagant flights of their imagination] (p. 112). Odysseus acknowledges the ambiguous nature of his tales – in much the same way that Vargas Llosa admits that he himself is unsure about his recollections of the past in relation to his fiction (as he states, for example, in *El pez*, see chapter 8 above):

> Tal vez no estés lejos de la verdad, Penélope. Te confesaré un secreto. Cuando me oigo refiriendo aquellas peripecias ante extraños, ya no estoy muy seguro si es mi memoria la que habla por mi boca, o mi imaginación. Contándolas, las vivo, cierto. Pero no estoy seguro si de veras las viví, o si, al contarlas, cambiaron tanto que es como si las estuviera inventando. (p. 112)

> [Perhaps you are not far from the truth, Penelope. I will tell you a secret. When I hear myself telling others these adventures, I am no longer sure whether it is my memory that is producing my words, or my imagination. When I tell these tales, I live them, that is certain. But I am not sure whether I had these experiences in reality, or whether they changed so much in the process of telling them that they end up more like inventions.]

Odysseus's storytelling gifts play an important role in Homer's *Odyssey*, but this particular theme of the shifting borders between reality and fiction is an individual note that Vargas Llosa has added to his storyteller protagonist.

On the last stage of his journey Odysseus wins over the Phaeacians with the tales of his adventures and convinces them to provide him with a ship to sail home on: 'Y hablé, hablé, no sé cuantas horas y días, en un palacio que a cada rato se llenaba de más y más gente. Escuchaban absortos. Reían, lloraban, se asustaban, se alegraban' [I talked and talked, I don't know for how many hours and days, in a palace which filled with more and more people. They listened, enthralled. They laughed, they cried, they became frightened, or happy] (p. 89). Nausicaa, daughter of the Phaeacian King, is so moved by the stories that she would have liked Odysseus to stay and become her husband: 'Todo el resto de la vida hubiera revivido esas aventuras gracias a tus cuentos. Hubiera sido como vivir varias vidas a la vez' [Thanks to your stories I would have been able to relive those adventures for the rest of my life. It would have been like living several lives at once] (p. 87). Vargas Llosa's stage version of Odysseus thus embodies the gift of storytelling with all the effects that Vargas Llosa ascribes to good literature: he moves his listeners' emotions, transports them into a different world, and enables them to live the many lives in their imagination that they cannot have in reality.

Inspired by his work on the *Odyssey*, the greatest example of storytelling in the history of Western civilization, Vargas Llosa has published a poem called *Padre Homero* [Father Homer].³³ It ends with lines that sum up Vargas Llosa's ideas about the role of the storyteller:

> Qué pobre sería nuestra historia
> sin tus historias,
> qué mediocres
> nuestros sueños
> sin tus sueños.
>
> [How poor would our history be
> without your stories,
> how mediocre
> our dreams
> without your dreams.]

Odiseo y Penélope and the dramatization of *Las mil noches y una noche* [*The Thousand and One Nights*] (better known in English under the title *Arabian Nights*), which followed in 2008, form an integral part of Vargas Llosa's exploration of the nature of fiction and the function of storytelling in the life of human beings. This subject matter, at the core of his literary theory and criticism, his narrative fiction and his plays, is also at the centre of his stage performances. *Las mil noches y una noche* was first presented in July 2008 in Madrid,³⁴ with Vargas Llosa in the role of the tyrannical king Shahryar and Aitana Sánchez-Gijón as his wife Scheherazade who manages to placate the vengeful king with her storytelling gifts. They first appear on stage as themselves, author and actress, greeting each other 'once again' to 'tell and live stories'. This is the outer level of the performance to which they return at the end. Vargas Llosa then briefly assumes the role of narrator, before they both take up their roles as Shahryar and Scheherazade. In the course of Scheherazade's storytelling they turn into the protagonists of her stories, as

---

³³ First published in *El Dominical. El Comercio*, 30 March 2008, this poem subsequently appeared in *Letras Libres*, 137 (May 2010), <http://www.letraslibres.com/print/64329> [accessed 21 October 2012]. This is one of Vargas Llosa's few – published – ventures into poetry, 'the most supreme of all literary genres', as he says; see Rosana Torres, 'Vargas Llosa: "La poesía es el género literario supremo"', *El País*, 13 May 2011, <http://cultura.elpais.com/cultura/2011/05/13/actualidad/1305237603_850215.html> [accessed 20 October 2012]. Hidden in his memoirs there is another poem inspired by Greek mythology called *Alcides*. See *El pez*, p. 449; *Fish*, p. 442.

³⁴ There are several clips on YouTube of various performances (in Spain, Mexico and Peru) with Vargas Llosa acting the role of King Sharyar. The most interesting clip of all is from the Madrid performance with Aitana Sánchez-Gijón in the role of Scheherazade: <http://www.youtube.com/watch?v=36gd0vC42FE> [accessed 10 October 2012]. The published text, as Vargas Llosa explains in the foreword, reflects the second round of performances in Seville and Tenerife in July 2008, with a number of modifications that developed out of the original performance earlier that month in Madrid.

if the king and his wife lived through them in their imagination during their thousand and one nights. These three levels of performance are distinguished by lighting and a leitmotif-like music that announces Scheherazade's storytelling. The episodes that Vargas Llosa has chosen for his 'minimalist adaptation' of the literary classic are less well known than those found in most collections for children. They deal with certain aspects of human nature that reflect recurring motifs of Vargas Llosa's work: beauty, love, eroticism, role-play, shifting gender, sexual transgression, betrayal, violence, the appearance of the devil amongst humans, human sacrifice and anthropophagy.

The tale of Scheherazade, who bewitches the king with her stories which, night after night, turn into more stories without ever coming to an end, illustrates better than anything one of Vargas Llosa's favourite narrative techniques, the 'cajas chinas' [Chinese boxes]. As long as the king is transfixed by Scheherazade's storytelling gifts and by the desire to hear the end of a story which always merges into another story, these tales within tales have a vital function for Scheherazade – in a very literal sense, since they divert the king from his intention to kill her at the end of the night as an act of revenge against all women. Little by little the king's emotions are brought back to life by the enchanting effect of Scheherazade's storytelling: 'Tu voz me apacigua y tus cuentos me vuelven bueno', he says [Your voice appeases me and your stories bring back the good in me] (p. 72). He feels curiosity, happiness, compassion, sadness and tenderness, and is able to smile and laugh again. This parable of the transforming quality of fiction ends with the king renouncing his plan to behead Scheherazade once her stories would finish. After three years, in which she has enriched every night with her tales, the king has lost his anger and vengefulness and reconciles himself with womankind. Fiction turns out to be a force for good in a world full of cruelty and violence, and the storyteller is the person who is able to encourage change. In Vargas Llosa's foreword to the book, 'Contar cuentos' [Telling Stories], he emphasizes this function of literature: 'con sus astucias de gran narradora, [Sherazada] desanimaliza al bárbaro que hasta antes de casarse con ella era puro instinto y pulsión y desarrolla en él las escondidas virtudes de lo humano. Haciéndolo vivir y soñar vidas imaginarias, lo enrumba por el camino de la civilización' [with her great storytelling skills, [Scheherazade] drives out the beastly nature of the barbarian who, until he married her, was pure instinct and impulsiveness, and develops in him the hidden virtues of humanity. By making him dream and live through imaginary lives, she sets him off on the path of civilization] (p. 11). This idea of the humanizing effect of literature is developed further in Vargas Llosa's essay 'El viaje a la ficción' [The Journey to Fiction][35] which also appeared in 2008, as a preface to his

---

[35] Mario Vargas Llosa, 'El viaje a la ficción', in *El viaje a la ficción. El mundo de Juan Carlos Onetti* (Lima: Alfaguara, 2008), pp. 11–32.

book on Juan Carlos Onetti (see chapter 2 above). This link between his theatrical work and his essay on literature is a clear indication of the strong connection between all areas of Vargas Llosa's writing.

Vargas Llosa's own narrative work has inspired many stage adaptations. He has himself been involved in a scenic reading opposite the singer Pastora Vega, when he introduced his novel *Travesuras de la niña mala* [*The Bad Girl*][36] in various Spanish cities during 2006.[37] Other novels such as *El Paraíso en la otra esquina*, with its dual structure, have also been presented in scenic readings. The list of theatrical adaptations of Vargas Llosa's narrative works is long – too long to be exhaustively documented here. Amongst the performances for which I found records are adaptations of *Los cachorros* [The Cubs][38] from 1982, 2009 and 2011;[39] a staging of *La ciudad y los perros* [*The Time of the Hero*][40] in 1982 in which Vargas Llosa was actively involved,[41] and a recent one in April 2012,[42] as well as a version of *La Fiesta del Chivo* [*The Feast of the Goat*][43] for the theatre in 2003[44] which he praised as very successful. Other adaptations were not altogether well received by the audience, such as the 1996 stage version of

---

[36] Mario Vargas Llosa, *Travesuras de la niña mala* (Madrid: Alfaguara, 2006); Mario Vargas Llosa, *The Bad Girl*, trans. Edith Grossman (London: Faber and Faber, 2008).

[37] Margot Molina, 'Vargas Llosa ofrece una lectura de su última novela en el Lope de Vega', *El País*, 5 June 2006, <http://elpais.com/diario/2006/06/05/andalucia/1149459743_850215.html> [accessed 20 October 2012].

[38] Mario Vargas Llosa, *Los cachorros* (Madrid: Cátedra, 1990); Mario Vargas Llosa, 'The Cubs', in *The Cubs and Other Stories*, trans. Gregory Kolovakos and Ronald Christ (London: Faber and Faber, 1991), pp. 1–43.

[39] Rosa María Pereda, 'El Teatro del Sol, de Perú, trae a España su versión de "Pichula Cuéllar", de Vargas Llosa', *El País*, 26 September 1982 <http://elpais.com/diario/1982/09/26/cultura/401839213_850215.html> [accessed 20 October 2012]; Asociación de Artistas Aficionados, 'Muestra Internacional de Teatro de Lima: "Los Cachorros"', <http://aaalima.blogspot.co.uk/2009/09/muestra-internacional-de-teatro-de-lima.html> [accessed 20 October 2012]; YouTube, <http://www.youtube.com/watch?v=uNVrWBLQDxI> [accessed 20 October 2012].

[40] Mario Vargas Llosa, *La ciudad y los perros* (Barcelona: Seix Barral, 1983); Mario Vargas Llosa, *The Time of the Hero* (London: Picador, 1986).

[41] Rosa María Pereda, 'Vargas Llosa supervisa en Madrid la versión teatral de "La ciudad y los perros"', *El País*, 12 November 1982, <http://elpais.com/diario/1982/11/12/cultura/405903606_850215.html> [accessed 20 October 2012].

[42] 'Mario Vargas Llosa habla de su primer amor: el teatro', *El Comercio*, 3 April 2012, <http://elcomercio.pe/espectaculos/1396721/noticia-mario-vargas-llosa-habla-su-primer-amor-teatro> [accessed 20 October 2012].

[43] Mario Vargas Llosa, *La Fiesta del Chivo* (Madrid: Alfaguara, 2000); Mario Vargas Llosa, *The Feast of the Goat*, trans. Edith Grossman (New York: Farrar, Straus and Giroux, 2001).

[44] Pilar Lozano, 'Vargas Llosa resalta la emoción del montaje teatral de "La fiesta del Chivo"', *El País*, 7 November 2003, <http://elpais.com/diario/2003/11/07/espectaculos/1068159601_850215.html> [accessed 20 October 2012].

Pantaleón y las visitadoras [*Captain Pantoja and the Special Service*].[45] This list would grow much longer if all the different adaptations of *La tía Julia y el escribidor* as a radio play in various countries around the world were taken into account. The temptation to adapt Vargas Llosa's novels for the theatre seems to be great, probably due to the visual quality of his descriptions but, as with the films that his books have inspired,[46] it is difficult to see how the formal aspects that play such an important part in complementing the content of his novels can be transposed to a different, dominantly visual medium. Even though he has acquired many of his narrative techniques from film, such as simultaneity and crosscutting, flashbacks, fading in and out of scenes, superimposition, and so on, he has reproduced these cinematic effects in language. To return this special characteristic of Vargas Llosa's novels to the visual level removes a whole dimension of his literature. This is particularly noticeable in the humour that develops out of his use of language in works such as *Pantaleón*. The criticism that the 1996 stage version of this novel received – 'Lo que en el libro era picardía, resulta obscenidad ... La sutileza y el encanto de la narración es metedura de paso' [What was mischievous in the book, becomes obscene ... The subtlety and charm of the narration turns into banal tactlessness][47] – mirrors my own reaction when I watched the film version by Francisco Lombardi which came out in 2000, a very steamy movie with lots of flesh on display, but very little sense of the comic clash between the outrageous nature of Pantoja's military mission and his self-characterization as a perfect bureaucrat. Multilayered plots become necessarily trimmed down in adaptations, multifaceted characters reduced without an insight into their minds, different levels of language, such as letters, dreams or stream of consciousness, cannot be adequately reproduced. As for the 'totalizing ambition' that has guided Vargas Llosa in his big novels,

---

[45] Mario Vargas Llosa, *Pantaleón y las visitadoras* (Barcelona: Seix Barral, 1986); Mario Vargas Llosa, *Captain Pantoja and the Special Service* (London: Faber and Faber, 1987). See Eduardo Haro Tecglen, 'Vargas Llosa y los adaptadores', *El País*, 26 January 1996, <http://elpais.com/diario/1996/01/26/cultura/822610808_850215.html> [accessed 20 October 2012].

[46] These include *Los cachorros*, a Mexican film of 1973, directed by Jorge Fons; *Pantaleón y las visitadoras* of 1976, a film for which Vargas Llosa wrote the script (he also co-directed it with José María Gutiérrez Santos, and acted in a minor role); *La ciudad y los perros*, a Peruvian film of 1985, directed by Francisco Lombardi; a 1990 Hollywood version of *La tía Julia* under the title *Tune in Tomorrow*, directed by Jon Amiel; a 2000 film of *Pantaleón y las visitadoras*, also by Lombardi; and the 2005 adaptation of *La Fiesta del Chivo* by Luis Llosa. For more information about these films, see <http://www.imdb.com/>. The last three films are available on DVD, and *La ciudad* and *Los cachorros* can be watched in instalments on YouTube; only the 1976 version of *Pantaleón* is hard to come by. See also Manuel Cuéllar, 'Mario Vargas Llosa y el cine', *El País*, 7 October 2010, <http://cultura.elpais.com/cultura/2010/10/07/actualidad/1286402424_850215.html> [accessed 22 October 2012], and the chapter on 'Film and the novels' by Carolina Sitnisky in Kristal and King, *The Cambridge Companion*, pp. 199–211.

[47] Tecglen, 'Vargas Llosa y los adaptadores'.

it is hard to imagine how the complexity of works such as *La casa verde*, *Conversación* or *La guerra del fin del mundo* [*The War of the End of the World*][48] – even though that last novel developed out of a movie project – can be transposed into film, let alone the theatre.

True to his vocation as a storyteller Vargas Llosa's own plays concentrate on the relationship between fantasy and reality, and attempt to show on stage the process of how fiction works. In September 2012 the Teatro Español in Madrid announced that it would produce all of his theatrical works within the next three years. Vargas Llosa has reacted with enthusiasm and declared this would give him the opportunity to revise some texts.[49] The theatrical project will undoubtedly raise the profile of Vargas Llosa's plays which have always remained in the shadow of his novels. The narrative work is definitely the first port of call for the reader who wants to find out about Mario Vargas Llosa, but his work for the theatre, his literary criticism, his theoretical writings on fiction, his journalism and his wide-ranging essays all form part of an oeuvre that attempts to understand the human condition in all its facets.

---

[48] Mario Vargas Llosa, *La guerra del fin del mundo* (Barcelona: Plaza y Janés, 1982); Mario Vargas Llosa, *The War of the End of the World* (London: Faber and Faber, 1986).
[49] Patricia Ortega Dolz, 'Vargas Llosa eclipsa el Español', *El País*, 14 September 2012, <http://ccaa.elpais.com/ccaa/2012/09/13/madrid/1347569905_899366.html> [accessed 21 October 2012].

SUGGESTIONS FOR FURTHER READING

The best place to start looking for further information about Vargas Llosa is the comprehensive documentation of his life and work on his official website: <http://www.mvargasllosa.com>, administered by Vargas Llosa's personal assistant Rosario M. N. de Bedoya. The individual sections – Biography, Work, Bibliography, Distinctions and Chronology – can be downloaded in PDF format, a very useful feature. The part of the bibliography dedicated to his own work includes all the items which would normally be hard to trace in an author as prolific as Vargas Llosa, such as prologues he has contributed to other authors' work, or lectures he has given around the world, sometimes repeatedly, but under different titles (these are cross-referenced). The chronological list of his output is helpfully categorized as covering 'literature', 'politics', 'art', 'religion', 'sport', amongst others, which enables easy searching. The second part of the bibliography lists books, articles and other material about Vargas Llosa and includes interviews, round-table discussions, and so on. The exhaustive chronology of his activities reveals a life spent travelling around the world, without letting this nomadic existence impede on his writing.

An invaluable tool for advanced research are the *Mario Vargas Llosa Papers* held at the Firestone Library, Princeton University. This archive comprises his 'notebooks, manuscripts of novels, plays and screenplays, short stories, nonfiction, documents, correspondence, and printed and recorded material, covering the period 1944–2010 (mostly 1958–1995)'. For example, researchers interested in the development of a novel through various drafts can access these papers in the Firestone Library.

Criticism in Spanish

Undergraduates and the general reader should start with the standard work by José Miguel Oviedo, *Mario Vargas Llosa: la invención de una realidad* (Barcelona: Seix Barral, 1982). Oviedo has also edited the volume *Mario Vargas Llosa* (Madrid: Taurus, 1981) and a more recent collection of his own articles, *Dossier Vargas Llosa* (Lima: Alfaguara, 2007). He has also contributed an excellent prologue to volume II of the complete works of Vargas Llosa (see 'Bibliography' below). Other standard works of criticism include Rosa Boldori de Baldussi, *Vargas Llosa: un narrador y sus demonios* (Buenos Aires: Fernando García Cambeiro, 1974); Sara Castro-Klarén, *Mario Vargas Llosa: análisis introductorio* (Lima: Latinoamericana Editores, 1988); Rita Gnutzman, *Cómo leer a Mario Vargas Llosa* (Gijón: Júcar, 1992); and Raymond Leslie Williams, *Vargas Llosa. Otra historia de un deicidio* (México: Taurus, 2001). The discussions in the *Semana de autor: Mario Vargas Llosa* (Madrid: Ediciones Cultura Hispánica, 1985) are very useful, as are the two book-length interviews about various aspects of Vargas Llosa's work: Ricardo Cano Gaviria, *El buitre y el ave Fénix. Conversaciones con Mario Vargas Llosa* (Barcelona: Anagrama, 1972); and Ricardo A. Setti, *... sobre la vida y la política: Diálogo con Vargas Llosa* (México: Kosmos Editorial, 1989). A recent volume edited and annotated by Jorge Coaguila brings together different interviews from 1964 to 2010: *Mario Vargas Llosa. Entrevistas escogidas* (Iquitos: Tierra Nueva Editores, 2010).

Technical and formal aspects are the focus of José Luis Martín, *La narrativa de Vargas Llosa. Acercamiento estilístico* (Madrid: Gredos, 1974); Casto M. Fernández, *Aproximación formal a la novelística de Vargas Llosa* (Madrid: Ed. Nacional, 1977); Inger Enkvist, *Las técnicas narrativas de Vargas Llosa* (Gothenburg: Acta Universitatis Gothoburgensis, 1987); and Helena Establier Pérez, *Vargas Llosa y el nuevo arte de hacer novelas* (Alicante: Publicaciones Universidad de Alicante, 1998).

The collection edited by Ana María Hernández de López, *Mario Vargas Llosa. Opera Omnia* (Madrid: Pliegos, 1994) varies in quality, but contains some good criticism. A number of journals have produced special issues dedicated to Vargas Llosa. These include *Antípodas*, 1 (1988); 8–9 (1996–7); and 17 (2006); *Explicación de textos literarios*, 25 (1996/97); *Ínsula*, 53 (1998); *Cuadernos Hispanoamericanos*, 574 (1998); *Letras Libres*, 106 (2007) as well as 143 (2010); and *Turia*, 97–8 (2011). Other authors who have contributed considerably to Vargas Llosa criticism in Spanish include Angel Rama, Ronald Christ, Albert Bensoussan, Marie-Madeleine Gladieu, José Morales Saravia, Roy C. Boland, Birger Angvik and Roland Forgues. Amongst Peruvian voices critical of Vargas Llosa's political opinions and his writing are Antonio Cornejo Polar, Julio Ortega, Mirko Lauer and Herbert Morote.

For a personal perspective on Vargas Llosa see, for example, José Donoso, *Historia personal del boom* (Barcelona: Seix Barral, 1972), especially the 1983 re-edition of this book which contains an appendix written by Donoso's wife María Pilar Serrano under the title 'El *boom* doméstico'. Readers interested in a domestic view of the author will also enjoy his first wife's riposte to *La tía Julia*: Julia Urquidi Illanes, *Lo que Varguitas no dijo* (La Paz: Khana Cruz, 1983), also available in an English translation by Catherine R. Perricone, *My Life with Mario Vargas Llosa* (New York: Peter Lang, 1988). The book by J. J. Armas Marcelo, *Vargas Llosa. El vicio de escribir* (Madrid:

Ediciones temas de hoy, 1991) is rich in anecdotes. A personal account of Vargas Llosa the presidential candidate comes from his son and campaign manager: Álvaro Vargas Llosa, *El diablo en campaña* (Madrid: Aguilar, 1991). Peruvian psychiatrist Max Silva Tuesta has published a *Psicoanálisis de Vargas Llosa* (Lima: Editorial Leo, 2005), as well as the recent *Mario Vargas Llosa. Interpretaciones de una vida* (Lima: Ed. San Marcos, 2012), which contains an appendix documenting what is known about the notorious incident in 1976 when Vargas Llosa knocked out his (until then) friend García Márquez. And whoever has not had enough personal background information about Vargas Llosa's novels from the author himself (for example, in *El pez en el agua*) will find further details about the 'real reality' behind *La ciudad y los perros* in Sergio Vilela Galván, *El cadete Vargas Llosa. La historia oculta tras 'La ciudad y los perros'* (Lima: Planeta, 2011), with astonishing photos of Vargas Llosa and his classmates in the Leoncio Prado military academy. Apart from a forensic reconstruction of the real people behind the novel's protagonists, there is a particularly interesting reproduction of a poem written by Vargas Llosa at the Colegio La Salle in the late 1940s, one of the few published of the many poems which Vargas Llosa seems to have composed during his life. In it he declares his intention to become a poet, or perhaps rather an actor – an ambition he realized sixty years later!

For readers keen to complement the written texts with a visual impression of the author, rich audiovisual material is but a mouse-click away: at the time of writing a search for 'Mario Vargas Llosa' on YouTube <http://www.youtube.com> brings up almost five thousand results, many of them interviews, TV appearances and lectures. This includes officially uploaded recordings of public events such as the conversation between Vargas Llosa and Juan Cruz in February 2012, published in full by TVCajaCanarias, in which Vargas Llosa talks for over an hour about his life and work: <http://www.youtube.com/watch?v=ElgE8SzEvbo> [accessed 4 November 2012]. One can also access a couple of highly interesting episodes of his early 1980s TV show *La Torre de Babel* [The Tower of Babel] (technically poor, but fascinating). The official website of the Nobel Prize makes available a video of Vargas Llosa's Nobel Lecture, 7 December 2010, <http://www.nobelprize.org/mediaplayer/index.php?id=1416> [accessed 4 November 2012], as well as a number of interviews, readings and other visual material.

Following the Nobel Prize, Latin American universities and other institutions rushed to honour Vargas Llosa with titles, symposia and subsequent publications. One of the more useful is the six-hundred-page volume of essays covering all aspects of the author's work, edited by Miguel Angel Rodríguez Rea, *Mario Vargas Llosa y la crítica peruana* (Lima: Universidad Ricardo Palma/Editorial Universitaria, 2011). It also contains a printed version of the Nobel Lecture in Spanish.

Criticism in English

Standard works in English include the early study by Luís A. Díez, *Mario Vargas Llosa's Pursuit of the Total Novel. A Study of Style and Technique in Relation to Moral Intention* (Cuernavaca: CIDOC, 1970); *Mario Vargas Llosa. A Collection of Critical Essays*, edited by Charles Rossman and Alan Warren Friedman (Austin: University of Texas Press, 1978); Marvin A. Lewis, *From Lima to Leticia: The Peruvian Novels of Mario Vargas Llosa* (Lanham: University Press of America, 1983); Dick Gerdes, *Mario Vargas Llosa* (Boston: Twayne Publishers, 1985); Raymond Leslie Williams, *Mario Vargas Llosa* (New York: Ungar, 1986); Sara Castro-Klarén, *Understanding Mario Vargas Llosa* (Columbia: University of South Carolina Press, 1990); and Efraín Kristal, *Temptation of the Word: the Novels of Mario Vargas Llosa* (Liverpool: Liverpool University Press, 1998). The recent *Cambridge Companion to Mario Vargas Llosa*, edited by Efraín Kristal and John King (Cambridge: Cambridge University Press, 2012) is a multi-authored volume covering the whole range of Vargas Llosa's work in a condensed way. Amongst many valuable articles it contains a review of Vargas Llosa's literary themes by Alonso Cueto and a chapter on 'Film and the novels' by Carolina Sitnisky.

Book-length studies of Vargas Llosa's work from a particular angle include the interesting Roy A. Kerr, *Mario Vargas Llosa: Critical Essays on Characterization* (Potomac: Scripta Humanistica, 1990); M. Keith Booker's view of *Vargas Llosa Among the Postmodernists* (Gainesville: University of Florida Press, 1994); and two studies highlighting the motif of the storyteller: Jean O'Bryan-Knight, *The Story of the Storyteller: 'La tía Julia y el escribidor', 'Historia de Mayta', and 'El hablador' by Mario Vargas Llosa* (Amsterdam and Atlanta: Rodopi, 1995); and Braulio Muñoz: *A Storyteller. Mario Vargas Llosa between Civilization and Barbarism* (Lanham: Rowman & Littlefield, 2000). The reader interested in a psychoanalytical interpretation of Vargas Llosa's work should turn to Roy C. Boland, especially his book *Mario Vargas Llosa: Oedipus and the 'Papa' State. A Study of Individual and Social Psychology in Mario Vargas Llosa's Novels of Peruvian Reality. From 'La ciudad y los perros' to 'Historia de Mayta'* (Madrid: Editorial Voz, 1990).

The multi-authored volume edited by Juan E. De Castro and Nicholas Birns, *Vargas Llosa and Latin American Politics* (New York: Palgrave Macmillan, 2010) looks at the political dimension of Vargas Llosa's writing, while a recent monograph by Juan E. De Castro focuses on the role of *Mario Vargas Llosa. Public Intellectual in Neoliberal Latin America* (Tucson: The University of Arizona Press, 2011).

Many valuable articles cannot be listed here individually, but authors with considerable contributions to criticism of Vargas Llosa in English include Roland Forgues, David Gallagher, John King, Gerald Martin and Peter Standish.

BIBLIOGRAPHY

Works by Mario Vargas Llosa in Spanish (in chronological order)

NARRATIVE

Los jefes (Barcelona: Rocas, 1959).
La ciudad y los perros (Barcelona: Seix Barral, 1963).
La casa verde (Barcelona: Seix Barral, 1966).
Los cachorros. Fotografías de Xavier Miserachs (Barcelona: Lumen, 1967).
Conversación en la catedral (Barcelona: Seix Barral, 1969).
Pantaleón y las visitadoras (Barcelona: Seix Barral, 1973).
La tía Julia y el escribidor (Barcelona: Seix Barral, 1977).
La guerra del fin del mundo (Barcelona: Seix Barral, 1981).
Historia de Mayta (Barcelona: Seix Barral, 1984).
¿Quién mató a Palomino Molero? (Barcelona: Seix Barral, 1986).
El hablador (Barcelona: Seix Barral, 1987).
Elogio de la madrastra (Barcelona: Tusquets, 1988).
Lituma en los Andes (Barcelona: Planeta, 1993).
Los cuadernos de Don Rigoberto (Madrid: Alfaguara, 1997).
La Fiesta del Chivo (Madrid: Alfaguara, 2000).
Narrativa breve. Obra reunida (Madrid: Alfaguara, 2000).
El Paraíso en la otra esquina (Madrid: Alfaguara, 2003).
Travesuras de la niña mala (Madrid: Alfaguara, 2006).
El sueño del celta (Madrid: Alfaguara, 2010).
La ciudad y los perros (Madrid: Alfaguara, 2012) [a special edition published under the auspices of the Real Academia Española to celebrate the fiftieth anniversary of the novel, for which Vargas Llosa has revised the text; it also contains new criticism, a bibliography, glossary and an index of names].
El héroe discreto (Madrid: Alfaguara, 2013).

CHILDREN'S FICTION

Fonchito y la luna, illus. Marta Chicote Juiz (México: Alfaguara Infantil, 2010).

POETRY

Padre Homero, El Dominical. *El Comercio*, 30 March 2008.

WORKS FOR THE THEATRE

La señorita de Tacna (Barcelona: Seix Barral, 1981).

Kathie y el hipopótamo (Barcelona: Seix Barral, 1983).
La Chunga (Barcelona: Seix Barral, 1986).
El loco de los balcones (Barcelona: Seix Barral, 1993).
Ojos bonitos, cuadros feos (Lima: PEISA, 1996).
Teatro. Obra reunida (Madrid: Alfaguara, 2006).
Odiseo y Penélope, photos Ros Ribas, illus. Frederic Amat (Barcelona: Galaxia Gutenberg, 2007).
Al pie del Támesis, photos Morgana Vargas Llosa (Lima: Alfaguara, 2008).
Las mil noches y una noche, photos Ros Ribas (Madrid: Alfaguara, 2009).

ESSAYS AND OTHER NON-FICTION

La novela. Conferencia pronunciada en el Paraninfo de la Universidad de la República, el 11 de agosto de 1966 (Montevideo: Fundación de Cultura Universitaria, 1969).
with Oscar Collazos and Julio Cortázar, *Literatura en la revolución y revolución en la literatura* (México: Siglo XXI, 1970).
García Márquez. Historia de un deicidio (Barcelona: Barral Editores, 1971).
Historia secreta de una novela (Barcelona: Tusquets, 1971).
with Angel Rama, *García Márquez y la problemática de la novela* (Buenos Aires: Corregidor-Marcha, 1973).
La orgía perpetua. Flaubert y 'Madame Bovary' (Barcelona: Seix Barral, 1975).
Entre Sartre y Camus (Río Piedras, Puerto Rico: Huracán, 1981).
Contra viento y marea, I (1962–1972) (Barcelona: Seix Barral, 1983).
La libertad de la cultura. La cultura de la libertad (Santiago de Chile: Fundación Eduardo Frei, 1985).
Contra viento y marea, II (1972–1983) (Barcelona: Seix Barral, 1986).
'Prólogo', in Hernando de Soto, *El otro sendero. La revolución informal* (Lima: El Barranco, 1986), pp. XVII–XXIX.
Contra viento y marea, III (1964–1988) (Barcelona: Seix Barral, 1990).
La verdad de las mentiras. Ensayos sobre literatura (Barcelona: Seix Barral, 1990).
Carta de batalla por Tirant lo Blanc (Barcelona: Seix Barral, 1991).
El pez en el agua. Memorias (Barcelona: Seix Barral, 1993).
Desafíos a la libertad (Madrid: El País/Aguilar, 1994).
'Dinosaurios en tiempos difíciles', in *Friedenspreis des deutschen Buchhandels 1996. Mario Vargas Llosa. Ansprachen aus Anlass der Verleihung*, ed. Börsenverein des Deutschen Buchhandels (Frankfurt am Main:Verlag der Buchhändler-Vereinigung, 1996), pp. 35–48.
La utopía arcaica. José María Arguedas y las ficciones del indigenismo (México: Fondo de Cultura Económica, 1996).
Cartas a un joven novelista (Barcelona: Planeta, 1997).
'La muerte de la novela', *Letras Libres*, 1 (1999), 14–16.
El lenguaje de la pasión (Madrid: Ediciones El País, 2000).
'Un mundo sin novelas', *Letras Libres*, 2 (2000), 38–44.
Bases para una interpretación de Rubén Darío, tesis universitaria 1958 (Lima: Universitaria Nacional de San Marcos, 2001).

'Agitador de conciencias', *ABC*, 16 May 2002, <http://www.abc.es/hemeroteca/historico-16-05-2002/abc/Cultura/agitador-de-conciencias_99723.html> [accessed 27 October 2012].
Diario de Irak, photos Morgana Vargas Llosa (Madrid: Aguilar, 2003).
La tentación de lo imposible. Victor Hugo y 'Los Miserables' (Madrid: Alfaguara, 2004).
Diccionario del amante de América Latina (Barcelona: Paidós, 2006).
'Günter Grass, en la picota', *El País*, 27 August 2006, <http://elpais.com/diario/2006/08/27/opinion/1156629605_850215.html> [accessed 26 August 2013].
Israel/Palestina: Paz o guerra santa, photos Morgana Vargas Llosa (Madrid: Aguilar, 2006).
'La civilización del espectáculo', *El País*, 3 June 2007, <http://elpais.com/diario/2007/06/03/opinion/1180821605_850215.html> [accessed 29 October 2012].
El viaje a la ficción. El mundo de Juan Carlos Onetti (Lima: Alfaguara, 2008).
Sables y utopías. Visiones de América Latina (Madrid: Aguilar 2009).
'Viaje al corazón de las tinieblas', *El País*, 11 January 2009, <http://elpais.com/diario/2009/01/11/eps/1231658814_850215.html> [accessed 29 October 2012].
Sueño y realidad de América Latina (Barcelona: Arcadia, 2010).
'Torear y otras maldades', *El País*, 18 April 2010, <http://www.elpais.com/articulo/opinion/Torear/otras/maldades/elpepiopi/20100418elpepiopi_11/Tes> [accessed 29 October 2012].
'Breve discurso sobre la cultura', *Letras Libres*, July 2010, <http://www.letraslibres.com/revista/convivio/breve-discurso-sobre-la-cultura> [accessed 29 October 2012].
'Catorce minutos de reflexión', *El País*, 10 October 2010, <http://www.elpais.com/articulo/opinion/Catorce/minutos/reflexion/elpepiopi/20101010elpepiopi_11/Tes> [accessed 27 October 2012].
'Elogio de la lectura y la ficción', Nobel Lecture, 7 December 2010, <http://nobelprize.org/nobel_prizes/literature/laureates/2010/vargas_llosa-lecture_sp.html> [accessed 27 October 2012].
'Lo privado y lo público', *El País*, 16 January 2011, <http://www.elpais.com/articulo/opinion/privado/publico/elpepiopi/20110116elpepiopi_10/Tes> [accessed 27 October 2012].
'La civilización del espectáculo', *El País*, 22 January 2011, <http://elpais.com/diario/2011/01/22/babelia/1295658733_850215.html> [accessed 29 October 2012].
'Piqueteros intelectuales', *El País*, 13 March 2011, <http://elpais.com/diario/2011/03/13/opinion/1299970811_850215.html> [accessed 29 October 2012].
'Los ensayos de Luis Loayza', *El País*, 10 April 2011, <http://elpais.com/diario/2011/04/10/opinion/1302386412_850215.html> [accessed 29 October 2012].
with Alfredo Bryce Echenique, Fernando Iwasaki 'y 104 escritores peruanos más', 'Escritores contra el fujimorismo', *El País*, 26 May 2011, <http://elpais.com/diario/2011/05/26/opinion/1306360807_850215.html> [accessed 29 October 2012].

'La derrota del fascismo', *El País*, 19 June 2011, <http://elpais.com/diario/2011/06/19/opinion/1308434411_850215.html> [accessed 29 October 2012].

La civilización del espectáculo (Madrid: Alfaguara, 2012).

OBRAS COMPLETAS/MARIO VARGAS LLOSA

An edition of the complete works of Vargas Llosa, edited by Antoni Munné under the general editorship of Mario Vargas Llosa, is in the process of being published by Galaxia Gutenberg: Círculo de Lectores (Barcelona, 2006–). The following volumes are available so far:

I Narraciones y novela 1959–67 **(2006)**
(with a prologue by Mario Vargas Llosa, 'Contar historias'; contains *Los jefes, La ciudad y los perros, La casa verde, Los cachorros* and *Historia secreta de una novela*).

II Novelas 1969–77 **(2007)**
(with a prologue by José Miguel Oviedo, 'La transición clave del realista'; contains *Conversación en la catedral, Pantaleón y las visitadoras* and *La tía Julia y el escribidor*).

III Novelas y teatro 1981–86 **(2007)**
(with a prologue by Efraín Kristal, 'Rebeldía y fantasía'; contains *La señorita de Tacna, La guerra del fin del mundo, Kathie y el hipopótamo, Historia de Mayta, La Chunga* and *¿Quién mató a Palomino Molero?*).

IV Novelas y teatro 1987–97 **(2008)**
(with a prologue by Juan Antonio Masoliver Ródenas, 'Fiel a una tradición literaria'; contains *El hablador, Elogio de la madrastra, Los cuadernos de Don Rigoberto, Lituma en los Andes, El loco de los balcones* and *Ojos bonitos, cuadros feos*).

V Novelas 2000–06 **(2010)**
(with a prologue by Albert Bensoussan, 'Sables, utopías y amores'; contains *La Fiesta del Chivo, El paraíso en la otra esquina* and *Travesuras de la niña mala*).

VI Ensayos literarios I **(2006)**
(with a prologue by Joaquín Marco; contains *Carta de batalla por Tirant lo Blanc, García Márquez. Historia de un deicidio, La orgía perpetua, La utopía arcaica* and *Cartas a un joven novelista*).

VII and *VIII* are announced as ***Ensayos literarios II*** and ***III***.

IX, X and *XI Piedra de toque I, II* and *III 1962–2012* **(2012)**

Works by Mario Vargas Llosa in English translation (in chronological order)

NARRATIVE

The Time of the Hero [*La ciudad y los perros*], trans. Lysander Kemp (New York: Grove Press, 1966).

The Green House [*La casa verde*], trans. Gregory Rabassa (New York: Harper & Row, 1968).

Conversation in the Cathedral [*Conversación en la catedral*], trans. Gregory Rabassa (New York: Harper & Row, 1975).
The Cubs and Other Stories [*Los cachorros, Los jefes*], trans. Gregory Kolovakos and Ronald Christ (New York: Harper & Row, 1975).
Captain Pantoja and the Special Service [*Pantaleón y las visitadoras*], trans. Ronald Christ and Gregory Kolovakos (New York: Harper & Row, 1978).
Aunt Julia and the Scriptwriter [*La tía Julia y el escribidor*], trans. Helen R. Lane (New York: Farrar, Straus and Giroux, 1982).
The War of the End of the World [*La guerra del fin del mundo*], trans. Helen Lane (New York: Farrar, Straus and Giroux, 1984).
The Real Life of Alejandro Mayta [*Historia de Mayta*], trans. Alfred MacAdam (New York: Farrar, Straus and Giroux, 1986).
Who Killed Palomino Molero? [*¿Quién mató a Palomino Molero?*], trans. Alfred MacAdam (New York: Farrar, Straus and Giroux, 1987).
The Storyteller [*El hablador*], trans. Helen Lane (New York: Farrar, Straus and Giroux, 1989).
In Praise of the Stepmother [*Elogio de la madrastra*], trans. Helen Lane (New York: Farrar, Straus and Giroux, 1990).
Death in the Andes [*Lituma en los Andes*], trans. Edith Grossman (New York: Farrar, Straus and Giroux, 1996).
The Notebooks of Don Rigoberto [*Los cuadernos de Don Rigoberto*], trans. Edith Grossman (New York: Farrar, Straus and Giroux, 1998).
The Feast of the Goat [*La Fiesta del Chivo*], trans. Edith Grossman (New York: Farrar, Straus and Giroux, 2001).
The Way to Paradise [*El Paraíso en la otra esquina*], trans. Natasha Wimmer (New York: Farrar, Straus and Giroux, 2003).
The Bad Girl [*Travesuras de la niña mala*], trans. Edith Grossman (New York: Farrar, Straus and Giroux, 2007).
The Dream of the Celt [*El sueño del celta*], trans. Edith Grossman (New York: Farrar, Straus and Giroux, 2012).

THEATRE

Three plays. The Young Lady from Tacna. Kathie and the Hippopotamus. La Chunga [*La señorita de Tacna, Kathie y el hipopótamo, La Chunga*], trans. David Graham-Young (London: Faber and Faber, 1990).

ESSAYS AND OTHER NON-FICTION

'The Latin American Novel Today', *Books Abroad*, 44.1 (1970), 8–16.
'Social Commitment and the Latin American Writer', *World Literature Today*, 52 (1978), 6–14.
'Inquest in the Andes', trans. Edith Grossman, *The New York Times Magazine*, 31 July 1983, pp. 18–23, 33, 36–7, 42, 48–51 and 56.
'In Nicaragua', trans. Edith Grossman, *The New York Times Magazine*, 28 April 1985, pp. 36–46, 76–7, 81–3 and 92–4.
The Perpetual Orgy. Flaubert and 'Madame Bovary' [*La orgía perpetua.*

Flaubert y 'Madame Bovary'], trans. Helen Lane (New York: Farrar, Straus and Giroux, 1986).
A Writer's Reality, ed. and intro. Myron L. Lichtblau (New York: Syracuse University Press, 1990).
'A Fish out of Water', trans. Helen Lane, *Vargas Llosa for President* (*Granta*, 36 (1991)), 15–76.
A Fish in the Water. A Memoir [*El pez en el agua. Memorias*], trans. Helen Lane (New York: Farrar, Straus and Giroux, 1994).
Literature and Freedom (St Leonards, Australia: Centre for Independent Studies, 1994).
Making Waves, ed. and trans. John King (London: Faber and Faber, 1996).
Letters to a Young Novelist [*Cartas a un joven novelista*], trans. Natasha Wimmer (New York: Farrar, Straus & Giroux, 2002).
The Language of Passion [*El lenguaje de la pasión*], trans. Natasha Wimmer (New York: Farrar, Straus & Giroux, 2003).
'Confessions of a Liberal', 2005 Irving Kristol Lecture AEI Annual Dinner, <http://www.aei.org/speech/22053> [accessed 27 October 2012].
Touchstones. Essays on Literature, Art and Politics, select., trans. and ed. John King (London: Faber and Faber, 2007).
The Temptation of the Impossible. Victor Hugo and 'Les Misérables' [*La tentación de lo imposible. Victor Hugo y 'Los Miserables'*], trans. John King (Princeton: Princeton University Press, 2007).
Wellsprings, trans. Kristin Keenan de Cueto, John King and Jonathan Titler (Cambridge, MA and London: Harvard University Press, 2008).
'In Praise of Reading and Fiction', Nobel Lecture, 7 December 2010, <http://nobelprize.org/nobel_prizes/literature/laureates/2010/vargas_llosa-lecture_en.html> [accessed 27 October 2012].
'Nobel Banquet Speech', 10 December 2010, <http://nobelprize.org/nobel_prizes/literature/laureates/2010/vargas_llosa-speech.html> [accessed 27 October 2012].
In Praise of Reading and Fiction. The Nobel Lecture, trans. Edith Grossman (New York: Farrar, Straus and Giroux, 2011).

Other works cited

Achebe, Chinua, 'An Image of Africa: Racism in Conrad's *Heart of Darkness*', *The Massachusetts Review*, 18 (1977), 782–94.
Actes du colloque Manuel Puig/Mario Vargas Llosa. Les Cahiers de Fontenay (Paris: ENS Éditions, 1982).
Alameda, Sol, interview with Mario Vargas Llosa, *El País*, 8 March 2000; also in <http://www.sololiteratura.com/var/entrevistapais1.html> [accessed 31 October 2012].
Allatson, Paul, 'Mario Vargas Llosa, the Fabulist of Queer Cleansing', in *Vargas Llosa and Latin American Politics*, ed. Juan E. De Castro and Nicholas Birns (New York: Palgrave Macmillan, 2010), pp. 85–102.
Asociación de Artistas Aficionados, 'Muestra Internacional de Teatro de

Lima: "Los Cachorros"', <http://aaalima.blogspot.co.uk/2009/09/muestra-internacional-de-teatro-de-lima.html> [accessed 20 October 2012].
Aubès, Françoise (ed.), *Lectures d'une oeuvre. 'La ciudad y los perros'. Mario Vargas Llosa* (Paris: Éditions du Temps, 1999).
Bernucci, Leopoldo M., *Historia de un Malentendido. Un Estudio Transtextual de 'La Guerra del Fin del Mundo' de Mario Vargas Llosa* (New York: Peter Lang, 1989).
Bodenmüller, Thomas, 'Yo no me voy a poner a juzgar la novela de Vargas Llosa', entrevista con Manuel Vázquez Montalbán, *Iberoamericana*, 1.3 (2001), 173–80.
Boland, Roy Charles, 'The erotic novels. *In Praise of the Stepmother* and *The Notebooks of Don Rigoberto*', in *The Cambridge Companion to Mario Vargas Llosa*, ed. Efraín Kristal and John King (Cambridge: Cambridge University Press, 2012), pp. 102–15.
——, *Mario Vargas Llosa: Oedipus and the 'Papa' State. A Study of Individual and Social Psychology in Mario Vargas Llosa's Novels of Peruvian Reality. From 'La ciudad y los perros' to 'Historia de Mayta'* (Madrid: Editorial Voz, 1990).
Börsenverein des Deutschen Buchhandels (ed.), *Friedenspreis des deutschen Buchhandels 1996. Mario Vargas Llosa. Ansprachen aus Anlass der Verleihung* (Frankfurt am Main:Verlag der Buchhändler-Vereinigung, 1996).
Cano Gaviria, Ricardo, *El buitre y el ave Fénix. Conversaciones con Mario Vargas Llosa* (Barcelona: Anagrama, 1972).
Carroll, Rory, 'Mario Vargas Llosa surprised and delighted by Nobel prize win', *The Guardian*, 7 October 2010, <http://www.guardian.co.uk/books/2010/oct/07/mario-vargas-llosa-nobel-prize-literature> [accessed 27 October 2012].
Chang-Rodríguez, Raquel and Gabriella de Beer (eds), *La historia en la literatura iberoamericana: Textos del XXVI Congreso del Instituto Internacional de Literatura Iberoamericana* (New York: Ediciones del Norte, 1989).
Cicero, *De oratore* (Cambridge, MA: Harvard University Press, The Loeb Classical Library, 1959).
Cifuentes Aldunate, Claudio Eugenio, *'Conversación en la catedral'. Poética de un fracaso. Análisis texto-estructural* (Odense: Odense University Press, 1983).
Collazos, Oscar, Julio Cortázar and Mario Vargas Llosa, *Literatura en la revolución y revolución en la literatura* (México: Siglo XXI, 1970).
Collectif autour de Mario Vargas Llosa, *De Flora Tristán à Mario Vargas Llosa* (Paris: Presses Sorbonne Nouvelle, 2004).
Cordero, Jaime, 'El Ejército "rehabilita" a Vargas Llosa', *El País*, 19 March 2011, <http://elpais.com/diario/2011/03/19/cultura/1300489206_850215.html> [accessed 29 October 2012].
——, 'La elección más reñida de la historia de Perú polariza a toda la sociedad', *El País*, 2 June 2011, <http://elpais.com/diario/2011/06/02/internacional/1306965607_850215.html> [accessed 29 October 2012].
Cornejo Polar, Antonio, *La novela peruana* (Lima: Editorial Horizonte,1989).
Crassweller, Robert D., *Trujillo: The Life and Times of a Caribbean Dictator* (New York: Macmillan, 1966).

Cuéllar, Manuel, 'Mario Vargas Llosa y el cine', *El País*, 7 October 2010, <http://cultura.elpais.com/cultura/2010/10/07/actualidad/1286402424_850215.html> [accessed 22 October 2012],
da Cunha, Euclides, *Os sertões* (Rio de Janeiro: Francisco Alves, 1982).
——, *Rebellion in the Backlands [Os sertões]*, trans. Samuel Putnam (Chicago: University of Chicago Press, 1992).
De Castro, Juan E., *Mario Vargas Llosa. Public Intellectual in Neoliberal Latin America* (Tucson: The University of Arizona Press, 2011)
—— and Nicholas Birns (eds), *Vargas Llosa and Latin American Politics* (New York: Palgrave Macmillan, 2010).
de Soto, Hernando, *El otro sendero. La revolución informal* (Lima: El Barranco, 1986).
Diederich, Bernard, *Trujillo. The Death of the Goat* (Boston and Toronto: Little, Brown and Company, 1978).
Dunkerley, James, *Political Suicide in Latin America and Other Essays* (London: Verso, 1992).
Fishburn, Evelyn, 'The plays', in *The Cambridge Companion to Mario Vargas Llosa*, ed. Efraín Kristal and John King (Cambridge: Cambridge University Press, 2012), pp. 185–98.
Forgues, Roland, 'La especie humana no puede soportar demasiado la realidad', in Michel Moner, *Les avatars de la première personne et le moi balbutiant de 'La tía Julia y el escribidor', suivi de 'La especie humana no puede soportar demasiado la realidad': entrevista a Mario Vargas Llosa por Roland Forgues* (Toulouse: Institut d' Études Hispaniques et Hispano-Americaines, 1983), pp. 67–80.
Franco, Sergio R., 'The Recovered Childhood', in *Vargas Llosa and Latin American Politics*, ed. Juan E. De Castro and Nicholas Birns (New York: Palgrave Macmillan, 2010), pp. 125–36.
Frank, Roslyn M., 'El estudio de "Los cachorros"', in *Mario Vargas Llosa*, ed. José Miguel Oviedo (Madrid: Taurus, 1981), pp. 156–75.
Galaz, Mábel, 'Es un honor ser marqués a la vez que Del Bosque', *El País*, 5 February 2011, <http://www.elpais.com/articulo/agenda/honor/ser/marques/vez/Bosque/elpepigen/20110205elpepiage_2/Tes> [accessed 27 October 2012].
Gallagher, David, 'Casement in Pentonville', *Times Literary Supplement*, 17 December 2010, 20–1.
Geisdorfer Feal, Rosemary, *Novel lives: The fictional Autobiographies of Guillermo Cabrera Infante and Mario Vargas Llosa* (Chapel Hill: University of North Carolina, 1988).
Gewecke, Frauke, '*La fiesta del Chivo* de Mario Vargas Llosa: perspectivas de recepción de una novela de éxito', *Iberoamericana*, 1.3 (2001), 151–65.
Grass, Günter, *Beim Häuten der Zwiebel* (Göttingen: Steidl, 2006).
Greenstein Altmann, Jennifer, 'Novelist Vargas Llosa imparts writing insights to students', *News at Princeton*, 4 October 2010, <http://www.princeton.edu/main/news/archive/S28/59/50G40/index.xml?section=featured> [accessed 27 October 2012].
Haro Tecglen, Eduardo, 'Vargas Llosa y los adaptadores', *El País*, 26 January

1996, <http://elpais.com/diario/1996/01/26/cultura/822610808_850215.html> [accessed 20 October 2012].

Hernández de López, Ana María (ed.), *Mario Vargas Llosa. Opera Omnia* (Madrid: Pliegos, 1994).

Hochschild, Adam, *King Leopold's Ghost. A Story of Greed, Terror and Heroism in Colonial Africa* (London: Pan Macmillan, 2006).

'Joaquín Sabina se pronunció en contra del veto a Mario Vargas Llosa', *El Comercio*, 16 March 2011, <http://elcomercio.pe/espectaculos/728391/noticia-joaquin-sabina-se-pronuncio-contra-veto-mario-vargas-llosa> [accessed 27 October 2012].

Jurado, Laura, 'Willy Toledo: "Vargas Llosa es un derechista muy peligroso"', *El Mundo*, 8 October 2010, <http://www.elmundo.es/elmundo/2010/10/08/baleares/1286554322.html> [accessed 27 October 2012].

Köllmann, Sabine, *Literatur und Politik – Mario Vargas Llosa* (Bern: Peter Lang, 1996).

——, 'Mistrust and mastery: Goethe, Victor Hugo, Mario Vargas Llosa and the art of rhetoric', *Rhetorica*, 2014.

——, 'Vargas Llosa as "the man who writes and thinks"', in *Vargas Llosa and Latin American Politics*, ed. Juan E. De Castro and Nicholas Birns (New York: Palgrave Macmillan, 2010), pp. 173–88.

——, *Vargas Llosa's Fiction & the Demons of Politics* (Oxford: Peter Lang, 2002).

König, Brigitte, 'Ama et impera! Linguistische (und andere) Betrachtungen zum erotischen Imperativ bei Mario Vargas Llosa', in *Das literarische Werk von Mario Vargas Llosa. Akten des Colloquiums im Ibero-Amerikanischen Institut, Berlin 5.–7. November 1998*, ed. José Morales Saravia (Frankfurt am Main: Vervuert, 2000), pp. 305–33.

Kristal, Efraín and John King (eds), *The Cambridge Companion to Mario Vargas Llosa* (Cambridge: Cambridge University Press, 2012).

Krauze, Enrique, 'La seducción del poder. Conversación entre Mario Vargas Llosa y Enrique Krauze', *Letras Libres*, 2 (2000), 22–6.

Levine, Robert M., *Vale of Tears: Revisiting the Canudos Massacre in Northeastern Brazil, 1893–1897* (Berkeley: University of California Press, 1992).

Lozano, Pilar, 'Vargas Llosa resalta la emoción del montaje teatral de "La fiesta del Chivo"', *El País*, 7 November 2003, <http://elpais.com/diario/2003/11/07/espectaculos/1068159601_850215.html> [accessed 20 October 2012].

Malloch Brown, Mark, 'The Consultant', in *Vargas Llosa for President* (*Granta*, 36 (1991)), 87–95.

'Mario Vargas Llosa habla de su primer amor: el teatro', *El Comercio*, 3 April 2012, <http://elcomercio.pe/espectaculos/1396721/noticia-mario-vargas-llosa-habla-su-primer-amor-teatro> [accessed 20 October 2012].

'Mario Vargas Llosa in conversation with Professor Efraín Kristal (UCLA) and Professor Michael Wood FBA (Princeton University)', video, British Academy, <http://www.britac.ac.uk/events/2012/MarioVargasLlosa.cfm> [accessed 15 September 2013].

'Mario Vargas Llosa Says Nobel Prize Changed His Life: "Death Will Find Me

With My Pen In Hand'", *Huffington Post*, 3 November 2010, <http://www.huffingtonpost.com/2010/11/03/vargas-llosa-says-nobel-p_n_778573.html> [accessed 27 October 2012].

Molina, Margot, 'Vargas Llosa ofrece una lectura de su última novela en el Lope de Vega', *El País*, 5 June 2006, <http://elpais.com/diario/2006/06/05/andalucia/1149459743_850215.html> [accessed 20 October 2012].

Moner, Michel, *Les avatars de la première personne et le moi balbutiant de 'La tía Julia y el escribidor', suivi de 'La especie humana no puede soportar demasiado la realidad': entrevista a Mario Vargas Llosa por Roland Forgues* (Toulouse: Institut d' Études Hispaniques et Hispano-Americaines, 1983).

Mora, Rosa, 'Vargas Llosa conquista el teatro con sus autores preferidos', *El País*, 6 October 2005, <http://elpais.com/diario/2005/10/06/espectaculos/1128549610_850215.html> [accessed 20 October 2012].

Morales Saravia, José (ed.), *Das literarische Werk von Mario Vargas Llosa. Akten des Colloquiums im Ibero-Amerikanischen Institut, Berlin 5.–7. November 1998* (Frankfurt am Main: Vervuert, 2000)

'Nobel de la literatura, Antinobel de la ética', *Granma*, 8 October 2010, <http://www.granma.cu/espanol/noticias/8octu-novel.html> [accessed 27 October 2012].

Oelker, Dieter, 'Cuando el mundo posee el sueño de una cosa (Para una lectura de *El Paraíso en la otra esquina* de Mario Vargas Llosa)', *Atenea*, 490 (2004), 59–85.

Ortega Dolz, Patricia, 'Vargas Llosa eclipsa el Español', *El País*, 14 September 2012, <http://ccaa.elpais.com/ccaa/2012/09/13/madrid/1347569905_899366.html> [accessed 21 October 2012].

Oviedo, José Miguel, *Espejo de escritores* (Hanover, NH: Ediciones del Norte, 1985).

——, 'Historia de la historia de la historia: conversación en Lima', *Escandalar*, 3 (1980), 82–7.

——, '*Historia de Mayta*: Una reflexión política en forma de novela', *Antípodas*, 1 (1988), 142–59.

—— (ed.), *Mario Vargas Llosa* (Madrid: Taurus, 1981).

——, *Mario Vargas Llosa: la invención de una realidad* (Barcelona: Seix Barral, 1982).

——, 'Travesuras de la niña mala, de Mario Vargas Llosa', *Letra Libres*, July 2006, <http://www.letraslibres.com/revista/libros/travesuras-de-la-nina-mala-de-mario-vargas-llosa> [accessed 29 October 2012].

Pereda, Rosa María, 'El Teatro del Sol, de Perú, trae a España su versión de "Pichula Cuéllar", de Vargas Llosa', *El País*, 26 September 1982 <http://elpais.com/diario/1982/09/26/cultura/401839213_850215.html> [accessed 20 October 2012].

——, 'Vargas Llosa supervisa en Madrid la versión teatral de "La ciudad y los perros"', *El País*, 12 November 1982, <http://elpais.com/diario/1982/11/12/cultura/405903606_850215.html> [accessed 20 October 2012].

Perreira, Armando, *La concepción literaria de Mario Vargas Llosa* (México: Universidad Nacional Autónoma de México, 1981).

Pinto, Ismael, 'La oscura fascinación por el poder', *Expreso* (Lima), 12 March

2000, <http://www.expreso.com.pe/ediciones/2000/mar/12/cultural/%5F01. htm> [accessed 17 May 2000].
Quintilian, *The Orator's Education* (Cambridge, MA and London: Harvard University Press, The Loeb Classical Library, 1963).
Rama, Angel and Mario Vargas Llosa, *García Márquez y la problemática de la novela* (Buenos Aires: Corregidor-Marcha, 1973).
Ramonet, Ignacio, 'Romancier flamboyant, doctrinaire convulsive. Les Deux Mario Vargas Llosa', *Le Monde Diplomatique*, November 2010, <http://www.monde-diplomatique.fr/2010/11/RAMONET/19856> [accessed 27 October 2012].
——, 'Vargas Llosa, neocon with a Nobel', *Le Monde diplomatique*, 23 December 2010, <http://mondediplo.com/2010/12/23vargasllosa> [accessed 27 October 2012].
Rhetorica ad Herennium (Cambridge, MA: Harvard University Press, The Loeb Classical Library, 1954).
Rilke, Rainer Maria, *Letters to a Young Poet* (London: Penguin, 2011).
Rodríguez, Emma, interview with Mario Vargas Llosa, *El mundo*, 7 March 2000, <http://www.el-mundo.es/2000/03/07/cultura/07N0128.html> [accessed 16 July 2000].
Rodríguez Marcos, Javier, 'El "terror feliz" de un premio Nobel', *El País*, 4 November 2010, <http://www.elpais.com/articulo/cultura/terror/feliz/premio/Nobel/elpepicul/20101104elpepicul_1/Tes> [accessed 27 October 2012].
Rodríguez Moncada, Carmen, *La ciudad y los perros. Mario Vargas Llosa. Estudio literario* (Bogotá: Panamericana, 2001).
Rodríguez Rea, Miguel Angel, *Tras las huellas de un crítico: Mario Vargas Llosa, 1954–1959* (Lima: Fondo Editorial de la Pontificia Universidad Católica del Perú, 1996).
Rossman, Charles and Alan Warren Friedman (eds), *Mario Vargas Llosa. A Collection of Critical Essays* (Austin: University of Texas Press, 1978).
Sarmiento, Domingo Faustino, *Facundo. Civilización y barbárie* (Santiago: Progreso, 1945).
——, *Facundo: Civilization and Barbarism* [*Facundo. Civilización y barbárie*], trans. Kathleen Ross (Berkeley: University of California Press, 2003).
Semana de autor: Mario Vargas Llosa (Madrid: Ediciones Cultura Hispánica, 1985).
Setti, Ricardo A., *... sobre la vida y la política: Diálogo con Vargas Llosa* (México: Kosmos Editorial, 1989).
Sienkiewicz, Henryk, *Quo Vadis* (Uhrichsville, OH: Barbour, 2000).
Sitnisky, Carolina, 'Film and the novels', in *The Cambridge Companion to Mario Vargas Llosa*, ed. Efraín Kristal and John King (Cambridge: Cambridge University Press, 2012), pp. 199–211.
Standish, Peter, 'A Novelist's Theatre', *Antípodas*, 1 (1988), 133–41.
——, *Vargas Llosa. La ciudad y los perros* (London: Grant & Cutler, 1982).
Taggart, Keith M., 'La técnica del contrapunto en ¿*Quién mató a Palomino Molero?*', in *Mario Vargas Llosa. Opera Omnia*, ed. Ana María Hernández de López (Madrid: Pliegos, 1994), pp. 151–8.

Thomson, Belinda (ed.), *Gauguin by Himself* (London: Little, Brown and Company, 2000).
Tiffert Wendorff, Liliana, *Camacho, c'est moi: parodia social y géneros literarios en 'La tía Julia y el escribidor'* (Lima: Editorial San Marcos, 2006).
Torres, Rosana, 'Vargas Llosa: "La poesía es el género literario supremo"', *El País*, 13 May 2011, <http://cultura.elpais.com/cultura/2011/05/13/actualidad/1305237603_850215.html> [accessed 20 October 2012].
Tristán, Flora, *The London Journal 1842* [*Promenades dans Londres*], trans. Jean Hawkes (London: Virago, 1982).
——, *Peregrinaciones de una Paria* (Selección), <http://digicoll.library.wisc.edu/cgi-bin/IbrAmerTxt/IbrAmerTxt-idx?type=HTML&rgn=div1&byte=11283680&q1=que%20gime%20bajo> [accessed 31 October 2012].
——, *Peregrinations of a Pariah: 1833–1834* [*Pérégrinations d'une paria*], trans., ed. and intro. Jean Hawkes (London: Virago, 1986).
Urquidi Illanes, Julia, *Lo que Varguitas no dijo* (La Paz: Khana Cruz, 1983).
——, *My Life with Mario Vargas Llosa* [*Lo que Varguitas no dijo*], trans. Catherine R. Perricone (New York: Peter Lang, 1988).
Vargas Llosa, Alvaro, 'The Press Officer', trans. Shaun Whiteside, *Vargas Llosa for President* (*Granta*, 36 (1991)), 77–85.
Vargas Llosa, Mario, 'Les Français vus de l'étranger par Jürg Altwegg, Mario Vargas Llosa et Stanley Hoffman', *Le rôle des intellectuels de l'affaire Dreyfus à nos jours* (*Magazine Littéraire*, 248 (1987)), 56–8.
Vargas Llosa, Morgana, *Las Fotos del Paraíso* (Madrid: Alfaguara, 2003).
Weber, Max, *Politik als Beruf* (Berlin: Dunker & Humblot, 1987).
Williams, Raymond Leslie, *Mario Vargas Llosa* (New York: Ungar, 1986).
Zapata, Miguel Angel (ed.), *Mario Vargas Llosa and the persistence of memory: celebrating the 40th anniversary of 'La ciudad y los perros' ('The Time of the Hero') and other works* (Lima: Universidad Nacional de San Marcos, 2006).
Zapata, Roger A., 'Las trampas de la ficción en *Historia de Mayta*', in *La historia en la literatura iberoamericana: Textos del XXVI Congreso del Instituto Internacional de Literatura Iberoamericana*, ed. Raquel Chang-Rodríguez and Gabriella de Beer (New York: Ediciones del Norte, 1989), pp. 189–97.

INDEX

absolute truth *see under* truth
abuse
   of power 5, 57–8, 129, 225, 236, 239
   of the indigenous population 106, 191, 257, 265–8
   of trust 240
   sexual 91, 122, 125, 182, 210, 225, 239 n. 30, 242, 287
added elements 18, 23–4, 27–8, 143, 176, 179, 281
adolescence 83, 85, 89–90, 96–100, 102, 116, 211, 214, 218
adventure story 112, 151, 166, 211, 217, 225, 295–6
alter ego 142, 179, 185, 205, 283
Amazon 60, 78, 101–12, 128–32, 136, 185–7, 189–93, 257–9, 264–71
ambiguity 88 n. 5, 104, 118, 125, 147–8, 158–9, 181–2, 190–1, 206, 207, 239, 248, 259, 260, 273, 291 n. 26
   ambiguous characterization 95, 162, 258, 274, 292
   ambiguous narrative voice 247, 253, 258, 275
   ambiguous relationship between reality and fiction 3, 7, 22, 28–31, 35, 41, 150, 167, 169, 262, 269, 288, 294, 296
   metafictional 179–80, 181–2
Andes 37, 47, 57, 59, 60, 75, 88, 130, 153 n. 7, 170, 175, 177, 186, 191, 193–9
animal metaphors 84, 108
   dog 86, 89, 91–4, 97, 99, 100, 114, 147, 156
Arequipa 1, 115, 242–3
Arguedas, José María 27 n. 29, 36–8, 60, 111 n. 20
art 44–8, 49, 68, 70, 73, 167, 200–5, 224, 242, 251, 254, 268, 284, 289, 290–1

authoritarianism 14, 21, 55, 73–4, 77, 117, 218–19, 224–5
autobiography 12, 20, 102, 140, 143, 149, 191, 209, 211, 214–17, 245
autonomous world of fiction 18, 27–9, 31, 36, 45, 115, 153, 274, 280

'barrio' *see* neighbourhood
Bataille, Georges 33, 41, 45, 197–8, 202 n. 33
beauty 39, 40, 44, 46, 51, 183, 199, 208, 210, 258, 268, 291, 298
Berlin, Isaiah 4, 40, 56–7, 64, 67, 165
betrayal 4, 5, 16, 17, 90, 91, 202, 206, 220, 281, 284, 298 (*see also* traitor)
Boom 3–4, 50–1, 81
Borges, Jorge Luis 33, 142
Botero, Fernando 45–6
brothel 102–4, 107, 113, 120, 127, 130, 132, 250 n. 43, 286, 287
bullfighting 48–9

cacique 106, 191, 266 (*see also* Jum)
Cahuide 2, 123, 216
'cajas chinas' *see* Chinese boxes
Camus, Albert 20, 27 n. 28, 49–51, 58
Canudos 59, 151–67, 191, 241
capitalism 18, 54
Casa de las Américas *see under* Cuba
Casement, Roger 192, 224, 256–75, 291 n. 26
Castro, Fidel 4, 17, 53–5, 61–2, 68, 226, 236
censorship 19, 51–6 (*see also* freedom of speech)
characterization 39, 120, 164, 291
Chávez, Hugo 6, 68, 226, 236 n. 26
Chinese boxes 28, 105, 142, 179, 189, 190–1, 289
'cholo' 100, 121, 122, 181, 184, 219
Church, the (Catholic) 62, 69, 75, 76,

101, 111, 112, 130, 132, 154, 157, 172, 232, 254
Cien años de soledad *see under* García Márquez, Gabriel
cinema 82, 89, 109, 110, 112, 148 n. 45, 151, 183, 300 (*see also* film)
circle of friends 123, 152
circular structure 85, 90, 130, 182, 188, 243, 260, 261, 289
civilization and barbarism 103, 108, 156
collectivism 6, 38, 65, 67, 204, 242
committed literature 37, 179 n. 12
communicating vessels 28, 42, 85, 101, 117, 171, 264
communication, lack of 12, 59, 153 n. 7, 162, 198–9
communism 82, 123–5, 173, 175, 180, 216, 220 (*see also* Marxism)
Conrad, Joseph 258–9, 263, 266, 273
Consejero, Antonio 151–66, 172, 224, 236, 237
contradictory truths *see under* truth
corruption
 of innocence 201, 207
 of society 73, 87, 91, 94, 103, 106, 117–20, 126, 181, 266
 of values 233–4, 259
counter-world, literature as a verbal 31, 45, 73, 199, 206, 219, 222, 224
crosscutting 89, 105, 137, 183, 300
Cuba
 Casa de las Américas 3, 4, 53, 54
 Cuban Revolution 3–4, 6, 15–19, 51–4, 56, 61, 113, 125, 150, 175, 178–9, 208–9
culture 3, 4, 36, 44, 48, 55, 123, 148, 186–7, 206, 209, 264
 cultural refinement 200, 203, 207, 268, 284
 French 2, 242, 284
 indigenous 189, 192, 195, 261
 trivialization of 13, 68–73

Da Cunha, Euclides 152–4, 159–60, 166
'dato escondido' *see* hidden fact
de Soto, Hernando 65–6, 180, 222
death 93, 97, 100, 105, 117, 130–1, 136, 139, 161, 209, 243, 250–6, 260–2, 275, 290
 violent death 88–90, 119, 162–3, 181–3, 193, 197, 226–35
deicide, literature as 24–7, 39

democracy 5, 6, 46, 55, 58, 60–8, 72, 73, 75, 77, 219–20, 236
'demonios' *see* demons
demons
 cultural 24, 31, 34, 35, 142, 191, 206
 exorcism of 24–5
 personal or individual 24, 146, 216, 240–1, 258, 283
 social and historical 24, 191
 the writer's 17, 23–5, 32, 37, 40, 102, 132, 150, 178, 213–14, 225, 249–51, 284, 287
devil 95, 98, 159, 214 n. 5, 221, 225, 232, 271, 298
 God and the Devil 157
 Lucifer 202, 271
 'muki' 195
 'pishtaco' 194–5
 Robert the Devil 166
 Satan 63, 232, 270
dictator 5, 18, 21, 24, 63, 68, 75, 115–19, 123, 141, 156–7, 177, 225
 as protagonist 225, 227–41
 dictatorship as a system 233, 236, 239, 240–1
 dictatorship novel 18, 225, 235
disillusionment 53, 55, 57, 89, 113, 125, 206, 220, 265, 271
dissidence 27, 52, 56, 220, 230
dogs *see under* animal metaphors
duality 202, 244–5
 dual concepts 36, 38, 90, 103, 108, 156, 169, 204
 dual role of writer and intellectual 4, 5, 18–20, 101
 structural duality 85, 86, 101, 140–1, 171, 178, 185–6, 211, 216, 242, 259, 299

ekphrasis 201–2, 207, 225, 245, 250, 253
'elementos añadidos' *see* added elements
entertainment 13, 71–3, 128, 141, 186, 204
epigraph 31, 42, 93, 115, 143, 214 n. 5, 216, 221, 261, 264, 288, 290
epilogue 89, 90, 101–2, 108–9, 140, 194, 202, 203, 206, 216, 261, 269, 274–5, 279, 295
eroticism 73, 200, 205, 207, 298
 erotic fantasies 121, 199–201, 203, 205–7, 249

erotic literature 47, 142, 183, 193, 199–200, 208, 212
European Left *see under* Left
evil as part of human nature 14, 40, 41, 45, 73, 95, 166, 181, 235, 239, 258, 259, 263, 266, 268, 273
Evil (Bataille's concept of 'Le mal') 33, 45, 202 n. 33
eyes, motif of striking 107–10, 158–60, 231, 236–7

fanatic, the type of 39, 49, 57, 108, 130–1, 145–6, 153, 155, 157–8, 164, 172–3, 187, 189, 192, 232, 237, 246, 268–72, 289–90
fanaticism 14, 21, 59, 67, 73, 128, 146, 150, 152, 156, 158–64, 246, 272
father
  fathers and daughters 181–5, 227–8, 239, 240–1, 242, 289
  fathers and sons 116, 118, 123, 125, 201–6, 240, 257
  in Vargas Llosa's biography 1–2, 86, 214, 217–18, 241
  the Father of the Fatherland 225, 237, 239, 240
  the motif of the authoritarian, abusive father 83–5, 89–94, 144, 147, 264
  religious and other father-figures 104, 156, 259–60, 265, 272, 297
Faulkner, William 30, 31, 42, 82, 87
film 24, 44, 48, 109, 110, 148, 151–2, 155, 181 n. 18, 210, 226, 241, 243, 300–1 (*see also* cinema)
Flaubert, Gustave 1, 26, 29, 31, 35–8, 95, 121, 139–40, 141, 142, 208, 253, 283
  Madame Bovary 35–6, 39, 95, 121, 140, 148 n. 45
form, literary or artistic 4, 24, 34, 46, 48, 71
free indirect style 36, 150, 162, 174, 228, 230, 272, 273, 275
free market 6, 64, 65, 67
freedom 5–7, 15, 19, 21, 41–2, 50, 51–3, 55–7, 61, 64–72, 157, 162, 165, 204–5, 219, 224, 232–4, 263, 274
  creative 15, 17, 52, 56, 242
  of speech and information 4, 52, 55–6, 64, 68, 72, 74, 120, 137
Freud, Sigmund 135, 149 n. 46

Fujimori, Alberto 5, 38, 58, 66, 74, 215, 221–2, 226

García Márquez, Gabriel 3, 4, 6, 22, 26, 30–1, 34, 86 n. 1, 127, 141, 225 n. 10, 226 n. 11, 235, 304
  Cien años de soledad 30, 34
Gauguin, Paul 47, 78, 224, 242–56, 275, 283, 285
genre 6, 49, 82, 149, 169, 182, 201, 208, 214, 223, 225, 294, 297 n. 33
God 27, 29, 40, 111, 125, 135, 184, 232, 237–8, 247, 256, 260
  and the Devil 157
gods 84, 194, 196, 249, 271, 295
Grass, Günter 20–1, 61–2

Hayek, Friedrich 65, 67, 219
hero 1 n. 1, 3, 13, 48, 56 n. 53, 86, 93, 124, 199, 206, 228, 236, 254, 256, 261, 265, 270, 272, 274, 295
  anti-hero 14, 41–2, 256
hidden fact 28, 34, 42, 85, 94, 95, 101, 103, 108, 118, 163
hierarchy 84, 92, 120, 129
historical fiction 166–7, 225, 234, 274
historiography 40, 150, 154, 167, 224, 230, 263–4
history 14, 23, 25, 31, 45, 52, 64, 67, 78, 101, 114–15, 125, 137, 151–2, 161, 164, 166–7, 169, 170–1, 174, 175, 176, 179, 187, 191, 256, 259, 263, 267, 290, 296–7
  and fiction 224–8
  idolatry of 160–1
homophobia 91, 178 n. 11
homosexuality 53, 118, 125, 173–5, 178–9, 250, 256–7, 260, 268–9, 274, 287, 291–2, 293
'huachafería' 206–7 n. 35, 208, 285 n. 17
Hugo, Victor 20, 29 n. 34, 38–40, 148, 166, 244, 283–5
  Les Misérables 38–40, 244 n. 36, 254
human condition 44, 48–9, 69, 72, 230, 256, 258, 301
human nature 31, 33, 49, 95, 223, 225, 235, 239, 244, 259, 298
humour 113, 127–8, 132–4, 139, 140 n. 43, 145, 149, 208, 300

idealism 21, 77, 125, 150, 157–8, 160, 164, 172, 178, 198, 232, 254, 257, 265, 289
identity 3, 47, 70–1, 91, 92, 97, 187, 204, 210, 265, 292–3
ideology 3, 20–1, 37–9, 50, 51–2, 56, 62, 66, 77, 120, 124–5, 151–62, 167, 174, 176, 180, 224, 262, 270–1
  anti-ideological position 4, 57, 150–1, 153, 166
imagination 16, 24, 27–8, 41, 93, 102, 104, 121, 123, 131, 135, 140, 144, 156, 165, 167, 178, 182–4, 186–8, 194, 199–202, 203, 206, 216, 249, 250, 252, 253, 264, 281, 283, 284, 286, 296, 298
implied author 170–9, 185–6, 192
imposture 46, 86, 93, 94, 96, 146, 234
'incomunicación' see communication, lack of
'Inconquistables' 31, 84, 103, 181, 194, 286–7
Indigenismo 36–8, 60, 73
individualism/the individual 5, 6, 54, 67, 71, 82, 84, 119, 127, 161, 204–5, 220, 223, 225, 228, 232–3, 242, 259
injustice, social 17, 35, 40, 52, 55, 63, 103, 106, 113, 122, 123, 127, 157, 161, 171–2, 177, 217, 219, 224, 232, 245, 256, 267, 290
intellectuals
  as protagonists 124, 141–2, 154, 165–6, 177, 230, 239–40, 272, 286
  criticism of 62–3, 221–2
  in society 4, 17, 19, 61–3, 152, 157
  Vargas Llosa as public intellectual 5–6, 11–20, 50, 53–4, 64, 75, 123, 213
intertextuality 188, 191, 207, 233–4, 243, 253, 258, 271, 283
irony 106, 108, 129, 130, 132, 162, 208, 210, 238, 247, 285 (*see also* self-irony)
Irving Kristol Award 19, 66

journalism 1, 2, 5, 14, 33, 44–78, 195, 198, 216–17, 222
  as theme in fiction 113, 116, 126, 136–7, 139, 150, 152, 154–6, 163–6, 169, 191, 226, 241, 266, 283, 286, 301
Jum 102, 106–8, 191, 192, 266

justice 16–17, 50–5, 160, 242, 245 (*see also* injustice, social)
juxtaposition 28, 95, 100, 111, 132, 163, 172, 188, 242

Latin American writer, situation of the 3, 19–20, 36–7, 54
Left, the 4, 6, 50, 55, 56, 69, 74, 75, 77, 150, 169, 176, 179–80
  European Left 20, 61
  left-wing 4, 19, 54, 56, 60–3, 74, 169, 175–6
leitmotif 65, 91, 114, 180, 285 n. 17, 298
Leoncio Prado Military Academy 2, 38, 86–96, 216, 304
liberalism 18–19, 53, 56, 64–8, 73, 75, 77 (*see also* neoliberalism)
  anti-liberal 38, 115 n. 30, 219
Lima 1–2, 64, 65, 81, 86, 90, 100, 101, 114, 119, 126–7, 129, 136, 140, 141, 145, 187, 208–9, 215, 243, 279–80, 281, 283, 287, 290, 292
littérature engagée see committed literature
Lituma 1 n. 1, 31, 83, 103–8, 147, 180–4, 193–9, 287

Machiguengas 185–93, 251 n. 46
machismo 84, 91, 94, 96, 108, 112, 129, 181, 183, 208, 218–19, 224, 225, 239, 287–8, 292
macrocosm/microcosm 30, 31, 90, 152, 218
Madame Bovary see under Flaubert
'malentendido' see misunderstanding
marginality 36, 170, 173, 177–8, 189, 272 (*see also* outsider)
Martorell, Joanot 30, 31, 33
  Tirant lo Blanc 30, 33
Marxism 2, 55, 60, 62–3, 76, 124–5, 171–2, 192, 220 (*see also* communism)
mediocrity 29, 32, 44, 123, 126, 145, 208, 211, 245, 284 n. 15, 286, 291, 297
melodrama 35, 139, 141–9, 209, 281, 283–4
  as ingredient of literature 35, 139
metafiction 5, 42, 140, 149, 151, 165, 166, 169, 171, 174, 176, 179–80, 186, 188, 194, 211, 212, 280–1
microcosm see macrocosm
military 30, 53, 56, 58, 63, 87 n. 3, 88–94, 101, 107, 113, 123, 127–39,

140, 150–63, 181, 183, 218, 225, 228, 257, 273, 300 (*see also* Leoncio Prado Military Academy)
Miraflores   83, 96, 97, 99–100, 124, 126–7, 208, 209, 211, 293
Misérables, Les   see under Hugo, Victor
Mises, Ludwig von   65
misunderstanding   58, 59, 150, 152, 154, 162, 165, 198, 221
montage   28, 105, 137
'muda'   *see* shift
multiperspectivism   77, 155, 166
myth   21, 24, 30, 31, 62, 63, 102, 104, 151, 158, 185, 187, 190, 191, 194, 196, 237, 244, 261, 263, 297

narrator   28–9, 33, 34, 36, 39, 42, 85, 92, 116, 153, 159, 174, 177, 186, 189, 191–2, 228, 229, 230, 241, 247, 248–9, 254, 270, 282–3, 297
   disappearance of   39, 97–8, 134
   first-person   89, 90, 95, 140, 143, 170, 175, 185, 209
   omniscient   38, 89, 150, 154, 247, 249, 256, 260, 268, 272, 273
   second-person   104 n. 18, 247, 253–5
nationalism   6, 13–14, 21, 66–7, 70–1, 73–4, 205, 224, 258, 268, 270–3 (*see also* patriotism)
nature   152, 191, 195, 196, 199, 254, 264
neighbourhood   83, 84, 96, 97, 98, 103, 142
neoliberalism   4 n. 10, 18–19, 219
nicknames   86, 89, 92, 97, 119, 189, 225, 248, 261
Nobel Lecture   1–2, 12–13, 15, 16, 21, 23, 50, 130
Nobel Prize in Literature   6–7, 11–12, 18, 50, 74, 87 n. 3
'novela total'   *see* total novel

Odría, Manuel   115, 117, 119, 120, 141, 177, 224
Onetti, Juan Carlos   30, 40–2, 299
orality   85, 96, 98, 99, 135, 166, 185, 187, 190, 294
outsider   84, 85, 88, 97, 120, 124, 154, 173, 189, 193, 196, 251 n. 46, 257, 260 (*see also* marginality)
Oviedo, José Miguel   32, 81 n. 1, 85, 102 n. 15, 115, 149 n. 46, 211
oxymoron   29

Padilla Affair   3–4, 15, 54, 150
parallels and contrasts   91, 117, 141, 150
Paris   2, 3, 81, 86, 104 n. 18, 142–3, 186, 209, 211, 242, 243, 248, 281
parody   63, 127, 131, 134–7, 139, 141, 143, 146, 149 n. 46, 204–5
patriotism   136, 205, 272 (*see also* nationalism)
PEN   4 n. 9, 56, 152 n. 7
perspective, narrative   85, 89–92, 97, 105, 109, 110, 115, 117, 121, 135, 154–5, 162, 164–5, 174, 204, 213, 224, 226–9, 234–5, 237, 239, 241, 249, 253, 256, 271–5, 288
Peru
   culture   36, 46, 201
   history   57, 171, 175–6, 209, 249, 262, 265–7
   indigenous population   37, 189–93, 198
   literature   81–2, 141
   motif of the divided country   59–60, 101–3, 112, 195, 219
   politics   5, 38, 52, 56–8, 63–6, 74–5, 115, 119, 122–3, 169, 186, 203, 213–21, 226
   presidential election in 1990   5, 38, 64, 66, 213–22, 226 n. 15
   society   2, 47, 84, 87, 90, 113–14, 119–21, 124, 127, 134, 209, 218
'Piedra de toque'   44, 66, 68, 75
Piura   1–2, 101–4, 106–8, 140, 181, 193, 195, 219, 279, 286, 288
pluralism, political   57, 67, 167
'poder de persuasión'   *see* power of persuasion
poetry   47, 48, 49, 73, 126, 166, 205, 222, 230, 261, 283, 290, 296–7, 304
polemic   6, 7, 20, 44 n. 2, 61, 63, 64, 69, 76, 179, 204
Popper, Karl   4, 64
popular fiction   140 n. 43, 148–9, 166, 185, 233
populist leader   6, 63, 68, 74
postmodernism   13, 46, 69–71, 179, 274
power of persuasion   28, 29, 127, 227
power structures   5, 6, 84, 92, 101, 239
progress   16, 36, 62, 67, 77, 157, 161, 192–3, 257, 258
purity   51, 123, 125, 158, 178, 202, 222, 257

qualitative leap   28, 143

racism   13, 14, 61, 67, 74, 83, 91, 121, 181, 182, 221, 259
radio   2, 4, 134, 136, 139–42, 145, 147–9, 185, 283, 290, 300
realism   3, 23, 28, 30, 34, 82–3, 84, 127, 141, 142, 146, 148, 149 n. 46, 166, 171, 202, 292
reality and fiction   3, 5, 38, 41, 104, 141, 143–4, 146, 179, 185, 188, 203, 206, 207, 211, 216, 258, 280, 282, 294, 296
  real reality/fictional reality   26–7, 34, 304
rebellion   2, 13, 26–7, 44, 46, 82, 84, 122, 139, 151–5, 162, 170–6, 186, 209, 218
  as an ingredient of literature   35, 139
religion   35, 68, 125, 130, 132, 140, 150, 151, 173, 224, 250, 251, 259–60, 262, 270–2 (*see also* the Church)
Revel, Jean-François   56, 64–5
revenge   83, 88, 121, 162, 195, 229, 231, 240, 291, 298
revolutionary politics   38, 49, 57, 59–63, 68, 70, 73, 74, 75–6, 123–4, 157, 161–3, 165, 169–80, 219–20, 244 (*see also* Cuban Revolution *under* Cuba)
rhetoric   16, 29 n. 34, 112, 136, 270, 285
Right (political)   5, 6, 50, 56, 69, 74, 75
role-play   83, 84, 93, 95, 146, 190, 201, 205, 208, 211, 283–6, 293–5, 298
Rómulo Gallegos Prize   15, 17, 22, 41, 101

'salto cualitativo'   *see* qualitative leap
San Marcos, National University of   2, 33, 123–4, 187, 216, 219
Sartre, Jean-Paul   4, 19–20, 49–50, 54, 93, 179, 289
self-irony   69, 89, 139, 141
self-referentiality   23, 140 n. 43, 191, 211, 212, 281, 283
'selva'   *see* Amazon
'Sendero Luminoso'   *see* Shining Path
Sertão   78, 151, 158, 162, 165
sex   128–30, 132–9, 158, 200–3, 204–5, 207–11, 219, 285, 287–8
  and creativity   250–2, 284–5
  and violence   92
  as an ingredient of literature   35, 139
  as an instrument of power   228, 238

shift   28 (*see also* qualitative leap)
Shining Path   38, 57, 59, 64, 175, 177, 193, 194, 195, 197, 198
simultaneity   95–6, 97, 105, 111, 115–16, 121, 300
single truth   *see under* truth
socialism   3–4, 16–17, 51–6, 57, 64, 76, 113, 123–5, 173, 176–8, 213, 242, 245, 285
storyteller, the   21, 166, 185–91, 193, 194, 196, 279, 296–8, 301
storytelling   105, 199, 241, 280, 294–8
stream of consciousness   89, 228, 300
Szyszlo, Fernando de   46–7, 201

telescopic dialogue   85, 105, 114, 230
terrorism   58, 178, 179, 193, 217
Tirant lo Blanc   *see under* Martorell, Joanot
total novel   24, 30, 33, 34, 38, 150–1, 166–7, 183, 209, 223, 225, 243, 253
totalitarianism   57, 58, 64, 65, 227, 228, 232, 234, 241
traitor   83–5, 88–9, 224, 237 (*see also* betrayal)
transgression   73, 81, 84, 88, 116, 144, 200–1, 208, 211, 287, 298
Tristán, Flora   224, 242–55, 282
Trujillo, Rafael Leónidas   120, 224–41, 246
truth
  absolute   68–9, 124, 190
  contradictory truths   40, 56, 165
  of lies   29, 146
  single   56–7, 125, 157, 167

Uchuraccay   57–60, 63 n. 72, 75, 169, 183, 193, 195–6, 198
utopia   49, 57, 73, 152, 180, 193, 202, 242–5, 249, 254, 256

Vargas Llosa, Mario
  Al pie del Támesis   292–4
  Los cachorros   81, 85, 96–100, 199, 299, 300 n. 46
  Carta de batalla por Tirant lo Blanc   33
  Cartas a un joven novelista   23, 25, 27, 28, 247
  La casa verde   22, 84, 101–13, 114, 117, 126, 128, 130, 140, 147, 156,

180, 186, 191, 192, 244, 266, 286, 301
La Chunga 194, 280 n. 9, 285–8
La ciudad y los perros 3, 82, 84, 86–96, 101, 140, 181, 208, 234, 299, 300 n. 46, 304
La civilización del espectáculo 7 n. 18, 13–14, 71 n. 104, 72 n. 107, 73, 200
Contra viento y marea 47, 51–66
Conversación en la catedral 2, 31, 82, 113–27, 172, 181, 216, 224, 234, 283
Los cuadernos de Don Rigoberto 47, 84, 193, 203–7, 295 n. 32
Desafíos a la libertad 66–8
Diario de Irak 76–7
Diccionario del amante de América Latina 285 n. 17
'Elogio de la lectura y la ficción', Nobel Lecture 1–2, 12–13, 15, 16, 21, 23, 50, 130
Elogio de la madrastra 47, 84, 183, 193, 199–203, 205, 207, 249, 271, 295 n. 32
Entre Sartre y Camus 49–51
La Fiesta del Chivo 18, 120, 167, 222, 223–41, 299, 300 n. 46
'A Fish out of Water' 66, 230
Fonchito y la luna 199
García Márquez. Historia de un deicidio 22, 26, 34, 36, 86 n. 1, 127, 222
La guerra del fin del mundo 4, 56, 59, 113, 125, 139, 150–68, 169, 172, 183, 191, 223, 241, 301
El hablador 60, 111, 185–93, 251 n. 46, 281
El héroe discreto 1 n. 1
Historia de Mayta 59, 125, 169–80, 185, 186, 223, 248, 251, 281
Historia secreta de una novela 22, 26, 101, 102–4, 106, 147, 244
'Inquest in the Andes' 59, 75
Israel/Palestina: Paz o guerra santa 77–8
Los jefes 3, 81–5, 96, 181
Kathie y el hipopótamo 280, 283–6, 288
El lenguaje de la pasión 49, 68–70
'La literatura es fuego' 15–17, 22, 41, 52, 82, 101, 115 n. 30

Lituma en los Andes 59, 60, 182, 184, 193–9
El loco de los balcones 48, 288–90
'Las mentiras verdaderas' 22, 29, 167, 280
Las mil noches y una noche 295, 297–9
La novela 22
Odiseo y Penélope 295–7
Ojos bonitos, cuadros feos 47, 288, 290–2
La orgía perpetua. Flaubert y 'Madame Bovary' 29, 35–6, 95, 139, 140, 148 n. 45, 170, 253
Padre Homero 297
Pantaleón y las visitadoras 113, 127–39, 140, 226, 300
El Paraíso en la otra esquina 47, 78, 223–5, 242–56, 275, 282, 299
El pez en el agua. Memorias 66, 127, 203, 213–22, 296, 297 n. 33
¿Quién mató a Palomino Molero? 180–5, 195, 211
Sables y utopías. Visiones de América Latina 73
La señorita de Tacna 22, 167, 281–3
El sueño del celta 78, 106, 168, 186, 192, 223–5, 250, 256–75
Sueño y realidad de América Latina 47 n. 12
'El teatro como ficción' 26, 32, 280, 281
La tentación de lo imposible. Victor Hugo y 'Los Miserables' 38–40, 244
La tía Julia y el escribidor 42–3, 82 n. 4, 139–49, 166, 185, 252 n. 47, 281, 283, 300
Touchstones. Essays on Literature, Art and Politics 70–1
Travesuras de la niña mala 207–12, 224, 239, 299
La utopía arcaica. José María Arguedas y las ficciones del indigenismo 36–8, 111
La verdad de las mentiras. Ensayos sobre literatura 23, 34, 294
El viaje a la ficción. El mundo de Juan Carlos Onetti 23, 40–2, 298
Wellsprings 71
A Writer's Reality 23, 33, 38, 102, 127, 128–9, 137–8, 148, 152–3, 169, 171

'vasos comunicantes' *see* communicating vessels
'verdad absoluta' *see* absolute truth *under* truth
'verdad de las mentiras' *see* truth of lies *under* truth
'verdad única' *see* single truth *under* truth
'verdades contradictorias' *see* contradictory truths *under* truth
violence
    as ingredient of literature   16, 35, 139, 209
    as part of human nature   13, 14, 77, 235, 298
    as social ill   83, 87, 91, 103, 127, 174–5, 198, 218, 219, 224, 234, 268, 298
    politically and ideologically motivated   21, 24, 57–61, 67, 117, 161, 169, 174–7, 193–5, 197–8
    sexual and domestic   92, 217–18, 287
visualization   102 n. 15, 109, 112, 139, 201, 287, 295
vocation of the writer   1, 7, 11, 18, 23–7, 49, 66, 144–5, 169, 181, 213, 215, 219, 301
voyeurism   7 n. 18, 71, 73, 205, 208, 210, 287

writer and intellectual   *see* dual role of writer and intellectual *under* duality
writer-protagonist   141, 147, 154, 166, 167, 169–80, 185–93, 223, 248, 281–2

yagunzo   153–6, 159, 161, 163–6

www.ingramcontent.com/pod-product-compliance
Lightning Source LLC
Chambersburg PA
CBHW051559230426
43668CB00013B/1908